DATE			

FOREIGN INTELLIGENCE
ORGANIZATIONS

FOREIGN INTELLIGENCE ORGANIZATIONS

JEFFREY T. RICHELSON

BALLINGER PUBLISHING COMPANY
Cambridge, Massachusetts
A Subsidiary of Harper & Row, Publishers, Inc.

International Standard Book Number: 0-88730-121-5 (CL)
0-88730-122-3 (PB)

Library of Congress Catalog Card number: 88-923

Printed in the United States of America

Library of Congress Cataloging-in-Publication Data

Richelson, Jeffrey.
  Foreign intelligence organizations.

  Includes index.
  1. Intelligence service. 2. Espionage—United States.
I. Title.
UB250.R53 1988   327.1'2   88-923
ISBN 0-88730-121-5
ISBN 0-88730-122-3 (pbk.)

CONTENTS

LIST OF FIGURES

LIST OF TABLES

LIST OF ABBREVIATIONS
AND ACRONYMS

AFMBW	Amt für Fernmeldwesen Bundeswehr
AMAN	Agaf Modiin
ANA	Arab News Agency
ASIS	Australian Secret Intelligence Service
BBC	British Broadcasting Service
BCRA	Bureau Central de Renseignement et d'Action
BEI	Bureau of Economic Intelligence
BfV	Bundesamt für Verfassungsschutz
BIAS	Bureau of Intelligence Analysis and Security
BND	Bundesnachrichtendienst
BSC	British Security Coordination
C, or CSS	Chief of the Secret Service
CBNRC	Communications Branch, National Research Council
CESIS	Executive Committee for Intelligence and Security Services
CIG	Current Intelligence Group
CINCPACFLT	Commander-in-Chief Pacific Fleet
CINCSDFLT	Commander-in-Chief Self-Defense Fleet
CIR	Comité Interministeriel des Renseignement
CND	Campaign for Nuclear Disarmament
CSE	Communications Security Establishment
CSID	Central Special Intelligence Department
CSIS	Canadian Security Intelligence Service
DEA	Department of External Affairs

DEA	Drug Enforcement Agency
DGED	Directorate General for Studies and Documentation
DGER	Direction Générale des Etudes et Recherches
DGI	Director General of Intelligence
DGSE	Direction Générale de la Sécurité Extérieure
DGSS	Direction Générale des Services Spéciaux
DIS	Defense Intelligence Staff
DSD	Defence Signals Directorate
DST	Directorate for Surveillance of the Territory
FBIS	Foreign Broadcast Information Service
FCO	Foreign and Commonwealth Office
FHO	Fremde Heere Ost–Foreign Armies East
FIB	Foreign Intelligence Bureau
FLN	Front de Libération National
FLNC	National Liberation Front of Corsica
FNLA	Front for the National Liberation of Angola
GCHQ	Government Communications Headquarters
GCR	Groupement de Communications Radio-Electriques
GIC	Groupement Interministeriel dès Communicationes
GRU	Chief Intelligence Directorate of the Soviet General Staff
GSS	General Security Service
HF-DF	High-Frequency Direction-Finding
IAC	Intelligence Advisory Committee
IDB	Inlichtingendienst Buitenland
IIC	Industrial Intelligence Centre
ILD	International Liaison Department
IPC	Intelligence Policy Committee
IRSIG	International Regulations on SIGINT
ISIC	Inter-Services Intelligence Committee
JETRO	Japanese External Trade Organization
JIB	Joint Intelligence Bureau
JIC	Joint Intelligence Committee
JIO	Joint Intelligence Organization
JRA	Japanese Red Army
JTLS	Joint Technical Language Service
LEKEM	Leshkat Kesher Madao
LRTS	Long-Range Technical Search
LSIB	London Signals Intelligence Board
LSIC(D)	London Signals Intelligence Committee (Defence)
MAD	Militarischer Abschirmdienst

MEW	Ministry of Economic Warfare
MfS	Ministry for State Security
MID	Military Intelligence Department
MINICULPOP	Ministry of Popular Culture
MITI	Ministry of International Trade and Industry
MOD	Ministry of Defence
MOS-1	Marine Observation Satellite
MPLA	Popular Movement for the Liberation of Angola
MPS	Ministry of Public Security
MSDF	Maritime Self-Defense Forces
MSS	Ministry of State Security
MVSN	Milizia Volontaria Sicurezza Nazionale
NCCL	National Council for Civil Liberties
NCNA	New China News Agency
NRC	National Research Council
NSA	National Security Agency
NSS	National Security Service
OEIC	Overseas Economic Intelligence Committee
OKW	Supreme High Command
OVRA	Voluntary Organization for the Repression of Anti-Facism
PFLP	Popular Front for the Liberation of Palestine
PIDE	Portuguese Internal Police for the Defense of the State
PSIA	Public Security Investigation Agency
PSIS	Permanent Under Secretaries Committee on Intelligence Services
RCMP	Royal Canadian Mounted Police
RG	Renseignement Générale
RSHA	Reichssicherheitshauptamt
SAC	Security Advisory Committee
SAD	Social Affairs Department
SAS	Special Air Service
SAVAK	National Security and Information Organization (Iran)
SBS	Special Boat Squadron
SDECE	Service de Documentation Extérieure et de Contre-Espionage
SHABAK	Sherut Bitachan Klali
SHAI	Sherut Ydioth
SIA	Servizio Informazioni Aeronautiche
SID	Servizio Informazioni Difesa
SIFAR	Servizio Informazioni Forze Armate
SIGSI	Servizio Informazioni Generali e Sicurezza Interna

SIM	Servizio Informazioni Militaire
SIOS	Servizio Informazioni Operativo Situazione
SIS	Servizio Informazioni Segreto
SISDE	Servizio per le Informazione e la Sicurezza Democratica
SISME	Servizio per le Informazioni e la Sicurezza Militare
SPARG	Security Planning and Research Group
SPOT	Systeme Probatoire d'Observation de la Terre
SIS	Secret Intelligence Service
SR	Service de Renseignement
TICV	Technische Informatie Centrale Verwerking
TR	Enterprise des Travaux Ruraux
UCI	Central Office of Investigations
UFWD	United Front Work Department
UNITA	National Union for the Total Independence of Angola

ACKNOWLEDGMENTS

A large number of individuals aided me in writing this book—providing articles, documents, critiques, leads, and the names of potential contacts. Included in this group are William Arkin, Desmond Ball, Duncan Campbell, Andrew Cockburn, Seymour Hersh, David Kahn, Steve Rosen, Paul Rusman, Roberto Suro, Wesley Wark, and Owen Wilkes. Paul Stares produced Figure 9-2. I'd also like to thank the Peace and Disarmament Strategy Study Unit in Tokyo as well as the historical sections of the Departments of National Defence and External Affairs in Canada for their assistance.

Special thanks go to Joseph Pittera, who translated books and articles in French, German, and Italian and thus allowed me to go beyond English-language sources.

John Martin, John Tucker, and Stephen Poston are also gratefully acknowledged for typing several drafts of the manuscript.

1 INTRODUCTION

One hundred years ago the intelligence and counterintelligence communities of major and middle-ranking powers were in a primitive stage of development. Intelligence units were underfunded and understaffed. They were subject to the technological limitations of their time, dependent on information from often unreliable human agents and from diplomatic intercepts. The type of information sought was also limited, involving mainly diplomatic maneuvering, military hardware, and war plans. Today, intelligence has become an integral part of the national security and international operations of even smaller nations. Both the scope and means of collection in the 1980s far surpass those of the 1880s.

The complexity and diversity of modern military hardware require a greater effort to collect information in order to produce a comprehensive order of battle, particularly regarding nations with highly secretive nuclear weapons programs.

The role of intelligence in conducting foreign policy has also grown as nations have broadened their contacts with the rest of the world. The ease of international communication and travel in today's world has encouraged closer global ties. More important, the numerous repercussions that events in a far corner of the world can have on a country's physical or economic security require that nations maintain a large number of diplomatic contacts. Finally, the advent of a variety of regional and international organizations has engendered a need for nations to determine the way in which member states are likely to align on specific issues.

Economic interests, too, have become a significant stimulant to intelligence activity. In some instances, the object is to determine the likely availability of natural resources, which might be affected by natural depletion, competition, political change, or military conflict. In other cases, participation in economic negotiations, or the acquisition of advanced technology may be the stimulus. On some occasions, the technology may be desired for its military applications—such as its role in the construction of an atomic bomb. But it is just as likely that technology is being sought to enhance industrial capabilities and to gain an advantage in the marketplace.

Intelligence concerning the sociological conditions of foreign nations has also gained importance. Internal strife, class conflicts, and morale all influence the course of a nation's foreign policy and its ability to conduct military operations.

Another concern that is far greater today than one hundred years ago is terrorism. Terrorist attacks may be motivated by ideological or ethnic conflict and carried out by domestic groups, exiles, or foreign groups. Intelligence and security services seek to identify such groups, their personnel, sources of support, weapons, and likely targets.

To deal with all of these concerns, intelligence communities engage in a wide range of activities—clandestine and open source collection, signals intelligence, ocean surveillance, photographic reconnaissance, counterintelligence, covert action, liaison, and analysis. The specific targets of such activities reflect both their national interests and their obligations under international intelligence or military alliances.

In intelligence matters, the United Kingdom is closely tied to the United States and several other Anglo-Saxon countries by such arrangements as the UKUSA signals intelligence treaty and the Commonwealth Signals Organization. Arrangements like these make the United Kingdom responsible for signals intelligence collection against some targets, such as Chinese space operations, that are not greatly relevant to British national security decision-making. At the same time, the activities of the Irish Republican Army—whether in Ireland, Britain, or overseas—are a matter of national concern and thus a target of British Security Service, Secret Intelligence Service, and Government Communications Headquarters operations. Likewise, international economic events that threaten the far from healthy British economy must be of critical interest to Her Majesty's government.

Although Canada may seem like a nation with little need for an intelligence service—for years it has done without a foreign clandestine collection agency—its proximity to the United States, both culturally and geographically, has given it a common interest in the defense of North America (as expressed in its participation in NORAD) and some common intelligence responsibilities. Canada is also concerned with the passage of U.S. and Soviet submarines through the Canadian Arctic. Moreover, Canada is a major home for expatriate Sikhs, including those who have visions of turning India's Punjab state into the independent Sikh nation of Khalistan. The most extreme Sikhs have resorted to a variety of terrorist acts inside and outside India, apparently including the destruction of an Air India flight that took off from Toronto, killing more than 300 people, as well as an attack on a Punjabi cabinet minister in Vancouver.[1] As a result, Sikh activity in Canada is a target of Canadian Security Intelligence Service surveillance.

Italy, too, has internal security concerns. Its role in NATO, its hosting of U.S. intelligence and military bases (including several at which nuclear weapons are stored), makes it a prominent target of Soviet bloc espionage activities. Italy has also been plagued by terrorist incidents, including assassinations, political kidnappings, and bombings. Some of these incidents were the responsibility of the Red Brigades. Others were the work of right-wing groups acting, unfortunately, with some degree of support from the very security services charged with preventing such actions. And although Italy's foreign intelligence concerns are somewhat less obvious, they surely include drug trafficking, Middle Eastern events that may affect the Italian oil supply, and the activities of foreign terrorist groups that may act against Italian targets.

West Germany's intelligence and security agenda is a function of its industrial status and its unique position in the East-West conflict. Intelligence related to West Germany's international trade position, as well as to its supply of energy and raw materials, is undoubtedly a key concern. At the same time, West Germany's intelligence network must focus a significant portion of its collection and analytical resources on events in the Soviet bloc, particularly East Germany, Czechoslovakia, and Poland. Events in those countries or in the Soviet Union can have notable implications for the success of Germany's policy of Ostpolitik as well as for its military security. Tactical military intelligence—produced by signals intelligence stations and aircraft—is also a necessity, given the imposing Warsaw Pact presence across the border.

Internally, West Germany is burdened by many of the same problems experienced by other Western European nations—threats of terrorist attacks (such as the attack on a West Berlin nightclub in April 1986) and Soviet bloc espionage activities. Indeed, West Germany because of rather obvious factors is a major target for both the Soviet and East German intelligence services. Additionally, West Germany has the burden of its Nazi past and the need to see that neo-Nazi groups do not attempt to do more than propagandize.

As a somewhat independent middle-ranking power with widespread interests, France has assigned to its intelligence and security services a broad range of responsibilities. Internally, France has had to deal with a large-scale Soviet intelligence effort, much of it directed at obtaining scientific and technical intelligence, as well as terrorist bombings. Externally, France's role in Africa and the Middle East has required the Directorate General of External Security (DGSE) to maintain substantial networks, particularly directed toward Chad and Libya. An even greater intelligence requirement is imposed by France's nuclear status. In 1983 France possessed 285 nuclear warheads, divided between strategic and tactical warheads and between land-based and sea-based weapons. It is projected that in the mid-1990s this number will grow to more than 1,000, of which approximately 700 will be strategic.[2] Such a force structure imposes a variety of intelligence requirements, target identification being one and Soviet ballistic missile defense and antisubmarine warfare efforts being two others.

Another aspect of France's nuclear activities that impose intelligence requirements is its South Pacific testing program. Even presuming that such follies as the *Rainbow Warrior* incident are avoided in the future, the DGSE will be expected to keep informed about the activities of peace and environmental groups opposed to France's nuclear-testing activities.

In the case of Israel, little explanation is needed of the central role played by intelligence in Israeli security policy. Since pre-Independence days, covert activity has been crucial to the Zionist movement. Israel has employed its intelligence community to conduct a variety of covert operations, including the assassination of Arab terrorists and the maintenance of relations with nations unwilling to officially recognize Israel.

More important, Israeli intelligence has been given the responsibility of providing up-to-date information on the activities of the PLO and Arab nations, both for combating their activities diplomatically and for providing warning of any impending attack. When Jordan, in a series of mediation missions, appears close to healing a six-year rift between Iraq and Syria, Israeli leaders want to be fully informed and may well approve a covert operation to block such an occurrence. When Syria begins digging trenches for tanks, bunkers for soldiers, and emplacements for artillery some ten to fifteen miles north of the Israeli-Lebanese border (as it did in May 1986), Israeli leaders expect to be kept fully informed of such activity.[3] When the Soviet Union and Syria sign a treaty—as they did with the October 1980 Soviet-Syrian Treaty of Friendship and Cooperation—some Israeli leaders worry whether there is a secret annex to the treaty allowing the stationing of Soviet forces in Syria.[4]

In the event that war does occur, Israeli strategic doctrine calls for the defense forces to achieve a rapid and decisive victory over the Arab forces. A rapid victory is imperative to avoid severe financial and manpower losses; a decisive victory is believed necessary to prevent the war from becoming a drawn-out slugging match and encouraging the adversary to try again at a later date. To accomplish such objectives, Israel's military leaders must have adequate early warning of attack and also detailed information on the military capabilities and tactics of the Arab forces. One crucial piece of information, attainable only by human sources or signals intelligence, is the extent to which Arab forces have mastered the advanced equipment provided by the Soviet Union and other countries.[5]

Japan's intelligence concerns involve both security and economic issues. Japan's aggressive export policy and its ability to compete in the production of high-technology items require, at the very least, analysts who can provide studies and estimates of foreign reactions to Japan's trade policies and advances in computer technology. Since Japan is virtually totally dependent on Middle Eastern oil to fuel its industrial machine, intelligence on political and military events in the Middle East, such as the Iran-Iraq war and the likely responses of Arab nations to any Japanese dealings with Israel is of considerable importance.[6]

Japan's military activities were highly restricted by the Peace Constitution imposed by the United States. And while Japanese government and ruling party leaders recently agreed to abandon a long-held policy that limited the military to one percent of the country's GNP, Japan is hardly likely to embark on a massive buildup requiring new intelligence activities.[7] But Japan's limited military forces and its status—due to the U.S. facilities there—as a major wartime Soviet target have made creation of an efficient intelligence and warning network imperative. Thus, Japan operates an extensive technical collection network to monitor Soviet activities in the Soviet Far East and the immediate vicinity of Japan.

China, unlike many European powers, meets some of the requirements for twentieth-century superpower status, including a large population and extensive natural resources. China is, however, a long way from such status—due in large part to its economic backwardness. The need to advance in great leaps fuels one portion of China's foreign intelligence activities: its focus on the acquisition of advanced technologies, often those which Western nations place off limits to the People's Republic of China. Of course, China's adversary status with the USSR also imposes intelligence requirements, one being the monitoring of Soviet military forces on the Sino-Soviet border and another being the acquisition of target data. China's adversary status with the USSR not only has made the Soviets a primary intelligence target but also has made the United States a major intelligence ally.

China's new openness to the West has produced an internal counterreaction, particularly within the Ministry of State Security. The ministry has been active in seeking not only to prevent foreign espionage activities but also to limit contacts between Westerners (particularly journalists) and Chinese citizens. The ministry's activities have often been the most visible sign of internal splits within the Chinese leadership over the question of modernization and relations with the West. In addition to real or imagined internal threats, China is obviously a target of both U.S. and Soviet intelligence activities, as evidenced by U.S. penetration of the Chinese nuclear program and the large number of Soviet agents periodically rounded up by the state security forces.

As a result of internal and external necessities, of threats real and imagined, all of these nations have engaged in extensive intelligence and security operations. In some cases, their activities have been dictated solely by national interest; in other cases, by international commitments. In some cases, their activities have marginally increased the intelligence available to the United States; in other cases, they have provided dramatic new information. As we will see in Chapter 10, future developments in these nations' intelligence capabilities could have a substantial impact on international relations.

NOTES TO CHAPTER 1

1. "Spies Under Fire," *Maclean's*, September 28, 1987, pp. 12–14.
2. Robbin F. Laird, "France's Nuclear Future," in Robbin F. Laird, ed., *French Security Policy: From Independence to Interdependence* (Boulder, Colo.: Westview, 1986), p. 69.
3. Charles P. Wallace, "Iraq-Syria Rift May Be Near End," *Los Angeles Times*, May 29, 1986, pp. 1, 10; Thomas L. Friedman, "Syria Is Said to Press Trench Work," *New York Times*, May 21, 1986, p. A12.
4. David Shipler, "To Israelis War in Gulf Is Opportunity for West," *New York Times*, November 1, 1980, p. 4.
5. Yoav Ben-Horin and Barry Posen, *Israel's Strategic Doctrine* (Santa Monica, Calif.: Rand Corporation, September 1981), pp. 6, 18.
6. William R. Campbell, "Japan and the Middle East," in Robert S. Ozaki and Walter Arnold, eds., *Japan's Foreign Relations: A Global Search for Economic Security* (Boulder, Colo.: Westview, 1985), p. 133.
7. Clyde Haberman, "Japan to Scrap Formula for Limiting Arms Budget," *New York Times*, January 24, 1987, p. 3.

2 UNITED KINGDOM INTELLIGENCE ORGANIZATIONS

ORIGINS

While the origins of today's British intelligence and security community can be traced to the early part of the twentieth century, Britain has been conducting organized intelligence activities since the late sixteenth century.

In 1570 Francis Walsingham (later Sir) was appointed Ambassador to France. During his tenure in Paris, he began to build up an intelligence network at home and abroad that included a number of agents in France. In 1573 Walsingham returned to England and became Principal Secretary and a member of the Privy Council. Among the duties assigned to him was "to have care to the intelligence abroad."[1]

By 1587 the system had become a full-fledged intelligence apparatus. Walsingham had sufficient reports concerning England's rival, Spain, to establish that Spain was amassing a vast fleet of ships to attack England. As a result, he drew up what was surely one of Britain's first intelligence requirement documents, the *Plot for Intelligence Out of Spain.* The *Plot* specified a variety of tasks for Walsingham's agents:

- The need to obtain some correspondence from the French Ambassador in Spain

- To take orders with some at Rouen to have frequent advertisements from such as arrive out of Spain at Nantes, Havre, and Dieppe
- Sir Edward Stafford (English Ambassador in France) to obtain information from the Venetian Ambassador
- To set up an Intelligence post in Cracow for receiving reports on Spanish matters coming from the Vatican
- To nominate persons (French, Flemish, or Italians) to travel along the Spanish coasts and report what preparations are being made at ports, furnishing them with letters of credit as a cover
- To obtain intelligence from the Court of Spain and from Genoa
- To arrange Intelligence at Brussels, Leydon and in Denmark [2]

When Walsingham died in 1590 Britain returned, for the time being, to the pre-Walsingham tradition of relying on its ambassadors for the bulk of intelligence.

The forerunner for Britain of a technical collection service was the agency involved in cryptanalysis. When the first such British agency, the Decyphering Branch, was created in 1703 there was no electronic means of transmitting diplomatic messages; messages to be deciphered had to be purloined and copied by British agents or obtained by recruiting a foreign cipher clerk. The Decyphering Branch was closed down in 1844, just at the time the electric telegraph was about to make the transmission and interception of diplomatic messages much easier. [3]

One hundred years after the formation of the Decyphering Branch, the first military intelligence organization was established by the Quartermaster General. Titled the Depot of Military Knowledge, the organization had as its primary function the collection from overt sources of maps and information on the military resources and topography of foreign powers. In 1855 a successor organization, the Topographical and Statistical Department of the War Office, was established. Its Topographical Section was responsible for collecting foreign military maps and plans, while its Statistical Section was responsible for gathering and collating intelligence on foreign military forces. The primary sources for the Statistical Section were the reports of military attachés and foreign publications. [4]

Beginning in the 1870s, the term *intelligence* began creeping into the titles of military organizations. Thus, in 1873 the Topographical and Statistical Department was renamed the Intelligence Branch (and subsequently the Intelligence Division and the Intelligence Department). In 1883 the Admiralty established a Foreign Intelligence Committee that eventually became the Naval Intelligence Department.[5] Subsequently, the Military Intelligence Department went through a series of mergers and separations with other departments before it reemerged, in 1939, as the Military Intelligence Department. In addition, an Irish Special Branch of the Metropolitan Police was formed in 1883 to combat Fenian bombing in London. Although the bombings ended on January 31, 1885, as of 1888 the activities of the branch went beyond the Irish and the word *Irish* was dropped from its title. Subsequently, the Special Branch became the most visible British organization involved in counterintelligence, counter-subversion, and VIP protection.[6]

The origins of the present Secret Intelligence Service (SIS) and Security Service can be traced to 1909, when a subcommittee of the Committee of Imperial Defence was established to examine "the nature and extent of the foreign espionage that is at present taking place within this country and the danger to which it may expose us."[7] Among the discoveries that alarmed the committee was Britain's lack of a single agent on the European continent. It was therefore recommended that a Secret Service Bureau be established. Initially divided into military and naval sections, the bureau's organization evolved within a year into a Home Section and a Foreign Section. Placed under the control of the War Office, the bureau had three functions:

1. to be a screen between the Service departments and foreign spies;
2. to be the intermediary between the Service departments and British agents abroad; and
3. to take charge of counterespionage.[8]

Over the subsequent years, the Home Section evolved into MO-5, MI-5 and finally the civilian Security Service. Likewise, the Foreign Section evolved into MI-1c, MI-6 and eventually the civilian SIS.[9]

World War I provided a major impetus for increasing the size of the services; by the armistice in November 1918, MI-5's original wartime staff of 19 had grown to 844.[10] The war also provided a considerable boost to technical collection activities. The Royal Flying Corps flew its first reconnaissance missions on August 19, 1915. The next day, it observed a column of troops passing through Louvain and "stretching as far as the eye could see." When trench warfare was superseded by a war of movement in the spring of 1918, aerial reconnaissance became more important than agent reports.[11]

Even more significant was the development of communications intelligence. Both the Army and the Navy established cryptographic units to attack diplomatic and military ciphers. The Navy organization, Room 40, became Britain's single most important intelligence asset during the war.[12] Among its accomplishments was the deciphering of the Zimmerman Telegram, in which Germany proposed that Mexico attack the United States to recover lost territory. The revelation of the contents of the telegram helped propel the United States into the war.[13]

In 1919 the remnants of Room 40 and MI-8 (the Army's cryptographic organization) were combined into the Government Code and Cypher School, located at Bletchley Park. The school's publicly announced function was "to advise as to the security of codes and cyphers used by all Government departments and to assist in their provision."[14] The school's unannounced function, of course, was to intercept the communications of foreign governments and to decipher the messages obtained. In this area the Government Code and Cypher School had several early successes. The American diplomatic code, which was reciphered quarterly, was broken in time to provide intelligence on U.S. policy during the Washington Naval Conference of 1921-22. Later in the decade the school achieved notable successes against Soviet diplomatic ciphers. Some of the deciphered messages were made public by British leaders to support their accusations of Soviet espionage/subversive activities in Britain—an act that led to Soviet adoption of the unbreakable "one-time pad" system.[15] In 1942 the school became the Government Communications Headquarters (GCHQ), which remains its present name.[16]

In 1928 the Industrial Intelligence in Foreign Countries Subcommittee of the Committee on Imperial Defense was established to report on foreign industrial mobilization plans in the event of war. In March 1931 the subcommittee established the Industrial Intelligence Centre (IIC), with responsibilities for studying the vulnerability of foreign nations' industry to attack, the potential expansion of arms industries in war, and the possibility of uncovering war preparations through the continuous study of imports of raw materials and machinery. Between 1931 and 1939 the IIC's responsibilities grew— replacing, for example, the Board of Trade as the principal authority on wartime trade questions. At the outbreak of World War II, it became part of the Ministry of Economic Warfare (MEW), and was abolished, along with MEW, at the end of the war.[17]

It was not until 1935 that the Air Ministry had any sort of intelligence organization. The resurgence of the German Air Force led to the establishment of a Deputy Director of Intelligence, subordinate to the Directorate of Operations and Intelligence. Upon outbreak of the war, an independent Air Intelligence Branch was established.[18]

In January 1936 an attempt was made to ensure better coordination of intelligence activities. An Inter-Services Intelligence Committee (ISIC) was established with the approval of the Chiefs of Staff and the Committee on Imperial Defence. The ISIC was stillborn, however, and in June 1936 was replaced by the Joint Intelligence Subcommittee of the Chiefs of Staff, which normally met at least once a month and included the head of the IIC,[19] The subcommittee subsequently became the Joint Intelligence Committee and included the heads of the Security Service and the SIS.

Naturally, World War II expanded the size of the British intelligence community. New organizations, such as the Special Operations Executive, established to conduct subversive operations, were formed and then dismantled after the war. In addition, the already-existing organizations—SIS, the Security Service, GCHQ, and the military service intelligence departments—grew in size. The most significant achievements were those of GCHQ, particularly its success in deciphering German military communications to produce ULTRA intelligence information.[20] To collect the German signals, GCHQ set up an extensive network of listening stations in England, Scotland, Northern Ireland, and other locations. Also of great importance was the Security Service's success in capturing every German agent infiltrated into Britain and then maintaining an elaborate double-cross system that permitted the British authorities to regularly pass disinformation back to German intelligence.[21]

In addition to the area of communications intelligence, World War II produced much British activity in other areas of what came to be known as technical collection. Much of this activity involved attempts to locate and destroy German radar and navigation stations. In order to guide their bombers to target, the Germans had developed a long-range blind bombing system named Knickebein. A ground transmitter radiated a beam to mark a flight path for aircraft, with Morse dots on one side of the beam and Morse dashes on the other. In the center lane, the dots and dashes merged to give a steady tone. To fly the beam, pilots had simply to stay in the zone where they heard the steady note signal.[22]

Armed with evidence that the Knickebein system used transmissions in the vicinity of 30 MHz, the British Air Ministry bought several receivers from ham radio enthusiasts that covered the 27- to 143-MHz band. One was installed in an Anson twin-engined reconnaissance aircraft to be used in what became the first British airborne electronics intelligence mission. During its third flight, on June 21, 1940, a full pattern of Knickebein signals aligned over Lincolnshire was found, with Morse dots to the south, dashes to the north, and a steady note signal running up the middle. With the information acquired, the Royal Air Force (RAF) began to jam the Knickebein system.[23]

The British employed both photographic reconnaissance and electronic intelligence (ELINT) as part of an operation code-named OCCULIST. RAF reconnaissance aircraft flew carefully planned tracks over occupied Europe, photographing the territory below so as to provide an accurate record of their tracks. In addition, German radio reports of the aircraft's flight paths were intercepted and decoded. By back-plotting the distances and bearings, given by the radar stations, intelligence officers were able to find the positions of several of the German stations.[24]

By the end of World War II, the three most important British intelligence and security agencies of the postwar era—SIS, GCHQ, and the Security Service—were in place. Additionally, Britain had become heavily involved in the types of technical collection activities that were to revolutionize postwar intelligence collection: airborne photographic and electronic reconnaissance and land-based signals interception.

One further significant change in the British intelligence community involved the military service intelligence departments. At the end of World War II, the Army War Office had its Military Intelligence Department, the Admiralty its Naval Intelligence Division, and the RAF the Air Ministry's Air Intelligence Directorate. In 1946 a small coordinating unit known as the Joint Intelligence Bureau (JIB) was created and headed by Kenneth Strong, who had been Dwight Eisenhower's chief intelligence officer in World War II. The scope of JIB went beyond providing analysis based on military considerations; rather, JIB was also to cover political, economic, and psychological factors connected with the national interest. In 1964 JIB was replaced by the Defense Intelligence Staff (DIS), which not only absorbed JIB's analytic and coordinating role but actually absorbed the service intelligence departments themselves.[25]

Thus, as of 1987 the British intelligence and security community consisted of a variety of collection, analytical, and management organizations, including the Government Communications Headquarters, the Secret Intelligence Service, the Defense Intelligence Staff, the Joint Air Reconnaissance Intelligence Centre, the Security Service, the Special Branch of Scotland Yard, and the Joint Intelligence Organization of the Joint Intelligence Committee.

INTELLIGENCE AND SECURITY ORGANIZATIONS

Government Communications Headquarters

The Government Communications Headquarters is located at Cheltenham, Gloucestershire, and maintains a London office at 2-8 Palmer Street, SW1. Between 5,000 and 8,000 individuals work at headquarters, with another 5,000 to 8,000 others (primarily servicemen) at field stations. GCHQ spends approximately $700 million a year. Its officially defined mission is the "reception and analysis of foreign communications and other electronic transmissions for intelligence purposes."[26] A more detailed description of GCHQ's communications intelligence (COMINT) role has been offered by Tony Bunyan: "GCHQ monitors and decodes all radio, telex and telegram communications in and out of Britain, including the messages of all foreign embassies in Britain, finance and industrial companies and individuals of interest to state agencies."[27]

In addition to its signals intelligence activities, GCHQ also "has the responsibility for developing codes and procedures to safeguard British Government communications."[28] A specialist unit of GCHQ, the Diplomatic Telecommunications Maintenance Service, has the responsibility for the debugging of Whitehall offices, outstations, and British embassies.[29]

At the top of the present GCHQ structure is the Director, subordinate to whom are four principal directorates—the Directorate of SIGINT Plans (DP), the Directorate of SIGINT Operations and Re-

Figure 2-1. Organization of the Government Communications Headquarters.

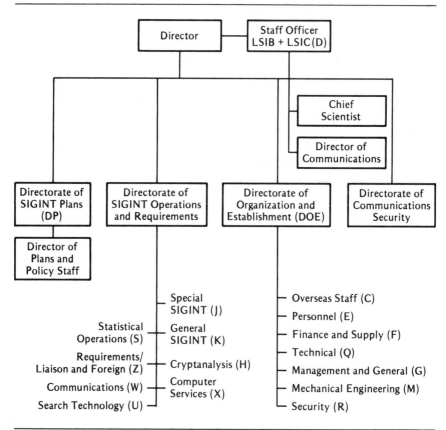

quirements, the Directorate of Organization and Establishment (DOE), and the Directorate of Communications Security. Attached to the Director's office is a staff officer representing the London Signals Intelligence Board and the London Signals Intelligence Committee (Defence), which are discussed later in this chapter. Figure 2-1 shows the organizational structure of the GCHQ.

The Directorate of SIGINT Operations and Requirements is central to GCHQ activities and is subdivided into eight divisions: Statistical Operations (S), Requirements/Liaison and Foreign (Z), Special SIGINT (J), General SIGINT (K), Communications (W), Cryptanalysis (H), Computer Services (X) and Search Technology (U). It is through Z Division that detailed UKUSA (discussed later in this chapter) as well as other SIGINT requirements are determined. Z Division receives target requests from the Ministry of Defence, the

Foreign Office, and the military services, as well as from trade and economic ministries. It also maintains liaison with a variety of foreign SIGINT agencies.[30]

J Division concentrates on the interception of Soviet bloc signals. With approximately 900 employees, it is one of the largest GCHQ divisions. K Division deals with all other geographical areas as well as with intercepted commercial messages. Among K Division sections are K25, which monitors the communications of sub-Saharan Africa, and K11, which coordinates the detailed monitoring and tasking of the intercept stations. Actual code-breaking activity is the responsibility of H Division, while X Division operates the GCHQ computer system. Among the computers employed are a variety of U.S.-built computers—including huge IBM 360 and IBM 370 machines, at least one Cray, and a computer known as Tandem Nonstop—that analyze the data collected at the GCHQ intercept stations.[31]

The Search Technology Division is concerned with the means of locating a signal rather than its interception—an activity known as Long-Range Technical Search (LRTS). This activity is intended to counter attempts by Soviet and other foreign communications bureaus to give further protection, beyond encryption, to their communications by concealing the very existence of the signal, either by spreading the signal so thinly across a range of frequencies that it becomes indistinguishable from the background noise or by burying it within other transmissions.[32] According to James Bamford:

> LRTS operators search for any unusual signal above 30 megahertz. Once they discover one which has not previously been logged they photograph it, take it down to the intermediate frequencies, and pass it through various specialized filters. . . . The "complete picture" of the signal is then studied . . . in order to develop equipment to better capture it and extract usable intelligence from it.[33]

Similarly, the Statistical Operations Division is not concerned with decryption, rather, its focus is on traffic analysis—studying the "externals" of a message (its source, destination, priority, etc.) as a means of obtaining information, even from encrypted messages that cannot be decrypted. Such externals can provide information about troop movements, for example, or the imminence of an attack or other military operations. The Communications Division is responsible for delivering the signals intelligence to its final consumer.[34]

The second most important directorate of the GCHQ is the Directorate of Communications Security. Until 1969 the functions of this directorate were performed by a separate agency, the London Communications Security Agency, which operated under "cover" as the Communications-Electronic Security Department of the Foreign Office. In 1969, however, it was decided to merge the agency into the GCHQ, partly as a means of ending the bitter and recurrent feuds between the two organizations.[35]

The Directorate of Organization and Establishment is the administrative directorate, responsible for Personnel (E), Mechanical Engineering (M), Finance and Supply (F), Management and General (G), Technical (Q), and Security (R). It is also responsible for the Overseas Staff (C), the division that assigns intercept operators to clandestine listening posts within British embassies. The Directorate of SIGINT Plans, consisting solely of the Plans and Policy Staff, is responsible for long-range planning for intercept stations and other SIGINT activities.[36]

Finally, subordinate to the GCHQ is the Joint Technical Language Service (JTLS), which consists of translators of a wide variety of languages who can transcribe the intercepted voice conversations resulting from COMINT activities.[37] These conversations may include, for example, those of Soviet pilots and army commanders on maneuvers or of oil ministers of the OPEC countries.

GCHQ directs the activities of all Army, Navy, and Air Force monitoring organizations and stations, having won a battle to take control of such stations in 1963. GCHQ set up the Composite Signals Organization to run the stations, which are located both in Britain and overseas. More than a dozen stations are located in Britain. Among the currently operating ground stations is a satellite ground station at Morwenstow, near Bude, Cornwall. One of the Morwenstow station's functions is the interception of COMSAT and INTELSAT communications. This task is accomplished with the aid of nine satellite dishes at the site, two of which are 100-foot aerials. Another four dishes are planned. A GCHQ London site at the Empress State Building in Earls Court has been used since the 1970s to intercept International Leased Carrier cable and telex traffic. A station at Culm Head hosts a 150-man CSO contingent. The antennas at Culm Head are of the rhombic variety, which can only listen to transmissions coming from a known direction.[38]

A fifty-man contingent at Brora uses High-Frequency Direction-Finding (HF-DF) equipment to listen to and pinpoint the location of Soviet ships in conjunction with Norwegian listening posts at Namdalen and Randaberg. The Norwegian stations can triangulate on a

Soviet ship by listening to its shortwave signals but have blind spots in the North Sea and North Atlantic that can conveniently be covered by Brora. A station at Irton Moor is primarily engaged in intercepting the communications of Soviet, East German, and Polish naval and shipping traffic in the Baltic Sea.[39]

Facilities at Hawklaw (in Fife) and Cheadle (in Staffs) have very different targets. Hawklaw intercepts international telecommunications traffic. Cheadle was set up during World War II to monitor the communications of the German Air Force, and its initial post-World War II duties were apparently the interception of the shortwave signals of Warsaw Pact aircraft. Currently, its staff of 340 is primarily involved in intercepting Irish communications.[40]

At Saxa Vord, Unst, Shetland, the RAF's 91 Signals Unit may monitor the electronic emissions from Soviet aircraft being tracked by the RAF radar site there. In addition there is a remote unmanned HF-DF installation at Saxa Vord to monitor naval movements in the Norwegian Sea.[41]

The primary mission of the Blakehill (Wilts) CSO station, which is tied into the NSA satellite communication intercept network, is to intercept Soviet Mohniya satellite communications. RAF Digby (Leicester) is responsible for the interception of Soviet and East European air communications.[42]

GCHQ also maintains several offices and stations outside of the United Kingdom. In addition to U.K. liaison offices at the Canadian Communications Security Establishment in Ottawa, the Australian Defence Signals Directorate (DSD) in Melbourne, and the U.S. National Security Agency (NSA) at Fort Meade, Maryland, GCHQ maintains several stations in Europe and Asia. Located in Birgelen, West Germany, is the Army's 13th Signal Regiment, which concentrates on the HF intercept of Soviet Army and related activity in the western USSR and Forward Area. The regiment maintains outstations at Dannenberg, Jever, and West Berlin (Teufelsberg).[43]

At Celle/Scheuen, Ironside Barracks, the Army's 14th Signal Regiment, specializes in mobile VHF/UHF and ELINT interception. Other intercept locations in West Germany include Langeleben and Wesendorf, which engage in VHF/UHF COMINT interception and tactical ELINT interception, respectively.[44]

A GCHQ unit established in 1983 at Gibraltar is engaged in COMINT and HF-DF monitoring. At Ayios Nikoaos near Farmagusta in Cyprus is the Army's 9th Signal Regiment, also known as the Mediterranean Field Intercept Station for GCHQ and as UKM 257 in the

UKUSA network. This facility operates against the communications of Mediterranean and Middle Eastern states, including the diplomatic and military communications of Libya, Egypt, and Iraq as well as NATO allies Italy, Greece, and Turkey. Other major targets are Saudi Arabia, Lebanon, Syria, and naval and aircraft movements in the eastern Mediterranean, particularly those of the USSR. Some signals are also intercepted from Israel and Iran.[45]

GCHQ also operates several joint sites overseas, including one with NSA and one with Australia. A site jointly operated with NSA is located at Two Boats on the Ascension Isles in the South Atlantic. This facility is primarily concerned with monitoring naval communications in the South Atlantic.[46]

The facility operated in conjunction with the Australian DSD was upgraded in 1976 with construction of a huge new complex at Tai Mo Shan in the New Territories. There are currently two intercept stations in Hong Kong. The Composite Signals Organization on Hong Kong itself houses administrative, signal recording, and cryptographic activities; it was originally located at Little Sai Wan but was moved to a new site on the south coast of Hong Kong Island in 1983, with Britain paying for the move.[47]

The New Territories outstation at Tai Mo Shan has an aerial farm that is even larger than the one formerly at Little Sai Wan. Until the mid-1970s, the Hong Kong operation was directed almost entirely against the People's Republic of China (PRC). The PRC, including its military communications and weapons and its space activities, is still very much a target, but the station is now also heavily involved in monitoring Soviet naval movements along East Asia from the major naval bases at Vladivostok and Petropovlovsk-Kamchatka to Cam Ranh Bay in Vietnam.[48]

Two sites activated in 1982–83 are located in Latin America. A small Army tactical SIGINT site was established in Belize, in Central America, and during 1983 an Army SIGINT collection unit was established on the Falklands.[49]

GCHQ also operates listening posts in a number of British embassies and High Commission offices overseas, including Moscow, Nairobi (Kenya), Pretoria, Lilongwe (Malawi), Lusaka (Zambia), Blantyre (Malawi), Gabarone (Botswana), Mbabane (Swaziland), and probably also Warsaw, Budapest, Prague, Cairo, Freetown (Sierra Leone), and Accra. In the early 1970s the GCHQ's African stations were involved in intercepting reports of regular tripartite security meetings among the Portuguese, Rhodesian, and South African intelligence organizations. In 1976, during South Africa's intervention in Angola, GCHQ intercepted and deciphered South African military communications.[50]

In addition to ground stations, GCHQ uses aircraft for signals intelligence collection. Under the tasking of GCHQ, the RAF's No. 51 Squadron, based at Wyton, operates a small number of BAe Nimrod aircraft modified for electronic reconnaissance.[51]

The Nimrod R1 was formally commissioned into squadron service on May 10, 1974. That aircraft was virtually indistinguishable from the standard maritime reconnaissance airframe, with the exception of the installation of radomes at the tail (replacing the Magnetic Anomaly Detector housing) and on the noses of the two external wing fuel tanks and extensive work around the original weapons bay, presumably to allow for the installation of the necessary electronics gear.[52]

Modification in the early 1980s resulted in three aircraft being redesignated Nimrod R2s. An array of nine "inverted L" shaped antennas above the forward fuselage, on both wing tanks, and above the tail planes were introduced, as were equipment pods on the wingtips. The cabin layout itself was revised by removal of the cabin windows forward of the wing, possibly indicating a reduction in the number of systems operations carried and the introduction of more automated equipment.[53]

The Nimrod R1/R2 aircraft have been most frequently spotted over the Baltic, suggesting interest in the activities of the Warsaw Pact air defense network in East Germany, Poland, Estonia, Latvia, and Lithuania and the Soviet naval installations around Leningrad. Further north, the installations around the White Sea and the launch site at Plesetsk would be of interest. Outside the European theater, Nimrod R2 aircraft can be expected to be active over the Mediterranean, with operating locations on Malta and Cyprus, together with the possible use of facilities in Turkey. Such a spread of rotational bases would be ideal for monitoring activities along the southern and eastern shores of the Mediterranean as well as activities of the Soviet Black Sea Fleet.[54]

Beginning in 1989, GCHQ may also have a satellite SIGINT capability. By that time GCHQ will probably have ZIRCON available for launch—a SIGINT satellite to be launched into a geosynchronous orbit and stationed at 53° east longitude, placing it over the Indian Ocean and giving it an electronic view of the eastern half of the Soviet Union. The satellite, expected to cost up to $750 million, was intended to be launched under the cover of the British SKYNET communications satellites, which also operate in geosynchronous orbit.[55]

GCHQ has had a number of security problems in the 1980s, the most noteworthy of which concerned Geoffrey Prime, a former GCHQ translator and section chief who was arrested in 1982 for having provided GCHQ material to the Soviet Union for fourteen years.[56] Earlier it was charged that numerous classified documents had disappeared from the GCHQ's station at Little Sai Wan in Hong Kong. In addition, it appears that code word documents classified TOP SECRET UMBRA disappeared in 1981 from the Stanley Fort Satellite Station in Hong Kong, a station built specifically to intercept signals from Chinese space and missile launches. According to one former GCHQ official, the lost documents contained details of how to detect, follow, and understand radio signals from Chinese missiles and satellites.[57]

Secret Intelligence Service

The Secret Intelligence Service has both internal and external functions. Internally, it seeks to spot, assess, and recruit foreigners residing in the United Kingdom for employment as agents when they return to their native countries. Externally, it conducts a wide range of activities, including the collection of intelligence by clandestine means, counterintelligence operations, covert action, and clandestine communications support. Naturally, it furnishes elements of the government with the products of its intelligence collection.

The SIS is headed by the Chief of the Secret Service, also known as C, or CSS. The second-ranking official in the SIS is the Director, who supervises its day-to-day operations. Under the Director are four directorates and a group of controllers for the supervision of foreign operations. The four directorates are the Directorate of Personnel and Administration; the Directorate of Special Support, which provides technical support for SIS activities; the Directorate of Counterintelligence and Security, which handles both SIS internal security and offensive counterintelligence operations; and the Directorate of Requirements and Production, which is responsible both for determining intelligence collection requirements and for producing intelligence reports.[58]

Figure 2-2. Organization of the British Secret Intelligence Service (MI-6).

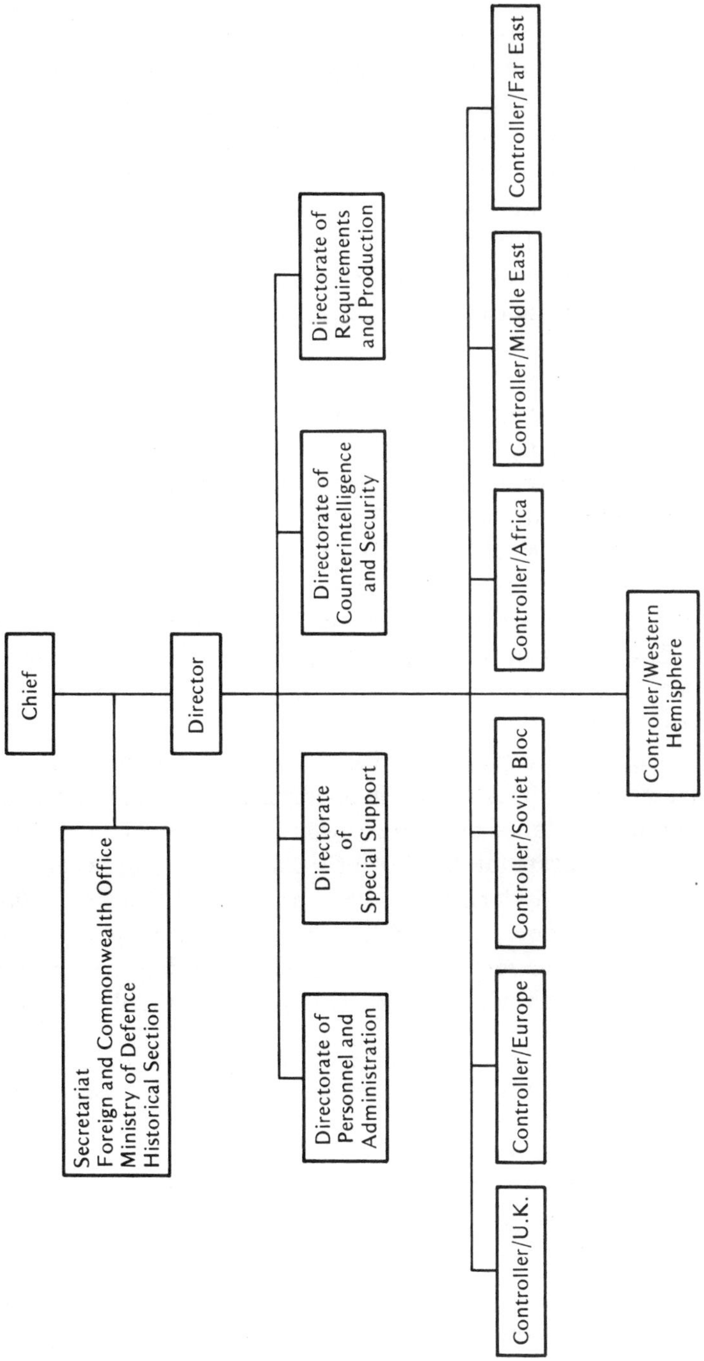

The SIS's foreign operations are under the supervision of seven controllers: Controller/U.K., Controller/Europe, Controller/Soviet Bloc, Controller/Africa, Controller/Middle East, Controller/Far East, and Controller/Western Hemisphere. The Controller/U.K. is responsible for spotting and recruiting foreigners residing in Britain to serve as agents in their native lands.[59] An organizational chart of the SIS is shown in Figure 2-2.

In pursuit of its postwar clandestine collection activities, SIS established extensive networks in Europe, Asia, and the Middle East, although those networks are probably substantially smaller now than in the 1950s and early 1960s, due to both limited resources and the betrayal of forty agents by George Blake. Among the East European countries where there were extensive networks are Czechoslovakia and East Germany.

One East German agent, Hans Joachim Koch, served SIS from 1951 until his arrest in 1955 while emptying a "dead-letter box" in Pankow Park. Koch, a wartime sergeant in the SS division Prine Eugen, had provided "good services" during the East Berlin uprising in 1953. Also arrested in 1955 was Johann Baumgart, an official of the East German railways; Baumgart had supplied the SIS with twenty-five extraordinarily detailed maps of the East German transport system.[60]

Of course, the greatest British success in the area of human intelligence gathering was the joint operation SIS conducted with the CIA in running Colonel Oleg Penkovskiy of the GRU, the Chief Intelligence Directorate of the Soviet General Staff. Between the time of his beginning to work for the SIS and the CIA in early 1961 and his arrest on October 22, 1962, Penkovskiy provided copies of large numbers of documents and manuals. According to Greville Wynne, the material with which Penkovskiy provided the West included:

- The names . . . and in many cases photographs of over 300 Soviet agents working in Western countries. In addition, several hundred agents under training in the Soviet Union, Czechoslovakia and other Eastern countries were made known to the West. . . .

- Details of Soviet rocket sites throughout the Soviet Union, together with statistical details of training manpower, weapon production, stock-piling and drawing board designs for future programs.

- . . . information that Khrushchev had allowed most important control equipment, which was in very short supply, to be sent with rockets to Cuba. . . .

- Photographic copies of reports which Khrushchev had given to the Soviet Praesidium, purporting to be an account of a meeting between Kennedy and himself, and the Italian Foreign Minister and himself.

- Statistics of agricultural production throughout the Soviet Union. . . .

- Production figures, location, lay-out and operating procedures for all the main Soviet industries, including the electronics industry, and the production of steel, aircraft and military equipment.

- Considerable information dealing with the Soviet Union's relations with Eastern European countries; photostatic copies of secret agreements; details of future policy of the Soviet Government towards those countries.[61]

In addition to purely human source operations, the SIS has conducted a number of technical operations on both small and large scales. According to George Blake, a Soviet penetration agent in the SIS from 1953 to 1961, he was involved in "Operation Contrary"—the placing of microphones in the office of the Polish Trade Mission in Brussels as well as the wiring of rooms at the Astoria Hotel in Brussels, used by trade representatives from Communist countries. A similar operation, according to Blake, was "Operation Fantastic"—the placing of hidden microphones at the office of the Soviet commercial attaché in Copenhagen. Other operations Blake claimed to have been involved in included tapping the telephones of the Czechoslovak Export Agency in Cairo and wiring the residence of a second secretary of the Bulgarian embassy in London.[62]

A technical SIS operation that occurred for certain and on a larger scale than the operations mentioned above was Operation SILVER. In 1949 the SIS purchased a house whose basement was about seventy feet from the two cables connecting Vienna's Imperial Hotel (the Soviet command center in then occupied Austria) with the Soviet command in Moscow. After resurfacing the driveway with reinforced concrete the SIS dug a tunnel from the basement out to the cables and tapped into the cables.[63]

In 1951 SILVER became a joint operation with the CIA. Both countries were able to benefit from the CIA's ability to read the plaintext of enciphered messages transmitted on land lines without subjecting the messages to cryptanalysis, by reading the "transients" or "artifacts" of the clear-text messages being enciphered by the Soviets at the Imperial Hotel. Among the intelligence produced was knowledge that the Soviet Union would not commit itself to a military advance through the Balkans, "a piece of intelligence holding enormous significance for the disposition of American troops during the fighting in Korea."[64]

The SIS has also been heavily involved in covert action, known as "special political action" in British terminology. In the 1950s and 1960s the SIS was engaged in substantial covert operations in the Middle East. The SIS financed the Sharq al-Adna broadcasting station (later named the Near East Arab Broadcasting Corporation), for example, to carry out pro-British propaganda. The SIS was also behind the Arab News Agency (ANA), which had been set up during the Second World War to engage in anti-Nazi propaganda, and the Near and Far Eastern News Agency (NAFEN). Both operated until 1968, when their assets were turned over to Forum World Features, a CIA proprietary.[65]

The SIS was heavily involved in the overthrow of Iranian Prime Minister Mossadeq in 1953 and his replacement by the Shah. It was Mossadeq's nationalization of the Anglo-Iranian Oil Company that led Britain to seek his overthrow. George Kennedy Young, the Deputy Director of the SIS, played a leading role in the day-to-day planning and liaison with the American CIA in the effort code-named "Ajax." Additionally, British agents played a significant role in day-to-day operations. When in April 1953 Mossadeq replaced the pro-American Chief of Police with a new chief and assigned him the task of purging pro-Americans, SIS agents kidnapped and killed the newly appointed police chief. Additionally, the British-controlled Iranian news media initiated a barrage of anti-Mossadeq propaganda.[66]

In the mid-1960s Iraq was also a target of SIS-inspired propaganda. The SIS stationed an experienced propagandist in Beirut to organize the publication of antigovernment pamphlets for circulation inside Iraq. In Yemen in the 1950s and 1960s the SIS was involved in British military activities directed against Egyptian-backed insurgents and antiroyalists. Imam Ahmad of North Yemen was overthrown by Nasser-backed nationalists in 1962. This led to a British attempt, with Israeli help, to tie down and harass large numbers of Egyptian troops. SIS officers aided Special Air Service soldiers in their operations.[67]

SIS operations in Ireland have included both intelligence collection and covert action. Its intelligence collection activities have been concentrated in three areas: (1) matters connected with the North, (2) the threat of the Soviet use of Ireland as a back door for spying on Britain, and (3) Irish politics and economics, especially in matters connected with the European Economic Community or relations with other countries. SIS has apparently had some success in establishing agents inside the Garda, the Irish Army, and government departments.[68]

One covert operation reportedly followed from the spotting, by an RAF maritime reconnaissance patrol, of a Soviet conventional submarine broken down on the surface within sight of the Donegal coast. Pictures taken by the patrol plane were passed to SIS, which then passed them to an agent who was a journalist. The agent was able to place them with a Belgian news agency that sold them to the British *The News of the World*, which published them on its front page with a story about the Soviet Union landing guns from submarines in Donegal.[69]

It has been alleged that two individuals, Kenneth and Keith Littlejohn, participated in a number of criminal acts at the behest of the SIS in order to pressure the Irish government to get tougher with the IRA. Included in the alleged acts were several bank robberies. SIS is also reported to have instructed the Littlejohns to petrol-bomb Garda stations.[70]

As with other intelligence services, the counterintelligence function of the SIS involves it in collecting and analyzing information concerning the intelligence services of hostile and friendly governments. In addition, it seeks to penetrate, when possible, the intelligence services of hostile governments. In that area it has achieved at least one major success. Oleg Gordievsky, who joined the KGB in 1962, began operating as a British agent in 1966, at his own instigation, shortly after arriving in Denmark. Gordievsky served two tours in Copenhagen as a press attaché in the Soviet Embassy, from 1966 to 1970 and from 1972 to 1978. After a four-year return to the Soviet Union, Gordievsky was reassigned to London in 1982 as deputy to the KGB resident. In April 1985 the KGB resident was expelled after his name came up in the trial of a British Security Service employee who tried to sell secrets to the Russians, and Gordievsky took the resident's place.[71]

While in Copenhagen, Gordievsky established a reputation as a specialist in the handling of East German illegals operating in West Germany and Denmark. During his tenure there, one Dane was arrested for spying for the KGB and seven Soviet diplomats were expelled. In addition, Gordievsky provided information vital to the arrest of Arne Treholt, the former Norwegian diplomat sentenced to twenty years in prison for spying for the Soviet Union. While stationed in London in 1982, Gordievsky alerted the British to the attempts of Security Service officer Michael Bettany to become a Soviet agent. Gordievsky was also able to provide SIS with positive intelligence concerning Soviet Secretary General Gorbachev, his wife, personal aides, and the working of the Politburo.[72]

After his promotion in 1985, Gordievsky was unexpectedly called back to the Soviet Union—a recall that he soon determined was due to his having fallen under suspicion. Gordievsky signaled British intelligence officers of his situation. SIS managed to exfiltrate Gordievsky clandestinely, spiriting him out of a Black Sea resort—reportedly via motorboat. When his defection was announced, twenty-five alleged spies were expelled from the United Kingdom.[73]

Another success in the counterintelligence area occurred in Geneva. A GRU officer, Vladimir Rezun, operating under cover of the UN World Health Organization, was under SIS control for several years prior to defecting. Subsequently, he wrote a number of books on the Soviet military and the GRU under the name of Viktor Surorov. While he was considered a valuable source by those who debriefed him, many of the claims in his books are considered questionable.[74]

The headquarters of the SIS are at Century House, 100 Westminster Bridge Road, SE1. Its London Station facility is at 60 Vauxhall Bridge Road, SE1, and its Training Centre is at 296–302 Borough High Street, SE1. Sabotage and demolition are taught in Gosport at an undercover establishment called Fort Monkton. Additionally, the SIS has a joint office with the Security Service at 140 Gower Street, WC1.[75]

Defense Intelligence Staff

At the head of the Defense Intelligence Staff (DIS) is the Director General of Intelligence (DGI), The Deputy to the DGI is also the Deputy Chief of the Defence Staff (Intelligence). Thus, in addition to his role as deputy, he reports directly on general and current intelligence matters to the Chief of the Defence Staff, the Chiefs of Staff Committee, and other staffs in the Ministry of Defence.[76]

The DIS is subdivided into four directorates: the Directorate of Management and Support of Intelligence (DMSI), the Directorate of Scientific and Technical Intelligence (DSTI), the Directorate of Service Intelligence (DSI), and the Directorate of Economic Intelligence.[77]

The DMSI provides the central staff support for the DGI and Deputy Chief of the Defence Staff (Intelligence) (DCDS(I)) in handling substantive intelligence business, with the exception of current intelligence. It coordinates the intelligence reporting required by DIS customers as well as the DIS input into the Joint Intelligence Committee (discussed later in this chapter). DMSI is also responsible for DIS long-term studies on such matters as U.S.–Soviet relations and the Strategic Arms Limitation Talks (SALT).[78]

The DSTI is responsible for producing intelligence concerning electronics, chemical and biological weapons, missiles, atomic energy, and the basic sciences. The DSI is responsible for producing intelligence on broad military aspects of the defense forces and policies of foreign countries; it also produces the coordinated DIS output of intelligence for the Assessment Staff. The Directorate of Economic Intelligence is responsible for studying the general economic developments in Communist countries; armaments production and supporting industries worldwide; and the military and economic aid activities of Communist countries.[79]

A job circular for DIS officers suggests that

> . . . specialist knowledge and experience is desirable in the fields of transportation systems, ports, beaches, power and water supplies, ammunition and ordnance, POL installations, airfields and supporting infrastructure command and control facilities, civil defence, telecommunications systems, the military applications of space, guided missile systems, anti-aircraft and other defensive systems as well as associated radars.[80]

DIS publications include *Air Intelligence Review, Army Technical Intelligence Digest, Army Weapons Intelligence Review,* and *Naval Intelligence Report.*[81]

Joint Air Reconnaissance Intelligence Centre

The Joint Air Reconnaissance Intelligence Centre, run by the RAF and located at Brampton, handles two aspects of Britain's airborne photographic reconnaissance activities. It manages the photographic reconnaissance missions conducted by Canberra aircraft and, until recently, Vulcan bombers. It also provides photographic interpretation of the imagery derived from British missions as well as some U.S. missions.[82]

In January and May 1982, two photographic reconnaissance units—
13 Squadron (which employed the Canberra PR MK 7 aircraft) and
3 Squadron (which employed the PR MK 9)—were disbanded. This
left the PR MK 9–equipped No. 1 Photographic Reconnaissance Unit
as the only strategic reconnaissance unit in existence. That unit operates from Wyton and Coltishal. Seven of its aircraft are to be fitted
with advanced radars in a program called CASTOR (Corps Airborne
Stand-Off Radar). The fixed wing jet will fly at an extreme altitude
of some sixty thousand feet, carrying a high-definition synthetic
aperture radar.[83]

Security Service

Just as the SIS evolved from the Foreign Section of the Secret Service Bureau, the Security Service evolved from the bureau's Home
Section. As noted earlier, the Home Section remained within the War
Office when the Foreign Section was transferred to the control of
the Admiralty. In 1916, when the War Office created the Military
Intelligence Department, the Home Section became part of the department, as MI-5.[84]

The Security Service is still best known by its MI-5 designation,
despite the fact that it has not been part of the Military Intelligence
Department for more than thirty years. In 1951 it was responsible
directly to the Prime Minister. At that time the Secretary of the
Cabinet, Sir Norman Brook, recommended that the responsibility be
transferred to the Home Secretary.[85] Shortly afterward, the Home
Secretary, Sir David Maxwell Fyfe, issued to the Director General a
directive making the Security Service responsible to the Home Secretary. Because the directive also serves as the charter for today's Security Service, it is worth quoting in full:

1. In your appointment as Director General of the Security Service, you will
    be responsible to the Home Secretary personally. The Security Service
    is not, however, a part of the Home Office. On appropriate occasions, you
    will have right of direct access to the Prime Minister.

2. The Security Service is part of the Defence Forces of the country. Its
    task is the Defence of the Realm as a whole, from external and internal
    dangers arising from attempts at espionage and sabotage, or from actions
    of persons and organizations whether directed from within or without the
    country, which may be judged to be subversive of the state.

3. You will take special care to see that the work of the Security Service is strictly limited to what is necessary for the purposes of this task.

4. It is essential that the Security Service should be kept absolutely free from any political bias or influence and nothing should be done that might lend colour to any suggestion that it is concerned with interests of any particular section of the community, or with any other matter than the Defence of the Realm as a whole.

5. No enquiry is to be carried out on behalf of any Government unless you are satisfied that an important public interest bearing on the Defence of the Realm, as defined in paragraph 2, is at stake.

6. You and your staff will maintain the well-established convention whereby Ministers do not concern themselves with the detailed information which may be obtained by the Security Service in particular cases, but are furnished with such information only as may be necessary for the determination of any issue on which guidance is sought.[86]

Despite its undeniable status as a government agency (as indicated by the Fyfe directive), the Security Service is not recognized by law. As the 1963 Denning Report on MI-5 stated: "The Security Service in the country is not established by Statute nor is it recognized by Common Law. Even the Official Secrets Act does not acknowledge its existence."[87] The report went on to note that:

The members of the Service are, in the eye of the law, ordinary citizens with no powers greater than anyone else. They have no special powers of arrest such as the police have. No special powers are given to them. They cannot enter premises without the consent of the householder even though they may suspect a spy is there. If a spy is fleeing the country, they cannot tap him on the shoulder and say he is not to go. They have, in short, no executive powers.[88]

With the exception of conducting liaison operations with Commonwealth and other security services through offices abroad, the primary functions of the Security Service are internal. These functions include conducting counterintelligence and counterespionage operations, supervising the security investigations of all employees who have access to sensitive information, and monitoring domestic movements and organizations for possible subversive elements. The Security Service is also in charge of countersabotage activity and the surveillance and control of resident and visiting foreign nationals, including those on diplomatic missions.

In the area of counterespionage, the Security Service's prime targets are the legal (diplomatic) and illegal (deep cover) operatives of the Soviet Union and other Warsaw Pact nations. In addition to their numerous penetrations of the British intelligence and security services themselves, the KGB and GRU have also had some successes against the British diplomatic and defense establishments. John Vassall, a British embassy employee in Moscow beginning in 1954, was caught in a KGB homosexual honeytrap and submitted to the resulting Soviet blackmail. In 1956 he returned to London and began abstracting secret documents, handing some over to his KGB controllers and photographing others. It was not until 1961 that his activities were discovered. During the same period, the British Underwater Weapons Establishment at Portland, Dorset, was penetrated by Harry Houghton, who reported to a Soviet illegal, Konon Molody, operating under the name of Gordon Lonsdale; Houghton passed on information concerning antisubmarine warfare and nuclear submarines.[89]

In the summer of 1986 the Security Service placed under surveillance an East German agent, Wolfgang Knoutzch, whose mission was to obtain information on British Aerospace's Hotol spacecraft and advanced computer technology. Knoutzch was eventually arrested in West Germany and convicted of espionage there.[90]

In the area of countersubversion, the Security Service has focused on a wide range of individuals and groups, many of whom would not be considered subversive by any reasonable definition of the word. Among those groups are the National Council for Civil Liberties (NCCL) and the Campaign for Nuclear Disarmament (CND). Groups may be designated by the Security Service as being subversive, subversive front, subversive dominated, or subversive penetrated; all but the last designation allows the Security Service to open files on all national and local officials as being at least subversive sympathizers. The Security Service may also engage in actions beyond file-opening; it has, for example, conducted surveillance of trade union leaders. In 1982 an MI-5 agent attended the national conference of the NCCL. According to a former Security Service officer, in the 1980s the organization infiltrated an experienced agent into CND's headquarters and tapped the home telephone of a leading official. The same officer also indicated that agents were infiltrated into the NCCL and that anyone who was on the National Executive of NCCL or who was a branch secretary would be placed on permanent record.[91]

The watching of foreign diplomatic establishments that may be involved in supporting terrorist operations rather than conventional espionage is a third function of Security Service operations. One eavesdropping operation, targeting the Syrian embassy, is reported to have produced "conclusive evidence" of Syrian involvement in the attempt on April 17, 1986, to place a bomb on board an El Al jumbo jet destined for Tel Aviv.[92]

A February 1986 message from the Syrian embassy in London to Air Force intelligence in Damascus requested further assistance for Nezar Handawi in putting the plan into operation. The communication was intercepted by GCHQ and decoded with the assistance of the NSA. Hindawi was then placed under twenty-four-hour Security Service surveillance. He was seen in frequent visits to the Syrian embassy and in meetings with Syrian diplomats. The Security Service was then given permission to bug some embassy rooms and telephone lines from the outside of the embassy.[93]

Operations against diplomatic establishments have included the bugging of the diplomatic missions of both friendly and hostile countries. In the late 1950s and 1960s the Security Service bugged the Soviet embassy and consulate in London as well as the Hungarian, Polish, Egyptian, Cypriot, and Indonesian missions there. An attempt to bug the West German embassy failed, while a similar effort against the French embassy succeeded. The latter action allowed Britain to listen to French discussions about Britain's application to enter the European Economic Community, as well as to gather and pass information to the CIA about the French independent nuclear force.[94]

Another target for many years has been the Irish embassy in Grosvenor Place. In addition to intercepting communications between Dublin and London, MI-5 has placed bugs within the embassy. It is also believed that at one point the electronic emanations of electronic typewriters were being overheard as well; as a result, the typewriters are no longer used for sensitive material. Additionally, since 1977 Irish diplomats have been sending all their correspondence to and from London by Aer Lingus pilots and army dispatch riders.[95]

The Security Service is organized into six directorates. Directorates A (Intelligence Resources and Operations), B (Staff Office and Administration and Finance), and S (Support Services, Registry, Computer Centre, and Training Office) are primarily administrative and evaluative directorates. Basic Security Service operations are carried out by directorates C (Protective Security), F (Domestic Subver-

Figure 2-3. Organization of the Security Service (MI-5).

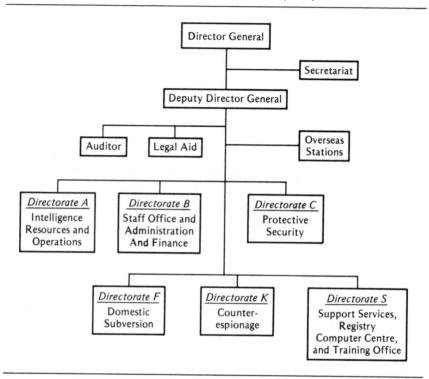

sion), and K (Counterespionage). These directorates are further divided into sections and subsections.[96]

Subsection A1A is responsible for official thefts and break-ins. A1B includes officials in other government departments, banks, and similar organizations who improperly pass on confidential personal information. A1D is staffed with locksmiths, carpenters, and other craftpersons who assist in break-ins and the installation of audio devices. Subsection A2A transcribes the product of telephone taps and bugs. Directorate K has two subsections of particular interest—K7 and K9. Subsection K7 is responsible for counterintelligence within the British intelligence services, while K9 investigates people who unexpectedly resign or retire from sensitive positions.[97]

An organizational chart of the Security Service is shown in Figure 2-3.

Headquarters for the Security Service are located at Curzon Street House, Curzon Street, W1, and 140 Gower Street (parts of F and K branches).[98]

Special Branch, Scotland Yard

Scotland Yard, or more properly the Metropolitan Police, performs a wide range of police activities throughout Britain. The Special Branch is a subdepartment of the C (Crime) Department. It was formed as the Irish Special Branch in 1883 to combat Fenian bombing in London. Although the bombings ended on January 31, 1885, by 1888 it was clear that the scope of the branch's activities went beyond the Irish and the word *Irish* was dropped from its title.[99]

The responsibilities of the Special Branch include the guarding of royalty, ministers, and visiting public dignitaries; the watching of ports and airports (for travelers of security interest); the watching and guarding of embassy buildings; the surveillance of subversive organizations; the monitoring of aliens entering the country and the vetting of applications for naturalization; the preparation of lists of potential internees in cases of war; and the investigation of offenses against the Official Secrets Act. In the area of counterespionage, the Special Branch serves as the Security Service's executive agent, making arrests at the appropriate times. It also assists in the last stages of surveillance, prepares evidence for court proceedings, and provides witnesses at trials.[100]

Special Branch headquarters are located on the top floor of Scotland Yard on Victoria Street. The branch also operates from offices around London. Organizationally, the Special Branch is divided into three sections—Ports, Administration, and Operations. Protection for royalty and others is provided by the Special Branch Personal Protection Squad. In 1975, of one thousand full-time Special Branch officers, about five hundred were stationed at headquarters, two-thirds of the officers being in the Ports and Administration sections.[101]

In addition to the Special Branch attached to Scotland Yard, special branches are attached to all local police forces and perform the same functions as Scotland Yard's Special Branch.

MANAGEMENT STRUCTURE

The management structure of the British intelligence community consists of the Permanent Under Secretaries Committee on Intelligence Services (PSIS), the Coordinator of Intelligence and Security in the Cabinet Office, and several committee structures—the Joint

Intelligence Committee (JIC), the Overseas Economic Intelligence Committee (OEIC), the London Signals Intelligence Board (LSIB), the Official Committee on Security, and the Ad Hoc Ministerial Group on Security.

The PSIS supervises the budgets of the intelligence organizations, exercises broad supervision over the British intelligence community as a whole, and approves interdepartmentally recommended intelligence priorities. The Secretary of the Cabinet is the Chairman of the PSIS. Other members are the Permanent Under Secretaries of the Foreign and Commonwealth Office, Defence, Treasury, and Trade and Industry, and the Chief of the Defence Staff. The Coordinator is an ex officio member.[102]

The office of the Coordinator of Intelligence and Security was created in 1970, although the function had been performed by various individuals in previous administrations. Thus, the functions performed by the present-day Coordinator were performed in the early 1960s by George Wigg, with the title of Paymaster General. The Coordinator is an adviser who provides guidance on intelligence priorities and resources and is appointed on the basis of long experience in intelligence. Two previous Coordinators were Sir Dick Goldsmith White (former head of MI-5 and MI-6) and Sir Leonard Hooper (former head of the GCHQ).[103] The Coordinator's basic responsibilities are to:

- prepare an annual review of intelligence for presentation to the PSIS. The review looks at intelligence in the previous 12 months and suggests the broad line of future requirements and priorities and proposes any necessary action;

- scrutinize the annual financial estimates and five-year forecasts of the individual intelligence agencies and present them to the PSIS with his recommendations;

- conduct enquiries on various intelligence subjects which he, the Secretary of the Cabinet or the PSIS may deem necessary; and

- generally advise and encourage the intelligence community, particularly the machinery within the Cabinet Office.[104]

In addition, since 1983 the Coordinator has served as Chairman of the Joint Intelligence Committee, which along with the Secretariat, provides him with staff support.

While the Coordinator is an adviser who provides general guidance, the Chairman of the JIC and the Chairman of the OEIC are responsible for the production of national intelligence and the day-to-day management of the inelligence community. The JIC and its subordinate elements are charged with the responsibility of ensuring efficiency, economy, and adaptation to changing requirements. They are also responsible for assembling and evaluating national intelligence for presentation to the Cabinet, individual ministers, and the Chiefs of Staff. The JIC was set up in 1936 under the Chiefs of Staff and transferred to the Cabinet Office in 1957. The rationale for the JIC's assessments function is to have final intelligence estimates and evaluations made by a body independent of the foreign and defense policy-making bureaucracies.[105]

Subordinate to the JIC are an Assessment Staff and a number of Current Intelligence Groups (CIGs), which collectively constitute the Joint Intelligence Organization(JIO). The Assessment Staff is responsible for preparing both short- and long-term assessments in support of government policy. In performing this function, it utilizes the output of various agencies both within and outside the intelligence community. Worldwide coverage of current intelligence is maintained by the CIGs, each of which has its own geographical area of responsibility. Each CIG is chaired by a member of the Assessment Staff.[106]

Membership of the JIC consists, in addition to the Coordinator as Chairman, of a Foreign and Commonwealth Office representative, the Chief of SIS, the Director General of Intelligence, the Director General of the Security Service, the DCDS(I), the Director of the GCHQ, and the Chairman and Deputy Chairman of the Assessments Staff.[107] In addition, liaison representatives from Australia, the United States, and Canada attend JIC meetings.

While the JIC is concerned primarily with diplomatic and military intelligence, the OEIC concentrates on economic and nonmilitary scientific and technical intelligence. The Chairman of the OEIC is a representative of the Treasury. Membership includes representatives of a variety of civil departments with an interest in overseas economic matters, as well as the heads of the intelligence-producing agencies.[108]

In addition to the JIC and OEIC, a third committee—the London Signals Intelligence Board—monitors the activities of the GCHQ. The LSIB was created in 1941 to increase the level of supervision of SIGINT activities. The board was presided over by C and attended by the Directors of Intelligence of each of the services and the Director of the Government Code and Cypler School.[109] Apparently, a subcommittee of the LSIB, the London Signals Intelligence Committee (Defence) (LSIC(D)), deals with military signals intelligence matters.

The highest level committee for the supervision of security matters is the Ad Hoc Ministerial Group on Security, chaired by the Prime Minister. Subordinate to the Ad Hoc Group is the Official Committee on Security, which supervises the Security Service. The Official Committee has three subordinate committees: the Security Policy and Methods Committee is a civil service group responsible for dealing with declassification policy and the physical security of documents and buildings; the Personnel Security Committee supervises the "positive vetting" system; and the recently created Electronic Security Committee is concerned with the protection of sensitive information stored in computer networks.[110]

Figure 2–4 shows the management structure of the British security and intelligence community.

LIAISON

In addition to its own collection activities, the United Kingdom receives intelligence information as part of several bilateral and multilateral cooperative arrangements entered into with foreign intelligence services, particularly those of the United States, Australia, New Zealand, and Canada. Indeed, the United Kingdom's SIGINT activities must be understood as part of larger collection network, with the United States and the National Security Agency at its head.

In addition to SIGINT, Britain's liaison and exchange arrangements involve human intelligence collection and reporting, ocean surveillance, and analysis.

The most important cooperative arrangement is, of course, the UKUSA Agreement, which followed from the intelligence relationship among Australia, Britain, Canada, New Zealand, and the United States that was forged by World War II. The year 1947 saw the formulation and acceptance of the UKUSA Agreement, also known as the UKUSA Security Agreement, or "Secret Treaty." The primary aspect of the agreement was the division of SIGINT collection responsibilities among the First Party (the United States) and the Second Parties (Australia, Britain, Canada, and New Zealand).[111] The specific agencies now involved are the U.S. National Security Agency

Figure 2-4. Management Structure of the Intelligence and Security Community.

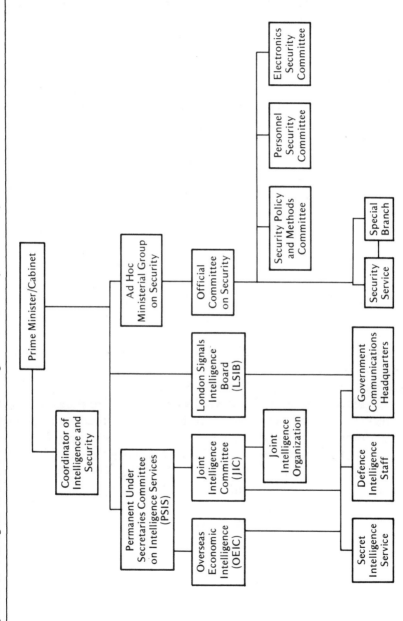

(NSA), Australian Defence Signals Directorate (DSD), British Government Communications Headquarters (GCHQ), Canadian Communications Security Establishment (CSE), and (until 1985) New Zealand Government Communications Security Bureau (GCSB).

Under the present division of responsibility, the Australian DSD is responsible for covering parts of the Indian Ocean, the South Pacific, and Southeast Asia. The United Kingdom's GCHQ is responsible for Africa and the Soviet Union west of the Urals. Canada is responsible for coverage of the northern Soviet Union.[112]

Britain's geographical position gives it a significant capability for long-range SIGINT collection against certain targets in the Soviet Union. Britain's historical role in Africa led to its assumption of SIGINT responsibility for that area. Canada's responsibility for the northern Soviet Union stems from Canada's geographical position, which gives it "unique access to communications in the northern Soviet Union." Australia's area of responsibility clearly results from its geographical location.[113]

The UKUSA relationship is more than an agreement to coordinate separately conducted intelligence activities and share the intelligence collected; the SIGINT aspect of the relationship is also more than that. Rather, the relationship is cemented by the presence of U.S. facilities on British, Canadian, and Australian territory; by joint operations (U.S.-U.K., Australian-U.S., and U.K.-Australian) within and outside UKUSA territory; and, in the case of Australia, by the presence of U.K. and U.S. staff at all DSD facilities.[114]

In addition to specifying SIGINT collection responsibilities, the agreement also concerns access to the collected intelligence and security arrangements for the handling of data. Standardized code words (e.g., UMBRA for signals intelligence), security agreements that all employees of the respective SIGINT agencies must sign, and procedures for storing and disseminating code word material are all part of the implementation of the agreement.[115] Thus, in an October 8, 1948, memo concerning the agreement, the U.S. Army Office of the Adjutant General advised the memo's recipients that:

> The United States Chiefs of Staff will make every effort to insure that the United States will maintain the military security classifications established by the United Kingdom authorities with respect to military information of U.K.

origin and the military security classifications established by the UK-US Agreement with respect to military information of joint UK-US origin.[116]

Similarly, in 1967 the "COMINT Indoctrination" declaration, which all British COMINT-cleared personnel had to sign, included in the first paragraph the statement:

> I declare that I fully understand the information relating to the manner and extent of the interception of communications of foreign powers by H.M. Government and other cooperating Governments, and intelligence produced by such interception known as Communications Intelligence (COMINT) is information covered by Section 2 of the Official Secrets Act 1911 (as amended).[117]

These requirements for standardized code words, security arrangements, and procedures for the handling and dissemination of SIGINT material are apparently detailed in a series of *International Regulations on SIGINT (IRSIG)*, which was in its third edition as of 1967.[118]

In addition to the highly formalized cooperative arrangement for signals intelligence, a second highly formalized arrangement concerns intelligence collection. This arrangement consists of an agreement between the United States and Britain to divide up, on a geographic basis, the responsibility for the monitoring of public radio and television broadcasts—mainly news and public affairs broadcasts. These broadcasts can provide valuable political intelligence, particularly because in so many nations the media, especially radio and television, are under government control. Monitoring of public radio broadcasts can yield intelligence about domestic political conflict and the propaganda line a government is taking internally as well as its pronouncements on foreign policy and international events. Such monitoring also allows a country to judge the effectiveness of its own propaganda operations.

The specific organizations involved in this arrangement are the British Broadcasting Corporation (BBC) Monitoring Service and the CIA's Foreign Broadcast Information Service (FBIS). Together, those two organizations monitor most of the world's most significant news and other broadcasts. As noted, both the BBC Monitoring Service and the FBIS have a network of overseas stations, operated with varying degrees of secrecy to gather their raw material.[119]

Cooperation between the BBC Monitoring Service and the FBIS began in 1948 as an openly acknowledged arrangement. Thus, the BBC Annual Report for 1948–49 noted:

> There [is] close cooperation between the BBC's Monitoring Service and its American counterpart, the Foreign Broadcast Information Branch of the United States Central Intelligence Agency, and each of the two services maintained liaison units at each other's stations for the purpose of a full exchange of information.[120]

The area of responsibility for the Monitoring Service is roughly equivalent to GCHQ's area of responsibility for SIGINT collection— Europe, Africa, and western Russia. Thus, the Monitoring Service maintains a remotely controlled listening post on the rooftop of the Vienna embassy to monitor VHF radio and television broadcasts originating in Hungary and Czechoslovakia. It also maintains listening posts in Accra in Ghana and in Abidjan in the Ivory Coast. In 1976–77 the Monitoring Service turned over responsibility for monitoring Far East broadcasts to the FBIS. To compensate, it had to provide additional coverage of Eastern Europe. In 1974–75 it also had to step up its reporting of events in Portugal and Spain to meet CIA requirements.[121]

The value of the monitoring arrangement has been summed up by Ray Cline, former CIA Deputy Director for Intelligence, as follows:

> This unique information service [covers] a worldwide beat, copying and translating hundreds of thousands of words daily and transmitting the product electronically for prompt availability wherever needed in Great Britain, the United States, and their outposts overseas.[122]

Britain also has significant liaison arrangements with the United States and Australia in the area of human intelligence. The original arrangements for cooperation between the Australian Secret Intelligence Service (ASIS) and the British SIS were made in May 1950 through an exchange of letters between the Australian and British prime ministers. The latter, after consultation with the Chief of SIS, agreed to provide facilities to assist in the setting up of an Australian organization on a professional basis.[123]

The main areas of cooperation between the two services are:

- cooperation in the field;
- exchange of intelligence reports and other information;

- assistance in training;
- cooperation in planning and preparation for clandestine activities in the event of emergency in the Far Eastern area; and
- provision of technical equipment and exchange of information on new developments.[124]

In countries where both ASIS and SIS are represented, the officers of both services keep in close but discreet contact, making it possible to exchange and discuss field intelligence reports and other information concerning the local situation on the spot. In other countries where only one service is represented, the service present may serve as the point of contact for the other service. Thus, the ASIS station in Manila also acts as a point of contact with the local intelligence authorities for SIS, as the British have no station there.[125]

The exchange of intelligence reports has also taken place on a large scale. Between 1950 and 1974, the SIS received ten thousand ASIS reports while transmitting forty-four thousand of their own reports in return (although both services have always excluded from the exchanges reports having a direct bearing on respective national interest or policies). With respect to countries in the Far East, this exchange has covered virtually their complete production. In addition, the SIS has also provided the ASIS with a copy of the whole of the SIS Far East Personality Card Index.[126]

ASIS officers have regularly been accepted as students in the SIS long training course. Further, some ASIS officers have received additional "on-the-job" experience in the SIS headquarters in London, or in Singapore when SIS maintained a large regional headquarters. ASIS technical staff members have also been trained by SIS and have been given access to British technical methods "of the utmost sensitivity."[127]

In November 1953, the then Australian Minister for Defence endorsed for planning purposes the concept of joint action between ASIS and SIS in all clandestine activity, including special operations, in the event of war or emergency in the Far East. As a result, the British have positioned in Australia, under ASIS control, quantities of operational stores and equipment that, in the event of an emergency, would be available to either Britain or Australia.[128]

In the area of intelligence analysis, Britain shares finished products with the four other Anglo-Saxon nations, has liaison arrangements, and participates in joint conferences. Thus, in 1974 the United Kingdom participated in the Annual Land Warfare Intelligence Conference, the Third International Scientific Intelligence Exchange, the Quadrapartite Intelligence Working Party on Chinese Guided Missiles, and the Tripartite Defense Intelligence Estimates Conference.

Held in London in May 1974, the Annual Land Warfare Intelligence Conference involved as participants the U.S., British, Canadian and Australian defense intelligence organizations, who gathered to discuss the armaments used by Communist armies.[129]

The Third International Scientific Exchange, involving U.S., British, New Zealand, and Australian defense intelligence organizations, was held in Canberra from June 18-27, 1974. Initially established to discuss Chinese scientific development, particularly with respect to nuclear weapons, the 1974 meeting also focused on technical developments in India and Japan, nuclear proliferation in Asia, development and military applications of lasers, and application of peaceful nuclear explosives.[130]

The Quadrapartite Intelligence Working Party on Chinese Guided Missiles met in London in 1974. The panel, consisting of representatives from the U.S., British, Australian, and Canadian defense intelligence agencies, focused on both Chinese guided missiles and satellite launch vehicles.[131]

The United Kingdom, and particularly GCHQ, has maintained liaison with the South African Directorate of Military Intelligence. Until 1974, when the Labour government abrogated the Simonstown Agreements, GCHQ staff members were openly posted to the Silvermine interception facility at Simonstown. Cooperation reached new heights with the installation of a Conservative government in 1979. Since 1981 the GCHQ has coordinated and assisted South African intelligence in monitoring and targeting the "frontline" African states and the African National Congress.[132]

From its listening post in Zambia, GCHQ can intercept communications to and from African National Congress (ANC) headquarters in Lusaka, in conjunction with South African stations in Namibia. GCHQ stations in Swaziland and Malawi are well positioned to intercept signals in Angola. The communications traffic of ANC training bases in Mozambique are monitored from a station on Ascension Island.[133]

In a 1980 conference at Cheltenham, South African representatives requested:

- political, military, and diplomatic intelligence about Zambia, Botswana, Tanzania, Angola, and Mozambique;
- intelligence about ANC's Oliver Tambo and ten members of his ANC high command staff;
- information on any flights Tambo took abroad on Soviet and Cuban airlines; and
- special attention by GCHQ (and NSA) to ANC communications.[134]

To make fulfillment of their first request easier, South Africa provided GCHQ with information about the radio frequencies used by the various nations.

In return, GCHQ (and NSA) asked South Africa for:

- continued monitoring of Soviet and Cuban activities in Angola and Mozambique;
- weekly reports on Soviet submarine and shipping activity around the Cape of Good Hope; and
- reports on Soviet commercial and economic activity in sub-Saharan Africa with special emphasis on support for rebel activity.[135]

THE FALKLANDS WAR

On April 2, 1982, the armed forces of Argentina invaded the British-run Falkland Islands and proceeded to install themselves in control. The invasion was the culmination of a dispute stemming from 1833, when Great Britain expelled the Argentine garrison of the Falkland Islands. Diplomatic and military moves by Great Britain followed the 1982 invasion, and within two months the Falklands were back in British hands.[136]

The war and the postmortem that followed cast light on the activities of the British intelligence community in three areas. First, British analytical activities were opened up to a large extent with respect to warning of an Argentine move. Second, knowledge about British intelligence operations that provided information to be used in conducting the war also emerged. And third, the utility of liaison arrangements—both standing and ad hoc—was clearly demonstrated.

The situation in the Falklands and possible Argentinean actions had been the subject of Joint Intelligence Committee estimates for many years prior to the 1982 invasion. Between 1965 and 1975, the JIC made assessments about once a year, more frequently at times of increased tension. In the earlier years, the conclusions were, basically, that official military action against the Falklands and the Dependencies was unlikely, at least until attempts at a diplomatic settlement had been exhausted, but that there was a continuing risk of unofficial action. In the early 1970s, during a period of improved relations with Argentina, the assessments were that direct military action could be discounted and that even the risk of an "adventurist" operation was very slight. Near the end of 1973, it was believed that Argentine attitudes were hardening, and for the first time there were indications that the Argentine government (of President Perón) might be preparing contingency plans for an occupation of the Islands. In 1974 the JIC assessed that "adventurist" operations were still the main threat, but with less likelihood of the Argentine government's discouraging them; although official military action was thought unlikely, as long as Argentina believed that the British government was prepared to negotiate on sovereignty, it was not ruled out.[137]

In November 1975 the JIC prepared a new assessment of the situation in the Falklands Islands. It concluded that a deliberately planned invasion in the near future still seemed unlikely but could not be completely dismissed. It followed earlier assessments in concluding that there was a greater possibility of some kind of "adventurist" operation, particularly if a British survey went ahead in the face of the continued opposition of the Argentine public. Opposition might be expressed by a propaganda campaign and possibly some practical harassment of the Falkland Islanders. For example, suspension of the air service would be an easy measure for Argentina to take.[138]

In another assessment, on January 8, 1976, the JIC concluded that although Argentina was unlikely to launch a sudden invasion in the near future, the likelihood of the Argentine government's intensifying political pressures and taking specific measures, such as the recall of ambassadors and the suspension of the air service had increased. The JIC concluded that physical aggression remained a remoter prospect but certainly could not be excluded.[139]

On January 22, 1976, in the wake of the withdrawal of ambassadors, a further assessment was prepared. It judged that the army and navy commanders were against any military action that might help Perón's regime stay in power, and noted that a January 8 announcement from the Argentine Ministry of Foreign Affairs, stating that the

Argentine government was going ahead immediately with the extension of the airstrip, suggested that the government did not wish, at least for the time being, to interfere with communications. The JIC concluded that, although there might be a short lull, further countermeasures against British interests, in the form of more hostile political and economic pressure, were possible in the future. The likelihood of an "adventurist" operation was believed to have increased. The estimate concluded that, while military operations were less likely than an adventurist operation, as the sequence of countermeasures proceeded, the prospect of military operations would need to be regarded more seriously. An intelligence report of January 23, 1976, referring to a meeting in December 1975, indicated that the armed forces commanders had at that stage ruled out invasion.[140]

On February 1976 an Argentine destroyer fired shots at the RRS *Shackleton* when the *Shackleton* was seventy-eight miles south of Port Stanley and attempted to stop the ship. Subsequently, intelligence data indicated that plans for the interception had been made not by the Argentine government but by the armed forces. The information also indicated that the Commander in Chief of the Argentine Navy had authorized firing into the ship but only in such a way as to avoid casualties or sinking of the ship. The JIC concluded that the purpose of the operation was to assert Argentine sovereignty over the Falklands and its surrounding waters in order to bring pressure to bear on the British government to negotiate.[141]

In July 1976 the JIC considered the political situation in Argentina following the military coup that had taken place three months earlier. The committee concluded that with respect to the Falklands, the military government might have unreasonable expectations about the negotiations in progress. The JIC believed that failure could be expected to lead to a more aggressive approach, at first in the United Nations, but that Argentina was unlikely to take military action. Intelligence had indicated that it was the view of President Videla and others that if bilateral negotiations were unsuccessful, Argentina was obligated to turn to the United Nations.[142]

In December 1976 the existence of an Argentine military presence on South Thule in the South Sandwich Islands was discovered. An intelligence report indicated that the presence was probably established in November with the approval of the Argentine Navy's Commander in Chief. Intelligence developed in January 1977 indicated that the Argentine presence was larger than Argentina claimed (in response to a query from British representatives) and that Argentina's original intention had been to announce the existence of the base in mid or late March, when it was too late for British ships to enter South Atlantic waters. In addition, intelligence indicated the existence of an Argentine Navy contingency plan for a joint Air Force-Navy invasion of the Falklands, combined with a diplomatic initiative at the United Nations.[143]

In light of this new evidence, the JIC produced an assessment of the situation on January 31, 1977. The committee considered it unlikely that the establishment of an Argentine presence on South Thule could have been mounted without the approval of the junta and concluded that the intentions of the Argentine government were

- to make a physical demonstration of Argentine sovereignty over the Dependencies;
- to probe the British Government's reaction to such a demonstration; and
- to obtain a bargaining counter in the forthcoming discussions.

The assessment concluded that Argentina was unlikely to withdraw until it suited the country to do so and, depending on the British government's actions, might be encouraged to initiate further military action.[144]

On February 14, 1977, intelligence indicated that the Argentine Navy's contingency plans had been shelved for the time being, on the grounds that while there were internal political benefits to be gained by an invasion, Argentina could not count on the support of the Third World or the Communist bloc.[145]

On October 11, 1977, a JIC assessment mentioned that another Argentine naval party was due to land on South Thule in the middle of the month. It judged that military action was still unlikely. A more extensive report on November 1 referred to increasing hostility in the Argentine Ministry of Foreign Affairs over what were perceived to be Britain's delaying tactics in the negotiations as well as to the militancy of the Navy—the October 11 assessment had raised the possibility of unilateral naval action. The assessment concluded that the military junta as a whole would prefer a peaceful settlement and that, as long as it believed that the British government was prepared to negotiate seriously on the issue of sovereignty, it was unlikely to turn to force; however, in the event that negotiations broke down or Argentina saw no likely prospect of negotiations producing a transfer of sovereignty, the probability of more forceful actions by the

Argentines—including military action—increased. The most likely action was thought to be action against British shipping, followed by the establishment of an Argentine presence on one or more of the Dependencies. Actual invasion was considered unlikely, although it could not be dismissed.[146]

The next JIC assessment of the Argentine threat to the Falklands took place in November 1979. It concluded that Argentine determination to gain sovereignty over the Falklands had remained steadfast and that the Argentine perception of Britain's willingness to negotiate was the key determinant in influencing the junta's course of action.[147]

On July 9, 1981, the JIC circulated a new assessment of the likelihood in the coming months of forcible Argentine action to resolve the dispute. The assessment covered a variety of relevant subjects, including the progress of Argentina's sovereignty dispute with Chile over the Beagle Islands and the improvement in Argentina's relations with the United States and Brazil. It also reviewed Argentina's options if the junta decided to resort to direct methods of resolving the conflict, and concluded that Argentina was likely first to try diplomatic and economic measures, the economic measures possibly to include the disruption of air and sea communications, of food and oil supplies,, and of the provision of medical treatment. The committee also thought it possible that Argentina might occupy one of the uninhabited Dependencies or even establish a military presence on the Falklands themselves, remote from Port Stanley. The harrassment or Argentine blockage of British shipping was now considered an unlikely option, unless the Argentine government felt severely provoked.[148]

This assessment, like the 1979 assessment, noted that Argentina was still determined to attain sovereignty over the Falklands but preferred to do so by peaceful means. Once again, the most important factor in determining Argentina's course of action was felt to be Argentina's perception of Britain's willingness to negotiate in good faith an eventual transfer of sovereignty. The assessment also noted evidence of impatience in Argentina over the absence of progress in negotiations and commented on minor actions taken by Argentina in the preceding year, notably a reduced number of flights to the Islands and a delayed supply ship. While small-scale military action could not be ruled out, the JIC believed that similar minor actions would be taken first. Finally, the JIC report stated that if Argentina concluded that there was no hope of a peaceful transfer, it might resort to forcible measures—acting swiftly and without warning.[149]

Intelligence in early March 1982 indicated the views of Argentine ministers and officials in the preceding weeks. The reports indicated that military action was not being contemplated, that it would not be contemplated unless talks broke down, and that invasion was an unrealistic option prior to the next Southern Hemisphere summer. Intelligence also reported that Argentina was planning to take the issue to the United Nations if no progress was attained by the end of the year, and that force was the likely alternative only if international diplomatic and political action failed and Argentina's sovereignty dispute with Chile remained unresolved.[150]

On March 10, 1982, an officer in the Defence Intelligence Staff circulated a paper throughout the Ministry of Defence; the paper was also sent to the Foreign and Commonwealth Office. It drew attention to recent intelligence indicating that belligerent (Falkland) press comments had been inspired by the Argentine Navy in an attempt to achieve an early settlement of the dispute. The intelligence also indicated that, if there was no evidence by June of progress toward a settlement, the Argentine Navy would push for a diplomatic offensive in international organizations, a break in relations with Britain, and military action against the Islands, but that neither President Galtieri nor the Army was thinking along those lines. In sum, the paper said that all other diplomatic and intelligence reporting confirmed that all elements of the Argentine government, apart from the Navy, favored diplomatic action to solve the dispute and that the military option was not under active consideration at that time. The DIS officer saw no reason to believe that the Argentine Navy had any prospect of persuading the president or other government members to adopt its proposed course of action or of going it alone, and did not therefore believe that the Argentine Navy's attitude posed any immediate or increased threat to the Falkland Islands beyond what was outlined in the JIC assessment of July 1981.[151]

In mid-March 1982, officials at the Foreign and Commonwealth Office received several intelligence reports. One report indicated that the U.S. Assistant Secretary of State for Latin America, Thomas Enders, had been told during a visit to Argentina that Argentina planned to mount an international diplomatic offensive if there were no immediate signs of British willingness to bring negotiations to a successful conclusion within the next year; according to the report, Enders indicated that there would be no U.S. objection. Another report on the views of the Argentine military concerned a plan to achieve gradual British withdrawal from the Falklands over a period of thirty years, at the end of which full sovereignty would pass to Argentina; the talk of invasion since the New York negotiations was said to have been part of a design to put psychological pressure on Britain. Yet another report indicated that senior Argentine naval officers doubted that Argentina would invade the Falklands, although it would be relatively simple to do so and they thought that Britain would not prevent it.[152]

Still other intelligence reports indicated that the junta had been displeased with the agreement reached in New York (in negotiations between British and Argentinian representatives to the United Nations) and that the unilateral Ministry of Foreign Affairs communiqué had been issued on the orders of the president. The view of the Ministry of Foreign Affairs was reported to be that the negotiating team in New York had properly carried out its instructions except in failing to obtain British agreement to a date in March 1982 for a meeting to begin the monthly series of talks. It had been decided that, if no reply were forthcoming from the British side on a date in March 1982, Argentina would retaliate by withdrawing the air or sea services to the Islands. An invasion, said the intelligence reports, had not been seriously considered, yet in the last resort, it could not be discounted, in view of the unpredictability of the president and some senior members of the armed forces.[153]

Intelligence reports circulated on March 23, 1982, indicated that there was still no serious intention of invading the Falklands by the Argentine government as a whole, although there were some differences of opinion, with the Navy being more hawkish and the Ministry of Foreign Affairs believing that a negotiated solution was preferable. The reports also indicated that while Argentina would try to raise the temperature, it would stop short of bloodshed. A report from the British embassy in Buenos Aires stated that based on information from another embassy, all submarines at the naval base of Mar del Plata had recently put to sea but that the event might not be sinister, since a joint naval exercise was taking place, probably in the River Plate area, with the Uruguayan Navy.[154]

Some of the intelligence gathered during this period may have been collected by the HMS *Endurance*, a patrol vessel that had been based in the area to demonstrate resolve over the Falklands. Lawrence Freedman suggests that the *Endurance* was critical in monitoring naval communications, which facilitated judgments on the overall level of military activity, coordination among the different services, and so on.[155]

According to one report, on March 24, 1982, the SIS in Buenos Aires picked up intelligence that an invasion was being planned. According to the report, this information was passed back to London and confirmed by other intelligence. Another account suggests that it is unlikely that such a firm conclusion was drawn, since it appears that the actual decision to invade was not taken until March 26; another account dates the decision at March 23.[156]

March 24 was also the first day that there was an Argentine military presence in the Falklands area. A detachment of Argentine marines landed at Leith in South Georgia, where a private Argentine party had landed five days earlier and established an Argentinian beachhead, flying the Argentine flag. British radio intercepts further indicated that two Argentinean frigates, the *Drummond* and the *Granville*, had broken away from maneuvers with Uruguay and were sailing toward the area.[157]

Signals intelligence obtained on March 25 picked up Argentine reports about the Royal Marines on the Falklands, the movements of the HMS *Endurance*, the overall deployments of the Royal Navy, and the Argentine decision that the civilians should stay on South Georgia. According to one report, there was a wealth of raw material in those few days for the cryptanalysts at GCHQ to work on, due to the Argentine Navy's having had to use their radios as a result of the presence of the two ships, the *Drummond* and the *Granville*, their later recall, being sent to South Georgia; and the bad weather-induced delays and reroutings of Argentinian forces, which necessitated the frequent use of radio.[158]

On March 29 intelligence was received indicating that (a) Argentine officials expected that some form of military action stopping short of a full-scale invasion would take place in the near future and (b) military action was planned in April, but in the form of occupation of one of the outlying islands, rather than of the main islands. It indicated that the Argentine Ministry of Foreign Affairs was making an assessment of the likely reactions of members of the UN Security Council to Argentine occupation of the Falklands; it was also learned, possibly via SIGINT, that a beach on the Falkland Islands was to be reconnoitered by the Argentines and that an amphibious task force was being prepared.[159]

March 30 brought a report from the naval attaché that five Argentine warships, including a submarine, were sailing toward South

Georgia and that another force had left Puerto Belgrano. In addition, travel restrictions had been imposed on personnel there.[160]

On the morning of March 31, an immediate assessment headed "Falkland Islands—the Incident on South Georgia" was prepared and circulated by the Latin American Current Intelligence Group. It concluded that although the landing on South Georgia had not been contrived by the Argentine government, the junta was taking full advantage of the incident to speed up negotiations on the transfer of sovereignty. An intercepted signal sent that day to the submarine *Santa Fe* ordered it to carry out a surface reconnaissance of landing beaches near Stanley. By the early evening of March 31, Ministry of Defence intelligence officials briefed John Nott, the Minister of Defence, that a time in the early morning of April 2 had been set by the Argentines to invade the Falkland Islands. Signals intelligence indicated that elements of the task force had turned toward the Falklands and would reach them in two days. In addition, there seems to have been a major increase in radio traffic among the varying branches of the Argentine armed forces.[161]

On April 1 an assessment prepared by the Latin American Current Intelligence Group was circulated, updating the information about Argentine military dispositions, which would enable Argentina to launch an assault on April 2. The destination, although not known for certain, appeared to be Port Stanley. The assessment said that, despite the military preparations and in contradiction to what Ministry of Defence intelligence officials indicated to John Nott, there was no intelligence suggesting that the junta had decided to invade the Falklands Islands—this despite information cited in the report indicating unusual cooperation among the three Argentine military services and their active involvement in the amphibious task force, which was considered disturbing. The report concluded that the assembled Argentine forces had the capability and logistic support required for an invasion of part of the Falklands and that by midday April 2 would be in a position to launch such an invasion. Later in the day, the defense attaché in Buenos Aires filed a report based on press reports indicating that Argentine Air Force transports were being prepared to lift troops to the south of the country and that a general mobilization seemed under way.[162]

Conclusive SIGINT on the morning of April 2 indicated that orders for an invasion had been issued the day before. Once that invasion occurred, several British intelligence agencies proceeded to produce both strategic and tactical intelligence. Employed as collection assets were open sources, ground stations, ships, aircraft, and human agents. Specifically, ships in the Royal Navy Fleet, Nimrod maritime reconnaissance aircraft, and a listening post (Two Boats) on the Ascension Islands (more than four thousand miles away), manned by fifty Britons monitored the Island.

Open sources of intelligence contributed to the British effort. Reference works such as *Military Balance* (published by the International Institute of Strategic Studies), *Jane's Fighting Ship's, Jane's Weapons Systems,* and *Jane's All the World's Aircraft* were examined by British intelligence personnel. The brigade intelligence officer of the 3rd Commando Brigade assembled an assessment of the Argentine order of battle using the Plymouth Public Library.[163]

Most valuable was the signals intelligence. According to the diary of a British naval officer who served on the HMS *Conqueror* (which, on May 2, 1982, sank the Argentine cruiser *General Belgrano*), throughout the 1982 Falklands War British interception of Argentine military radio and even private international telephone transmissions was "impressive, indeed [and] without it we would never have achieved what we have." The diary went on to state, "We are evidently able to intercept much, if not, all of the enemy's signal traffic.[164] An Argentinean military analyst agreed, writing that "the British intercepted all our radio transmissions, and almost certainly broke our codes," and noted that the reason the Argentine headquarters on the Falklands was never bombed was that "its destruction would have deprived the British of its source." Messages that could not be decoded on the spot were sent to the GCHQ, where teams of specialists worked twenty-four hours a day "to monitor, analyze and decode thousands of Argentine operational and other messages."[165]

In various entries, the British naval officer's diary records advance warning of aircraft attacks and messages from top Argentine military officers on the status of their forces. One intercepted message was a phone conversation from the United States to a Peruvian admiral, wherein the officer's son "intimated" some agreement for Peru to provide submarine support to Argentina, a situation that "seems unlikely."[166]

British controlled or partly controlled assets employed for SIGINT collection included a GCHQ SIGINT station, operated jointly with NSA, on Ascension Island. As noted earlier, the HMS *Endurance* targeted Argentine communications and also received reports from

Islanders (via radio) on the numbers and dispositions of Argentine troops. Intelligence was further provided, in part, by Ascension Island-based Nimrod surveillance planes that carried high-frequency receivers. Similarly, British ships such as the carriers *Hermes* and *Invincible* were also equippped with high-frequency receivers. These were tuned in to listen to the Argentines' tactical signals transmitted by voice, and also to highly secret operational orders coded and sent in Morse. A Royal Navy vessel parked 1,000 miles off the Argentine coast would have been able to pick up literally hundreds of signals coming in simultaneously.[167]

British overhead reconnaissance involved photographic, SIGINT, and maritime surveillance operations. Six Victor tankers arrived at Ascension on April 18, at least one fitted with aerial cameras. Victors were also employed for radar reconnaissance missions. On April 20, a fourteen-hour mission was flown from Ascension Island to make a radar search of the area up to 250 miles out from the South Georgia coast to make sure that no Argentinean ships were in the vicinity. The Victor covered a distance of more than 7,000 miles, setting a record for the longest-range operational reconnaissance mission ever undertaken. The radar photographs indicated no warships of any size off the coast in the area searched. Two further missions were flown during the operation to regain South Georgia.[168]

Initial photographic reconnaissance missions may have been less successful. One mission was forced to turn back because of operating problems. Another reconnaissance attempt—to discover the effectiveness of the bombing of Stanley airfield by Vulcan bombers in May—failed. An attempt by a Harrier to take photos of the damage was unsuccessful due to heavy antiaircraft fire and bad weather. Some information, indicating damage, was obtained by visual observation. According to some accounts, the first photos relevant to the land campaign were not available until June 6, a week prior to the Argentine surrender.[169]

Thus, according to Brigadier Julian Thompson, commander of the 3rd Commando Brigade: "Not until the very end of the campaign were there any air photographs showing enemy dispositions, defensive positions, strong positions, gun positions and so forth. Even they arrived so late and were so poor that they had no influence on planning."[170]

Nimrod maritime reconnaissance flights were used to track Argentine Navy movements. A nineteen-hour, 8,300-mile flight was undertaken on May 15. Using their Searchwater radar, the Nimrod crew scrutinized a 1,000-mile long, 4,000-mile wide swath of the Argentinean coast. They were able to determine that there was no Argentine Navy task group at sea in the area they examined. Another such mission was conducted up the Argentine coast on May 27, setting a new record of 8,453 miles flown.[171]

Intelligence was also provided by Special Air Service (SAS) and Special Boat Squadron (SBS) commandos. From May 1, patrols were landed on the Falklands at night by helicopter, submarine, or fast inflatable boats. Operating in Argentina itself, SAS patrols monitored Super-Entendard bases in southern Argentina to advise on departures of the aircraft to attack the British task force. On East Falkland a trio of four-man SAS patrols was landed in the Port Stanley, Bluff Cove, and Darwin areas. Four patrols were landed on West Falkland to watch Port Howard and Fox Bay, among other locations.[172]

As soon as they landed, the patrols set off on a long march to their prearranged observation post positions, selected from the little information available on the whereabouts of the main Argentinean posts. For days on end they watched and noted the behavior of the Argentinean soldiers, the coming and going of aircraft, and generally the Argentineans' offensive and defensive preparations. The picture built up was of a fairly low-caliber, young, and inexperienced opposition that was poorly led although superbly armed.[173]

While the SAS was engaged in collecting data on Argentine land forces, SBS reconnaissance patrols were busy examining beaches on both islands to assess their suitability for the main landing. SBS information led to the selection of San Carlos Bay, fifty miles east of Port Stanley. SBS found no Argentine troops around San Carlos and no evidence of mines on the shore or minelaying at sea.[174]

In addition to its own intelligence, Great Britain was able to rely on long-term and ad hoc exchange agreements. Most significant was the information provided by the United States. Two different types of satellite systems were reported to have been employed to provide the British with data: the KH-11 imaging system and the White Cloud ocean surveillance satellite. KH-11 satellites launched in 1980 and 1981 passed over the Falklands and South Pacific areas as a result of their normal operations. With their real-time capability, these satellites' data could have been of significant use to the British forces. According to the *The Economist*, U.S. photographic satellite data were available only during the later stages of the conflict, after the British had persuaded the United States to alter the orbit of a satellite to cover the Falklands. Other sources claim that the British never received any satellite photography of the Falklands. Additionally, it was also reported that early in the Falklands crisis, the United States flew a special SR-71 mission from California over Argentina and the Falklands at British request.[175]

The United States also contributed a significant amount of SIGINT from its stations on Galeta Island, Panama, and around the South Atlantic. Said one report: "The Americans are believed to have broken the Argentine military codes, thus adding to the British intelligence gathered by HMS *Endurance*. The Americans claim 98 percent of British intelligence of Argentine movements came from them.[176]

CIA collection against the Argentine High Command probably also benefited Britain's war effort. The CIA's Buenos Aires station was located in the same block as the offices of the Argentine High Command. The CIA was able to monitor High Command discussions through both human intelligence penetration and electronic eavesdropping.[177]

New Zealand was another benefactor. The New Zealand Government Communications Security Bureau's Irirangi station was able to monitor Argentine naval traffic in the South Pacific, providing intelligence that was used by Britain to form a clearer and more comprehensive picture of the Argentine Navy's Order of Battle and its deployments.[178]

A third foreign source was Chile. According to Duncan Campbell, a major aspect of Britain's arrangement with Chile was the transfer of long-range RAF spy planes to Chile. In mid-April, half a squadron of Canberra PR 9 aircraft, normally based at RAF Wyton near Huntingdon, were flown secretly to Belize, the former British colony and military base in Central America. The Canberra PR 9 is specially built for long-range, high-altitude photography. At their normal operating height in excess of sixty thousand feet, the Canberras were immune to attack by the Argentine Air Force. Once in Belize, they were repainted in Chilean Air Force markings and flew on, illegally and without clearance, over Central America and on to Punta Arenas.[179]

At least six Canberras were involved. Their operation was concealed at Punta Arenas, while Chilean F5 jet fighters were in continual operation to keep Argentine defenses stretched toward the west and south as well as toward the Falklands. By April 10, before the

Canberras arrived, all the windows of the Civil Air terminal at Punta Arenas airfield were whitewashed, with guards posted to prevent anyone looking through cracks. Flight crews aboard Chilean civil airliners were instructed to ensure that passenger blinds were pulled down during landings and takeoffs "for reasons of national security."[180]

With an operating range of about 2,000 miles, the Canberras would be able to cover all important Argentine targets. The three main southern Argentine air bases—Rio Grande, Rio Galligas, and Ushvaia—are all less than 160 miles from Punta Arenas, amounting to twenty minutes' flying time. Port Stanley and the Falklands are about 400 miles away, less than an hour's flying time.[181]

Britain also received direct intelligence help from Chile. Included were the monitoring and code-breaking of signals carried out by the Chilean Naval Intelligence Staff. Among the information provided was notification of when the *General Belgrano* left port.[182]

In return, according to Campbell, Chile received between two and six of the Canberra PR-9s for the Chilean Air Force. Additionally, Chile obtained Britain's support in undermining United Nations investigations into Chilean human rights abuses by opposing reappointment of UN special investigators; gained the dropping of British restrictions on arms sales to Chile; and received a squadron of RAF Hawker Hunter aircraft.[183]

NOTES TO CHAPTER 2

1. Richard Deacon, *A History of British Secret Service*, 2d ed. (London: Granada, 1980), pp. 24–25, 27.
2. Ibid., pp. 33–34.
3. Christopher Andrew, *Secret Service: The Making of the British Intelligence Community* (London: Heinemann, 1985), pp. 3, 6.
4. Ibid., pp. 9–10.
5. Ibid., pp. 11, 13–14.
6. F. H. Hinsley, E. E. Thomas, C. F. G. Ransom, and R. C. Knight, *British Intelligence in the Second World War*, Vol. 1 (New York: Cambridge University Press, 1979), p. 11; Tony Bunyan, *The Political Police in Britain* (New York: St. Martin's Press, 1976), pp. 104–5; see also Rupert Allason, *The Branch: A History of the Metropolitan Police Special Branch 1883–1983* (London: Secker & Warburgh, 1983).
7. Andrew, *Secret Service*, p. 53.

8. Hinsley et al., *British Intelligence in the Second World War*, p. 16; Nigel West, *MI-6 British Secret Intelligence Service Operations 1909-1945* (London: Weidenfeld and Nicolson, 1983), p. 4; Andrew, *Secret Service*, pp. 58-59.

9. Andrew, *Secret Service*, pp. 139, 174.

10. Ibid., p. 174.

11. Ibid., pp. 133, 137.

12. See Patrick Beesly, *Room 40: British Naval Intelligence 1914-1918* (New York: Harcourt, Brace and Jovanovich, 1984).

13. Ibid., pp. 204-24.

14. Andrew, *Secret Service*, p. 259.

15. Ibid., pp. 260, 332.

16. Ibid., p. 488.

17. Wesley Wark, *The Ultimate Enemy: British Intelligence and Nazi Germany, 1933-1939* (Ithaca, N.Y.: Cornell University Press, 1985), pp. 158-61; Andrew, *Secret Service*, p. 472.

18. Hinseley et al., *British Intelligence Operations in the Second World War*, Vol. 1, pp. 11-12.

19. Andrew, *Secret Service*, p. 409.

20. See F. W. Winterbotham, *The Ultra Secret* (New York: Harper & Row, 1974); Gordon Welchman, *The Hut Six Story* (New York: McGraw-Hill, 1982); Ronald Lewin, *Ultra Goes to War* (New York: Pocket, 1980).

21. J. C. Masterman, *The Double-Cross System* (New Haven: Yale University Press, 1972); Nigel West, *MI-5* (New York: Stein and Day, 1972).

22. Alfred Price, *The History of U.S. Electronic Warfare* (Washington, D.C.: Association of Old Crows, 1984), Vol. 1, *The Years of Innovation Beginnings to 1946*, p. 12.

23. Ibid.

24. Ibid., p. 117.

25. Bunyan, *The Political Police in Britain*, p. 186.

26. The figures for GCHQ employees are based on comments by two knowledgeable sources. The quote is from Duncan Campbell, "The Threat of the Electronic Spies," *New Statesman*, February 2, 1979, pp. 142-45 at p. 142.

27. Bunyan, *The Political Police in Britain*, p. 191.

28. Richard Walsh and George Munster, *Documents on Australian Foreign Policy, 1968-1975* (Sydney: J. R. Walsh and G. J. Munster, 1980), p. 96.

29. Chapman Pincher, *Inside Story: A Documentary of the Pursuit of Power* (New York: Stein & Day, 1979), p. 32.

30. Duncan Campbell, "Inside the 'SIGINT' Empire," *New Statesman*, October 29, 1982, p. 4.

31. Duncan Campbell and Patrick Forbes, "U.K.'s Listening Link with Apartheid," *New Statesman*, August 1, 1986, pp. 10-11; Campbell, "Inside the

'SIGINT' Empire"; James Bamford, *The Puzzle Palace: A Report on NSA, America's Most Secret Agency* (New York: Penguin, 1983), pp. 494–500; statements concerning the computers at GCHQ is based on "News Digest," *Aviation Week and Space Technology*, November 1, 1982, p. 27 (Tandem Nonstop) and a knowledgeable source (IBM 360, 370, and Cray).

32. Bamford, *The Puzzle Palace* (Penguin), p. 494.

33. Ibid., p. 494.

34. Ibid., p. 495.

35. James Bamford, *The Puzzle Palace: A Report on NSA, America's Most Secret Agency* (Boston: Houghton Mifflin, 1982), p. 335.

36. Campbell, "Inside the 'SIGINT' Empire"; Bamford, *The Puzzle Palace* (Penguin), p. 493.

37. Ibid.

38. Duncan Campbell and Mark Hosenball, "The Eavesdroppers," *Time Out*, May 21–27, 1976, p. 8; Nick Anning, "A Battery of Hearing Aids Listening to the World," *The Leveller* 37 (April 1980): 18–19; Duncan Campbell, "Secrecy for Its Own Sake," *New Statesman*, July 23, 1982, pp. 6–8; "Britain's World Spy Network," *Sunday Times*, July 18, 1982; "Diplomacy by Satellite: Foreign Office Link with Embassies," *The Times* (London), February 2, 1967; Bamford, *The Puzzle Palace* (Houghton Mifflin), p. 333; Steve Connor, "How Cheltenham Entered America's Backyard," *New Scientist*, April 5, 1984, pp. 8–9; and information provided by Duncan Campbell.

39. Connor, "How Cheltenham Entered America's Backyard."; private information.

40. Private information.

41. Malcom Spaven, *Fortress Scotland: A Guide to the Military Presence* (London: Pluto Press, 1983), pp. 56–57; correspondence from Duncan Campbell, July 20, 1987.

42. Private information.

43. Anning, "A Battery of Hearing Aids"; "On Watch in Berlin," *Inscom Journal* 5, no. 5 (May 1982): 13.; private information.

44. Private information.

45. Duncan Campbell, "Eavesdroppers on a Dusty Plain," *New Statesman*, November 1, 1985, p. 11.

46. "Britannia Scorns to Yield," *Newsweek*, April 19, 1982, pp. 13–16.

47. "Cipher," *Defense Electronics*, March 1982, p. 30.

48. Joint Intelligence Organization (JIO), *Fourth Annual Report 1974*, Pt. 2 (Canberra: JIO, 1974), p. 7; Desmond Ball, "The U.S. Naval Ocean Surveillance System (NOSIS)—Australia's Role," *Pacific Defence Reporter*, June 1982, p. 42.

49. Private information.

50. Anning, "A Battery of Hearing Aids"; information provided by Duncan Campbell; Campbell and Forbes, "U.K.'s Listening Link with Apartheid."

51. Martin Streetly, "Royal Air Force's Nimrod Electronic Intelligence Aircraft," *Jane's Defence Weekly*, October 19, 1985, pp. 869-71.

52. Ibid.

53. Ibid.

54. Ibid.

55. Duncan Campbell, "The Parliamentary Bypass Operation," *New Statesman*, January 23, 1987, pp. 8-12; Duncan Campbell, "The Cost of Zircon," *New Statesman*, February 27, 1987, pp. 13-14; subsequent stories indicated that plans for ZIRCON had been cancelled in favor of a new project relying on U.S. technology (e.g., Peter Almond, "Britain Gives Up Effort to Develop Own Spy Satellite, Will Turn to U.S.," *Washington Times*, August 7, 1987, p. A6). However, ZIRCON was never an all-British project and, although it was to be built by British companies, was intended to rely on U.S. technology. In particular, use of the technology developed by TRW was part of the ZIRCON program from the beginning.

56. "The Treason of Geoffrey Prime," *The Economist*, November 13, 1982, pp. 63-64.

57. Duncan Campbell, "The Spies Who Spend What They Like," *New Statesman*, May 16, 1980, pp. 738-44; Duncan Campbell, "GCHQ's Lost Secrets," *New Statesman*, November 5, 1982, p. 5.

58. Duncan Campbell, "Friends and Others," *New Statesman*, November 26, 1982, p. 6.

59. Ibid.

60. E. H. Cookridge, *George Blake: Double Agent* (New York: Ballantine, 1982), pp. 139-40.

61. Greville Wynne, *The Man from Moscow* (London: Hutchinson, 1967), pp. 7-9.

62. Cookridge, *George Blake*, pp. 115-16.

63. David C. Martin, *Wilderness of Mirrors* (New York: Ballantine, 1981), pp. 72-75.

64. Ibid., p. 75.

65. Andrew Weir, Jonathan Bloch, and Pat Fitzgerald, "Sun Sets Over the Other Empire," *The Middle East*, October 1981, pp. 39-42.; correspondence from Duncan Campbell, July 20, 1987.

66. Weir, Bloch, and Fitzgerald, "Sun Sets Over the Empire," p. 40.

67. Ibid., p. 40.

68. Frank Doherty, "Her Majesty's Spies in Ireland," *Intelligence/Parapolitics* (reprinted from *The Phoenix*), May 1987, pp. 2-5.

69. Ibid.

70. Ibid.

71. "Spies: One for the West," *Newsweek*, September 23, 1985, p. 37; "What Russia Lost," *The Economist*, September 21, 1985, pp. 46-47.

72. "Spies: One for the West"; "What Russia Lost"; Murrey Marder, "Defector Told of Soviet Alert," *Washington Post*, August 8, 1986, pp. A1, A22; Leslie Gelb, "K.G.B. Defector Helped the C.I.A. Brief Reagan Before Summit Talks," *New York Times*, August 9, 1986, pp. 1, 4.

73. "Spies: One for the West"; Gelb, "K.G.B. Defector Helped the C.I.A."; private information.

74. Private information.

75. Duncan Campbell, "Big Brother's Many Mansions," *New Statesman*, February 8, 1980, pp. 194-97.

76. Munster and Walsh, *Documents on Australian Foreign Policy*, pp. 95-96.

77. Ibid.

78. Ibid.

79. Ibid.

80. Job Circular: "Ministry of Defense (Central Staffs) Intelligence Officers," G/7264/87.

81. National Defense University, *Intelligence for Joint Forces* (Washington, D.C.: NDU, 1985).

82. Correspondence from Duncan Campbell, July 20, 1987.

83. *History of Royal Air Force* (Rawlings/Temple Newhes Books), pp. 317-18; Bill Gunston, *An Illustrated Guide to Spy Planes and Electronic Warfare Aircraft* (New York: Arco, 1983), p. 79.

84. Hinsley et al., *British Intelligence in the Second World War*, Vol. 1, p. 16.

85. J. Ll., J. Edwards, *Ministrial Responsibility for National Security* (Hull, Quebec: Canadian Government Publishing Centre, 1980), p. 60.

86. Lord Denning, *Report* (London: Her Majesty's Stationery Office, 1963), para. 238.

87. Ibid.

88. Ibid., p. 91.

89. Chapman Pincher, *Inside Story: A Documentary of the Pursuit of Power* (New York: Stein & Day, 1978), p. 65; Chapman Pincher, *Their Trade Is Treachery* (London: Sidgwick & Jackson, 1981), pp. 56-57.

90. Barrie Penrose, David Connett, and Anthony Terry, "Spy Network Builder Shadowed in Britain," *Sunday Times*, March 29, 1987, p. 3.

91. Duncan Campbell, Patrick Forbes, and Jocelyn Jenkins, "The MI5 Affair: Can the Spooks Be Trusted?" *New Statesman*, December 5, 1986, pp. 14-15; "MI 5's Official Secrets," transcript of 20/20 Vision television program, pp. 3, 10.

92. Francis X. Clines, "British Say They Heard Syrian Envoy Discuss Plot," *New York Times*, October 26, 1986, p. 6.

93. David Horovitz, "How Syrian Tie with Terrorism was Exposed," *Jerusalem Post International Edition*, November 8, 1986, pp. 1, 2.

94. Karen De Young, "British Spy Agency Criticized," *Washington Post*, May 3, 1987, pp. A1, A23.
95. Alexander Cockburn, "Beat the Devil," *The Nation*, February 7, 1987, pp. 134–35.
96. Bunyan, *The Political Police in Britain*, pp. 175–77; Campbell, "Friends and Others."
97. Duncan Campbell, "Spymaster (2): Chief of 'A' Branch," *New Statesman*, August 17, 1984, p. 5; Bunyan, *The Political Police in Britain*, pp. 175–77.
98. Campbell, "Big Brother's Many Mansions."; private information.
99. Bunyan, *The Political Police in Britain*, pp. 104–5.
100. Ibid., pp. 131–32.
101. Ibid., pp. 129, 134.
102. Munster and Walsh, *Documents on Australian Foreign Policy*, pp. 92–93.
103. Duncan Campbell, "Unaccountable Empire Building," *New Statesman*, November 19, 1982, pp. 8–9; "Britain's Foreign Office," *The Economist*, November 27, 1982, p. 29.
104. Munster and Walsh, *Documents on Australian Foreign Policy*, pp. 93–94.
105. "Britain's Foreign Office," *The Economist*, November 27, 1982, pp. 27–28.
106. The Rt. Hon. Lord Franks, Chairman, *Falkland Islands Review: Report of a Committee of Privy Counsellors* (London: Her Majesty's Stationery Office, 1983), pp. 94–95.
107. Munster and Walsh, *Documents on Australian Foreign Policy*, p. 94; Campbell, "Unaccountable Empire Building."
108. Munster and Walsh, *Documents on Australian Foreign Policy*, p. 94; Campbell, "Unaccountable Empire Building."
109. Ronald Lewin, *The American Magic: Codes, Ciphers and the Defeat of Japan* (New York: Farrar, Straus, Giroux, 1982), p. 121n.
110. Campbell, "Unaccountable Empire Building"; "Making Whitehall Mole Proof," *The Economist*, June 5, 1982, p. 37.
111. See Jeffrey Richelson and Desmond Ball, *The Ties that Bind: Intelligence Cooperation Among the UKUSA Countries* (London: Allen & Unwin, 1985).
112. Campbell, "Threat of the Electronic Spies"; John Sawatsky, *Men in the Shadows: The RCMP Security Service* (New York: Doubleday, 1980), p. 92; Transcript of "The Fifth Estate—The Espionage Establishment," broadcast by Canadian Broadcast Company, 1974.
113. Pincher, *Inside Story*, p. 157; Sawatsky, *Men in the Shadows*, p. 9n.
114. Desmond Ball, *A Suitable Piece of Real Estate: American Installations in Australia* (Sydney: Hale & Iremonger, 1980), p. 40.
115. Campbell, "Threat of the Electronic Spies."
116. Department of the Army, Office of the Adjutant General, "United States—United Kingdom Security Agreement," memorandum dated October 8, 1948.

117. Richelson and Ball, *The Ties that Bind*, pp. 148–49.
118. Ibid.
119. Duncan Campbell and Clive Thomas, "BBC's Trade Secrets," *New Statesman*, July 4, 1980, pp. 13–14.
120. Ibid., p. 14.
121. Ibid., pp. 13–14.
122. Ray Cline, *Secret Spies and Scholars* (Washington, D.C.: Acropolis, 1976), p. 12.
123. Royal Commission on Intelligence and Security, *Fifth Report* (Canberra: Australian Government Printer, 1977), app. 5-E, para. 2.
124. Ibid., app. 5-E, para. 3.
125. Ibid., app. 5-E, para. 4.
126. Ibid., paras. 211–12.
127. Ibid., app. 5-E, para. 15.
128. Ibid., app. 5-E, para. 17.
129. Joint Intelligence Organization (JIO), *Fourth Annual Report*, 1974, pt. 1 (Canberra: JIO, 1974), p. 36.
130. Ibid.
131. Ibid., app. F.
132. Campbell and Forbes, "U.K.'s Listening Link with Apartheid."
133. Ibid.
134. Ibid.
135. Ibid.
136. Arthur Gavshon and Desmond Rice, *The Sinking of the Belgrano* (London: Secker & Warburg, 1984), p. 3; Max Hastings and Simon Jenkins, *The Battle for the Falklands* (New York: W. W. Norton & Co., 1983).
137. Lord Franks, *Falkland Islands Review*, pp. 8–9.
138. Ibid., p. 11.
139. Ibid.
140. Ibid.
141. Ibid., p. 12.
142. Ibid., pp. 13–14.
143. Ibid., pp. 14–15.
144. Ibid., p. 15.
145. Ibid.
146. Ibid., p. 18.
147. Ibid., p. 22.
148. Ibid., p. 26.
149. Ibid., pp. 26–27.
150. Ibid., pp. 43–44.
151. Ibid., pp. 44–45.
152. Ibid., p. 47.
153. Ibid., p. 47.
154. Ibid., p. 59.

155. Lawrence Freedman, "Intelligence Operations in the Falklands," *Intelligence and National Security*, 1, no. 3 (1986): 309–35.
156. Ibid., Martin Middlebrook, *Operation Corporate* (New York: Viking, 1985), p. 40.
157. Middlebrook, *Operation Corporate*, pp. 37–38.
158. Ibid., p. 39.
159. Franks, *Falkland Islands Review*, p. 63.
160. Freedman, "Intelligence Operations in the Falklands."
161. Franks, *Falkland Islands Review*, p. 66; Freedman, "Intelligence Operations in the Falklands"; Middlebrook, *Operation Corporate*, p. 43.
162. Franks, *Falkland Islands Review*, p. 68.
163. Julian Thompson, *No Picnic* (Glasgow: Fontana & Collins, 1985), pp. 12–13.
164. Walter Pincus, "British Got Crucial Data in Falklands, Diary Says," *New York Times*, December 23, 1984, pp. A1, A20.
165. J. C. Murquizur, "The South Atlantic Conflict, an Argentinian Point of View," *International Defense Review* 2 (1983): 138, 140–42; Gavshon and Rice, *The Sinking of the Belgrano*, p. 161.
166. Pincus, "British Got Crucial Data in Falklands," p. A20.
167. Gavshon and Rice, *The Sinking of the Belgrano*, p. 101; Middlebrook, *Operation Corporate.*
168. Middlebrook, *Operation Corporate*, p. 104; Jeffrey Ethell and Alfred Price, *Air War South Atlantic* (New York: Jove, June 1986), pp. 32, 34–35.
169. Freedman, "Intelligence Operations in the Falklands."
170. Ibid., p. 325.
171. Ethell and Price, *Air War South Atlantic*, pp. 93, 128.
172. William Seymour, *British Special Forces* (London: Sidgwick & Jackson, 1985), pp. 311–12; Max Hastings and Simon Jenkins, *The Battle for the Falklands* (London: Pan Books, 1983), p. 206; Freedman, "Intelligence Operations in the Falklands."
173. Seymour, *British Special Forces*, p. 312.
174. Ibid.; Hastings and Jenkins, *The Battle for the Falklands*, p. 215.
175. Max White, "U.S. Satellite Reconnaissance During the Falklands Conflict," Earth Satellite Research Unit, Department of Mathematics, University of Aston, Birmingham; "America's Falklands War," *The Economist*, March 3, 1984; Duncan Campbell, "How We Spy on Argentina," *New Statesman*, April 30, 1982, p. 5; correspondence from Duncan Campbell, July 20, 1987.
176. "America's Falklands War."
177. Gavshon and Rice, *The Sinking of the Belgrano*, p. 205, n. 5.
178. Richelson and Ball, *The Ties that Bind*, p. 77.
179. Duncan Campbell, "The Chile Connection," *New Statesman*, January 25, 1985.

180. Ibid.
181. Ibid.
182. Ibid.; Freedman, "Intelligence Operations in the Falklands."
183. Campbell, "The Chile Connection."

3 CANADIAN INTELLIGENCE ORGANIZATIONS

ORIGINS

Although the Canadian intelligence and security community is the product of more than sixty years of evolution, its modern structure is largely due to changes after World War II and then again from 1975 to the present.

The first bonafide intelligence organization established by the Canadian government was a military one—the Directorate of Military Operations and Intelligence, established in 1920. Subsequently, a naval intelligence unit was established. But it was World War II and its aftermath that served as a catalyst for expansion of the Canadian intelligence and security community. Even before Canada established its own cryptographic unit, it was making a COMINT contribution to the British war effort. Canadian naval intelligence officers were studying German naval telecommunications. Messages were intercepted by Army, Air Force, Navy, and Department of Transport Radio Division stations, such as those at Forest (later Winnipeg), Manitoba, and Point Grey, British Columbia. As France collapsed, the Canadian Navy monitored French naval frequencies at British request to discover the fate of the French fleet. Intercepted communications helped the British in mounting a successful attack on Germany's giant battleship, the *Bismarck*.[1]

In June 1941 the Examination Unit of the National Research Council (NRC) was established under the supervision of Herbert O. Yardley, the former head of the American "Black Chamber," and grew to a staff of twenty-five in the following months. One initial function was the interception and decoding of communications traffic between German Abwehr controllers in Hamburg and their agents in South America. Due to favorable reception conditions, the small intercept station established at the Rockliffe base near Ottawa in 1939 by a Royal Canadian Signal Corps officer was able to intercept such traffic. Further, because of the simplicity of the cipher system employed between the Abwehr and its agents, the Examination Unit was able to read the messages. By the end of 1941, the activities of fifty-two agents were being monitored and 740 messages had been read. These messages warned of danger, instructed agents to stop transmitting immediately, and told of invisible ink, shipping activities, or bribes needed to pay off police officers.[2] Another initial function was to intercept and decode messages to and from the Vichy delegation in Ottawa. Because Vichy was suspected of propaganda activities in Quebec, interception of the mission's messages appeared to be the best means of determining the nature and extent of those activities. At first, some Canadian officials believed the emphasis for a Canadian cryptographic unit would be the identification of German agents and U-boats operating in Latin America, since Ottawa's wireless interception facilities happened to be one of the best locations for picking up messages to Latin America; however, arrangements had already been made for the United States to perform this task.[3]

In January 1942, at the insistence of the British, Yardley was replaced. His replacement by a British designee, Oliver Strachey, led to closer cooperation with the United States and Britain, which now shared their keys to Vichy codes as well as copies of intercepts that British Security Coordination (BSC) obtained from their receiving stations. In addition, BSC acquired actual copies of the Vichy codebooks and passed them on to the Examination Unit, which was thus able to identify important intercepts that would assist Allied planning for the invasion of North Africa in November 1942.[4]

Subsequently, the Examination Unit added the interception of Japanese communications and ocean surveillance to its functions. At British request, the unit started work on intercepted Japanese messages in August 1941. The Canadian Navy had developed expertise in the interception of Japanese communications; with Allied assistance, the Examination Unit was able to read low-level Japanese codes by November 1941. In December 1941 a further emphasis on Japanese traffic ensued when the British High Commissioner in Ottawa requested that the Canadians immediately switch their signals intelligence focus to the Pacific theater, particularly to Japanese agent traffic.[5]

In 1942 several operations were moved under the control of the Examination Unit. The Army's Discrimination Unit, which distinguished significant from insignificant messages, was moved into the same building as similar units from the Navy and Air Force. The Foreign Intelligence Section of the Navy, which was working on low-grade Japanese traffic, was transferred to the Examination Unit. The Signals Corps was given permission to upgrade its interception facilities, and all messages received from the nineteen Canadian receiving stations were channeled to the Examination Unit.[6]

In addition, a Special Intelligence Section of the Department of External Affairs was established within the Examination Unit in September 1942. Its function was to prepare from the Examination Unit's material and other sources intelligence reports on Japan and the Far East. Soon the Special Intelligence Section was being given specific research topics, such as the possible effects of Germany's acquisition of Spanish wolfram for use in hardening steel. What the section could produce, however, was limited by its size—it never had more than two officers and three support staff. In January 1945 External Affairs pulled the section out of the Examination Unit, partly because its experienced personnel were needed elsewhere and partly because of the disintegration of effective interception.[7]

The single most important message that the Examination Unit worked on during the war was the Vichy signal to Admiral Robert to scuttle the French fleet lying at anchor off the Caribbean island of Martinique. The presence of French facilities and equipment in the Caribbean became a vital factor in the struggle against German submarine activities in 1942. A German submarine had visited Martinique in February. In May the United States demanded that Robert's ships be totally immobilized by the removal of all ordnance; in addition, all merchant ships and gold that had been transferred to Martinique were to be turned over to the Allies. In return for these concessions the United States was to recognize Robert as the ultimate governing authority of Martinique and other French possessions. To prevent this arrangement from coming to pass, the Germans persuaded Vichy Prime Minister Pierre Laval to scuttle the French fleet immediately, and it was the Ottawa interception station that picked up Laval's orders. Once deciphered and decoded by the Examination Unit, the message was given to Norman Robertson of External Affairs, who alerted the Americans. In the end, no intervention was required, as Robert refused to carry out Laval's orders.[8]

The overall Canadian contribution was assessed by F. H. Hinsley et al.:

> Canadian . . . intercept stations and DF [Direction-Finding] organization . . . made an indispensable contribution to the Allied north Atlantic Sigint network since the early days of the war. In May 1943, as well as receiving the intelligence summaries issued by Whitehall to the naval commands at home and overseas, the Tracking Room in Ottawa began to receive a full series of Enigma decrypts and from that it carried on a completely free exchange of ideas by direct signal link with the Tracking Room in OIC [Operational Intelligence Center].[9]

In the aftermath of the war, the Examination Unit was saved from probable extinction by the revelations of Igor Gouzenko, a Soviet cipher clerk before his defection, concerning Soviet intelligence activities in Canada and the United States. At a December 1945 meeting of officials from the Department of External Affairs, the Army, and the NRC, it was decided to keep the unit in operation. By March 1946 plans had been prepared for the establishment of five hundred service personnel at one hundred high-speed monitoring positions. Although the initial target was the wireless traffic of the Soviet embassy, operations were soon expanded to include radio communications in the northern USSR.[10] Subsequently, the unit was renamed the Communications Branch, National Research Council (CBNRC).

The year 1946 also saw other changes in the Canadian intelligence and security community. Prior to that year, counterintelligence and countersubversion functions were the responsibility of the Intelligence Section of the Royal Canadian Mounted Police (RCMP) Criminal Investigation Branch. Gouzenko's revelations led to the creation of a separate Special Branch to handle such functions.[11]

Thus, as of 1946 the Canadian intelligence and security community consisted of the Examination Unit of the NRC, the Special Branch of the RCMP, the Army's Directorate of Intelligence, the

Navy's Directorate of Intelligence, the Air Force's Directorate of Security, and the Directorate of Scientific Intelligence of the Department of National Defence. A December 1945 proposal by the chief of the General Staff for the establishment of a National Bureau of Intelligence was never accepted, and thus Canada remained without a central intelligence agency.[12]

A proposal that fared better than that for a National Bureau of Intelligence called for the establishment of a Joint Intelligence Bureau (JIB). In 1950, four years after its establishment was first proposed, the JIB came into being. Administered by the Defence Research Board, it was responsible for intelligence common to all users on such subjects as topography, communications, economics, and logistics. Subsequently, the JIB was split in two, with its nondefense functions performed by a Special Research Bureau (later called the Economic Intelligence Bureau) and transferred to the Department of External Affairs.[13]

The Canadian intelligence and security community continued to evolve over the years. In 1956 the Special Branch was renamed the Directorate of Security and Intelligence, or I Directorate. In 1970, as the result of a report by the Mackenzie Commission, the directorate was given enhanced status within the RCMP and renamed the Security Service. In 1965 the military service headquarters were unified, eliminating individual services and thus their separate intelligence units. Instead, a Director General for Intelligence and Security in the Department of National Defence oversaw all intelligence and security functions for the military. Subsequently, the Directorate of Scientific Intelligence of the Defence Research Board was absorbed into the Director General's unit.[14]

On April 1, 1975, the CBNRC was transferred to the Department of National Defence and renamed the Communications Security Establishment. At that time it had approximately 250 to 300 civilian employees and a budget of Can$5 million per year. In 1976 the RCMP Security Service was given "National Division" status, resulting in more administrative responsibilities being delegated to the Director General of the Security Service and to Security Service headquarters in Ottawa, rather than to the heads of the RCMP's geographic divisions—an independence that was somewhat curtailed in later years. The intelligence and security components of the Defence Director General of Intelligence and Security were separated on October 29, 1982—approximately twelve years after they had been joined—resulting in a Director General, Intelligence, separated from the Chief, Intelligence and Security.[15]

The biggest change in the Canadian intelligence and security community came as a result of the 1981 McDonald Commission's inquiry into Security Service abuses. Among the commission's recommendations was the establishment of a civilian security service separated from the RCMP. The idea of a separate civilian (as opposed to RCMP-controlled) security service had been suggested by the 1969 Mackenzie Commission, but was not adopted by the government of the time, then headed by Prime Minister Trudeau. The Mackenzie Commission felt that RCMP recruitment, training, and promotion procedures resulted in a Security Service dominated, in terms of operational decision-making and action, by those who had spent earlier years in conventional police work and gone through training at the RCMP academy in Regina.

Given the composition of RCMP recruits and a policy of recruitment for only the lowest levels of RCMP regular members, it was considered unlikely that Security Service members charged with operational duties would have more than a high school education or would be representative of more than a narrow segment of the community. It was suggested that the Security Service needed personnel with broader backgrounds, including university backgrounds, to properly deal with the problems confronting it.

In August 1981, in response to the recommendation of the McDonald Commission's report on RCMP activities, the Solicitor General announced that the Security Service would be detached from the RCMP and would become the civilian Canadian Security Intelligence Service (CSIS). Although Frederick E. Gibson, the Assistant Deputy Minister of Justice, was named to head the service, he was replaced by Ted D'Arcy Finn as head of the Security Intelligence Transitional Group and future head of the CSIS. The transitional period extended considerably beyond the intended time. In November 1982 the enabling legislation, along with a package of other measures, such as amendments to existing laws to permit mail interception in national security cases, had been before a Cabinet committee for several months.[16]

In May 1983 the Liberal government introduced a bill, C-157, authorizing the establishment of the CSIS. The bill immediately ran into a prolonged storm of criticism over provisions that were considered by many to give the CSIS far too much discretion in the investigation of domestic subversion. The bill proposed to give the CSIS the authority to seek judicial warrants to conduct intrusive surveillance (that is, buggings, wiretaps, break-ins, mail openings) with respect to "activities within . . . Canada directed toward or in support of . . . acts of violence . . . for the purpose of achieving a political objective within Canada or a foreign state." Likewise, "activities . . . intended ultimately to lead to the destruction or overthrow of the constitutionally established system of government in Canada "were also a justification for intrusive surveillance.[17]

The first provision could have been used to justify surveillance of groups supporting resistance movements abroad, whether Afghan or Salvadoran. The "intended ultimately" portion of the second provision could have been used as a pretext for investigating a wide range of nonviolent groups whose activities the CSIS believed might lead to violence.

In addition to the criticisms voiced by the Canadian Civil Liberties Association, strenuous objections were raised by the Conservative party and the provincial attorneys general. The latter group denounced C-157 as a "massive threat to the rights and freedoms of all Canadians." The Special Senate Committee on the CSIS recommended a dozen major amendments to the bill; as a result, a modified version, designated C-9, was submitted. Despite strong opposition from some groups, C-9 became law in May 1984, thus effecting the creation of the CSIS.[18]

The most recent change in the Canadian intelligence community occurred in 1986, when two External Affairs intelligence units—the Bureau of Intelligence Analysis and Security and the Bureau of Economic Intelligence—were merged to become the Foreign Intelligence Bureau.[19]

INTELLIGENCE AND SECURITY ORGANIZATIONS

Canadian Security Intelligence Service

The Canadian Security Intelligence Service bears a strong relationship to its predecessors, having retained most of its two thousand members as well as its functions. Its budget is in the area of Can$134 million, a substantial increase from the approximately Can$68 million budget of the Security Service.[20]

The CSIS Act (Bill C-9) allows CSIS to collect information related to "threats to the security of Canada." The act specifies that information may be collected to the extent that it is "strictly necessary" to deal with activities that can reasonably be suspected of being threats. "Threats to the security of Canada," according to the act, include

- espionage or sabotage that is directed against Canada or is detrimental to the interests of Canada or activities directed toward or in support of such espionage or sabotage,

- foreign-influenced activities within or relating to Canada that are detrimental to the interests of Canada and are clandestine or deceptive or involve a threat to any person,

- activities within or relating to Canada directed toward or in support of the threat or use of acts of serious violence against persons or property for the purpose of achieving a political objective within Canada or a foreign state, and

- activities directed toward undermining by covert unlawful acts, or directed toward or intended ultimately to lead to the destruction or overthrow by violence of the constitutionally established system of government in Canada

but do not include lawful advocacy, protest, or dissent, unless carried on in conjunction with any of the above activities.[21]

The functions of the CSIS will differ from those of the RCMP Security Service in several ways. Unlike the Security Service, the CSIS will not have law enforcement powers, an absence recommended by both the Mackenzie and the McDonald commissions. Rather, in matters of arrest and seizure, it will cooperate with a special group within the RCMP and with other forces when necessary.[22]

Further, the CSIS will apparently have permission to function abroad to collect information through its own sources for foreign intelligence purposes. While the RCMP did, on occasion, operate abroad, it apparently did so on an ad hoc basis and primarily in pursuit of internal security cases rather than foreign information. One case has come to light, however, in which Security Service agents traveled to Basel, Switzerland, and New York City in an attempt to recruit a middle-level Soviet trade representative, Anatoly Maximov.

These meetings occurred shortly after Prime Minister Trudeau had publicly vowed that the force was engaged in no clandestine operations outside of Canada. According to Canadian officials, the CSIS will not engage in covert operations abroad that seek to influence or alter the politics of another nation.[23]

Within Canada, the CSIS is permitted, under section 16 of the CSIS Act, to conduct espionage (for example, by means of telephone taps or other forms of electronic surveillance) to obtain economic or national security intelligence. Targets could include foreign diplomats, trade officials, foreign business enterprises, and foreign visitors. As of 1986 the CSIS had not conducted any such operations.[24]

Counterespionage is a more prominent part of the CSIS mission. According to the CSIS, about 60 percent of some of the members of Toronto's forty-seven trade missions or consulates, particularly those from Soviet bloc and other Communist countries, are actually intelligence officers. In the summer of 1985 the Assistant Trade Commissioner at the Bulgarian Consulate General in Toronto was declared persona non grata for alleged espionage activities. In many instances the targets of Soviet bloc espionage may be restricted technological information residing in the industrial and scientific centers of the "Golden Horseshoe" area bounded by Hamilton, Toronto, and Oshawa. The CSIS monitors the staff of Soviet bloc trading companies operating in the Toronto area. Included are Belarus Equipment of Canada (which sells and services Soviet agricultural equipment), Stan-Canada Inc. (which sells and services Soviet machine tools in Canada and the United States), Omintrade Ltd. (which sells and services a wide range of Czechoslovakian industrial products), Pekao Trading Company (Canada) Ltd. (which sells Polish consumer and manufactured products), and Dalimpex Ltd. (which sells and services Polish consumer and industrial products).[25]

Also active in Canada are the intelligence operatives of countries such as India, Israel, South Korea, and the Philippines. In addition to collecting intelligence on the activities of dissidents or violence-prone expatriate groups (such as the Sikhs from India), the intelligence officers of these countries may also engage in covert action operations to influence opinion in their ethnic communities in Canada. Thus, Croatians in Toronto were asked by the Yugoslav security service to gather information about fellow Croats living in Toronto. In 1979 the Department of External Affairs expelled the Yugoslav vice-consul in Toronto, charging that he "had used his position in

Canada to exert improper pressure on Canadians of Yugoslav origin in order to obtain information and to influence developments in the Canadian Yugoslav community."[26]

The CSIS has also conducted operations on Canadian college campuses, with the object of detecting foreign agents. These operations have centered on recruiting informers, although no faculty have been involved. The CSIS also keeps on file the names of MPs who "unwittingly" come in contact with foreign agents.[27]

CSIS counterterrorist operations are undoubtedly aimed at violence-prone expatriate groups residing in Canada as well as the foreign intelligence services that might take violent measures against them. Of particular concern are extremist Sikh groups in pursuit of making Punjab an independent Sikh state, "Khalistan" and alleged to be behind political violence in Canada and India. One operation— a wiretap of a Canadian Sikh's telephone—ultimately led to the resignation of the first director of the CSIS, Ted Finn, when it was revealed that the CSIS had used information from an informant it knew to be unreliable to obtain a warrant for the wiretap. In anticipation of the 1988 Winter Olympics in Calgary CSIS is pouring extra effort into its counterterrorism operations.[28]

It is in the area of countersubversion that CSIS has generated the most concern. The CSIS claims to maintain files on 3,867 individuals, 450 of those files having been opened since July 1984. The Canadian Security Intelligence Review Committee (SIRC), an official watchdog agency, has expressed misgivings about CSIS attempts to penetrate and curtail the activities of student groups, political fringe groups, environmental coalitions, and peace movements that CSIS believes represent a threat to national security. The SIRC has identified what it calls "virtually ludicrous" cases of CSIS investigating and plotting the disruption of alleged subversive groups and "intimidation" by CSIS agents of individuals associated with some of the groups under investigation.[29] One group targeted by the CSIS has been *This Magazine*, described by the SIRC as "a magazine that deals with a wide range of topics—the arts as well as social policy and other issues—from the perspective of the far left." The committee also noted that "some members . . . advocated violent action by this group, but they were brushed aside by others."[30]

The structure of the CSIS is similar to that of the RCMP Security Service, shown in Figure 3-1. The two most important units are the Counterintelligence Branch and the Counterterrorism Branch. The Counterintelligence Branch corresponds to B and H Ops units in the

Figure 3-1. Organization of the RCMP Security Service, 1978.

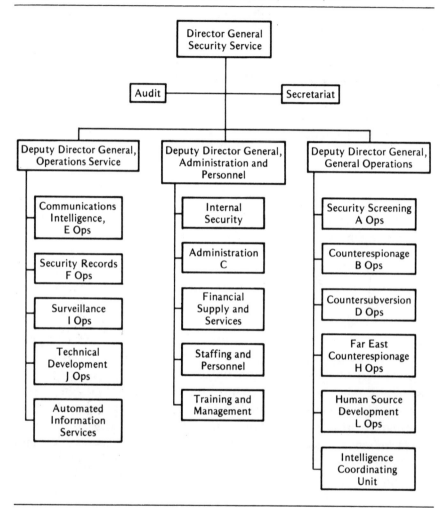

RCMP Security Service. The Counterterrorist Branch is unique to CSIS.[31] Recently, the Countersubversion Branch, which corresponded to the D Ops Section, was abolished—with its responsibilities being divided between the Counterintelligence and Counterterrorism branches. According to the SIRC, the Countersubversion Branch was primarily concerned with (1) the potential ability of foreign powers to manipulate Canadian policy through social institutions or legitimate protest groups and (2) the possibility that certain groups might undermine Canadian institutions and bring about the violent over-throw of the state.[32]

Corresponding to the A Ops unit is the Security Screening Branch, responsible for checking the backgrounds of individuals who would have access to classified information. The branch seeks to determine whether the individual is who he or she claims to be (that is, not an "illegal" posing as someone who had actually died years earlier) and whether there is a "character weakness" (use of drugs, excessive use of liquor, large debts) that might make the individual a target for blackmail, or evidence of extremist political associations or disloyal-ty to the existing political structure that would preclude having access to official secrets. In 1985 the branch received 69,647 re-quests for security assessment—14,647 for Top Secret clearance and over 48,000 for Secret and Confidential clearances.[33]

The CSIS Human Sources Branch corresponds to the Security Services' L Ops. Human Sources serves all CSIS operational branches, seeking to ensure that informers are reliable as well as establishing rules about what paid sources can and cannot be asked to do. The branch probably also serves as the repository for information on all CSIS informers.[34]

New to CSIS is the Open Source Information Centre, with a tech-nical services section, an Open Source Research Unit, an Emergency Operations Centre, and two reference units. Among the shortcomings that the McDonald Commission found in the RCMP Security Service was an almost complete reliance on 'information' from covert sources. The commission noted the value of collecting and analyzing information from public sources, such as scholarly journals and mass media, as an alternative to intrusive activities, such as wiretaps and infiltration. The Open Sources Research Unit compiles and distrib-utes open-source information to operational desks. The Emergency Operations Centre assures that information in the mass media about fast-breaking events is transmitted to the proper branches and desks of CSIS. Information is also drawn from clippings and computerized data bases.[35]

Finally, there is a Target Approval and Review Committee (TARC), composed of senior CSIS managers that considers requests by the operational (that is, Counterterrorist and Counterintelligence) branches to target individuals or groups. TARC authorizes targets for specific periods of time, approving or rejecting new targets and re-newing, in some cases, old targets.[36]

Communications Security Establishment

The Communications Security Establishment (CSE) operates under a secret directive signed by the Minister of National Defence in 1975, when CBNRC became CSE. Similar to the relationship between the U.S. National Security Agency and the U.S. Department of Defense, the CSE is a "separately organized establishment under general management and direction of the Department of National Defence."[37]

One function of the CSE is to manage and direct a communications security (COMSEC) program for the entire government. Another function is to collect communications intelligence (COMINT) and electronic intelligence (ELINT). In addition to its signals intelligence responsibilities under the UKUSA agreement, the CSE intercepts electronic communications between foreign embassies in Ottawa and their capitals.[38]

Since 1975, the CSE has expanded to over 700 employees. It is currently headed by P. R. Hunt, who has three major units subordinate to him—Production, Security, and Technology—each headed by a Director General. In addition, there are units for Administration and Finance and for Personnel.[39]

During the hearings on the establishment of the CSIS, the CSE also became a subject for debate. The Solicitor General, Robert Kaplan, testified that there was nothing illegal about the interception of microwave and satellite communications, and therefore no need for the CSE to obtain a judicial warrant to intercept such communications if it desired to do so. Kaplan stated, however, that as a matter of policy the CSE did not intercept microwave signals, "target" Canadians for eavesdropping operations, or intercept private telephone calls.[40] (All Canadian long-distance calls that travel farther than 372 miles are on a microwave link at some point.)

Other aspects of CSE's operations were revealed later in 1984. The CSE maintains a personal information data bank on people who are considered security risks. The CSE is also involved in attempting to protect the interception of high-frequency radio signals leaking from computer equipment. These signals sound like interference when picked up on standard radios but can be intercepted by sensitive receivers, recorded, and later unscrambled by sophisticated electronic devices, including other computers. In some circumstances, sophisticated equipment can pick up signals from computer equipment within a two-block area. CSE is responsible for protecting certain computers that process classified information, such as computer communications with other nations of NATO. CSE security measures include shielding equipment with copper to block emissions.[41]

Canadian signals intelligence facilities are located on both coasts as well as in the far northern regions of Canada. Manning and operation of the actual stations is the responsibility of the military-run Canadian Forces Supplementary Radio System (CFSRS), with 400 to 500 military and civilian personnel.[42]

Present CSE facilities on the East Coast include the Argentia Naval Station in Newfoundland, and the 770 Communications Research Squadron at Gander in Newfoundland. The Argentia facility is an ELINT/HF-DF station, while the Gander Station is the home of the 770th Communications Research Squadron. A more centrally located facility is the one at the Leitrim Canadian Forces Station in Ontario. Additionally, the 1st Canadian Signals Regiment is located at Kingston, Ontario. A West Coast monitoring station is located at the Masset Canadian Forces Station in British Columbia.[43]

Until 1986 the CSE had at least two listening posts in the northern regions of Canada for monitoring the northern Soviet Union: the Canadian Forces Station at Alert, Northwest Territories, and the Canadian Forces Station at Inuvik. The Inuvik station was closed in 1986. Among the probable targets of the Alert station are northern Soviet Air Force communications.[44]

Finally, there is a Canadian Forces Station in Bermuda, formerly titled a "Communications Research Station." This endeavor may be a joint operation with the United States, as there is a U.S. naval air station in Bermuda as well as a listing for "Bermuda activities" in the U.S. Department of Defense Automatic Voice Network (AUTOVON) telephone directory.[45]

Department of National Defence Intelligence

As noted earlier, in 1982 a separation was effected between the intelligence and security components of the Defence staff. Until that time, both functions were the responsibility of the Chief, Intelligence and Security, who oversaw defense intelligence production, foreign liaison operations, and military security. Subordinate to the Chief were directors for Defence Intelligence, Foreign Liaison, Scientific and Technical Intelligence, and Security. The Director of Defence

Intelligence published a quarterly journal, the *Canadian Intelligence Quarterly*, classified secret. The Director of Foreign Liaison was responsible for maintaining liaison with allied military intelligence services such as U.S. Defense Intelligence Agency and Australian Joint Intelligence Organization. The Director of Scientific and Technical Intelligence was charged with producing studies on the applications of science to and the technical characteristics of weapon systems. The Director of Security was responsible for security standards and procedures for the protection of information, for the physical security of materials and units, and for the security clearance of personnel and supervision of security staff.[46]

Under the present structure, the Chief, Intelligence and Security, is responsible for security and foreign liaison and is assisted by a Director, Security, and a Director, Foreign Liaison. The Director General, Intelligence, is responsible for the production of foreign intelligence and is assisted by the Director, Defence Intelligence; the Director, Scientific and Technical Intelligence; the Director, Intelligence and Security; the Director, Current Intelligence; and the Director, Imagery Exploitation.[47]

Foreign Intelligence Bureau, Department of External Affairs

The January 6, 1986, creation of the Foreign Intelligence Bureau (FIB) was part of a restructuring of Department of External Affairs (DEA) intelligence and security operations. The FIB was created by merging the Bureau of Economic Intelligence (BEI) with the Bureau of Intelligence Analysis and Security (BIAS), less the security and emergency preparedness components of BIAS, which became the Security Services Bureau. The FIB is headed by a Director General and responsible to the Assistant Deputy Minister (Political and International Security Affairs). It is responsible for collecting, analyzing, and distributing political and economic intelligence both for policymakers within the DEA and for other departments concerned with foreign policy. As currently structured, subordinate to the FIB's Director General are four divisions: the Economic Intelligence Division, the Interview Division, the Political Intelligence Division, and the Intelligence Services Division.[48]

The Economic Intelligence Division, the new incarnation of the BEI, is divided into four units—Europe, Africa and the Middle East,

Figure 3-2. Organization of the Foreign Intelligence Bureau, Political Intelligence Division.

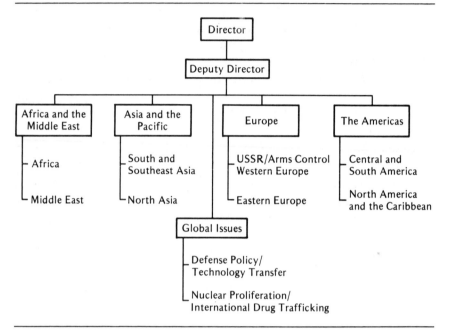

the Americas and Asia and the Pacific. As was the BEI, it is responsible for the collation, storage, and reporting of economic intelligence. Previously the BEI prepared assessments relevant to departments and agencies such as Finance, Industry, Trade and Commerce, Energy, Mines and Resources, and the Bank of Canada.[49] Presumably, priorities for the Economic Intelligence Division are established by the Economic Intelligence Subcommittee of the Intelligence Advisory Committee, which established priorities for the BEI.

The Intelligence Services Division performs administrative, data management, communications, and liaison (within the Canadian government) functions, as indicated by its some of its subunits: Management and Resources, Registry and Production Planning and Coordination, Clearances and Control, and Client Relations. The Interview Division gathers information by means of voluntary interviews conducted in Canada with individuals who have lived or worked abroad and may possess information of interest to the FIB. Representing an expansion of DEA intelligence focus is the Political Intelligence Division, which consists of a combination of geographical and functional units, each divided into three sections, as shown in Figure 3-2.[50]

Not transferred to the FIB were the Emergency Preparedness Division and the Security Division of BIAS. The two divisions became the basis of a newly created Security Services Bureau. The Emergency Preparedness Division of BIAS became two divisions under the Security Services Bureau: its Operations Centre became Emergency Preparedness—Operations and the remainder stayed as the Emergency Preparedness Division. The Security Division retained its name, function, and organization.[51]

Police and Security Branch

The Police and Security Branch, in the Office of the Solicitor General, is somewhere between being a member of the management structure and being an analytical unit. The branch was created in 1971 as the Security Planning and Research Group (SPARG) of the Office of the Solicitor General.[52] In announcing its formation, the Solicitor General, Jean Pierre Goyer, stated that its functions would be:

- to study the nature, origin and causes of subversive and revolutionary action, its objectives and techniques, as well as the measures necessary to protect Canadians from internal threats;

- to compile and analyze information collected on subversive and revolutionary groups and their activities, to estimate the nature and scope of internal threat to Canadians and to plan for measures to counter these threats; and

- to advise me on these matters.[53]

SPARG was to have only research, analysis, and planning functions, with no field security or operational intelligence duties, which some feared to be among its intended functions. Subsequently, SPARG added law enforcement and police matters to its security functions and became, in December 1972, the Police and Security Planning and Analysis Group. In 1974 it was retitled the Police and Security Planning and Analysis Branch and subsequently the Police and Security Branch.[54]

The initial intention to have SPARG serve as an assessor of RCMP security intelligence reports and perform long-term research was never implemented, because of the difficulty of obtaining the required information from the RCMP. By 1974 the branch had assumed primary responsibility for research and development in relation to the government's capacity to respond to civil emergencies and natural disasters.[55]

As currently constituted the Police and Security Branch consists of three sections: a Security Planning and Coordination Directorate; a Director General, Security Policy and Operations (with subordinate directors for Security Policy and Security Operations); and a Director General, Police and Law Enforcement Policy (with subordinate directors for RCMP Policy and Programs and Law Enforcement Policy).[56]

At present the branch is responsible for analyzing and proposing measures in response to:

- threats to the internal security of Canada from organizations, groups and individuals either in Canada or elsewhere;
- policy formulation for the protection of personnel, property and equipment in the federal government, including the security of government information;
- the role of the federal government in law enforcement in Canada;
- contingency planning for Ministry crisis handling in emergency situations.[57]

Implementation of this responsibility has included projects involving the following:

- development of contingency planning procedures in the event of internal security crises such as riots, the hijacking of aircraft, kidnapping and the holding of hostages;
- studies to assess Canada's vulnerability to possible acts by international terrorist organizations;
- studies on establishing national police research and training capabilities;
- formulation of government policy and recommendations on the physical security of information and property; and
- studies on the practical implementation of legislation, such as the Protection of Privacy Act.[58]

MANAGEMENT STRUCTURE

Control and supervision of the Canadian security and intelligence community are exercised at both the ministerial and deputy ministerial levels. The most senior supervisory body is the Cabinet Committee on Security and Intelligence, formed in 1963 and chaired by the Prime Minister.[59]

It is likely that the Cabinet committee exercises only general guidance, dealing extensively only with the most sensitive matters, especially with regard to security policy. This would be consistent with former Prime Minister Trudeau's view that:

> The politicians who happen to form the government should be kept in ignorance of the day-to-day operations of the police force and even of security. . . . It is a matter of stating, as a principle, that the particular minister of the day should not have a right to know what the police are doing constantly in their investigative practices, in what they are looking at and what they are looking for, and in the way they are doing it.[60]

Staff assistance to the Prime Minister is provided by the Privy Council Secretariat for Security and Intelligence, headed by the Assistant Secretary to the Cabinet for Security and Intelligence. In addition to the Assistant Secretary, there were, in 1980, seven officers assigned to the secretariat. On the security side were a security policy adviser and two officers responsible for personnel and physical security within the Privy Council office. In addition, there were four intelligence officers seconded from the Department of External Affairs, and the Department of National Defence, and the RCMP. These officers, under the direction of the Intelligence Advisory Committee, perform staff work involved in collating intelligence reports and participate in working groups that prepare long-term intelligence assessments.[61]

As of 1972, the vehicles for deputy ministerial control of the intelligence community were the Security Panel and the Intelligence Policy Committee (IPC). The Security Panel was formed under the auspices of the Privy Council in 1946 and chaired by the Secretary to the Cabinet. It was established as a result of a proposal by Norman Robertson, the Under Secretary of the Department of External Affairs, to create a committee that brought together representatives of the Department of External Affairs and the RCMP, the directors of the intelligence agencies of the armed services, and the Director General of Defense Research for the purpose of directing intelligence and security activities.[62]

The function of the Security Panel was to formulate security policy, including the security screening process, for approval by the Cabinet. Initial membership included the directors of the military intelligence services and representatives from the Department of External Affairs and the RCMP. Membership was later expanded to include the departments of Manpower, Immigration, and Supply and Services; the Office of the Solicitor General; and the Public Service Commission. The military was eventually represented by the Deputy Minister for National Defence and the Chief of the Defence Staff. After 1953 all representatives on the Security Panel were of deputy minister rank or its equivalent.[63]

The IPC was formed in 1960 to determine general intelligence policy. Under the chairmanship of the Under Secretary of State for External Affairs, the IPC was "to maintain general control and policy direction over all aspects of Canadian intelligence activity, determine what general intelligence objectives and priorities should be, . . . recommend what financial and manpower priorities and resources . . . should be . . . and assess performance." Until 1963 the IPC reported to the Defence Committee of the Cabinet (while Security Panel proposals went to the full Cabinet). With the formation of the Cabinet Committee on Security and Intelligence, both the IPC and the Security Panel were subordinated to that body.[64]

In 1972 the Security Panel and the IPC were merged to form the Interdepartmental Committee on Security and Intelligence, chaired by the Secretary of the Cabinet/Clerk of the Privy Council. The primary motivation for the merger was a desire to coordinate the external intelligence function with counterterrorist activities.[65]

Under the Interdepartmental Committee on Security and Intelligence are two subcommittees, the Security Advisory Committee (SAC) and the Intelligence Advisory Committee (IAC). Membership in the SAC includes the head of the Police and Security Branch as chairman, the Director General of the CSIS as vice-chairman, and the heads of the intelligence units in the External Affairs, National Defence, and Supply and Service Departments as well as the Canada Employment and Immigration Commission. The Canada Employment and Immigration maintains an Analysis and Intelligence Directorate while the Supply and Service Department operates a Security

Branch. Also included is the Assistant Secretary to the Cabinet for Security and Intelligence. Support staff is provided by the Police and Security Branch.[66]

The SAC has two functions. One is to review the adequacy of policies concerning personnel and physical security in government departments. To aid in this task, the SAC has a network of subcommittees dealing with specific substantive areas—communications and computer security, protection of nuclear materials, and crisis management. The second function is to assess the Canadian situation via weekly reports to the Interdepartmental Committee on Security and Intelligence and the Cabinet Committee on Security and Intelligence. These reports are based largely on information provided by the CSIS.[67]

The IAC is responsible for external intelligence matters. It collates and disseminates external intelligence weekly and prepares periodic assessments on particular subjects. Its Review and Priorities Group has primary responsibility for developing annual intelligence priorities. The IAC is chaired by the Deputy Under Secretary of State (Security and Intelligence) of the Department of External Affairs and consists of the head of the CSIS as well as the heads of the other units concerned with external intelligence.[68]

Among the products of the IAC is the April 25, 1983, study entitled "Soviet Intelligence-Related Organization, Structure and Methods." Classified SECRET, with foreign access limited by the CAN/AUST/NZ/UK/US EYES ONLY designation, the report is a straightforward and unexceptional summary of the subject. As indicated by its table of contents, reproduced in Table 3-1, the report deals with the organizations involved in Soviet intelligence collection (the KGB, the GRU, the International Department of the Central Committee, the Academy of Sciences, and the State Committee for Science and Technology), the methods of operation (including SIGINT, satellite imagery, and the use of illegals), and the implications for Canada.[69]

Perhaps the most notable aspect of the study is the overclassification of numerous paragraphs. For example, one paragraph classified SECRET reads:

Following the death of Stalin, CPSU [Communist Party of the Soviet Union] leaders brought the KGB under party control, ending its role as his personal organ of terror. They restored its original political role as the principal arm of the Party for the protection of the revolution at home and the creation of favourable conditions for the implementation of CPSU policies abroad.[70]

Table 3–1. Table of Contents of "Soviet Intelligence–Related Organization, Structure and Methods."

SECRET
CAN/AUST/NZ/UK/US EYES ONLY

IAC ASSESSMENT 3/83
Approved: 16 March 1983

SOVIET INTELLIGENCE–RELATED ORGANIZATION,
STRUCTURE AND METHODS

Figure 3-3. Management Structure of the Canadian Intelligence and Security Community.

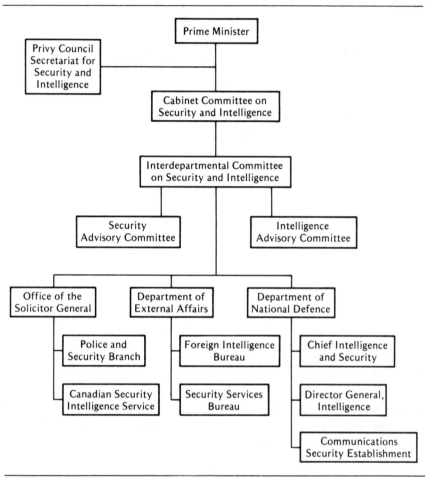

The management structure of the Canadian security and intelligence community is shown in Figure 3-3.

LIAISON

Canada maintains an intelligence liaison with various nations, especially the Anglo-Saxon countries. As detailed in Chapter 2, Canada is a participant (through CSE) in the UKUSA agreement and (through

Department of National Defence intelligence) in a variety of multi-lateral intelligence conferences, such as the Annual Land Warfare Intelligence Conference and the Quadripartite Intelligence Working Party on Chinese Guided Missiles.

In addition, Canada has a variety of bilateral intelligence agreements with the United States. The U.S.-Canadian joint estimates produced in the late 1950s focused on Soviet capabilities and likely actions in the event of a major Soviet attack on North America. Thus, *Soviet Capabilities and Probable Courses of Action against North America in a Major War during the Period 1 January 1958 to 31 December 1958*, as well as a similarly titled document for the period July 1, 1958 to June 30, 1959, prepared by the Canadian-U.S. Joint Intelligence Committee, assessed the Soviet threat to North America. Factors considered include Communist bloc political stability and economic support; the internal threat to North America; Soviet nuclear, radiological, biological, and chemical weapons; aircraft, including bombers, transport aircraft, and tanker aircraft; guided missiles; naval weapons; electronics; ground, naval, and surface strength and combat effectiveness; Soviet worldwide strategy; and capabilities to conduct air and airborne missile, naval, amphibious, and internal operations against North America. Preparation of such estimates continue on a yearly basis under the title *Canadian-United States Intelligence Estimate of the Military Threat to North America.*[71]

In addition to its UKUSA participation, Canada's SIGINT relationship with the United States is defined by the CANUS agreement. On September 15, 1950, Canada and the United States exchanged letters giving formal recognition to the "Security Agreement between Canada and the United States of America" (which was followed exactly two months later by the "Arrangement for Exchange of Information between the U.S., U.K. and Canada").[72]

Negotiations for the CANUS agreement had been taking place since at least 1948. There was some concern on the part of U.S. intelligence officials that original drafts of the agreement provided for too much exchange. Thus, a 1948 memorandum by the Acting Director of Intelligence of the U.S. Air Force noted that paragraph 6a of the proposed agreement was "not sufficiently restrictive. In effect, it provides for the complete exchange of information. Not only is it considered that the Canadians will reap all the benefits of complete exchange but wider dissemination of the information would jeopardize the security of the information. It is believed that the exchange should be related to mutually agreed COMINT activities on a 'need to know' basis"[73]

A more recent agreement is the "Canadian-United States Communications Instructions for Reporting Vital Intelligence Sightings" (CIRVIS/MERINT), signed in March 1966. This agreement specifies the type of information to be reported by airborne or land-based observers—that is, information concerning:

- Hostile or unidentified single aircraft or formations of aircraft which appear to be directed against the United States or Canada or their forces.
- Missiles.
- Unidentified flying objects.
- Hostile or unidentified submarines.
- Hostile or unidentified group or groups of military vessels.
- Individual surface vessels, submarines, or aircraft of unconventional design, or engaged in suspicious activity or observed in a location or on a course which may be interpreted as constituting a threat to the United States, Canada or their forces.
- Any unexplained or unusual activity which may indicate a possible attack against or through Canada or the United States, including the presence of any unidentified or other suspicious ground parties in the Polar Region or other remote or sparsely populated areas.[74]

The agreement also specifies eleven types of information that should be provided in any report, among them a description of the object(s) sighted (of which nine aspects are specified), a description of the course of the object and the manner of observation, and information on weather and wind conditions.[75]

The agreement further specifies that reports (known as MERINT reports) are to be forwarded by seaborne vessels concerning:

- Movement of Warsaw Pact/unidentified aircraft (single or in formation).
- Missile firings.
- Movement of Warsaw Pact/unidentified submarines.
- Movement of Warsaw Pact/unidentified group or groups of surface combatants.
- Any airborne, seaborne, ballistic or orbiting object which the observer feels may constitute a military threat against the United States or Canada, or may be of interest to military and civilian government officials.

- Individual surface ships, submarines or aircraft of unconventional design, or engaged in suspicious activities or observed in unusual location.

- Any unexplained or unusual activity which may indicate possible attack against or through the United States or Canada, including the presence of any unidentified or other suspicious ground parties in the Polar Region or other remote or sparsely populated areas.[76]

Canada has been trying to establish an intelligence-sharing arrangement with India, primarily with regard to Sikh activities that would affect both countries' security. During an early 1987 trip to India, the Minister for External Affairs stated that "it would help [Canada] to have additional information" and that an agreement would give Canada "access to things that might be in the hands of the Indians that wouldn't be in the hands of anyone else."[77]

Apparently, conclusion of an agreement was blocked by India's refusal to accept certain conditions—a refusal that also blocked implementation of an agreement formulated in December 1985. Joe Clark, the Canadian Minister for External Affairs, would not (in 1987) specify the areas of disagreement but simply said: "If there is going to be a security arrangement with India, it's going to be according to the same rules that apply to other countries. . . . The rules principally have to do with . . . keeping the game on the field and not allowing a latitude that is not generally available to other countries with which we have an agreement."[78]

MONITORING THE OCEANS

The Soviet Union (and the United States) has devoted increasing attention to the exploitation of the Arctic for submarine patrols. The most modern Soviet submarine, the Typhoon, armed with the SS-N-20 missile, can fire through the ice. Canada's Department of National Defence has recently noted the Arctic's importance: "The Arctic Ocean, lying between the two superpowers, is also an area of growing strategic importance. In the past it served as a buffer between the Soviet Union and North America. Technology, however, is making the Arctic more accessible, Canadians cannot ignore that what was once a buffer could become a battleground."[79] Despite the growing importance of the Arctic, the Pacific and Atlantic Ocean areas near Canada remain significant areas of Soviet naval activity.

Canada is involved in several ways in monitoring the naval movements in all three oceans.

One form of monitoring is underwater surveillance. The Canadian defense white paper notes that

> in all three oceans, underwater surveillance is essential to monitor the activities of potentially hostile submarines. Greater emphasis will be placed on underwater detection by continuing to develop Canadian sonar systems, by requiring array-towing vessels to provide an area surveillance capability in the northeast Pacific and northwest Atlantic, and by deploying fixed sonar systems in the Canadian Arctic.[80]

At present, Canada operates three SOSUS-type stations, one at CFS Bermuda, near Hamilton, Bermuda; another on Masset, Queen Charlotte Island, in British Columbia; and the third at Shelburne, Nova Scotia.[81] SOSUS installations are sets of ocean-bottom hydrophones that receive sound waves from distant submarines. The sounds, when relayed from the hydrophones to the associated shore stations and processing stations, can be used to determine the approximate location of the submarines as well as the specific submarine. According to one report, the detection capabilities of SOSUS are sufficient to localize a submarine to within a radius of fifty miles at ranges of several thousand miles. Among the signals being picked up by the British Columbia array are probably signals from Soviet attack and missile submarines that have been prowling off Canada's Pacific Coast near Juan de Fuca. The Soviet subs may be involved in monitoring the Trident submarine base at Bangor, Washington.[82]

From bases on both coasts, Canada operates eighteen CP-140 Aurora aircraft as well as eighteen CP-121 Tracker aircraft. The Aurora is a variant of the P-3C, is built to Canadian specifications, and incorporates the sensor and processing systems of the S-3A Viking. The sensors include a high-resolution radar (APS-116) for maritime reconnaissance, a magnetic anomoly detector, and sixty sonobuoys. The primary data display serves as a real-time link between the Aurora's crew of four and the various surface and underwater sensors. Information is stored, updated, and selectively displayed by an on-board digital computer.[83]

Of the eighteen Auroras, fourteen are based on the Atlantic coast (at Greenwood CFB, Nova Scotia); according to the Department of National Defence, this barely achieves effective surveillance. The four Auroras based on the Pacific coast (at Comox CFB, British Columbia) are judged to yield less than adequate surveillance. Surveillance of the Arctic has increased but is confined to a three-day patrol once every three weeks. Plans to increase surveillance capabilities include the acquisition of six P-3 aircraft and possibly the installation of synthetic aperture radar in existing aircraft to permit all-weather surveillance.[84]

Canada may also institute space-based systems for ocean surface (and land) surveillance. A RADARSAT project is intended to yield an ability to cover 34, 62, and 300 mile swaths at resolutions of 32, 81, and 325 feet, respectively.[85]

NOTES TO CHAPTER 3

1. Peter St. John, "Canada's Accession to the Allied Intelligence Community 1940-45," *Conflict Quarterly* 4, no. 4 (1984): 5-21.

2. Wesley Wark, "Cryptographic Innocence: The Origins of Signals Intelligence in Canada in World War Two," University of Calgary, 1987, mimeo.; Stevie Cameron, "Forming Canada's Intelligence Service Wasn't Easy," *Ottawa Citizen*, March 15, 1986, p. B5; Stevie Cameron, "Documents Reveal Canada's Wartime Intelligence Role," *Ottawa Citizen*, March 15, 1986, pp. B1, B5.

3. St. John, "Canada's Accession to the Allied Intelligence Community"; J. L. Granatstein, *A Man of Influence: Norman A. Robertson and Canadian Statecraft, 1929-1968* (Ottawa: Deneau, 1981), p. 181; David Kahn, "Introduction," in Herbert O. Yardley, *The American Black Chamber* (New York: Ballantine, 1981), p. xv; R. Harris Smith, *OSS: The Secret History of America's First Central Intelligence Agency* (New York: Dell, 1972), pp. 245-46.

4. St. John, "Canada's Accession to the Allied Intelligence Community."

5. Ibid., J. L. Granatstein, "The Enemy Within?" *Saturday Night*, November 1986, pp. 32 ff.; Wark, "Cryptographic Innocence."

6. St. John, "Canada's Accession to the Allied Intelligence Community."

7. Ibid.

8. Ibid.

9. F. H. Hinsely, E. E. Thomas, C. F. G. Ransom, and R. C. Knight, *British Intelligence in the Second World War*, Vol. 2 (New York: Cambridge, 1981), p. 551n.

10. Granatstein, *A Man of Influence*, p. 180; Robert Sheppard, "Lack of Quick RCMP Action Upset Gouzenko, Papers Say," *Toronto Globe and Mail*, October 17, 1981, p. 5; Robert Bothwell and J. L. Granatstein, eds., *The Gouzenko Transcripts: The Evidence Presented to the Kellock Taschereau Royal Commission of 1946* (Ottawa: Deneau, 1983), p. 20.

11.   Commission of Inquiry Concerning Certain Activities of the Royal Canadian Mounted Police (hereafter Commission of Inquiry, also known as the McDonald Commission), *Freedom and Security Under the Law*, Vol. 1 (Hull, Quebec: Canadian Government Publishing Centre, 1981), pp. 62–63.

12.   Lawrence R. Aronsen, " 'Peace, Order and Good Government' During the Cold War: The Origins and Organization of Canada's Internal Security Program," *Intelligence and National Security* 1, no. 3 (1986): 357–80.

13.   Department of External Affairs, *Co-ordination of Intelligence* (Ottawa: DEA, May 3, 1946); R. L. Raymont, *The Evolution of the Structure of the Department of National Defence, Report to the Task Force on Review of Unification of the Canadian Armed Forces* (Ottawa: Department of National Defence, November 30, 1979), app. A, pp. 23–24.

14.   Commission of Inquiry, *Freedom and Security Under the Law*, Vol. 1, p. 63; Royal Commission on Security (hereafter Mackenzie Commission), *Report of the Royal Commission on Security*, Abridged (Ottawa: Ministry of Supply and Service, 1969); Raymont, *The Evolution of the Structure of the Department of National Defence*, app. A, p. 24.

15.   "Secret Listening Agency Expands Its Operations," *Toronto Globe & Mail*, November 2, 1983, p. 3; Commission of Inquiry, *Freedom and Security Under the Law*, Vol. 2 (Hull, Quebec: Canadian Government Publishing Centre, 1981), p. 71; "Canada Gives Intrepid Intelligence Role," *Toronto Globe and Mail*, August 6, 1982, p. 3.

16.   "Mounties to Lose National Security Role," *Los Angeles Times*, August 26, 1981, p. 4; *Government of Canada Telephone Directory, National Capital Region* (Hull, Quebec: Canadian Government Publishing Centre, November 1982), p. 229E; Jeff Sallot, "Transition to a Civilian Security Agency Incomplete 15 Months After Promised," *Toronto Globe and Mail*, November 23, 1982, p. 9.

17.   Canadian Civil Liberties Association (CCLA), *Submissions to Special Committee of the Senate on the Canadian Security Intelligence Service Re: Bill C-157* (Toronto: CCLA, 1983), p. 1.

18.   Linda McQuaig, "Insecurities About Security," *Maclean's*, June 6, 1983, p. 13; "Controlling the Spies," *Maclean's*, November 14, 1983, pp. 23–24.

19.   Letter to the author from G. A. Calkin, Director, Intelligence Services Division, Foreign Intelligence Bureau, January 28, 1987.

20.   Jeff Sallot, "Anti-Spy Budget is 67.7 Million," *Toronto Globe and Mail*, September 22, 1983, p. 1; "Security Body to Get $6.9 Million to Bolster Counter-Terrorism Work," *Toronto Globe and Mail*, March 3, 1987, p. A10.

21.   Security Intelligence Review Committee, *Annual Report 1986–87* (Ottawa: Minister of Supply and Services, 1987), p. 21.

22.   Robert Sheppard, "Ottawa Yields on Civilian Agency, Other Moves Delayed," *Toronto Globe and Mail*, August 26, 1981, p. 13.

23. Henry Giniger, "Ottawa Pledges Tight Rein on Security Force," *New York Times*, August 27, 1981, p. A6; "The Mole that Slipped Away," *Maclean's*, January 24, 1983, p. 13; "Restrict Role to Spying, Kaplan Says of Agency" *Toronto Globe and Mail*, September 11, 1981, p. 8.

24. Jeff Sallot, "Spying on Foreign Diplomats Part of Security Bill," *Toronto Globe and Mail*, September 23, 1983, p. 4; Security Intelligence Review Committee, *Annual Report 1985-86*, p. 43.

25. Peter Moon and Geoffrey York, "Spies at Work in Many Toronto Consulates, CSIS Says," *Toronto Globe and Mail*, February 22, 1986, pp. A1, A4.

26. Moon and York, "Spies at Work in Many Toronto Consulates," p. A4.

27. David Viennau, "Security Agency Hunting Spies on Campuses, Official Tells MPs," *Toronto Star*, December 12, 1986, pp. A1, A4.

28. "Canada Security Chief Quits," *New York Times*, September 13, 1987, p. 22; Terence Wills, "Watching the Watchdogs: These 5 Monitor Spy Services for US," *Ottawa Citizen*, May 2, 1987; Ross Howard, "CSIS Powers of Secrecy Called Threat to Freedom," *Toronto Globe and Mail*, May 9, 1987, p. A3.

29. Victor Malarek, "Only 3,867 'Subversive' Files Active, Not 30,000 Says CSIS," *Toronto Globe and Mail*, July 4, 1987, p. A5; Ross Howard, "Security Agency Alarming Critics," *Toronto Globe and Mail*, May 11, 1987, pp. A1, A2.

30. Victor Malarek, "CSIS Probe of Leftist Magazine Called Threat to Freedom of the Press," *Toronto Globe and Mail*, July 9, 1987, pp. A1, A2; Security Intelligence Review Committee, *Annual Report 1986-87*, p. 40.

31. Security Intelligence Review Committee, *Annual Report 1986-87*, pp. 33-34, 39; John Sawatsky, *Men in the Shadows: RCMP Security Service* (New York: Doubleday, 1980).

32. Jeff Sallot, "Spy Service to Undergo Major Shakeup," *Toronto Globe and Mail*, December 1, 1987, pp. A1, A4; John F. Burns, "Canada to End Subversion Unit," *New York Times*, December 2, 1987, p. A3; Security Intelligence Review Committee, *Annual Report 1986-87*, p. 39.

33. Security Intelligence Review Committee, *Annual Report 1985-86* (Ottawa: Minister of Supply and Services, 1986), p. 24; Richard French and Andre Beliveau, *The RCMP and the Management of National Security* (Montreal Institute for Research on Public Policy, 1977), p. 77; Sawatsky, *Men in the Shadows*, pp. 21-22.

34. Security Intelligence Review Committee, *Annual Report 1986-87*, p. 35; Sawatsky, *Men in the Shadows*, p. 28.

35. Security Intelligence Review Committee, *Annual Report 1985-86*, p. 25; Security Intelligence Review Committee, *Annual Report 1986-87*, pp. 12-13.

36. Security Intelligence Review Committee, *Annual Report 1986-87*, p. 35.

37. Commission of Inquiry, *Freedom and Security Under the Law*, Vol. 1, p. 88; Jeff Sallot, "Kaplan Protects Top-Secret Spy Agency," *Toronto Globe and Mail*, April 11, 1984, p. 5.
38. Transcript of "The Fifth Estate—The Espionage Establishment," Canadian Broadcasting Company, 1974.
39. "Secret Listening Agency Expands Its Operations"; *Government of Canada Telephone Directory, National Capital Region* (Hull, Quebec: Canadian Government Publishing Centre, July 1987), p. 170E; Peter Moon, "Canadian Agency Safeguards Secrecy," *Toronto Globe and Mail*, March 30, 1987, p. A11.
40. Jeff Sallot, "Microwave Not Secure: Kaplan," *Toronto Globe and Mail*, April 6, 1984, p. 3; Jeff Sallot, "Top-Secret Eavesdropping Agency Doesn't Tap Phones, Kaplan Says," *Toronto Globe and Mail*, April 7, 1984, p. 3; testimony of Robert P. Kaplan, *Minutes and Proceedings and Evidence of the Standing Committee on Justice and Legal Affairs*, House of Commons, No. 11, April 4–5, 1984, pp. 68–79.
41. Jeff Sallot, "Defence Agency Keeps Data on Individual 'Security Risks,'" *Toronto Globe and Mail*, November 21, 1984, p. 1; Jeff Sallot, "Ottawa Tries to Protect Computers Against Spies with Sensitive Radios," *Toronto Globe and Mail*, October 13, 1984, pp. 1, 2.
42. "Canadian Forces Communications Command" (Ottawa: CFCC, n.d.).
43. Ibid., p. 3.
44. Ibid.; private information.
45. *Global Autovon Defense Communications System Directory* (Washington, D.C.: Defense Communications Agency, March 1981), p. 96; "Canadian Forces Communications Command," p. 3.
46. *Government of Canada Telephone Directory*, November 1982, p. 161E; Mackenzie Commission, *Report*, p. 87.
47. *Government of Canada Telephone Directory, National Capital Region*, July 1987, p. 171E.
48. Ibid., p. 100E; letter from G. A. Calkin.
49. Commission of Inquiry, *Freedom and Security Under the Law*, Vol. 2, p. 493; *Government of Canada Telephone Directory, National Capital Region* (Hull, Quebec: Canadian Government Publishing Centre, July 1987), p. 100E.
50. *Government of Canada Telephone Directory, National Capital Region*, February 1987, p. 100E; letter from G. A. Calkin.
51. *Government of Canada Telephone Directory, National Capital Region* (Hull, Quebec: Canadian Government Publishing Centre, December 1985), p. 100E; *Government of Canada Telephone Directory, National Capital Region*, July 1986, p. 102E.
52. French and Beliveau, *The RCMP and the Management of National Security*, p. 15.

53. Ibid.

54. Chris Belfour, "Super-Snooper or Security Analyst?" *Toronto Globe and Mail*, September 10, 1971; Commission of Inquiry, *Freedom and Security Under the Law*, Vol. 1, p. 84.

55. Commission of Inquiry, *Freedom and Security Under the Law*, Vol. 1, p. 83.

56. *Government of Canada Telephone Directory, National Capital Region*, July 1987, p. 247E.

57. Commission of Inquiry, *Freedom and Security Under the Law*, Vol. 1, p. 84.

58. *Organization of the Government of Canada, 1980* (Hull, Quebec: Canadian Government Publishing Centre, 1980).

59. Commission of Inquiry, *Freedom and Security Under the Law*, Vol. 2, p. 845.

60. *Transcript of the Prime Minister's Press Conference in Ottawa* (Ottawa: Prime Minister's Office, December 9, 1977).

61. Commission of Inquiry, *Freedom and Security Under the Law*, Vol. 2, pp. 847–48.

62. Bothwell and Granatstein, *The Gouzenko Transcripts*, p. 19.

63. Commission of Inquiry, *Freedom and Security Under the Law*, Vol. 1, pp. 89–90.

64. Ibid.; Raymont, "The Evolution of the Structure of the Department of National Defense," app. A, p. 13.

65. Commission of Inquiry, *Freedom and Security Under the Law*, Vol. 1, pp. 89–91.

66. Ibid., pp. 91–92.

67. Ibid.

68. Commission of Inquiry, *Freedom and Security Under the Law*, Vol. 1, p. 92; Commission of Inquiry, *Freedom and Security Under the Law*, Vol. 2, p. 856.

69. Intelligence Advisory Committee, *Soviet Intelligence–Related Organization, Structure and Methods* (Ottawa: IAC, April 25, 1983).

70. Ibid., p. 13.

71. Canadian-U.S. Joint Intelligence Committee, *Soviet Capabilities and Probable Course of Action Against North America in a Major War Commencing During the Period 1 January 1958 to 31 December 1958* (Washington, D.C.: Central Intelligence Agency, March 1, 1957) in Declassified Documents Reference System, 1981–169A.

72. *Canada-U.S. Arrangements in Regard to Defence, Defence Production, Defence Sharing* (Washington, D.C.: Institute for Policy Studies, 1985), p. 31.

73. Walter Agee, Acting Director of Intelligence, "Memorandum for the Co-ordinator of Joint Operations: Proposed U.S. Canadian Agreement," Mod-

ern Military Branch, National Archives, R341, Entry 214, File Nos. 2–1900 through 2-1999.

74. Joint Chiefs of Staff (JCS), *Canadian-United States Communications Instructions for Reporting Vital Intelligence Sightings (CERVIS/MERINT)* (Washington, D.C.: JCS March 1966), p. 2-1.

75. Ibid., pp. 2-4-2-6.

76. Ibid., p. 3-1.

77. Bryan Johnson, "Ottawa Seeks Pact with India." *Toronto Globe and Mail*, February 7, 1987, p. A8.

78. Ibid.

79. Department of National Defence, *Challenge and Commitment: A Defence Policy for Canada* (Ottawa, Canada: DND, June 1987), p. 6.

80. Ibid., p. 51.

81. Private communication with Owen Wilkes; Robert Gordon, "ASW Developments," *Jane's Defence Weekly*, November 21, 1987, p. 1192.

82. Owen Wilkes, "Strategic Anti-Submarine Warfare and Its Implications for a Counterforce First Strike," in *SIPRI Yearbook, 1979* (London: Taylor and Francis, 1979), p. 430; Ron Lowman, "Soviet Missile Subs Prowling Off West Coast May Be Guided by Spy Ring's Information," *Toronto Star*, April 10, 1987, p. A19.

83. David Miller, *An Illustrated Guide to Modern Sub Hunters* (New York: Arco, 1984), pp. 122, 126; "Old Age of Air Force Fleet Complicates Modernization," *Aviation Week and Space Technology*, September 21, 1987, pp. 69–79.

84. Department of National Defence, *Challenge and Commitment*, p. 57.

85. Ibid., p. 58; Theresa M. Foley, "Canada Approves Development of Scaled Back Radarsat," *Aviation Week and Space Technology*, July 13, 1987, pp. 51–53.

4 ITALIAN INTELLIGENCE ORGANIZATIONS

ORIGINS

A unified Italian state dates back only to 1861, when a number of separate kingdoms were unified around the Kingdom of Piemonte. The Kingdom of Piemonte, as well as the other kingdoms incorporated into the new Italian state, had a variety of foreign and domestic intelligence services that formed the basis for the intelligence and security establishment of the unified Italian state.

In 1854 Piemonte established a secret service within its Foreign Ministry. Among the activities it conducted in the next five years was financing portions of the French press to support Piemonte foreign policy initiatives. In 1855 two military secret services were established, a Service for Special Missions and a Secret Service. Whereas the Service for Special Missions was a tactical organization for conducting reconnaissance of enemy territory, the Secret Service was interested in broader strategic political and military information. In 1856 a Military Office was created in the Royal Corps of the High Command, and it served as an office of documentation. Also in operation were two domestic intelligence organizations, including the information service of the Carabinieri.[1]

In 1861 several security and political police organizations were set up, among them a Directorate General of Public Security and a High Office for Political Surveillance. The Carabinieri also continued to conduct domestic intelligence operations and in 1866 was assigned military counterespionage responsibilities as well.[2]

Foreign intelligence became the responsibility of both civilian and military organs, as was the case before unification. The Foreign Ministry's secret service sent Count Alessandro Malaguzzi to Vienna in 1865 to provide information on Austrian troop concentrations and was subsequently involved in the negotiations over the Italian-Prussian treaty. Military intelligence was the responsibility of the *Ufficio de Informazione* (Office of Information) under the Army High Command. This office, established in 1863, apparently performed poorly in the war of 1866, resulting in its abolition in 1867. Two new military intelligence organizations were established in its place during 1867, one an Office of Reserved and Secret Affairs under the Ministry of War and the other a Statistical Office subordinate to the High Command. In 1869 the Statistical Office became the Special Office of Military Statistics.[3]

Between the time of their initial establishment and 1900, the civilian intelligence and security units of the Interior Ministry underwent numerous name changes. The Office of High Political Surveillance eventually became the Office of Reserved Affairs for the Cabinet, while the Directorate General of Public Security became the Corps of City Guards.[4]

In 1900 the Office of Information within the Army High Command was reestablished, consisting only of the head of the office and two officers. With its limited resources, the office could pay for some information and send occasional "mobile informers" to collect additional information; in 1906 there were three such informers operating. In 1907 the office created a telegraphic cipher office, which was apparently used strictly for encipherment purposes. The year 1907 also saw the establishment of frontier operating posts.[5]

During the war with Libya that began with the Italian invasion in 1911, the Office of Information managed to put together an expedition of chartographers to chart the topography of the region, note sea and desert defenses, and pinpoint Turkish forces and their location near population centers. All of the office's information was sent to the Office of Monographs in the High Command, which was gathering military and logistical data.[6]

In 1915 Italy entered World War I, producing further changes and growth in the Italian intelligence community. After mobilization the Office of Information was transferred from the High Command to

Rome. A Territorial Information Office was established under the High Command to coordinate with the various intelligence services headquartered in Rome. A Special Territorial Office in Milan was charged with collecting information along the Swiss frontier and engaging in sabotage and smuggling operations. In addition, the Navy Ministry formed its own information service. By 1916 there were seventeen locations from which the military was collecting intelligence: Athens, Salonica, Cairo, Corfu, Valona, Lugano, Bern, Paris, London, Madrid, The Hague, Copenhagen, Stockholm, St. Petersburg, Cristiana, Bucharest, and Buenos Aires.[7]

World War I served as the impetus for an expansion of the functions and personnel of the Italian intelligence community. It led to the establishment of an effective counterespionage service and to the expansion of the Office of Information to one hundred personnel. It also resulted in the formation of a service for telephone and telegraph interception and cryptanalysis, as well as the employment of aircraft for photographic reconnaissance.[8]

In 1919 Benito Mussolini came to power. Mussolini's rise, along with the impact of the end of World War I, brought about a variety of changes within the intelligence and security structure. As of 1919 the Ministry of the Interior was still operating the Division of General and Reserved Affairs (Political) and the Central Office of Investigations (UCI), the latter with one foreign office, in Bern. That year saw the replacement of the Corps of City Guards with the Corps of Royal Guards for Public Security, composed of 25,000 men and 337 officers in 1919 and growing to 40,000 men in 1922, when it became part of the Carabinieri. In 1925 the unit was removed from the Carabinieri and became the Corps of Agents for Public Security, with many undercover operatives.[9]

In 1923 two additional units were established: the Voluntary Militia for National Security (Milizia Volontaria Sicurezza Nazionale—MVSN) and the Voluntary Organization for the Repression of Anti-Fascism (OVRA). In 1926 a Political Investigative Office of the MVSN was set up as a secret information service.[10]

In these years there was also significant change in the military intelligence and security structure. In August 1919 the Office of Information and the High Command were reunited in Rome. In 1925 the Office of Information was recreated as the *Servizio Informazioni Militaire* (Military Information Service), or SIM, with responsibility for all aspects of military intelligence: land, air, and sea. In addition,

SIM was assigned counterespionage duties. On February 6, 1927, it was placed directly under the head of the High Command and charged with responsibility for internal and external security for all three armed forces.[11]

In 1925 a Ministry of Aeronautics was formed and in turn instituted an information service, the *Servizio Informazioni Aeronautiche* (Aeronautical Information Service), or SIA. The Navy's *Servizio Informazioni Segreto* (Secret Information Service, or SIS) completed the set of military service intelligence units.[12]

From the late 1920s to the beginning of World War II, the Italian military service intelligence units established a large foreign representation, both through the stationing of attachés and through the creation of information centers. In 1928 the Army, Navy, and Air Force had seventeen, thirteen, and seventeen military attachés, respectively, in overseas posts. In 1930 SIM established its first information centers on foreign territory, setting up centers in Basel, Brussels, and Barcelona. Subsequently, centers were installed in Vienna, Geneva, Munich, Egypt, Syria, Palestine, Tunisia, Algeria, and Morocco.[13]

By 1940 all three military service intelligence units were still operating, with SIM at the apex, reporting directly to the High Command. The organization of SIM's headquarters included an "offensive," or espionage section; a counterespionage section; a "special services" section that engaged in sabotage and assassination; and a *situazoini* section that compiled intelligence summaries (daily, weekly, monthly) as well as order-of-battle analyses, country books, and intelligence assessments on particular issues.[14]

The espionage section maintained a network abroad, particularly in such areas as Egypt and North Africa. It did not, however, acquire a reliable network of clandestine foreign stations with adequate radio communications with Rome until late 1940. In June 1940, when Italy entered the war, SIM had permanent stations only at Sofia, Salonika, Athens, and Basel. It had no agents and little information on Great Britain, Germany, the Soviet Union, and the United States.[15]

The *situazioni* section had a regional organization. Four groups dealt with (a) Western Europe, the British Empire, and the Middle East, (b) Central and Eastern Europe, (c) the Balkans, and (d) Asia and America. The section also ran a number of "statistical centers" for collecting and processing order-of-battle information—in Turin (for France), in Milan (for Switzerland and Germany), and in Trieste (for Yugoslavia).[16]

In addition, SIM had two sections involved in intercepting communications and trying to decipher them. *Sezione 6* was the intercept unit, and *Sezione 5*, with fifty members, was the deciphering unit. *Sezione 6* maintained a monitoring network centered at Forte Braveita on the outskirts of Rome, and provided Mussolini and other top figures in the regime with a daily bulletin of decrypts of British, French, Turkish, Yugoslav, and Greek diplomatic and military traffic. Many of the decrypts were the result not of brilliant cryptanalytical work but of a highly successful program of embassy break-ins and diplomatic bag interceptions that began in 1935.[17]

By the time the war was at its peak, SIM's interception and decryption operations had taken on immense proportions. In a typical month *Sezione 6* intercepted eight thousand radiograms, about six thousand of which were considered worthy of study. Of those six thousand, *Sezione 5* would reduce about thirty-five hundred to plaintext. The flow was so large that General Cesare Ame, the head of SIM, began to publish a daily—*Bulletin I*—that summarized the most significant information. It had only three subscribers: Mussolini, the Chief of the General Staff, and the King (via his aide-de-camp).[18]

As was the case before the war, many of the deciphering solutions resulted from SIM's theft of cryptologic documents. In 1941 SIM obtained possession of about fifty such items, among them the U.S. Black Code, a new and secret code for military attachés. Thus, the Foreign Minister, Count Ciano, gloated in his diary on September 30 30, 1941, that "the military intelligence service has come into possession of the American secret code; everything that U.S. Ambassador [William] Phillips telegraphs is read by our decoding offices."[19]

The Navy's SIS directed its efforts toward answering four questions:

- What is the composition of the enemy's naval forces?
- Where are they located?
- What are they doing?
- What are the enemy's plans?[20]

During 1942–43 the SIS was divided into six sections and a Center for Training. The sections were *Sezione A* (Administration),

Sezione B (Interception and Cryptanalysis), *Sezione C* (Naval Monographs), *Sezione D* (Espionage), *Sezione E* (Counterespionage), and *Sezione F* (Technical).[21]

The most productive was *Sezione B*, responsible for interception and cryptanalysis. SIS cryptographers routinely read Yugoslav and French naval messages. SIS was also, for a period of time, a vehicle for British disinformation. Beginning in December 1939 the British sent out, presumably in a relatively low-grade cipher, a long series of reported intelligence summaries for subordinate commands, including reports of German designs on Italian territory (January 1940), hints that the British leadership would relish the chance to strike at Italy (early May 1940), and suggestions that Hitler intended to ally himself with France and drop Italy (July 1940). All were apparently believed by Mussolini.[22]

In 1942, however, SIS scored a major success against Britain. In early 1942, SIS penetrated the British naval ciphers in the Mediterranean—ciphers so poor that Admiral Sir Andrew Cunningham apparently threatened, after the invasion of Crete, to transmit entirely in the clear if he were not given better ciphers. The Italian deciphering of a British scout plane report enabled the Italian High Command to warn one of its task force commanders at 6:00 P.M. on March 27, just before the Battle of Cape Matapan, that the British had sighted him soon after he put to sea. The following day the decryption of an order to Cunningham from Alexandria made the Italians certain that the British torpedo planes would attack. They did—and so prepared were the Italian forces that the intensity of their anti-aircraft defense made it almost impossible for the British planes to identify their targets or observe the results of the attack.[23]

SIS was less successful in producing intelligence assessments on enemy naval forces. Its concentration on naval cryptography and current tactical intelligence apparently precluded SIS from devoting much effort to assessment. A handful of overworked officers and clerks were overwhelmed by a mountain of clippings, news from the Italian merchant marine, and agent reports.[24]

Outside the military, intelligence operations of one form or another were conducted by several ministries. In addition to the civilian Ministry of External Affairs, the civilian Ministry of Popular Culture (MINCULPOP) also had a foreign intelligence responsibility. MINCULPOP monitored foreign radio broadcasts and twice daily produced foreign press summaries. Moreover, its press attachés abroad also served as collectors of political intelligence.[25]

The Ministry of the Interior and security organs continued to conduct both counterintelligence and political police operations. The units included the Carabinieri, the Directorate General of Public Security, and the OVRA. The OVRA tapped telephones and surveilled foreign embassies, diplomatic personnel, and foreign nationals. The taps furnished Mussolini with daily batches of intercepts; those relevant to foreign affairs ranged from German embassy communications with Berlin to a diplomatically vital March 1940 conversation between Roosevelt and his special envoy, Sumner Welles.[26]

The July 1943 coup that overthrew Mussolini led eventually to the establishment of Fascist and anti-Fascist Italian states operating in the north and south of Italy, respectively. Each government then organized its own secret services, with the Fascist government in the north reestablishing several of the services existing prior to the coup, as well as new services, such as the *Servizio Informazioni Difesa* (Defense Information Service).[27]

The Italian intelligence community that reemerged after World War II was much smaller (in terms of numbers of organizations) and stripped of its political police functions, although lack of legal authority did not stop a number of Italian secret services from engaging in a variety of illegal activities.

The organization that became the primary Italian intelligence service in the postwar period was established on September 1, 1949. Placed under the Ministry of Defense, the organization, called the *Servizio Informazioni Forze Armate* (Armed Forces Information Service), or SIFAR, was to be a strategic defense intelligence service operating for the Army, Navy, and Air Force. For tactical intelligence purposes, a *Servizio Informazioni Operativo Situazione* (Information Service for Operations and Situations), or SIOS, was established within each of the armed forces. SIFAR was to be responsible for coordinating the tactical information services.[28]

SIFAR, when first established, consisted of three major offices. Office D (Defense) operated internally; its first section monitored subversive political activity, and its second section was responsible for counterespionage. Office R (Research) was responsible for actual intelligence collection, from human sources and from technical sources. Subordinate to Office R were components for radio inter-

cept, cryptography, and human intelligence operations. Office S
(Situations) was responsible for analyzing the data collected.[29]

In the early 1950s, SIFAR responded to the Cold War situation
and directed a considerable amount of attention to the Italian left.
Under the command of General Giovanni De Lorenzo and his two
successors, SIFAR collected private information on various public
figures and private citizens. By 1964 SIFAR had accumulated at least
157,000 files on deputies, senators, union leaders, managers, party
heads, government employees, and 4,500 priests. The information
was used by De Lorenzo to enhance his private interests and personal
career. In 1964 De Lorenzo was also involved in planning a coup
attempt. He and some twenty other senior military officials drew up
plans for a coup involving the assassination of Premier Aldo Moro
and his replacement by a right-wing Christian Democrat. The plan,
"Plan Solo," was called off at the last minute as a result of a political
compromise between the Socialists and the right-wing Christian
Democrats. Lorenzo was also heavily involved in another attempt to
create a coup d'état. Heading the planning group, known as "Rose of
Winds," were eighty-seven officers representing all branches of the
military and secret services. SIFAR was given the job of collecting
dossiers on Italian "subversives" who were to be neutralized.[30]

The abuses associated with SIFAR led to a variety of cleanup
operations, including the transfer of several officers out of the most
sensitive divisions. In 1965 the intelligence service was renamed the
Servizio Informazioni Difesa (Defense Information Service), or SID.
According to President of the Republic Decree No. 1477 of November 18, 1965, the SID was:

> ... to carry out, through its offices and units, intelligence duties relating to
> the protection of the military secret and to every other activity of national
> interest for the defense and security of the country; and to take appropriate
> measures for the prevention of actions harmful to the defense potential of the
> country.[31]

A Ministry of Defense circular dated June 25, 1966, assigned to
SID the following operational duties:

- to collect at home and abroad all useful information for defense and national security;

- to organize and conduct operations against foreign intelligence activities and against every other activity that might be dangerous or damaging to national defense and security;

- to follow and keep abreast of the political, economic, industrial, military and scientific condition of foreign countries of interest;

- to insure the protection of the military secret and other state secrets.[32]

To carry out these functions, SID was organized into three branches. Section I was responsible for intelligence collection abroad, including political and military intelligence. Section S was responsible for the processing and analysis provided by Section I. Section D was the counterintelligence unit, encompassing all operations in Italy and territorially subdivided into twenty-three counterespionage groups.[33]

Like SIFAR, SID was involved in questionable activities, particularly while under the command of General Vito Miceli. Some SID informers became involved in judicial investigative proceedings related to presumed or actual rightist conspiracies. Delays in the preparation of SID reports on such conspiracies led to speculation that SID agents may have infiltrated these groups more to participate in than to report on their activities.[34]

Indeed, according to one account, SID was involved in a variety of right-wing terrorist activities as part of a "strategy of tension." The objective was to blame the Left and to make the far Right appear as the only force that could restore order. In December 1969 the bombing of the Milan Banca dell'Agricoltura killed or injured ninety persons, signaling what was seen as a terrorist strategy to destabilize the country. The bombing was blamed on New Left organizations that had emerged in the late 1960s, and a series of arrests followed. According to this account, after various trials many of the charges were found to be baseless, and it was established that the attacks were the work of the extreme right, acting with the assistance of SID.[35]

The bombing was, according to the account, only one of several terrorist acts that SID was involved in between 1968 and 1973. Guido Giannettini, who had acted as liaison between SID and the neo-Fascist bombers, was given a life sentence for his involvement in the explosion at the Bologna train station that left eighty-five dead and two hundred injured. General Miceli, in charge of SID during that period, was asked to resign, and after a short period of time in prison he became a neo-Fascist (MSI) deputy.[36]

In November 1984 former SID agent Robert Cavallero told the Italian weekly *Europeo* that "the security services make special alliances both with organized crime and with terrorism. The secret services exercised a strict control over the terrorist groups, both left and right." A similar claim is made by Broadhead, Friel, and Herman in their study of the "Bulgarian connection": "In most of the great terrorist massacres in Italy in the 1960s and 1970s, virtually all of them rightwing in origin, the security services played some sort of role: sometimes as instigator, sometimes protecting the killers from apprehension, often deliberately diverting suspicion onto convenient (leftwing) scapegoats."[37]

Other SID activities that might be considered questionable involved Colonel Qaddafi, whom, because of the substantial Italian presence in Libya, the government wanted to placate. In January 1970, when the nephew of the deposed King Idris prepared an operation to send mercenaries into Libya to set up an internal revolt, SID's counterespionage section blocked the operation by informing the Libyan secret service of the plan. On March 21, 1971, SID blocked the departure from Trieste of a boat carrying agents intending to rescue political prisoners in Libya.[38]

While SID operated under the Ministry of Defense, several domestic intelligence units operated under the Ministry of the Interior. Within the ministry's Directorate General of Public Security an Office of Reserved Affairs operated until its abolition on May 29, 1974. The office was replaced first by the General Information Service for Internal Security (Servizio Informazioni Generali e Sicurezza Interna, or SIGSI) and then by the Service of Information Security (Servizio Informazioni e Sicurezza—SIS).[39]

In 1977 the Italian intelligence and security services were restructured in response both to the abuses committed by the services and to the terrorist situation in Italy. Both SID and SIS were replaced. The new services—the *Servizio per le Informazioni e la Sicurezza Democratica* (Service for Information and Democratic Security), or SISDE, and the *Servizio per le Informazioni e la Sicurezza Militare* (Service for Information and Military Security), or SISMI—were established by Law No. 801 of October 24, 1977. This law also set forth four major innovations:

1. a more stringent oversight of the intelligence services by the government and parliament;
2. separation of intelligence and internal security functions into two services;
3. additional separation of intelligence and security functions from judicial police functions;
4. new regulations governing state secrecy.[40]

INTELLIGENCE AND SECURITY ORGANIZATIONS

Service for Information and Democratic Security (SISDE)

SISDE—the successor to SIS—is subordinate to the Ministry of the Interior. Estimated to have about fifteen hundred personnel, SISDE has as its mission all intelligence and security functions related to the defense of the Italian democratic state.[41] Specifically, SISDE is responsible for nonmilitary counterespionage, countersubversion investigations directed against both right- and left-wing extremist groups, and counterterrorist intelligence.

A report prepared in late 1978 for the Italian Executive Committee for Intelligence and Security Services (CESIS) severely criticized SISDE's performance since its creation. The report, in the words of a U.S. military liaison officer and based on what he was told by a source with high access, said:

> SISDE had not been functioning according to the law, had not been carrying out its assigned mission, had not been able to develop a viable structure and was still in the process of organizing; was being led by unqualified persons who ignored the professionally qualified personnel; and based on its one year of operations as borne out by approximately 225 SISDE reports forwarded to CESIS, had to be considered almost totally ineffective.[42]

Particular criticism was directed at Major General Giuilo Grassini, the Director of SISDE. Several Italian military personnel who had served in SISMI or the Carabinieri praised Grassini both as a person and as a manager of an already functioning organization, but not as the person to preside over the establishment of a new organization. It was reported that a field-grade Carabinieri officer and SISMI official who considered himself a friend of Grassini's felt that Grassini lacked "the initiative, imagination, operational knowledge and creativity to organize a SISDE from nothing," as well as the forcefulness needed to organize and move SISDE personnel into the field and keep the pressure on obtaining results.[43]

The report also attributed the state of SISDE to factors other than Grassini. Grassini was not, said the report, receiving the level of government cooperation required with the counterterrorist operation being run by Major General Dalla Chiesa, the Coordinator for Anti-Terrorism, and the investigator of the Aldo Moro murder. While Dalla Chiesa's operation was receiving the personnel it requested, SISDE was being denied requested personnel.[44]

As part of its functions, SISDE prepares reports on the structure and operations of the Red Brigades, hostile intelligence operations conducted in Italy and directed against the Italian government as well as NATO and U.S. facilities; on terrorist operations conducted by foreign governments (e.g., Libya) or groups (e.g., the Palestine Liberation Organization); and on the harassment or murder of exiles from Libya or other countries residing in Italy.

A 1986 report prepared by SISDE in the aftermath of the *Achille Lauro* hijacking challenged the assertion by the prosecution in the case that it had uncovered the true authors of the action. In the report the Director of SISDE, Vincenzo Parisi, said: "It is indeed difficult to believe the hypothesis that the operation was managed only by those whose responsibility has been ascertained by the magistrates."[45]

Although the prosecution identified Mohammed Abbas, leader of a small faction of the PLO, as the person responsible for the plan, SISDE's report argued that Abbas's small group was incapable of carrying out the plan unassisted:

> The concept, the planning, the management and the conclusion of the hijacking are on a highly professional level. So much so as to make one suspect the involvement of particularly qualified "intelligence" structures, capable of planning the various phases of action and subsequent options, both on an operative level and on a disinformation and propaganda level. . . . From this angle the *Achille Lauro* operation assumes a completely different and more threatening aspect.[46]

The report further argued that pursuing the goals of Palestinian nationalism is not the aim of groups such as those of Abbas or Abu

Nidal, but rather, "the Palestinians have abandoned their original irredentist aims of Palestinian nationalism, and have become, instead instruments in a political struggle . . . aimed at enlarging the range of Libyan and Syrian regional intervention and also, at reducing the negotiating power of Western countries by undermining their commitments for equitable solutions of the problems in the area."[47]

The report also stated that the hijacking was not a success, but maintained that it "undoubtedly achieved positive results in further weakening Arafat's leadership and in creating dissension among allied and friendly countries (such as Italy, the U.S.A. and Egypt)."[48]

In another report SISDE examined the links between drugs and terrorism, stating that "the high profits coming from the drug trade are some among the financing forms of the PLF (Palestinian Liberation Front), headed by Abu Abbas . . . organizer of the *Achille Lauro* hijacking." With respect to the Tamil insurgency in Sri Lanka, the report noted:

> The financing of the Tamil groups, obtained with bank robberies and illegal drug trades achieved by the Tamil dislocated in the West, allows the above terroristic group to carry out an intensive subversive activity in its own country. Some important police operations accomplished in Italy and France, in 1984 and 1985, resulted in the confiscation of several kilos of heroin and in the arrest of a considerable number of "couriers" belonging to the above ethnic group.[49]

Service for Information and Military Security (SISMI)

Law No. 801 assigned SISMI all intelligence and security functions pertaining to Italian military defense. Included in SISMI's domain of responsibility are political, military, and economic intelligence; counterintelligence; and counterespionage. SISMI is subordinate to the Ministry of Defense, which determines its structure.[50]

U.S. and NATO military facilities in Italy are a target for both the Soviet and other Warsaw Pact intelligence services. Included among the facilities are "Site Pluto" at Longare (the main nuclear weapons storage site for U.S. Army units in Italy); Avians Air Base, where two hundred nuclear bombs are estimated to be stored; and a variety of U.S. and NATO command centers.[51]

Evidence of Soviet espionage activities includes the operation of a large network headed by Giorgi Rinaldi Ghislieri, recruited by the

GRU in 1956 to spy on U.S. military bases. Until his arrest in 1967, Ghislieri and his wife—who ran an antique shop—set up and managed a network of agents and informers who reported on NATO bases in Italy and U.S. Air Force bases in Spain. Ghislieri's sources apparently extended into France, Greece, and Cyprus. In 1983 an Aeroflot official was charged with military espionage, having been caught with NATO documents and plans for the twin-engine, all-weather Tornado fighter.[52]

SISMI's collection responsibilities include both technical collection and human espionage. SISMI oversees and directs the SIGINT activities of the individual military services. It will also have a significant role in managing Italian participation in the French Helios military reconnaissance satellite program. Evidence of its agent activities occurred in 1983, when Switzerland protested violation of its sovereignty by Italian agents.[53] SISMI is also responsible for producing analytical reports.

In 1986, after the December 27, 1985, attack on the Rome airport, the head of SISMI told a Rome newspaper that the terrorists represented the Abu Nidal faction, a Palestinian splinter group, and had been trained in Iran, and entered Italy, through Syria. A later SISMI report stated that Syria had provided the group with passports and money and arranged transportation to Belgrade and that the group had been accompanied by Syrian agents to Bucharest, Rumania, and then to Vienna.[54]

The same 1978 evaluation that was so critical of SISDE was also critical of SISMI. According to the U.S. military liaison officer whose report was based on his source at CESIS, the evaluation would have been used by Premier Andreotti to further his desire to have a single service, except that on the basis of the three hundred reports SISMI submitted to CESIS, it was censured equally harshly.[55]

A particular problem that the liaison officer found with SISMI pertained to the operation of its First Division. The First Division was the former D-Office, or Department II, of SID, less the department's First Section, which was transferred to SISDE. The official responsibilities of the First Division included both counterespionage and counterterrorism; however, the liaison officer, reported that the Vice Chief of SISMI's First Division, while discussing the physical security and espionage threat to U.S. military personnel and installations in Italy, indicated that:

In recent months, SISMI's orientation, particularly that of the First Division, had been changed to an almost complete anti-terrorist stance. Unfortunately, the counterespionage operations, once primary to First Division functions, now occupied the place of secondary priority after terrorism. Therefore, it was now difficult for [the Vice Chief] to speak in an authoritative manner about the counterespionage situation. It was not that there was not a continuing and deep interest in the counterespionage area, it was just that SISMI did did not have the qualified personnel to concentrate throughout the country for thorough counterespionage operations.[56]

The Vice Chief further indicated to the liaison officer that while "the First Division still had a counterespionage capability to conduct limited field operations against specific and important targets with seasoned and qualified agents, . . . it could no longer provide the country-wide counterespionage coverage previously available. Even if released from anti-terrorist operations, it would require the assignment of a greater number of qualified field agents to the field before SISMI could regain its former counterespionage posture."[57]

SISMI has also been criticized for the legitimacy of some of its activities. A 1985 court report indicated that high officials of SISMI, like their predecessors in SIFAR and SID, had engaged in a number of questionable activities. Included in these activities were articles secretly subsidized by SISMI and planted in the press that smeared a variety of individuals and an attempt to split the Italian Communist Party (PCI) by supporting a hard-line, pro-Soviet faction within the party. In addition, the court charged that a SISMI plane was used to transport a man wanted for crimes out of the country. The court also concluded that SISMI fabricated reports linking drugs and arms traffic to the Arabs and Bulgaria to divert attention from SISMI's abuses by providing evidence of productive activity.[58]

In addition, SISMI, through a group called Super S, was responsible for luring Billy Carter into a compromising relationship with Qaddafi during the 1980 Presidential campaign. SISMI provided the tape recorder and hired a photographer to take pictures of Billy Carter with a Libyan representative.[59]

Military Service Intelligence Units

Each military service continues to maintain an intelligence or security department known as the *Secondo Reparto* (Second Department), or SIOS, subordinate to the individual service Chiefs of Staff and coordinated by SISMI.[60]

Among the activities possibly supervised by the naval intelligence unit are the operation of Brequet Atlantique maritime patrol aircraft, the same aircraft employed by West Germany for monitoring the Baltic. The aircraft are employed to monitor the activities of Soviet surface vessels and submarines in the Mediterranean.[61]

Signals intelligence activities assigned to the Army are managed by the Army's Electronic Defense Information Center (Centro Informazioni Difesa Elletronica) at Anzio. Three units conduct intercept operations: the 8° Battaglione Ricerea Elettronica (8th Electronic Research Batallion) "Tonale" at Anzio, the 9° Battaglione Guerra Elettronica (9th Electronic Warfare Battalion) "Rombo" at Anzio and the 33° Battaglione Guerra Elettronica "Falzarego" at Congeliano.[62]

Airborne signals intelligence activities are managed by the Air Force via the 14° Stormo Radiomisure (14th Radio Measurement Squadron) a Practica di Mare Air Base. The 8th Electronic Callibration Squadron flies SIGINT missions employing PD-808, MB-339, and G-222 RM aircraft while the 71st Electronic Warfare Squadron flies PD-808 and G-222 aircraft. The G-222 is a twin-engine transport with a ninety-four-foot wing span, a length of just over seventy-four feet, an operational ceiling of 29,000 feet, a standard ten-hour endurance, and a maximum speed less than normal (336 mph) for transports. A French report suggests that two of the G-222s are of the VS version, employed primarily for electronic intelligence missions. The G-222 RM is a version for calibrating navigational aids and ILF systems.[63]

Office of Foreign Statistics, Foreign Ministry

The Foreign Ministry operates an Office of Foreign Statistics that analyzes information and produces reports, which it then stores or passes on to Parliament. The office is organized into five sections: Political, Economics, Cultural-Scientific, Immigration, and Economic Development.[64]

MANAGEMENT STRUCTURE

One of the purposes of Law No. 801 in October 1977 was to enhance supervision by the government and Parliament. As a result of the law, the Prime Minister is now responsible for intelligence and security policy as well as for supervision of the intelligence and security services. The Prime Minister is also empowered to issue directives and to control the application and protection of state secrecy.[65]

The Prime Minister is assisted by the Interministerial Committee on Intelligence and Security. Chaired by the Prime Minister, the committee has as members the ministers of Foreign Affairs, the Interior, Clemency and Justice, Defense, Industry, and Finance. The committee advised the Prime Minister on general directives and fundamental objectives of intelligence and security policy and makes proposals. The Prime Minister may invite other ministers, the directors of the intelligence and security services, civilian and military officials, and experts to meetings of the committee.[66]

Law 801 also established, the *Comitato Esecutivo per i Servizi di Informazioni e di Sicurezza* (Executive Committee for Intelligence and Security Services), or CESIS, under the authority of the Prime Minister. CESIS is chaired either by the Prime Minister or by an Undersecretary of State appointed by him. The Prime Minister determines the composition of CESIS, with the exception of the directors of the intelligence and security services, who are members by right.[67]

CESIS is responsible for providing the Prime Minister with all the data needed to coordinate the intelligence and security services, as well as with processed and analyzed intelligence. Liaison with foreign intelligence and security services is also conducted by CESIS.[68]

The structure of CESIS is determined by the Prime Minister, who is authorized to establish whatever offices are deemed necessary. The only office required by law is a General Secretariat, also headed by the Prime Minister.[69]

Parliamentary supervision is attained in part by the requirement that the Prime Minister report in writing to Parliament every six months on intelligence and security policy and its results. In addition, a parliamentary committee of four deputies and four senators monitors the application of the principle set forth by Law No. 801. The committee is entitled to request basic information about the structure and activities of the intelligence and security services and to make observations and recommendations. The Prime Minister can deny information based on a claimed need for state security but must briefly substantiate the need.[70]

LIAISON

Italian intelligence maintains close relations with several intelligence services; foremost is the liaison with the United States. During the tenure of General De Lorenzo at SIFAR, the CIA received photocopies of all major files compiled by SIFAR, and, according to one source, "De Lorenzo would hand two copies of each file to [CIA station chief Thomas] Karamessines, who would keep one for himself while sending the other to Langley."[71]

A particular area of present cooperation concerns terrorist groups. The SISDE report on the *Achille Lauro* hijacking was presented at a meeting in June 1986 of a United States-Italian committee on drug trafficking and terrorism. During that meeting, the United States and Italy signed an agreement to pool intelligence resources concerning terrorist activities. Italian intelligence reports about the December 1985 attack on the Rome airport have also been shared with the United States.[72]

In September 1986 Italy was one of the twelve governments of the European Communities who agreed to pool their intelligence about terrorists so that their police forces could "search out the vital links in terrorist operations and disrupt them."[73] In March 1987 it was reported that the Italian security services were also attempting to tighten their contacts with Israel and Morocco in the belief that European terrorists had links with Arab extremists.[74]

P-2, ITALIAN INTELLIGENCE, AND MEHMET ALI AGCA

Of the scandals associated with SISDE and SISMI since their creation, the one involving Propaganda Due (P-2) was one of the largest. P-2 was one of hundreds of masonic lodges in Italy, with total membership running into the tens of thousands. P-2, however, was a secret lodge and therefore illegal in Italy. It was also neo-Fascist. Moreover, its membership consisted of a large segment of the Italian government, both military and civil factions, as revealed following discovery of P-2's membership list during a raid on the house of Licio Gelli, the head of P-2.

Gelli, a life-long supporter of Fascist causes, fought for Franco in the Spanish Civil War and served Mussolini devotedly during World War II. After the war, disclosures that Gelli had been involved in the torture and murder of Italian partisans resulted in his fleeing to Argentina, where he became involved in the Fascist AAA Anticommunist League. Gelli remained in Argentina for twenty years before returning to Italy as an Argentine counsel.[75]

Upon his return to Italy, Gelli was initiated into Freemasonry— secret, anticlerical organizations that draw their members from the middle class and technocracy. In 1971 he was made organizing secretary of the Loggia Propaganda, which then became known as the Gelli P-2 Group. Gelli proceeded to politicize the organization and to target numerous generals and colonels from the Italian military for recruitment, in the belief that P-2 would have to engage in political action against the left. By 1974 Gelli had recruited 195 military officers, including 92 generals and colonels.[76]

By 1979 P-2 consisted of 953 members, including 3 Cabinet ministers, 43 military police officers, 43 generals, 8 admirals, the police chiefs of Italy's 4 main cities, and 36 members of Parliament. The P-2 membership list seized in 1981 listed 245 individuals from government ministries. The breakdown is shown in Table 4-1.[77]

P-2's membership list also included some prominent intelligence officials. Not only was Gelli a member of the intelligence services, but the Director of SISDE (General Grassini), the Director of SISMI (General Santovito), and the chairman of CESIS (Prefect Peolosi) *were all members of P-2.* Further, within P-2 was a group of secret service "plumbers," headed by SISMI agent Francesco Pazienza, that used the resources of SISMI and answered only to General Santovito. The group was known as Super S (for Super SID since it was founded before the establishment of SISMI and SISDE).[78]

Super S indulged in black bag and disinformation operations and was deeply involved in the SISMI projects discussed earlier. In addition, five days after Mehmet Ali Agca wounded the Pope on May 13, 1981, SISMI circulated a secret report saying that the assassination attempt had been inspired by the Warsaw Pact powers in a meeting attended by Soviet Defense Minister Ustinov and that the plan had been to wound the Pope in order to intimidate Solidarity.[79]

It has been suggested that SISMI was directly involved in persuading Agca to point the finger of blame for the attempted assassination

Table 4-1. Number of Individuals by Government Ministry on P-2 Membership List, 1981.

Ministry	Number
Interior	19
Foreign Affairs	4
Public Works	4
Public Instruction	32
State	21
Treasury	67
Health	3
Industry and Commerce	13
Finance	52
Justice	21
Cultural Affairs	4
Scientific and Technological Research	3
Transportation	2
Total	245

at Bulgaria and thus at the Soviet Union. As suggested, this action involved three components: (1) identifying for Agca the preferred culprits, (2) inducing him to cooperate either by promised benefits if he did or by threatened harm if he did not, and (3) supplying him with information that would allow him to specify a scenario and name coconspirators.[80]

Suggestions of SISMI coaching revolve around visits made by SISMI personnel to Agca in late 1981. On December 29, 1981, Agca was visited in his cell at Ascoli Prison by Major Petrocelli of SISMI. The significance of that visit and whether there were any others have been a matter of dispute. The judge and prosecutor in the case both claimed that a single insignificant visit took place. The December 29 visit lasted five hours. It has been reported that there were other visits—an August 1982 police report stated that the secret services had conducted "interviews" with Agca to determine if there were any "international connections" in the case, and the Italian press referred to repeated visits by the secret service to Ascoli Prison and Agca.[81]

Among those reported to have been among Agca's visitors were Lieutenant General Giuseppi Belmonte of SISMI and former SISMI officer Francesco Pazienza, the latter on several occasions during the time when Agca was assembling his thoughts in preparation for implicating the Bulgarians. Agca has asserted that Pazienza (who in 1985 was in a U.S. jail, awaiting extradition to Italy) visited him in prison and offered him his freedom in return for evidence of the KGB-Bulgarian connection.[82]

In addition, Giovanni Pandico, the state's main witness in a trial in Naples against the Mafia, asserted that Pietro Musumeci, Deputy Chief of SISMI, had used a Mafia chieftain who was an inmate at Ascoli Prison to get Agca to cooperate. According to Pandico, the Mafia chieftain, a prison chaplain, and a prison official explained to Agca that he could expect trouble if he failed to cooperate, but if he did cooperate, he might be released within six or seven years. At this point, according to Pandico, Agca was given detailed instructions about his "confession." Pandico also claimed that Musumeci came to Ascoli Prison with note cards indicating both possible motivations Agca might offer as the reason for his confession and what he was to say about Soviet and Bulgarian involvement.[83]

Pazienza has denied Agca's claim, contending that he was no longer a member of SISMI at the time and could not have gained access to the high-security prison, and stating that he has never met or talked with Agca. However, another Mafia inmate-turned-informer is reported to have claimed that Pazienza was a frequent visitor to the prison and that Pazienza personally gave Agca instructions concerning the identification of photos of the Bulgarians.[84]

Pandico's testimony has also been challenged. Under cross-examination Pandico was unable to explain numerous discrepancies between his account and earlier versions of the events that he gave in interviews and when questioned by Italian magistrates. The discrepancies involved differing accounts of the people who were alleged to take part in the meetings with Agca and the dates of the gatherings. As a result of the contradictions and a lack of corroborating evidence, official investigations into Pandico's charges were dropped.[85]

The trial of the Bulgarians who were arrested on the basis of Agca's charges ended with a dismissal of the charges. The dismissal was urged by the prosecutor on the grounds of insufficient evidence—grounds that became inevitable when the star witness changed his story several times and claimed to be Jesus Christ.[86]

SISMI's actual role, if any, in Agca's claims of a "Bulgarian connection" may never be established with certainty. But it is clear that

SISMI, SISDE, and their predecessors have proved quite hospitable to those with right-wing, even Fascist, sympathies and those individuals have been able to use the resources and authority of the intelligence services to promote their own political objectives.

NOTES TO CHAPTER 4

1.   Ambrogio Viviani, *Servizi Segreti Italiani*, Vol. I (Rome: Adnkronos, 1985), p. 86.
2.   Ibid., p. 101.
3.   Ibid., p. 108; Giuseppe De Lutis, *Storia dei Servizi Segreti in Italia* (Rome: Editori Reunite, 1985), p. 7.
4.   Viviani, *Servizi Segreti Italiani*, Vol. I, p. 116.
5.   Ibid., p. 128; De Lutis, *Storia dei Servizi Segreti in Italia*, p. 8.
6.   De Lutis, *Storia dei Servizi Segreti in Italia*, pp. 8–9.
7.   Viviani, *Servizi Segreti Italiani*, Vol. I, pp. 152, 155.
8.   De Lutis, *Storia dei Servizi Segreti in Italia*, pp. 9–12.
9.   Viviani, *Servizi Segreti Italiani*, Vol. I, pp. 173–74.
10.   Ibid., pp. 176–78.
11.   Ibid., pp. 183, 187, 191; De Lutis, *Storia dei Servizi Segreti in Italia*, p. 12.
12.   Viviani, *Servizi Segreti Italiani*, p. 189.
13.   Ibid., p. 192.
14.   Mac Gregor Knox, "Fascist Italy Assesses Its Enemies, 1935–1940," in Ernest R. May, ed., *Knowing One's Enemies: Intelligence Assessment Before the Two World Wars* (Princeton, N.J.: Princeton, 1985), pp. 347–72.
15.   Ibid.
16.   Ibid.
17.   Ibid.; David Kahn, *The Codebreakers: The Story of Secret Writing* (New York: MacMillan, 1967), pp. 470–72.
18.   Kahn, *The Codebreakers*, p. 472.
19.   Ibid.
20.   Knox, "Fascist Italy Assesses Its Enemies," p. 351.
21.   Viviani, *Servizi Segreti Italiani*, Vol. II (Rome: Adnkronos, 1985), p. 25.
22.   Knox, "Fascist Italy Assesses Its Enemies," p. 351.
23.   Kahn, *The Codebreakers*, pp. 468–69.
24.   Knox, "Fascist Italy Assesses Its Enemies," p. 352.
25.   Ibid., p. 353.
26.   Ibid., p. 352.
27.   Viviani, *Servizi Segreti Italiani*, Vol. II, pp. 49–105.
28.   Vittorfranco S. Pisano, *A Study of the Restructured Italian Intelligence and Security Services* (Washington, D.C.: Congressional Research Service, 1978), p. 15; Viviani, *Servizi Segreti Italiani*, pp. 122–23.

29. Viviani, *Servizi Segreti Italiani*, Vol. II, p. 125.
30. Pisano, *Restructured Italian Intelligence and Security Services*, pp. 15–16; Edward S. Herman and Frank Brodhead, *The Rise and Fall of the Bulgarian Connection* (New York: Sheridan Square, 1986), pp. 79–80; De Lutis, *Storia dei Servizi Segreti in Italia*, p. 29.
31. Pisano, *Restructured Italian Intelligence and Security Services*, p. 17.
32. Ibid., pp. 17–18.
33. Ibid., p. 18.
34. Ibid., p. 19.
35. Paolo Caligaris, "Italy's Secret Service Wars," *The Middle East*, July 1981, pp. 17–19.
36. Ibid.
37. Frank Broadhead, Howard Friel, and Edward S. Herman, "The 'Bulgarian Connection' Revisited," *Covert Action Information Bulletin* 23 (Spring 1985): 3–38.
38. Viviani, *Servizi Segreti Italiani*, Vol. II, p. 148.
39. Ibid., pp. 165–66.
40. Pisano, *Restructured Italian Intelligence and Security Services*, p. 21.
41. Viviani, *Servizi Segreti Italiani*, Vol. II, p. 179.
42. Dominic Perrone, "I & SS, Status SISDE/SISMI Anti-Terrorist Orientation," *Covert Action Information Bulletin* 4 (1979): 6–9.
43. Ibid.
44. Ibid.
45. Vicenzo Parisi, *Assessment of the Terrorist Threat of Middle East Origin/ Cooperation Through the Exchange of Intelligence* (Rome: Servizio per le Informazioni e la Sicurezza Democratica, June 23, 1986), pp. 10–11.
46. Ibid., p. 11.
47. Ibid., pp. 9–10.
48. Ibid.
49. Servizio per le Informazioni e la Sicurezza Democratica (SISDE), *Drugs and Terrorism* (Rome: SISDE, 1986), pp. 34, 35.
50. Pisano, *Restructured Italian Intelligence and Security Services*, p. 24; Vittorfranco S. Pisano, *Terrorism and Security: The Italian Experience* (Washington, D.C.: Senate Subcommittee on Security and Terrorism, 1984), p. 53; Franco Villalba, "The Organizational Structure of the Italian Counterterrorist Forces," *International Defense Review* 6 (1985): 915–17.
51. William Arkin and Richard Fieldhouse, *Nuclear Battlefields: Global Links in the Arms Race* (Cambridge, Mass.: Ballinger, 1985), pp. 222–23.
52. Harry Rozitske, *KGB: Eyes of Russia* (Garden City, N.Y.: Doubleday, 1981), p. 156; "Crop of Soviet Agents Apprehended in Europe," *Toronto Globe and Mail*, March 7, 1983, pp. 1, 2.
53. Viviani, *Servizi Segreti Italiani*, Vol. II, pp. 204–5; "Italy to Share in French Satellite System," *Aviation Week and Space Technology*, June 22, 1987, p. 66.

54. Leslie Gelb, "Italy Now Linking Syrians to Attack at Rome Airport," *New York Times*, May 21, 1986, pp. A1, A12.
55. Perrone, "I & SS, Status SISDE/SISMI Anti-Terrorist Orientation."
56. Ibid.
57. Ibid.
58. Herman and Brodhead, *The Rise and Fall of the Bulgarian Connection*, pp. 92–93.
59. Ibid., p. 96.
60. Information provided by Defense Intelligence Agency.
61. Institute for Research in Disarmament, Development and Peace, *What the Russians Know Already and the Italians Must Not Know* (Rome: IRDISP, 1984), p. 11.
62. Ibid., pp. 52, 58.
63. Ibid., p. 95; Bill Gunston, *Spy Planes and Electronic Warfare Aircraft* (New York: Arco, 1983), pp. 64–65.
64. Private information.
65. Pisano, *Restructured Italian Intelligence and Security Services*, p. 21.
66. Ibid., pp. 21–22.
67. Ibid., p. 22.
68. Ibid.
69. Ibid.
70. Ibid., p. 23.
71. De Lutis, *Storia dei Servizi Segreti in Italia*, p. 69.
72. Gelb, "Italians Now Linking Syrians to Attack at Rome Airport"; "U.S., Italy Sign Antiterror Agreement," *Washington Post*, June 25, 1986, p. A26.
73. Stanley Meisler, "Europeans Agree to Share Data on Terrorists," *Los Angeles Times*, September 26, 1986, pp. 1, 16.
74. Andrew Borowiec, "Italy Warns West to Brace for New Wave of Terrorism," *Washington Times*, March 26, 1987, pp. 1A, 8A.
75. Herman and Broadhead, *The Rise and Fall of the Bulgarian Connection*, p. 81.
76. Ibid., p. 82.
77. Ibid., pp. 83, 84 n. 50.
78. Broadhead, Friel, and Herman, "The 'Bulgarian Connection' Revisited"; Philip Jenkins, "The Assassins Revisited: Claire Sterling and the Politics of Intelligence," *Intelligence and National Security* 1, no. 3 (September 1986): 459–71.
79. Broadhead, Friel, and Herman, "The 'Bulgarian Connection' Revisited."
80. Herman and Broadhead, *The Rise and Fall of the Bulgarian Connection*, p. 102.
81. Ibid., p. 104.

82. Alexander Cockburn, "The Gospel According to Ali Agca," *The Nation*, July 6–13, 1985, pp. 1, 6–7.

83. Herman and Broadhead, *The Rise and Fall of the Bulgarian Connection*, pp. 105–6.

84. Ibid., p. 106; Ralph Blumenthal, "Ex-Italian Agent Ordered Extradited from U.S.," *New York Times*, September 12, 1985, p. A12.

85. John Tagliabue, "Italian Says Intelligence Service Tried to Influence Agca Testimony," *New York Times*, December 4, 1985, p. A8; Michael Dobbs, "Italian Court Ends Probe of Papal Plot," *Washington Post*, December 22, 1985, p. A30.

86. John Tagliabue, "Rome Prosecutor Urges Acquittal of 3 Bulgarians," *New York Times*, February 28, 1986, pp. A1, A10; John Tagliabue, "An Unsettling Question at Rome Trial," *New York Times*, March 1, 1986, p. 5; John Tagliabue, "Verdict on Papal Plot, but No Answer," *New York Times*, March 31, 1986, p. A3.

5 WEST GERMAN INTELLIGENCE ORGANIZATIONS

ORIGINS

The beginnings of organized German intelligence activity can be traced to the period just before Prussia's war with Austria in 1866. On March 25, 1866, the chief of the Army General Staff established an Intelligence Bureau on an emergency basis to acquire information that was lacking about the prospective enemy.[1]

Over the next fifty years the Intelligence Bureau was shuffled from component to component of the General Staff. In 1889 it became Section b of the IIIrd *Oberquartiermeister* (Chief Quartermaster) and hence became known as IIIb—a designation it was to maintain throughout World War I. By 1901 it had grown significantly, with 124 officers and men directing agent activities from War Intelligence Posts in Belgium, Switzerland, England, Italy, Spain, Luxembourg, Denmark, Sweden and Rumania.[2]

As might be expected, World War I produced another major expansion of German intelligence activity. IIIb continued to operate and by mid-December 1915 had 337 agents in the West. By 1917 it had 150 officers running those and other agents. In addition to the Army, the Imperial German Navy was also involved in a variety of intelligence activities. Its Intelligence Branch conducted reconnaissance and ran agents, and its Observation and Cryptanalytic Service produced communications intelligence. The latter organization evolved into a 458-man unit headquartered at Neumünster and possessing about two dozen intercept and direction-finding posts along the German coasts and inland by floating units aboard German naval vessels. The material produced by the collection units was in turn analyzed by the Military-Political Branch and the Foreign Navies Branch.[3]

In addition to communications intelligence, Germany was involved in airborne photographic reconnaissance, made possible by the introduction of vertical photography in 1915. By 1918 an area larger than Connecticut was being photographed each week by German cameras. Aerial photography became Germany's single most important source of information.[4]

At the highest levels of the German military was an organization established for the general analysis of operational and strategic intelligence for the entire German Army. Created upon mobilization of the Army as the Intelligence Branch of General Headquarters, it was renamed the Foreign Armies Branch in mid-1917. Its function was to keep track of the nature and capabilities of foreign armies and to predict their movements. Thus, the Foreign Armies Branch produced a twenty-three-page overview of the war organization of the French Army. It accurately provided warning of the Allied offensive on the Somme in the summer of 1916.[5]

Germany's defeat in World War I produced the harsh Versailles treaty, which virtually stripped Germany of any true military capability. In hope of preventing future German aggression, the treaty prohibited such organizations as a General Staff or foreign secret service. As a result, the German military that was permitted resorted to a series of subterfuges. The General Staff was abolished on September 30, 1919, and recreated the very next day as the Troops Department. Intelligence functions were assigned to its 3rd Branch, T3.[6]

The Navy also established intelligence units. While the Signals Section of the Naval Command contained a small unit of cryptanalysts, the Fleet Section produced overt intelligence, clandestine intelligence, and counterintelligence reports. By 1928 the Navy was also operating a monitoring and deciphering service, the *B-Dienst* (*Beobachtungs Dienst*, or Observation Service), a Naval Supply Organization with intelligence functions, and the World Intelligence Service.[7]

In 1928, partly as a result of revelations about the Army's covert activities in the Soviet Union and the links between naval intelligence and right-wing extremist organizations, a consolidation of intelligence functions took place under the Ministry of Defense. A central military intelligence organization, the Abwehr (literally: Defense), was formed and consisted of three sections—Espionage (I), Cipher Unit (II), and Counterespionage (III)—in addition to a Navy Group. The Navy Group included the World Intelligence Service, which was subsequently abolished in 1929.[8]

Hitler's coming to power led to the renouncing of the Versailles treaty and a massive expansion in military, economic, and foreign policy establishments within the German government. Along with that expansion came a similarly huge increase in the personnel and organizations of the German intelligence community.

The intelligence community that resulted foreshadowed the post-war intelligence community of the United States in several ways. It involved a large number of agencies spread across numerous departments. Intelligence was assiduously collected from open sources, via human agents, from radio broadcasts, via signals intelligence operations, and from overhead photography. The intelligence collected went far beyond traditional military intelligence—political, military, sociological, and economic intelligence were all produced as a result of collection activities.

Economic intelligence was provided by units of the Economics Ministry and the Supreme High Command (OKW). Within the Economics Ministry were the Foreign Economy Bureau (with its Central Desk for Foreign Statistics and Foreign Research) and the Reich Statistical Department. Both organizations passed material on to the OKW's War Economy and Armaments Department. From 1939 to 1942 a War Economy Branch of the department examined a number of subjects related to Britain, Russia, the United States, and several other nations; among the topics considered were foreign trade, food production, the armaments industry, and energy. Subsequently, the War Economy Branch became the Foreign Bureau of the Field Economy Department.[9]

Radio broadcast monitoring was undertaken on a large scale, first by the *Sonderdienst Seehaus* (Lake House Special Service) and then by the German Foreign Broadcast Interradio, Inc. By the beginning of 1942 the *Seehaus* was monitoring broadcasts from thirty-three countries on a regular basis and fourteen countries on an occasional basis. The monitored stations broadcast in a total of thirty-seven languages, including Afrikaans, Icelandic, Hindustani, Persian, Gaelic, Maghreb, and Latin.[10]

These monitoring activities produced a large number of reports. Included were a daily digest, the *Radio Mirror* of a few pages, and the *Weekly Radio Mirror* for government agencies that did not need complete coverage. In addition, there were reports on individual topics. The basic publication produced as a result of radio monitoring activities was *Radio Intercept Reports: Transmissions of Foreign Radio Broadcasts*, a daily report that ran to more than a thousand pages an issue for most of the war.[11]

Of course, of far more importance than the interception of public radio broadcasts were the interception and cryptanalysis of the coded diplomatic and military communications of foreign governments. To conduct such activities, a number of civilian and military organizations were created. One civilian organization was *Per Z* (the Z section of the Personnel and Administrative Branch of the Foreign Office), which, during its existence, broke some of the codes of thirty-four nations. Codes of Britain, France, Japan, Italy, Spain, the United States, and the Vatican were all successfully attacked by Per Z. Only those of the Soviet Union remained immune.[12]

A second civilian organization involved in communications interception was the Research Post (*Forshungstelle*) of the Postal Ministry. Its highly directional rhombic antennae were employed to intercept the scrambled messages sent between Great Britain and the United States. The Research Post was then able to unscramble the messages to provide a clear-text message. Included in the intercepted and unscrambled conversations were those between President Roosevelt and Prime Minister Winston Churchill.[13]

Four strictly military organizations were involved in communications interception: the Army's Main Post Communications Reconnaissance, the Navy's *B-Dienst*, the Air Force's Radio Reconnaissance Battalion 350, and the OKW's Cipher Branch. The Cipher Branch, with three thousand employees at its peak, was the military organization that probably undertook the widest range of interception operations. It attacked both military and diplomatic communications, its greatest success being the U.S. BLACK Code for military attachés, which it solved analytically.[14]

Of all the interception operations, the most important was the *Forschungsamt* (Research Office), under the direct command of Hermann Göring. The Research Office began operation in 1933 with six men working in an attic; by the peak of World War II, it had expanded by a factor of a thousand. The office gathered information via the interception of wireless transmissions and teletypewriter transmissions, through telephone tapping, and by monitoring the speeches of key politicians. The "take" associated with these activities was monumental. At the height of the office's activity, the evaluation branch of the foreign politics bureau received on a monthly basis 2,400 cryptanalyzed messages, 42,000 clear-text radio and wire messages, 11,000 broadcast transcripts, 14,000 Z reports, and 150 newspapers. Among the Research Office's greatest successes was its deciphering of the system used between Soviet armament centers in the Urals, a success that produced considerable information of value.[15]

As was the case in World War I, aerial reconnaissance also played a major role. In 1936 a Squadron for Special Purposes was created and subordinated to the General Staff of the Luftwaffe's 5th Branch (Intelligence). The squadron began to conduct operations to provide information that could be used in an attack. Reconnaissance missions were flown over England, Czechoslovakia, France, and the Soviet Union. On some missions the planes flew at thirty-two thousand feet—high enough to be unseen by ground observers. With the outbreak of the war, the Squadron for Special Purposes became the Reconnaissance Group of the Commander in Chief of the Air Force and expanded to three squadrons of twelve planes each. At its peak it had about fifty planes and between two hundred and three hundred men. Its wartime targets included all the European and African areas where German forces were involved—England, France, North Africa, Italy, the Balkans, and the Soviet Union.[16]

In the area of conventional intelligence activities—human intelligence, sabotage, and counterespionage—two organizations were significant. The Reich Main Security Office (*Reichssicherheitshauptamt*—RSHA) was the result of a merger in 1939 of Nazi party and government intelligence, security, and criminal police organizations. *Amt II* was the internal party security service—the *Sicherheitsdienst-Inland*, or SD-Inland. SD-Inland collected information concerning ethnic, cultural, education, labor, and other domestic matters. *Amt IV* was the dreaded Gestapo—a contraction of *Geheime Staats Polizei* (Secret State Police)—the Reich's political police. In addition to hunting down opponents of National Socialism, the Gestapo handled counterespionage duties within the Reich and the conquered countries of Scandinavia and Europe.[17]

Amt VI—SD-Ausland—was the party's foreign intelligence organization. Run by Walter Schellenberg, its headquarters operation em-

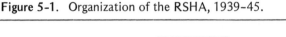

Figure 5-1. Organization of the RSHA, 1939–45.

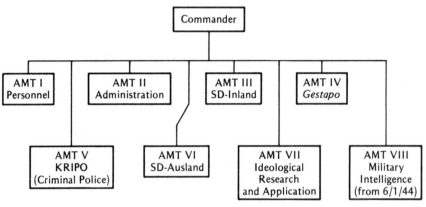

Source: Leslie B. Rout Jr. and John F. Bratzel, The *Shadow War: German Espionage and United States Counterespionage in Latin America during World War II* (Frederick, Md.: University Publications of America, 1986), p. 12.

ployed between three hundred and five hundred agents, depending on the period of time. Although a party organization, it was concerned with all types of intelligence: political, military, economic, and sociological. Among its agents was Eliazar Banza, code-named CICERO, the valet to the British ambassador in Turkey. Banza was able to gain access to the ambassador's safe and turn over to SD-Ausland copies of a variety of documents. Included in the material he provided was a copy of a discussion between the ambassador and Turkish officials concerning Turkey's possible entrance into the war on the Allied side. Subsequently, when the Abwehr was dissolved in 1944, *Amt VI* became the major military intelligence organization in the Reich.[18] Figure 5-1 shows the organization of the RSHA.

Probably the best known of all German foreign intelligence organizations was the Abwehr. When World War II began, the Abwehr, headed by Admiral Wilhelm Canaris, had responsibility for conducting espionage, counterespionage, and sabotage operations for the entire German armed forces. Internally, the World War II Abwehr, which lost its reconnaissance and cipher functions in 1937, consisted of four sections (*Abteilungs*)—*Abteilung I* (Military Espionage), *Abteilung II* (Sabotage), *Abteilung III* (Counterespionage), and *Abteilung Z* (Administration)—and the *Amstgruppe Ausland* (Foreign Division), which controlled the military services' attaché offices and maintained contact with foreign attachés.[19] The subdivisions of the various Abwehr sections are shown in Figure 5-2.

The Abwehr's espionage network was extensive. Its agents operated in countries that Germany was at war with or expected to be at war with—Russia, France, the United States, Norway—as well as in neutral countries such as Portugal and Sweden. In England the Abwehr had numerous agents—all under the control of the British Security Service. In addition, the Abwehr had large networks in Mexico, Chile, Argentina, and Brazil.[20]

Reporting to the Army High Command were two units concerned with foreign armies: Foreign Armies West and Foreign Armies East. During 1940 the main function of Foreign Armies West was to build up a picture of enemy orders of battle; in the absence of enemy troop movements, there was none to predict. Foreign Armies West worked from varied sources, including prisoners of war, aerial reconnaissance, communications intercepts, and traditional espionage. When full-scale war broke out, the unit sought to identify the location and composition of the enemy's forces.[21]

Foreign Armies East (*Fremde Heere Ost*—FHO) was run from 1942 on by Lieutenant Colonel Reinhard Gehlen. It was combination of man and position that was to influence German intelligence for many years after the conclusion of the war. Gehlen's organization was divided into six groups. The two most important were Group I, which produced daily situation reports on the strength, location, and equipment of the Soviet forces, and Group II, which evaluated secret service reports and prepared general assessments on the Soviet Union, other than those provided in the daily reports.[22]

By virtue of the methodical sifting of information, Gehlen had, by the end of the war, built an enormous data base concerning the USSR. In addition, he had gained a certain degree of control over espionage operations against the Soviets. He was able to parley these assets into a bargaining chip in dealing with U.S. occupation forces.

As the end of the war approached, Gehlen knew he had a valuable commodity: an incredibly detailed set of files on the Soviet Union and an agent network to provide new information. In March 1944 he ordered all important documents microfilmed in triplicate, stored in steel containers, and placed in safe locations. After his surrender, Gehlen was able to make himself known to General Edwin L. Sibert, the chief intelligence officer of General Omar Bradley's 12th Army Group.[23]

Figure 5-2. Organization of the Abwher.

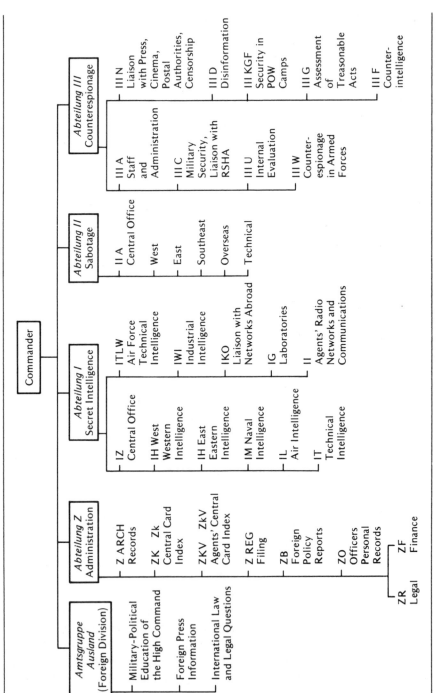

Source: Heinz Höhne, *Canaris: Hitler's Master Spy* (Garden City, N.Y.: Doubleday, 1979), frontispiece.

Eventually Sibert put Gehlen on a plane bound for the United States to consult with American intelligence officials. After several weeks of negotiations, Gehlen and U.S. intelligence authorities reached an agreement in which Gehlen consented to conduct intelligence operations targeted against the Soviet Union and Eastern Europe. U.S. officials agreed to four conditions specified by Gehlen:

1. [The] organization would not be regarded as part of the American intelligence services but as an autonomous apparatus under Gehlen's exclusive management. Liaison with American intelligence would be maintained by U.S. officers whose selection Gehlen would approve.

2. The Gehlen Organization would be used solely to procure intelligence on the Soviet Union and satellite countries of the communist bloc.

3. On the establishment of a German government, the organization would be transferred to it and all previous agreements and arrangements cancelled, subject to discussions between the new sovereign authority and the United States.

4. Nothing detrimental or contrary to German interest [would] be required or expected from the organization, nor [would] it be called upon for security activities in West Germany.[24]

In July 1946 Gehlen returned to Germany to establish "the Org," or "Gehlen Organization," per his agreement with U.S. intelligence. The Org then began a program of seeking to penetrate Eastern Europe and the Soviet Union.

In a "Police Letter" of April 14, 1949, the Allied Military Governors authorized the formation of an agency, directly subordinate to the Federal Chancellor, for the collection and distribution of information concerning state security. The term *Verfassungsschutz* ("Protection of the Constitution") was used in the Basic Law to designate both the agency and the scope of its operations. Modeled on the British Security Service (MI-5), the agency was to be kept strictly separate from the police and to have no power to arrest, to search houses, or to seize seditious literature.[25]

The Agency was eventually designated the Federal Office for the Protection of the Constitution (*Bundesamt für Verfassungsschutz—* BfV), Before it could be established, however, the Interior ministries in Lower Saxony and North Rhine-Westphalia created Internal Security sections that had already begun to operate. When the federal government was finally able to submit the legislation for the BfV in the spring of 1950, a heated debate ensued. As desired by the

Allies, the BfV was made responsible to the Federal Chancellor's office. The Social Democrats objected to what they considered a reinforcement of the personal power of the Chancellor.[26]

The result was a decision by the *Bundestag* to give authority over the BfV to the Federal Interior Ministry. In a law of September 27, 1950, the *Bundestag* defined the duty of the BfV as the "acquisition and evaluation of information and intelligence . . . concerning tendencies aiming at suspension, alteration or disturbance of the constitutional order in the Federal Republic or in a Land." The BfV was instructed to concentrate at first on the observation of Communist or extreme right-wing plots.[27]

Konrad Adenauer, in an attempt to maintain influence over the BfV, issued a "Federal Government Instruction on the Formation of a Federal Internal Security Office" on November 7, 1950. This document declared that the Chancellor's consent was required for the nomination of the president of the BfV. But despite his instruction, Adenauer was less than happy with the final choice to head the office: Dr. Otto John, a liberal-conservative lawyer and survivor of the anti-Hitler resistance.[28]

On April 1, 1956, the Gehlen Organization became the *Bundesnachrichtendienst* (BND), the Federal Intelligence Service of the Federal Republic of Germany. The Cabinet of Dr. Konrad Adenauer had decided, on July 11, 1955, to "attach the Gehlen Organization as a separate department to the Federal Chancellery, after which it is to be known as the *Bundesnachrichtendienst.*"[29] The BND, along with the intelligence units established within the military and the BfV, formed the West German intelligence community.

INTELLIGENCE AND SECURITY ORGANIZATIONS

Federal Intelligence Service (BND)

Today's BND, with about seven thousand officers and headquartered at Pullach, is very much different from that which existed when Gehlen retired in 1968. Gehlen's successor, General Gerhard Wessel, reorganized the BND by consolidating, by 1972, its large number of autonomous sections and departments into four main divisions, as shown in Figure 5-3.

Figure 5-3. Organization of the BND, 1972.

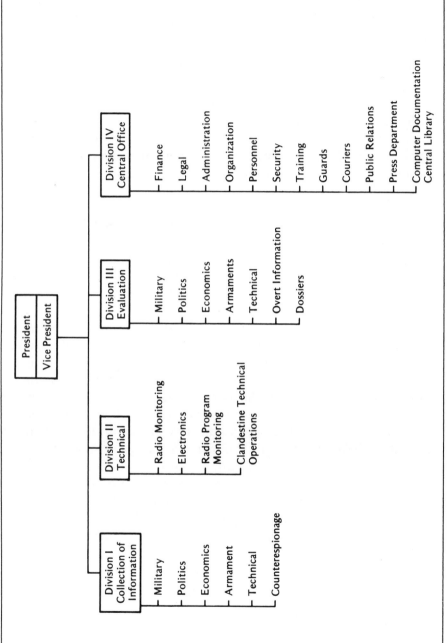

| President |
| Vice President |

Division I
Collection of
Information
- Military
- Politics
- Economics
- Armament
- Technical
- Counterespionage

Division II
Technical
- Radio Monitoring
- Electronics
- Radio Program Monitoring
- Clandestine Technical Operations

Division III
Evaluation
- Military
- Politics
- Economics
- Armaments
- Technical
- Overt Information
- Dossiers

Division IV
Central Office
- Finance
- Legal
- Administration
- Organization
- Personnel
- Security
- Training
- Guards
- Couriers
- Public Relations
- Press Department
- Computer Documentation Central Library

Source: E. H. Cookridge, *Gehlen: Spy of the Century* (New York: Random House, 1972), p. 362.

Division I, Collection of Information, is responsible for collecting information in six areas: military affairs, politics, economics, aramaments, technical matters, and counterespionage. Each functional subdivision is further divided by countries or regions. Division II, Technical, is involved in technical collection, technical support, and countermeasures work. It monitors the confidential communications of foreign governments as well as foreign public radio and television programs of intelligence value. It maintains major SIGINT collection sites at several locations and shares beams with the military at other sites. Division II is also involved in a variety of clandestine technical operations entailing photography, bugging, debugging, invisible ink, and special radio equipment.[30]

Division III, Evaluation, produces analytical studies and estimates on military, economic, and political subjects related to countries throughout the world; its reports are based on information derived from open and clandestine sources. Division III is organized into seven functional subdivisions (Military, Politics, Economics, Armaments, Technical, Overt Information, and Dossiers), which are further subdivided into country or regional sections. Division III is responsible for publication of the *BND Intelligence Review*, the daily *BND Foreign Situation Report*, the *BND Weekly Report*, *Situation Reports East*, and *Situation Reports West.* In 1981 a brief official survey specified the main areas of BND study as follows: military policy and armaments in the Eastern bloc countries, the war in Afghanistan, the Iran-Iraq conflict, Chad's civil war, energy problems, developments in Poland, and the development of new technologies. It has been reported that the BND accurately forecast the Israeli attack on and quick victory over Egypt in 1967 but failed to predict the Soviet invasion of Afghanistan, Constantin Cherneko's rise to power, and General Jaruzelski's seizure of power.[31]

Division IV, the Central Office, is responsible for various administrative functions, including finance, legal matters, security, training, and personnel.

The BND has been involved in numerous famous and infamous operations. Prior to becoming the BND, while it was still the Gehlen Org, it achieved several penetrations of the East German government. Captain Durt Heinz Wallesch was elected to the East German party's national committee and became a member of the Leipzig municipal council. Org recruit Karl Laurenze had a fiancée who worked for East Germany's first Minister-President—from her Laurenz was able to obtain copies of government decrees and minutes from ministries, letters from the Soviet High Command, and directives from the East German Politburo. In 1948 the Org recruited Herman Kastner, the Vice President of the German Democratic Republic, who proceeded to report on the Central Committee of the Liberal Democratic Party, the Economic Commission, the Presidency of the People's Congress, the National Council of the National Front, and the Cabinet. Kastner also described his conversations with Soviet politicians, diplomats, and generals and passed their views on to the Org.[32]

In Czechoslovakia, the Org placed an agent in the Skoda arms factory. It also recruited a shorthand typist in the Ministry of Commerce (who provided information on trade between Czechoslovakia and East Germany) and a technical draftsman (who handed over the plans for an important component of a guidance mechanism used in weapons and missiles).[33]

Operation Pfiffikus was directed against the Soviet Union. Informers in East Germany would contact any German who had reason to travel to the Soviet Union, including students, professors, engineers, and scientists. The operation also involved training a special group of individuals—those with knowledge of one or more East European countries and languages—who were then sent to international congresses and scientific meetings outside Germany, and sent to the Soviet Union, Poland, Czechoslovakia, Hungary, Rumania, and Yugoslavia whenever the opportunity arose.[34]

As Soviet and East European security operations eliminated some of the opportunities that arose from postwar chaos, Org and BND human intelligence (HUMINT) operations met with a lower rate of success. There were, however, some achievements—the BND obtained advance warning of the Israeli decision to attack Egypt, Syria, and Jordan in 1967 as well as advance knowledge of the Soviet decision to invade Czechoslovakia the following year.[35]

In 1979 East German authorities revealed that Rear Admiral Winfried Baumann-Zakrzowski had been a BND agent. Baumann-Zakrowski was arrested, convicted, and executed.[36]

It appears that, at least from the mid-1970s until 1985, the BND was receiving military and scientific secrets from a prominent Soviet journalist, Ilya M. Suslov. Suslov, an editor for the Novosti Press Agency and the former host of a television program on space exploration, is alleged to have cajoled "well-known people who had done much for Soviet science" into providing him with secret information in exchange for promises of publicity, and then to have given the information to Pavel Arsene, the Moscow representative of a West German company that was a front for the BND.[37]

In counterespionage, the BND had a major success in 1979 in the form of Warner Schiller, an officer in the East German Ministry for State Security (MfS), who provided information to the BND before "exfiltrating" in that same year. Schiller furnished information on the structure of the MfS, confirmation of the existence of a Military Intelligence Service, and material that led to the arrest of East bloc agents in West Germany and other Western European countries.[38]

Years earlier, the BND had suffered a counterespionage fiasco of monumental proportions. Heinz Felfe was born in 1918 and served as a member of the Nazi SS Security Service. As a result of being an SS officer, he was imprisoned by the Allies and sent to Canada. He was released in 1946, probably because he had offered his services to British intelligence and they had accepted.[39]

Upon his return to Germany, Felfe became an informer at the University of Bonn. In his informant role, Felfe joined a variety of Marxist and left-wing student groups. He was classified by the British as "uninvolved" in Nazi activities, allowing his acceptance into the BND; his entrance was arranged by an already operating KGB agent, Hans Clemens. Felfe became chief of Department IIIF, Counterespionage, which operated against all East bloc services. As senior intelligence officer of a department, Felfe had access to the reports of several intelligence and security agencies. In addition, he was regularly informed of those individuals who were suspected of being Soviet agents and those who were being investigated and placed under surveillance.[40]

Felfe photographed practically every document that passed through his hands. Included were personnel reports on the BND staff, minutes of classified meetings, and reports on clandestine field operations. Based on information from an East German intelligence officer who defected in 1961, Felfe was arrested in November 1962. At their trial, Felfe and Clemens admitted to delivering fifteen thousand photographs of classified West German intelligence documents. Additionally, Felfe admitted that he had betrayed ninety-four agents.[41]

In 1969 Felfe was freed as part of a prisoner exchange between the Germanys and has been living in East Berlin ever since. In 1986 he resurfaced to promote his memoirs, *In the Service of the Adversary*, which were published in West Germany but not in the East, presumably because of his Nazi past. In the book he claims that the BND spied on fifty-four West German politicians.[42]

The BND is reported to have built up a huge signals intelligence apparatus to listen in on the telephone conversations, radio communications, and radar systems of the Warsaw Pact nations. One particular target is the communications associated with SS-20 deployments. BND SIGINT sites have been established at Bad Sachsa, Bischotsgram, Kassel, Bonn, Heiligenhafen Holst/ Todendorf, and Braunschweig Flughafen. Additionally, there is an experimental station at Steinbrach/Schöningen and a site at Breisach (code named "PACKHORSE") involved in intercepting satellite communications.[43]

The diplomatic ciphers of a variety of nations are also the target of BND interception and deciphering activities. The BND is reported to have cracked Libyan ciphers several years prior to the March 25, 1986, cable sent to eight Libyan People's Bureaux, including one in East Berlin, and provided that information to the U.S. National Security Agency. The decipherment was used as evidence of Libyan involvement in the bombing of an American-frequented night club in Hamburg.[44]

Office for Radio Monitoring, Bundeswehr

The Office for Radio Monitoring of the Bundeswehr (*Amt für Fernmeldwesen Bundeswehr,* or AFMBW) occupies a position within the German Ministry of Defense akin to that occupied by the National Security Agency in the U.S. Department of Defense: "within but not part of." Headquartered at Bad Neuenahr-Ahrweiler, near Bonn, the office is responsible for coordinating an extensive network of electronic signals intelligence sites operated by West Germany along its 519-mile border with the Warsaw Pact nations. It also maintains a SIGINT analysis center at its headquarters.[45]

The network began to develop in 1956, when West Germany acquired equipment from the United States on a grant-in-aid basis, although ownership was restricted. During this time, U.S., British, and French resident forces operated all the collection sites. Many of the sites in the present network were originally built by the United States for its own purposes.[46]

The only site actually run by the Office for Radio Monitoring is at Hof. The office acquired it in May 1962 by paying the U.S. government $75 million for equipment deployed on its soil, including the purchase of the AN/FLR–12 antenna at Hof for $1. In exchange, the United States acquired the right to share the data obtained.[47]

The Navy's Marine Fernmeldebereich (Naval Signal Section) operates one site in the northern German area of Neustadt, employing a Watkins-Johnson QRC-259 antenna for collection in the 1-40 GHz range. It also "operates" a wooden dummy site in another northern German area. The Air Force's Fernmeldebereich 70 (Signals Section 70) operates five sites in the middle to northern regions of the country, with the principal collection asset being the QRC-259. In the late 1970s the sites were being outfitted with a newer HF/VHF system. Among the sites are those run by Fermelderegiment (Signals Regiment) 71 at Osnabrück and Fermelderegiment 72 at Schneeberg.[48] *

The Army has several Communications Reconnaissance Batallions, subordinate to the Army's Fermeldebreich 94 (Signals Section 94) in the south of Germany that collect signals intelligence on the electronics and communications capabilities of Warsaw Pact countries. The sites are reportedly located at Kornberg, Marklethen, in the southern Oberfranken region of Germany. The standard equipment at the sites is the Watkins-Johnson QRC-259 and the newer HF/VHF DF systems developed by GTE-Sylvania and German Rohde & Schwarz under the terms of a $50 million contract signed in April 1977. The Army also utilizes microwave vans built by Italia Electronic SpA that operate in the 1-18 GHz range.[49]

Typically the entire radio spectrum is surveyed with the antennas located for optimal line-of-site interception. Thus, from strategic positions atop the Fechtel mountains, northeast Nuremberg observers can see Czech radar sites, complete with their Soviet-built Cake series height-finders, as well as numerous Barlock GCI radars.[50]

Federal Armed Forces Intelligence Office (Amt Für Nachrictenwesen der Bundeswehr)

The origins of West German military intelligence date back to 1950, when Konrad Adenauer decided that he wanted to be informed about the military situation in East Germany prior to making a decision on West German militarization. The assignment was given to former Major Joachim Oster, who recruited former officer Lieuten-

---

*The Air Force has begun flight testing a high-altitude surveillance platform, codenamed EGRETT, based on the Grob G 109 motorglider, prior to procuring a squadron of eight to ten for monitoring Soviet and Warsaw Pact military communications and radars, as well as

ant Colonel Friedrich Wilhelm Heinz to assist him. Oster organized the headquarters while Heinz ran the external operation. Camouflaged as the "Institute for Contemporary Research," Oster and Heinz conducted military espionage in East Germany.[51]

Reinhard Gehlen, however, reacted sharply to having another organization conduct clandestine collection operations, particularly in the East bloc. Gehlen fought for his turf and was able to induce the resignations of Oster and Heinz. As a result, Gehlen's deputy took charge of the Ministry of Defense's intelligence section, today known as the Amt für Nachristenwesen der Bundeswehr, or Federal Armed Forces Intelligence Office. Its only human intelligence operations are those conducted by military attachés, such as those in Cairo, Lisbon, Oslo, Stockholm, and Tokyo. In addition, it conducts naval and aerial reconnaissance, particularly in the Baltic.[52]

The intelligence office also supervises the intelligence section of each military service—the Staab Abteilung II, or Staff Section II, under each service's Chief of Staff. The staff sections are responsible for the service attachés such as the Navy attachés in Buenos Aires, The Hague, London, Moscow, Paris, Rome, and Washington. The Air Force's Staff Section II supervises the activities of the Air Force reconnaissance wings that fly RF-4E and Alpha jet aircraft.[53]

Military Screen Service (MAD)

The Military Screen Service (*Militarischer Abschirmdienst*—(MAD) was created in 1956, along with the West German armed forces. It was not established by a specific law. Its organization and working methods are guided by internal regulations of the Minister of Defense.[54]

MAD has no foreign intelligence functions. Rather, it is responsible for preventing espionage, subversion, and sabotage directed against the West German armed forces. In carrying out these functions, MAD conducts personnel security investigations according to guidelines established in coordination with other NATO countries.[55]

MAD's activities are conducted in secrecy and, because of the lack of legislation delineating its responsibilities and powers, are subject to controversy. While MAD has no police powers and is limited to the collection of information, that collection can focus on West Ger-

---

conducting thermal imaging. Flying at nine to eleven miles altitude, the plane could "see" thirty-five miles into Warsaw Pact territory and eavesdrop over longer distance. The Tornado ECR will carry out reconnaissance missions, where deeper surveillance is required.

man civilians if it is believed that they are involved in activities directed against the German armed forces that MAD is responsible for preventing. Among the intelligence collection tools employed by MAD are wiretapping and mail opening.[56]

MAD has more than two thousand employees and is divided into seven groups.[57]

Federal Office for the Protection of the Constitution (BfV)

In 1972 new legislation was passed, expanding the powers of the BfV to conduct surveillance over aliens while specifying the limits of the BfV's powers with respect to West German citizens. The federal law describes the functions of the BfV and its Land units as the "collection and evaluation of information, intelligence and other data" on:

1. Efforts directed against a free and democratic basic order or against the existence or security of the federation or one of the *lander* or efforts aiming at illegally impairing the official functions of members of constitutional organs of the federation or the *lander*;

2. Security-endangering or intelligence activities carried out within the jurisdiction of this law on behalf of a foreign power;

3. Efforts within the jurisdiction of this law which endanger foreign affairs interests of the Federal Republic by the use of force or through actions preparatory therefore.[58]

The 1972 legislation also provided more detailed guidelines concerning personnel security investigations. The BfV and its Land units are to "participate" in:

1. The investigation of persons who, in the public interest, are entrusted with facts, objects or knowledge that require secrecy, or who are to be granted access to these or can otherwise obtain it;

2. The investigation of persons who are about to be employed in security-sensitive positions in installations that are important to defense or in other ways essential.[59]

As shown in Figure 5-4, the structure of todays' BfV, which has more than a thousand employees, involves eight sections: Administration, Background Inquiries, Right-Wing Radicals, Left-Wing Radicals, Counterespionage, Secrets Protection, Foreign Surveillance, and Terrorism.[60]

Figure 5-4. Organization of the BfV.

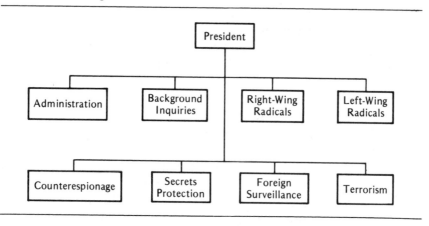

The eight sections carry out the responsibilities assigned to the BfV by the *Bundestag*. Background Inquiries is responsible for security checks, while the Right-Wing Radicals and Left-Wing Radicals deal with extremist groups. The Counterespionage section tries to combat the large-scale espionage activities conducted by East bloc agents. Between 1953 and 1970, there were at least thirty-three thousand attempts by East bloc agents to recruit West Germans. In the first ten months of 1986, thirty-two suspected Soviet bloc spies were arrested. In addition, the East German Ministry of State Security has successfully planted several moles in various parts of the West German government, included among them was Gunter Guillaume, a key aide to Willy Brandt when he was Chancellor. More recently, a former secretary in the President's office was charged with having spied for the Soviet Union since 1971. The secretary, Margarete Höke, worked for West German presidents from 1959 until her arrest in August 1985. From 1972 until her arrest, she saw 1,717 classified security documents from various government ministries as well as from the BND. In addition, she is believed to have passed reports from West German embassies on to the Soviets.[61]

The Foreign Surveillance section monitors the movements of foreign diplomats and other foreign nationals who might be hostile to West German, NATO, or Western interests. Upon the bombing of a discotheque in West Berlin in April 1986, the section stepped up its surveillance of Libyan diplomats stationed in West Germany. Syrian diplomats and intelligence operations are another target of the Foreign Surveillance section, as links have been established between Syrian representatives and the two terrorists who planted a bomb that injured seven persons at the German-Arab Friendship Society gathering on March 29, 1986. Among those sought by West German police in connection with aiding the convicted terrorists was the deputy chief of Syrian Air Force intelligence, Lieutenant Colonel Haithem Saeed; Saeed is accused of having provided the bomb and given instructions on its use.[62]

The Terrorist section operates against both "homegrown" terrorist groups and foreign groups.

Techniques employed by the BfV include the infiltration of groups, the use of audio devices and wiretaps, the monitoring of rallies, and the utilization of open sources such as group publications. Occasionally, the use of some techniques has proved embarrassing for the BfV. In 1975 and 1976 the BfV conducted an eavesdropping operation in the prison of Staffheim to overhear conversations between terrorists and their attorneys. Another operation was directed against Dr. Klause Traube, a scientist. Along with the BND, the BfV planted eavesdropping devices in Traube's home, believing it was monitoring conversations between terrorists and a nuclear physicist who had access to nuclear facilities. Traube, however, was a mechanical engineer who had no contacts with terrorists.[63]

Over the years the BfV has suffered two major defections. The first involved Otto John, the BfV's first president. On July 30, 1954, he announced over East German radio that he had defected and shortly afterward held a news conference, open to both Eastern and Western reporters, to explain the reason for his defection. On December 12, 1955, John reappeared in West Germany, claiming that his defection was the result of having been drugged and kidnapped. In August 1956 he was charged with treason and subsequently spent seven years in prison.[64]

The second breach occurred in August 1985, when Hans-Joachim Tiedge, a senior counterintelligence official, defected to East Germany. A forty-eight-year-old widower, Tiedge apparently fled impulsively to escape mounting debts and the responsibility for three troubled teenage daughters who were becoming involved in the Cologne drug scene. Tiedge was also considered a "hard-drinker" and had recently been denied a promotion.[65]

Tiedge apparently betrayed two Western agents who had infiltrated the inner circle of the ruling Communist establishment in East

Berlin. In addition, he evidently warned three highly placed East German agents that they were under suspicion and should flee to the East; the three were Ursula Richter, a fifty-two-year-old secretary in an organization for former refugees, Herbert Willner, a senior official at a foundation close to the liberal Free Democratic Party, and his wife, Astrid Willner, a longtime secretary in the Chancellor's office.[66]

MONITORING OF THE BALTIC

West German monitoring of the Baltic is done via both airborne and seaborne methods. In the 1970s survey ships A-51 and A-52, *Trace* and *Oste*, monitored East bloc naval movements.[67] The *Oste* still appears to be operating.

The West Germans conduct signals intelligence missions in the Baltic using Breguet Atlantique special-mission aircraft. The Atlantiques were converted in the early 1970s under the code name PEACE PEEK to become flying signals intelligence platforms. They were further modernized in 1980. Onboard the planes are a battery of multitrack recorders for the interception of radio and radar signals originating from the communication networks and warning systems of the Warsaw Pact. The antennas used to intercept these signals are located in a large black dome under what was previously the bomb bay, in longitudinal pods on the wingtips, and in a small cone on top of the vertical fin. Flying over the Baltic at a significant distance from the coast, the intercept operators on the Atlantiques can monitor signals hundreds of miles into the Eastern bloc.[68]

Using intercepted radio communications from such missions, the West Germans are able to develop a picture of the organizational structure of the military units in the Warsaw Pact countries. Troop movements can be monitored, as can military exercises. Thus, in 1982 the Atlantiques detected increased states of readiness of Soviet troops in three military districts on the Polish eastern border.[69]

In addition to intercepting radio communications, the Atlantiques are employed for the monitoring of radar systems—coastal radars near a naval base, an air defense radar, or a target-tracking radar associated with a surface-to-air missile (SAM) battery.[70]

A recent target for the Atlantiques was the construction of Soviet anti-aircraft sites with SA-5 Gammon missiles, near the East German town of Rostock, this was the first time the SA-5, with its 150-mile range, had been stationed outside the USSR. Another target is the Swedish air defense network. The West Germans fly closer to Swedish airspace than the Swedes would like and are regularly intercepted by Swedish fighters.[71]

More conventional Breguet Atlantique planes, armed with detection and strike equipment, are used for maritime surveillance and submarine detection in the North Sea and the Baltic.[72]

NOTES TO CHAPTER 5

1. David Kahn, *Hitler's Spies: German Military Intelligence in World War II* (New York: Collier, 1985), p. 32.
2. Ibid.
3. Ibid., pp. 35–38.
4. Ibid., p. 34.
5. Ibid., pp. 38–39.
6. Ibid., pp. 50–51.
7. J. W. M. Chapman, "No Final Solution: A Survey of the Cryptanalytical Capabilities of German Military Agencies, 1926-1935," *Intelligence and National Security* 1, no. 1 (1986): 13–47.
8. Ibid.
9. Kahn, *Hitler's Spies*, pp. 55, 373–75.
10. Ibid., pp. 162–63.
11. Ibid., p. 165.
12. Ibid., p. 185.
13. Ibid., pp. 173–75.
14. Ibid., pp. 169, 192–93.
15. Ibid., pp. 178–81.
16. Ibid., pp. 117–20.
17. Jacques Delarue, *The Gestapo: A History of Horror* (New York: William Morrow, 1964), pp. 357–59.
18. Ibid., pp. 359–60; Kahn, *Hitler's Spies*, pp. 238, 270.
19. Leslie Rout, Jr., and John F. Bratzel, *The Shadow War: German Espionage and United States Counterespionage in Latin America During World War II* (Frederick, Md.: University Publications of America, 1986), p. 4.
20. John Masterman, *The Double-Cross System* (New Haven: Yale University Press, 1972); Rout, Jr., and Bratzel, *The Shadow War*, chs. 3-8.
21. Kahn, *Hitler's Spies*, p. 421.
22. Heinz Höhne and Hermann Zolling, *The General Was a Spy* (New York: Coward, McCann and Geohagen, 1971), p. 14.

23. E. H. Cookridge, *Gehlen: Spy of the Century* (New York: Random House, 1972), p. 121.
24. Ibid., pp. 134-35.
25. Höhne and Zolling, *The General Was a Spy*, p. 191.
26. Ibid., p. 192.
27. Ibid.
28. Ibid.
29. Cookridge, *Gehlen*, p. 287.
30. Ibid., p. 362; "West Germans Eavesdrop on Warsaw Pact Nations," *Defense Electronics*, November/December 1977, pp. 51-53.
31. Cookridge, *Gehlen*, p. 362; Walter Lacquer, *A World of Secrets* (New York: Basic Books, 1985), p. 217; "Dieser Dilettanten-Verein," *Der Spiegel* 12 no. 19 (March 1984): 38-52.
32. Cookridge, *Gehlen*, p. 171.
33. Höhne and Zolling, *The General Was a Spy*, p. 149.
34. Ibid., p. 156; Cookridge, *Gehlen*, p. 177.
35. Lacquer, *A World of Secrets*, p. 219.
36. "Bonn Trades Spy for East German," *New York Times*, August 13, 1987, p. A6.
37. William J. Eaton, "Soviet Journalist Gets 15 Years as Spy for West," *Los Angeles Times*, July 31, 1986, p. 5.
38. Lacquer, *A World of Secrets*, p. 218.
39. Höhne and Zolling, *The General Was a Spy*, pp. 245-66, 277-80.
40. Ibid.
41. Ibid.
42. James M. Markham, "German Spy Comes in from the Cold," *New York Times*, March 13, 1986, p. A3.
43. Private information.
44. Catherine Feld, Tony Catterall, and Ian Mather, "Disco Bomb Evidence 'Massaged,'" *The Observer*, April 27, 1986, p. 14.
45. "West Germans Eavesdrop on Warsaw Pact"; *Die Bundesrepublik Deutschland Staatshardbuch 1985/86* (Bonn: Bundesdruckerei, 1985), p. 404.
46. "West Germans Eavesdrop on Warsaw Pact."
47. Ibid.
48. Ibid.
49. Ibid.
50. Ibid.
51. Höhne and Zolling, *The General Was a Spy*, pp. 197-98.
52. Ibid., p. 201; Lacquer, *A World of Secrets*, p. 218.
53. "German Defense Hierarchy Outlined," *Defense Electronics*, November/December 1977, p. 62; Ronald Zedler, *Die Bundeswehr eine Gesamtdarstellung, Band 7: Planungs-und Führungssystem* (Regensburg: Walhalla U. Praetoria Verlag 1978), pp. 271-72.

54. Edith Palmer, "Personnel Security in the Federal Republic of Germany," in Senate Committee on Governmental Affairs, *Federal Government Security Clearance Programs* (Washington, D.C.: U.S. Government Printing Office, 1985), p. 1226.
55. Ibid.
56. Ibid., pp. 1226–27.
57. Höhne and Zolling, *The General Was a Spy*, p. 238.
58. Palmer, "Personnel Security in the Federal Republic of Germany," p. 1225.
59. Ibid.
60. "Eine Merkwürdige Art von Dienstaufischt," *Der Spiegel* 36 (1985): 19–32.
61. Palmer, "Personnel Security in the Federal Republic of Germany," pp. 1213–14; "32 Soviet Bloc Spies Captured, Bonn Says," *Los Angeles Times*, November 7, 1986, p. 21; "Bonn Charges Ex-Aide with Spying for Soviet," *New York Times*, December 12, 1986, p. A5.
62. John Tagliabue, "West Germany Steps Up Watch on Libyans After Berlin Bombing," *New York Times*, April 8, 1986, pp. A1, A8; Robert J. McCartney, "Two Arabs Convicted in Berlin Bombing," *Washington Post*, November 27, 1986, pp. A5, A61; Robert J. McCartney, "Bonn Adopts Sanctions Against Syria," *Washington Post*, November 28, 1986, pp. A1, A50.
63. Palmer, "Personnel Security in the Federal Republic of Germany," p. 1223.
64. Höhne and Zolling, *The General Was a Spy*, pp. 192–96, 203.
65. James M. Markham, "Bonn and Its Many Enemies Within: Spy Scandals Bare Its Vulnerability," *New York Times*, December 10, 1985, p. A6.
66. Ibid.
67. Höhne and Zolling, *The General Was a Spy*, p. 238.
68. Dick Van der Aart, *Aerial Espionage: Secret Intelligence Flights by East and West* (New York: Arco/Prentice Hall, 1986), pp. 104–5.
69. Ibid.
70. Ibid.
71. Ibid.
72. Ibid.

6 FRENCH INTELLIGENCE ORGANIZATIONS

ORIGINS

Until its 1870 war with Germany, France maintained no permanent full-scale intelligence service. The only military information unit in existence at that time was the Statistical Section of the War Depot, which performed historical and geographical studies and obtained information from open sources, military attachés, and the occasional use of secret agents. Even so, as of 1870 France did not have a single agent in Germany.[1]

At the end of the war, a Statistical and Military Reconnaissance Section was established and given the task of obtaining information on the German troops occupying Alsace-Lorraine. After the occupation ended in 1873, the section grew and was alternately known as the Information Service (*Service de Renseignement*—SR) or Special Service. Its Frontline Bureau was responsible for the collection of foreign intelligence. Although its headquarters staff was small, by 1880 the SR had agents in Berlin, Vienna, Dresden, Leipzig, Frankfurt, Cologne, and Mannheim. Among these agents' accomplishments was the acquisition of German mobilization plans.[2]

As a result of the Dreyfus affair, the SR was abolished as a separate entity in 1899. Its counterespionage functions were assigned to the Sûreté Générale of the Interior Ministry, while its intelligence role was reduced and assigned to the Deuxième Bureau of the Army General Staff. The latter section began to expand in 1905 because of tensions between the Triple Alliance (Germany, Italy, and Austria-Hungary) and the Triple Entente (Britain, France, and Russia). Intelligence posts were set up to operate against Italy and Austria, and additional posts were established to focus on Germany. By the time war broke out, French intelligence had obtained detailed information on the number of reserve corps, Germany's employment of heavy artillery and mortars, and even the Schlieffen Plan itself.[3]

The Deuxième Bureau and its information section were not the only intelligence and security service operating for France at the beginning of the war. One of the most important French intelligence units, the *Cabinet Noir*, was the responsibility of the Foreign Ministry. This unit had functioned intermittently since the days of Cardinal Richelieu and had been revived during the 1880s. By the beginning of the next decade, it was able to decrypt significant quantities of Italian, Spanish, English, German, and Turkish diplomatic telegrams.[4]

In addition to the *Cabinet Noir*, several other organizations were engaged in cryptology. Because of its desire in the 1890s to break anarchist codes, the Sûreté Générale had developed an interest in the subject but then went on to attack diplomatic traffic. In 1909 the ministries of War, Marine, Interior, Colonies and Posts, and Telegraph jointly established the *Commission Interministériel de Cryptographie*, whose purpose was to prepare for the interception and decryption of German Army radio communications in the event of war. Finally, in 1912 the War Ministry set up its own *Section du Chiffre*. The Sûreté also had a significant budget (one million francs) for "agents' secrets." Although the bulk of the Sûreté's work was in internal security, it gathered foreign intelligence as a by-product of its counterintelligence function, its cooperation with foreign police forces, and its black chamber.[5]

Also in operation was the Naval Information Service (SR Marine), set up in 1891 after a reorganization of the Naval General Staff. The SR Marine was charged with studying the coastal defense facilities of foreign powers and obtaining information via attachés and open sources. Among its accomplishments was the acquisition, in 1917, of secret instructions destined for commanders of submarines. The SR Marine was, however, of far less importance than the Deuxième Bureau, having about 20 percent of the bureau's budget of a half-million francs.[6]

In 1936 the SR was separated from the Deuxième Bureau (although it continued to report to it) and consisted of two major sections, the Intelligence Section (*Section de Renseignements*) and the Counterintelligence Section (*Section de Centralization des Renseignements*). The Intelligence Section was further divided into four geographical sections—the German Section (Germany and Central Europe), the Middle Section (Italy and Mediterranean countries other than Spain), the Russian Section (which also covered Japan and China), and the Spanish Section—and two functional sections for War Materials and Air. War Materials was responsible for providing technical information on weaponry and other war materials and also had the job of researching sabotage methods. The Air Section was the embryo of the future air intelligence service. The SR's Counterintelligence Section was divided into German and Italian sections.[7]

In addition, several support sections were common to both branches of the SR. The Cipher Section was responsible for furnishing special codes, as well as for penetrating the ciphers of other nations. Section Nemo was involved in telephone tapping, while the clandestine uses of chemistry, radio, and photography were the responsibility of the Section of Chemistry-Radio-Photography. Finally, the Administrative Section was charged with personnel and finance functions.[8]

Within France, the SR maintained five posts, three of them targeted at Germany, one at Italy, and one at Spain. The posts focusing on Germany were located at Lille, Metz, and Belfort. At Lille the Bureau of North/East Studies worked through Belgium and Holland and had an antenna in Rotterdam and an auxillary antenna at Anvers. At Metz the Bureau of Regional Military Studies worked through Luxembourg as well as directly against Germany and had antennas at Luxemburg, Furbach, and Thionville. At Belfort the Service of Military Communications had antennas at Mulhouse, Basel, Zurich, and Saint-Louis. The Section of Regional Studies focused its antenna on Italy, as well as Libya and Algeria, and the Bureau of Pyrenees Studies had Spain, as well as German and Italian activities in Spain, as its target.[9]

The SR also maintained posts abroad—in Prague, Warsaw, Bucharest, Sofia, Copenhagen, Moscow, Berlin, Madrid, and Rome. Shortly before the war, auxillary antennas were installed in the consulates in Dresden, Leipzig, Dusseldorf, Cologne, Karlsruhe, Munich, Nuremberg, Stuttgart, Innsbruck, Sarrelbruck, Milan, Naples, Florence, Lugano, and Zagreb.[10]

In 1937 the Directorate for the Surveillance of the Territory (*Direction de la Surveillance du Territoire*—DST) was established within the Ministry of the Interior and assigned the function of combating foreign intelligence agents in France.[11] Also formed in 1937 was the SR Intercolonial, the intelligence service of the Ministry of Colonies. Given France's worldwide empire at the time and the designs of other countries on various parts of that empire, the eight sections of the SR Intercolonial operated on all five continents.[12]

By 1938 virtually all important intelligence functions were concentrated in the War Ministry and under the supervision of the Deuxième Bureau. Although the Air Ministry had its Air Intelligence Bureau and the Navy Ministry its Naval Intelligence Service, the Army's Deuxième Bureau was the major actor. The bureau had two principal components, the SR and the *Section des Armées Etrangères*, charged with preparing studies and reports based on the intelligence collected. The latter section produced the near-daily summaries of intelligence received from the SR and the weekly reports on intelligence received from all sources. It also produced the lengthy *Bulletins de Renseignements Mensuels*, comprehensive summaries that were disseminated to both higher and lower levels.[13]

After the German invasion, the services remained in Vichy France and continued to operate under a variety of covers. The counterespionage services set up as a cover a company called *Enterprise des Travaux Ruraux* (TR), headquartered in Marseilles. The company's ostensible purpose was the development of rural districts, and its "executives" set up branches all over the country. The TR was extremely efficient in the detection of Nazi agents. It was, however, working for the Petain government, hoping that Marshal Petain would choose to resist.[14]

In London, Charles de Gaulle set up a French government-in-exile. As part of his government de Gaulle established an intelligence and covert action agency, the Central Bureau for Information and Action (*Bureau Central de Renseignement et d'Action*—BCRA). Headed by Andre Dewavrin, alias Colonel Passy, the BCRA collected intelligence on the German forces occupying France, and it directed and aided resistance groups as well.[15]

In the aftermath of the U.S. landing in North Africa, the Germans proceeded to occupy the rest of France while the non-Gaullist intelligence services fled to Algiers, under the command of General Giraud. When de Gaulle arrived in Algiers in March 1943, among his objectives was the merger of his BCRA with the Giraudist SR and Military Security Service. Attainment of this objective was no easy task, as General Giraud and the intelligence services under his command were resistant to any suggestion of a merger. After a considerable battle with Giraud, de Gaulle emerged the winner, with the SR becoming the Technical Division of the new *Direction Générale des Services Spéciaux* (DGSS), or General Directorate of Special Services.[16]

Decisions concerning the direction and support to be given to the underground movements were made by the Committee for Action in France, presided over by de Gaulle and populated by a small number of his trusted aides, along with some representatives of the movements involved. The decisions of the committee were given to the DGSS to be carried out by the London branch of the BCRA for all actions concerning Paris and the northern part of France, and by the Algiers branch for all actions concerning the southern part of France.[17]

The political importance of the Special Services increased with the prospects of the liberation of France. Whereas a new administration was to take over, the Special Services made recommendations to the committee of candidates to fill all the key positions. The candidates were generally chosen from members of the underground committees working under the direction of the Committee for Action, with the recommendations inevitably being approved. The Special Services were selecting an administration that would be subservient to de Gaulle.[18]

The DGSS had been set up to work within France, but also ran intelligence networks outside of France. Hence, with the exception of several networks in the Balkans and the Middle East, the only sources of information were benevolent informers. The DGSS also operated, to a small extent, in the United States. A founder of the BCRA sent press clippings and reports on the activities of French refugees in the United States. Two of the refugees, Camille Chautemps and Genevieve Tabouvis, who actively opposed de Gaulle, were believed to have the ear of President Roosevelt. Also among the targets was U.S. training of officers for the administration of formerly occupied areas, including France, after the defeat of Germany.[19]

With the return of de Gaulle and his government to Paris in 1944, the DGSS was renamed the General Directorate of Studies and Research (*Direction Générale des Etudes et Recherches*—DGER) and inherited the networks that had been established within France by the DGSS. As a result, the DGER's focus was internal. A January 1945 memorandum issued to the top officials of the DGER called for the organization to focus on three domestic targets: (1) the internal situation in the country and public opinion, (2) political parties, and (3) resistance movements. In addition, via the Directorate of Technical Control, the DGER intercepted letters and telephone communications that were suspect. To accomplish the required surveillance, the DGER built up a force of ten thousand agents.[20]

The controversy generated by such domestic operations, together with charges by the Communist party that the DGER had initiated a series of operations designed to weaken the Communist Party of France, was substantial. The impact was felt in three ways. First, Dewavrin reorganized the DGER, ridding the agency of its more unprincipled members and reducing the size of bloated departments. Second, he set up two main divisions within DGER, one responsible for administration and the other for collection and analysis; the latter division included sections for intelligence, counterintelligence, and studies. Third, the organization was renamed the Service for External Documentation and Counterespionage (*Service de Documentation Extérieure et de Contre-Espionage*—SDECE) and given a charter that prohibited it from operating within France. Thus, the SDECE's founding decree specified that the organization was "meant to seek, outside national boundaries, all information and documents which might inform the government" and that it was to "carry no power on French territory, but operate only in foreign countries. Any counter-intelligence operation in France will rest with a special division of the Department of the Interior."[21]

The intelligence section of the SDECE was referred to as the Geographic Division, and its only task was the collection of positive intelligence on other nations' military potential, orders of battle, and political and economic situations. The requirement for a particular type of information was determined by computations of questionnaires received from various departments of the government.[22]

Stations were then set up in various countries. Usually they functioned under diplomatic cover and were linked to the assistant military attaché who controlled a certain number of agents and tried to establish networks to operate in specific fields (e.g., military, or science and technology). At headquarters, the heads of the Geographic Division supervised and channeled instructions to the stations under their command.[23]

The mission of SDECE's counterintelligence section was to protect France from interference by foreign intelligence services through gathering information on the structure and organization of those services, their members, and the operations they conducted. Additionally, an Action Service was set up to carry out covert operations.[24]

Over the years the SDECE expanded in personnel, budget, and mission. The Action Service grew in response to French involvement in Indochina. Subsequently, covert operations became a major means of carrying out French foreign policy, although at times the operators got out of hand, embarrassing the national government and leading to the dismissal of the SDECE chief. Of particular importance was the 1973 takeover by the SDECE of the French SIGINT agency, the Radio-Electric Group (*Groupement de Communications Radio-Electriques*—GCR).[25]

During the tenure of Count Alexandre de Marenches as Director General of SDECE (1970–81), several significant changes were made in the service. Originally saddled with a staff whose members ranged from gangsters and fascist Gaullists to incompetent military men and Soviet agents, he quickly fired half of the two-thousand-man force and began recruiting younger, more talented civilians. He also computerized much of SDECE's data processing. In addition, on the pretext of collecting information related to terrorism, he reestablished internal stations in the northern Basque country and Corsica.[26]

INTELLIGENCE AND SECURITY ORGANIZATIONS

General Directorate of External Security

As a result of the 1981 election of Socialist Francois Mitterrand, the SDECE became the General Directorate of External Security (*Direction Générale de la Sécurité Extérieure*—DGSE). Mitterrand appointed Pierre Marion, the former head of Air France and the SNAS aerospace company, to replace de Marenches, authorizing Marion to clean up the DGSE and reorient some of its operations.[27]

Marion proceeded to alter the service's personnel and organization—both on his initiative and at the request of Mitterrand. He removed fifty top officials suspected of being unsympathetic to the left. He also reorganized the service along more centralized lines, limiting the independence of its divisions and tightening up the command structure. At the behest of Mitterrand, he sought to improve the agency's capability to gather economic, financial, industrial, and scientific information.[28]

Marion met great resistance, however, from within the DGSE. His management ideas were particularly unpopular at headquarters, and as many as five hundred of the service's employees may have left. Some officers were alienated by his irascibility and unwillingness to delegate authority. More fatally for Marion's tenure, he lost the confidence of President Mitterrand in 1982. For one thing, the DGSE (unlike the other major intelligence services) failed to predict the Israeli move into Lebanon as well as a wave of terrorist attacks in France, some of which appear to have been planned abroad. For another, Mitterrand reportedly dismissed one set of intelligence reports as being "no better than press clippings." The final incident was Marion's unsuccessful attempt to find out what France's domestic counterespionage service was doing. On November 10, 1982, Marion's resignation was accepted.[29] Although Vice Admiral Pierre Lacoste was appointed in his place, in 1985 Lacoste was fired in the wake of the *Rainbow Warrior* affair and replaced by General Rene Imbot.

The decree of April 2, 1982, that created the DGSE also defined the organization's role:

> The Direction Générale de la Sécurité Extérieure, in order to conduct its mission for the benefit of the Government and in strict collaboration with other organizations concerned, [is] to seek and exploit intelligence advantageous to the security of France, also to detect and disrupt, throughout the national territory, espionage activities directed against French interests in order to prevent the consequences.[30]

To carry out this mission, the DGSE is specifically charged with:

- assuring the necessary liaisons with other services or organizations concerned;
- carrying out, with[in] the limits of its powers, all action entrusted to it by the Government;
- [producing] synthesis of the intelligence at its disposal.[31]

Figure 6-1.   The SDECE in 1971.

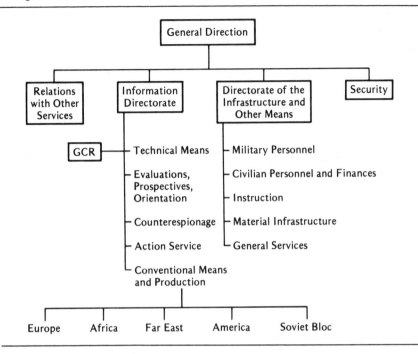

With respect to intelligence collection, the top priorities of the DGSE have been established as the Soviet Union, economics, and terrorism. In addition, when Vice Admiral Lacoste took over the DGSE, Defense Minister Charles Hernu (Lacoste's immediate superior, who also was removed from his position due to the *Rainbow Warrior* incident) requested that the organization increase its intelligence collection operations in Latin America, a region where government policymakers believed France could establish itself as a leading European political influence and arms supplier. Hernu also asked Lacoste to prepare the DGSE for a greater operational role in the Mediterranean and Middle East countries.[32]

The internal structure of the DGSE may be similar to that of the SDECE in 1971 (with the exception of its acquisition of the GCR), which is shown in Figure 6-1. The two principal directorates were the Information Directorate and the Directorate of the Infrastructure and Other Means. The Information Directorate was really an operations directorate, as it included the sections responsible for human collection, technical collection, analysis, counterespionage, and covert operations. Two additional branches were responsible for security and for liaison with foreign intelligence services.[33]

The activities of the DGSE have subjected President Mitterrand to substantial embarrassment. In November 1984 the DGSE informed him that Libya was honoring the mutual withdrawal pact from Chad, and Mitterrand ordered his forces back. When told by the United States that the forces were still in Chad, Mitterrand refused to believe it until the United States provided him with satellite photographs.[34]

A more serious embarrassment was the *Rainbow Warrior* incident (discussed later in this chapter). Prior to that time, the Action Service consisted of three sections: Air Support, Formation of Commandos, and Naval Missions. Subsequent to the *Rainbow Warrior* incident, the 11th Parachute Shock Battalion, which had been dismantled after the Algerian war, was re-formed. The revised 11th Parachute Shock Batallion will absorb two secret units that served the DGSE until the sinking of the *Rainbow Warrior:* the Cercottes parachute center near Orleans and the underwater combat center at Aspretto, in Corsica. The unit at Aspretto supplied at least six agents known to have taken part in the New Zealand operation.[35]

Additional changes in DGSE structure and personnel may have resulted from the *Rainbow Warrior* incident. In the aftermath President Mitterrand, in a letter to Prime Minister Laurent Fabius, ordered such changes, stating that "the moment has come to proceed without delay to changes in the personnel and, in case of need, in structure."[36]

In pursuit of intelligence to advance French interests and to inform national decision-makers, the DGSE and its predecessors have used both human and technical means of collection and have operated against Eastern, Third World, and Western targets.

Thus, at the direct request of then Finance Minister Giscard d'Estaing, the French intelligence services spied on American delegates to the Kennedy round of talks of 1964. D'Estaing desired a preview of the position of U.S. negotiator George Ball. To obtain that preview, the SDECE bugged Ball's hotel room at the Hotel Majestic in Cannes; in addition, SDECE Service 7 set up a clandestine laboratory for photographing documents at the hotel. An SDECE operative broke into Ball's room and, while Ball slept, rummaged through his pockets for notes, which were then microfilmed and later returned.[37]

SDECE Service 7 was originally created to open diplomatic correspondence between countries and their embassies in France. During the same period as the Ball incident, Service 7 was opening between twenty and twenty-seven diplomatic pouches a day, intercepting and decoding embassy mail. Among the materials opened were the diplomatic pouches of Egypt, Japan, and African countries considered friendly to France. The Japanese diplomatic luggage that was opened produced a wealth of data on Japanese political options, economic espionage, and liaison with the CIA. Among the information acquired by opening Egyptian diplomatic mail was the fact that Egypt had intercepted a French valise in Great Britain.[38]

Service 7 operations were conducted at airports and train stations; its agents were operating on national territory without the knowledge of the DST. Service 7 would photograph the documents and then distribute them to be developed in one of five geographical divisions: the Free World, Eastern countries, Arab countries, Africa, and the Orient. In addition, Service 7 conducted special operations, such as stealing a jet engine from a Tupolev airliner in Paris. Service 7 also prevailed upon Air France pilots to go off course and take photographs of sensitive installations in other countries.[39]

One technical operation that was conducted outside of France took place in Tunisia, where thirteen technicians were able to tap into the Tunisian telephone and telecommunications systems. Among the products of this operation was the taping of President Hans Bourgiba's telephone conversations.[40]

The SDECE also played a role in the Cuban missile crisis. When the first Soviet technicians began to flow into Cuba, French sources gave estimates varying from two thousand to fifteen thousand men, while the true number was about seven hundred. Likewise, reports mentioning the landing of MiGs and missiles in Cuban harbors turned out, largely, to be fairy tales.[41]

In July 1962 French sources began mentioning the arrival of Soviet ships in Havana and Mariel. Inclusion of the latter was particularly strange, since Mariel was a small harbor that rarely appeared on maps of Cuba. In addition, the Mariel harbor was closed to Cubans, and Soviet service personnel were seen unloading the cargoes themselves. Other ships were apparently landing people and cargoes in harbors where the Soviet flag had, until this point, been a rarity.[42]

P.L. de Vosjoli—the chief of the SDECE station in the United States—was skeptical because of previously exaggerated reports, but flew down to Havana to investigate. One source, however, helped convince de Vosjoli—a young man who had served in the French Army in Germany as a noncommissioned officer and was spending some time in Havana. He reported seeing a missile transported by truck. His description of the scene—a huge, multiwheeled trailer transporting Russian rockets under canvas cover—was considered accurate and reliable by de Vosjoli. The rockets were, said the young man, "bigger, much bigger than anything the Americans had in Germany."[43]

A more recent espionage case involving France revolved around a group of free-enterprising Indian civil servants and military officers selling information about Indian military equipment—a great deal of it from the Soviet Union—to several foreign intelligence services. Data sold also included confidential reports from the Prime Minister's office, intelligence notes on the security situation in Pakistan and Sri Lanka, and details about negotiations on military procurement.[44]

Fifteen persons, including three aides in Prime Minister Rajiv Gandhi's office, were arrested and accused of selling military secrets and other classified information to a foreign power. The key figure in the ring was T. N. Kher, a personal secretary to a top official in the Prime Minister's secretariat. In the aftermath of the arrests and the report by an Indian newspaper that a French diplomat was being deported for involvement in the ring, France recalled its deputy military attaché, Colonel Alain Bolley. In addition, it was reported that two French businessmen had left India a few days earlier because government investigators were about to deport them.[45]

Other targets of DGSE collection operations have included the United States and European Economic Community (EEC) departments. The French sale of Mirage aircraft to India is reported to have been facilitated by French knowledge of the U.S. offer during the final phases of the negotiations. DGSE agents also reportedly sought to penetrate some major businesses in the United States but were detected by the FBI. In addition, the DGSE reportedly sought to infiltrate EEC offices in Brussels to obtain information on the economics and technology of its European partners.[46]

The intelligence collected by the DGSE through human and other sources is transmitted to government departments in a variety of forms, including the approximately twenty-page "International Events Evaluation Notes," "Current Intelligence Notes," and notes on particular subjects—for example, the note of October 1983 on the arms traffic with Iran.[47]

Since its inception, the DGSE has engaged in a series of covert operations directed against a number of targets. Between 1949 and 1954, about one hundred parachutists were sent to Czechoslovakia, Yugoslavia, Romania, Byelorussia, and Lithuania. The parachutists—émigrés equipped by the SDECE with radios, rations, and light weapons—were part of Operation MINOS, in which agents were parachuted at night from planes that took off from the airports at Innsbruck and Lahr in Germany. Operation MINOS was carried out with heavy logistical help from the CIA—and, like a similar CIA operation, was a failure.[48]

A particularly deadly covert operation was the "Red Hand" operation. The Red Hand Organization was actually a cover for a series of assassination and sabotage operations intended to aid France's effort to suppress the Algerian National Liberation Front (Front de Libération National, or FLN) in its attempt to terminate France's colonial rule. The brain trust of the organization were drawn from the DST and three SDECE branches—Research, Service 7, and the Action Service. After an officer was selected and given plans of a target, he would formulate a plan and submit it for approval to the brain trust, who would then discuss it and pass it on to the President of the Parliament, who would ratify it.[49]

Table 6-1 lists the assassinations carried out by the Red Hand. Among them was the November 1958 assassination of Ait Ahcene, a representative of the Algerian revolutionaries in West Germany. One day Ahcene got into his Peugeot with a female friend at 8:30 A.M. and headed for the autobahn that would take him to Bonn. Once on the highway, he accelerated to a maximum speed and was followed closely by two Mercedes. After about two miles, one of the Mercedes began a maneuver to pass, then got back in line in front of the Peugeot and reduced its speed, forcing the Peugeot to slow down. The second Mecedes immediately came up alongside as if it too were going to pass, but instead, a machine gun fired at the Peugeot, sending it out of control. The Peugeot swerved wildly, then turned over and came to rest in a ditch alongside the road. Ahcene suffered serious injuries and died a few months later in a Tunisian hospital. He had on several occasions received threatening letters, showing in place of a signature the imprint of a red hand.[50]

Table 6-1. Red Hand Assassination and Sabotage Operations.

Date	Action
September 28, 1956	The Hamburg sales office of Otto Schlutter is blown up, an associate killed
June 3, 1957	Schlutter's mother is killed in an explosion of his car
July 18, 1957	The boat of German arms dealer Georg Puchert is blown up in Tangiers
July 21, 1957	The ship *Typhoon* is blown up in Tangiers
July 30, 1957	The cargo ship *Emma* suffers an explosion between Tangiers and Gibraltar
September 9, 1957	Georges Geiser, a maker of detonators, is stabbed in Geneva
September 19, 1957	Marcel Leopold, an arms merchant, is assassinated in Geneva
October 1, 1958	The ship *Atlas* explodes in Hamburg
November 5, 1958	Ait Ahcene, an FLN leader, is assassinated in Bonn
November 28, 1958	Algerian lawyer Auguste Thuveny is killed by a bomb in his car in Rabat
January 19, 1959	Abd-El Soulaem is killed on his way to Sarrebruck
March 3, 1959	George Puchert is killed by a bomb placed in his car
April 13, 1959	The cargo ship *Alkaira* blows up at Ostend
May 21, 1959	The police discover the body of Ould Aoudia
January 1, 1960	Abd El Kader Noasri loses both hands in an explosion
March 9, 1960	Akli Aissou, a student, is shot in Brussels
March 25, 1960	University professor Georges Laperches, a supporter of the FLN, is killed in Brussels by a package-bomb
October 15, 1960	Wilhelm Beissner loses both legs in an explosion of his car in Munich

Similarly, in 1959 George Puchert became a victim of the Red Hand. Puchert was an arms dealer who had been doing business with the Algerian nationalists. An explosive device was placed under the hood of his car. The following morning, a few seconds after he had begun driving, a violent explosion blew up the entire front of the vehicle, killing Puchert instantly. Inside the car, investigators discovered the imprint of a red hand.[51]

In addition to arms traffickers and FLN representatives, prominent supporters of the Algerian rebels were also eliminated by the Red Hand. One such victim was Georges Laperche, Professor of Philosophy in Liege, Belgium. Laperche, a leftist intellectual, was known to have made several contacts with Algerian nationalists. One day a package that apparently contained books arrived in the mail. The name of the apparent sender—*Presses Universitaires de France*—was printed clearly. Upon opening the package, Laperche was blown up by a terrible explosion. He died several hours later.[52]

Red Hand sabotage activities resulted in the sinking of at least fourteen ships with two thousand tons of weapons headed for the Algerian rebels. Those activities were effected using aircraft, a minisubmarine, and two minesweepers. A less violent operation involved the setting up of black radio stations disguised as the "Voice of the Arabs" and the "Voice of Free Algiers" near Chartres on land purchased by the SDECE. Speakers from those Arab countries were used to add authenticity to the transmissions.[53]

Assassination was also used to eliminate economic rivals, as in the case of Enrico Mattei. Mattei was president of ENI, the Italian National Hydrocarbon Authority. His accurate estimate, in 1946, concerning the presence of a large deposit of natural gas in the Po Valley led ENI to attain prominence in the utilization of methane as a low-cost source of energy for Italian industry. ENI also occupied a prominent position in the construction of pipelines and the creation of new petrochemical industries and oil refineries all over the world. Moreover, ENI diversified even further, moving into such areas as textiles, restaurants, motels, and newspapers.[54]

In late 1962 ENI was preparing to fight the large foreign companies in the Middle East. It was offering 75-25 percent contracts, compared with the 50-50 percent contracts offered by the other companies. But Mattei's plans caused problems for Charles de Gaulle, who had assured the French people that France would retain economic prominence in the former French colonies in sub-Saharan Africa and Algeria. That promise helped de Gaulle attain public support or tolerance for his policy of independence. Further, the support of many small French private investors was crucial to de Gaulle, and to retain that support he felt it necessary to demonstrate that France would keep control of North African oil.[55]

ENI—having concluded agreements with the governments of Senegal, Mali, Cameroon, the Ivory Coast, and Madagascar to set up a distribution network for its oil and oil products—was at work throughout Africa. In Tunisia ENI had obtained authorization to search for oil; in Bizerte, the company was building a refinery. Similarly, in Morocco a refinery had recently been completed, and an ENI subsidiary was prospecting for oil.[56] In addition, looking toward dealing with an independent Algerian government, Mattei had agreed to give the Algerian rebels all the financial and shipping assistance for their arms purchases that he could. In exchange, the rebel leaders promised him the right to build a refinery in Algeria and to take over the search for oil in the Sahara in place of the French.[57]

When approached directly by a French diplomat and told he was a nuisance, Mattei laughed in the diplomat's face. As a result, it was decided to bring pressure against Mattei. He received a message, presumably from the Red Hand, threatening him with assassination if he did not curtail his help to the Algerian rebels. When such tactics didn't work, it was decided to sabotage Mattei's plane. On October 27, 1962, Mattei flew from Catania, headed for Milan. Also on his private plane was William McHale, the chief of the *Time* magazine Rome bureau. The weather forecast indicated a low ceiling and a heavy fog over Milan. Because the altimeter and other instruments had been tampered with, the pilot emerged from the fog into a line of poplars, and the plane plunged to the ground and exploded, killing Mattei, McHale, and the pilot.[58]

Probably the best known incident involving a French covert operation, until the *Rainbow Warrior* incident, was the 1965 Ben Barka affair. Ben Barka, a Moroccan dissident living in Geneva, was active in speaking out against the Moroccan government and was involved as well in Third World activities, such as planning a meeting of revolutionary groups, to be held in Havana. When an attempt was made in 1963 to assassinate King Hassan of Morocco, the authorities claimed that Ben Barka was part of the conspiracy and sentenced him to death *in absentia*. When he supported Algeria during the brief Algerian-Moroccan conflict later that same year, Ben Barka was again sentenced to death *in absentia*.[59]

Having heard King Hassan frequently complain that "this man disturbs me," Interior Minister Mohammed Oufkir began planning to eliminate Ben Barka. In early 1965 Oufkir began a new round of meetings with French officials and found a great deal of cooperation. To lure Ben Barka to Paris, some "friends" told Ben Barka of plans for an anticolonial film and offered to arrange a meeting, to which Ben Barka agreed. On his way to the meeting, Ben Barka was intercepted at a restaurant by an SDECE agent and two French police officers and was then driven to a villa, where he was imprisoned and guarded by approximately thirty men, including Moroccan agents and French gangsters.[60]

On the evening of October 30, 1965, Ben Barka was fatally shot by either Oufkir or one of the Moroccan agents at the villa. An inquiry showed that Ben Barka's abductors had acted with the assent, if not the encouragement, of top people in the SDECE. Six French agents were convicted, two were given prison terms, and four were sentenced to life imprisonment. In addition, several members of the SDECE, including the Director, were forced to resign.[61]

French covert operations have also been directed against various governments, particularly African governments. An early target was Gamal Abdel Nasser and his government. In 1954 an agent was dispatched with the assignment of assassinating Nasser. In 1956 another attempt was made as part of the Suez invasion. Additionally, the 11th Choc was employed for a variety of purposes, including blowing up a Voice of the Arabs radio station that was broadcasting revolutionary propaganda for Algerian nationalists.[62]

Two years later Sekou Toure of Guinea became a target. On August 27, 1958, de Gaulle and Toure met in Guinea. De Gaulle revealed his plans for a French commonwealth, with France at the center and the former colonies circling it. Toure refused to become a member and thus started a long break with de Gaulle. As a result, the SDECE made repeated attempts to overthrow Toure—the leader of the independent nation of Guinea from October 2, 1958.[63]

France did not recognize Guinea until January 2, 1960. SDECE plotting turned into a joint operation with the BND, the CIA, and the Portugese security service (PIDE) involved. SDECE tried to destabilize the economy by sabotaging its pullout from the Common African Franc system as well as by printing fake money. While Toure was on a London voyage, SDECE tried to foment a coup; however, rumors that the French were up to something led to its being called off. In April 1960 commando raids from Senegal and the Ivory Coast began but were neutralized by Toure's security service.[64]

A recent target of French covert action has been Colonel Qaddafi. In 1980 an attempt was made to instigate a coup d'état. Several

SDECE agents were dispatched to Libya through the Tripoli embassy (which had been partially burned down in January) and the Benghazi consulate. Others arrived in Libya under cover of the ELF oil company, as "special engineers." They were to contact disenchanted officers in the Libyan Army.[65]

Psychological operations against Qaddafi were organized for six months prior to the date set for the coup. Included were numerous interviews in the French press with opponents of the Libyan regime as well as elaborate leaks and stories planted by SDECE-connected journalists. Additionally, a massive publicity drive was undertaken within France to promote *The Fifth Horseman*, a novel by two French writers wherein Qaddafi obtains an atomic bomb and blackmails the President of the United States.[66]

Also injected into the media were statements and other items portraying Qaddafi as the mastermind of all terrorist groups. Among the statements was that by Interior Minister Christian Bonnet, hinting that Libya was responsible for a bombing campaign undertaken by the National Liberation Front of Corsica (FLNC). A more violent approach was taken in conjunction with the British SIS, whose operatives set up a phony "Maltese Liberation Front" that in July 1980 claimed responsibility for a series of bomb attacks against Libyan telecommunication centers and other commercial buildings.[67]

On August 5, 1980, a military uprising was to be organized at the garrison of Tobruk, to be followed by guerilla action on both the eastern and western borders. The head of military security in Tobruk had been recruited by the French to lead the uprising. No uprising occurred, however, and the commandant fled.[68]

In 1984 two major operations to assassinate or overthrow Qaddafi were launched by the DGSE. Teams of Libyan exiles were armed with Israeli and other third-party weaponry, brought to the Sudan for combat training and infiltrated through Tunisia into Libya. Although neither plot succeeded, one resulted in a May 1984 battle with Qaddafi loyalists near the El-Azziziya Barracks. Libya later reported that fifteen members of the exile group had been slain.[69]

Radio-Electric Communications Group (GCR)

The GCR was set up in 1941 by Lieutenant Colonel Paul Labat. In addition to intercepting foreign diplomatic and military communications from overseas posts, it also listened to communications from embassies in Paris. Initial listening sites were at Alluets-Feucherolles, Velaineren-Haye, Domme, Berlin, Djibouti, Guadeloupe, and Maurice Island.[70]

Subsequently, the GCR has been heavily involved in Africa. By arrangement with King Hassan in the 1960s, it was able to set up a facility to monitor the communications of a U.S. base in Morocco. During the war in Algeria, the GCR intercepted, transcribed, and decoded the communications of the FLN as well as determined the position of FLN forces. Both ground and airborne listening posts were employed.[71]

GCR listening posts within France include Les Alluets-de-Roi, Le Mont Valerien, La Courtine (Creuse), and Larcay, near Tours. The La Courtine post focuses on the Middle East, while the Larcay station is targeted on Southeast Asia. Stations outside of France include Berlin (targeted on the Warsaw Pact countries) as well as Djibouti, Mayotte, and Reunion, the latter three being employed to monitor Soviet military movements around the horn of Africa and in the Indian Ocean. Two listening posts are operated at Saint-Barthélémy (Guadeloupe) and Tromelin (Maurice Island) under the cover of meteorological stations. Additionally, a base at Bouar in the Central African Republic was developed as a supply post and an electronic listening post.[72]

Military Intelligence

The French armed forces and defense establishment operate a variety of defense and service intelligence and security organizations. Subordinate to the Supreme Council of Defense is the National Defense Staff. Reporting to the defense staff are the Security and Defense Division (*Division de Sécurité et Défense*) and the Second (Intelligence) Division (*Division du Renseignement*). Within the latter division are two centers: the Center for the Exploitation of Scientific and Technical Intelligence (*Centre d'Exploitation du Renseignement Scientifique et Technique*) and the Center for Intelligence Exploitation (*Centre d'Exploitation du Renseignement*).[73]

The Second Division is also responsible for coordinating the activities of the Deuxieme Bureau of each of the major services—the Army, Navy, and Air Force. These bureaus also provide the attachés who serve in French embassies and seek to acquire military intelligence.[74]

One of the more advanced means of gathering military intelligence is overhead reconnaissance. The French Air Force's 33rd Reconnaissance Wing has three types of airplanes—all Mirage variants—that are employed in such activities. The Mirage F1.CR is a single-seat tactical reconnaissance aircraft derived from the Mirage F1 fighter. The F1.CR, first flown in 1981, is a replacement for the Mirage IIR/RD. The plane is equipped with an Omera 35 oblique frame camera, an Omera 40 panoramic camera, an infrared sensor, and a sight recorder. An external pod houses additional sensors. A total of sixty-four F1.CRs are planned.[75]

A second single-seat tactical reconnaissance aircraft employed by France is the Mirage IIIR. The IIIR can fly at a maximum speed (clean) of 1,450 mph and has a combat radius of 745 miles. The Mirage IVR, of which there are a dozen, is France's sole strategic reconnaissance aircraft and a modification of the Mirage IVR that first flew in 1959. The Mirage IVR is equipped with optical sensors, an infrared (IR) line scan, and possibly a side-looking airborne radar (SLAR) in the underside of the fuselage. At 40,000 feet the plane can attain a maximum speed of 1,454 (Mach 2.2) in a "dash" mode, while in a sustained pattern of operation at 60,000 feet it can fly at speeds up to 1,222 mph (mach 1.7). Its range for strategic missions is 2,485 miles.[76]

France also operates electronic reconnaissance aircraft—specifically, two Gabriel C-160 Transalls. The Transalls replaced the modified Nord 2501, transports that had been performing "special mission" duties from Evreux Air Base in eastern France, where the 51st Electronic Squadron (51 Escadrille Electronique) is located. The Gabriels are equipped with UHF and direction-finding antennas.[77]

France is one of several smaller countries that has considered the operation of a photographic reconnaissance satellite. The satellite that was originally planned, designated SAMRO, was to be a modified version of a nonmilitary French satellite known as SPOT (*Systeme Probatoire d'Observation de la Terre*).

In 1978 the French government decided to undertake the development of SPOT. The satellite, meant to be similar to the U.S. LANDSAT system and to transmit its data to ground receiving stations, was planned to make fourteen-plus revolutions of the earth each day, at an inclination of 98.7 degrees and at a mean altitude of approximately 500 miles.[78]

The capabilities of the satellite include 20-meter (66-foot) ground resolution of color images recorded in three (visible and near-infrared) bands and 10-meter (33-foot) resolution of black-and-white images recorded in a broader spectral band—three times better than LANDSAT's resolution. SPOT's mirrors can be pointed 27 degrees to the east or west of its track, allowing viewing of any location within a 950-kilometer-wide corridor (and increased revisit coverage ranging from one to several days). SPOT is thus capable of producing stereoscopic pairs of images by simply recording the same area during different orbital passes from different angles and then combining them.[79]

Present plans call for four SPOT spacecraft. SPOT 1 was launched in February 1986, with some of its data being used for intelligence purposes by the French military. Early in 1986 the French government approved the production of SPOT 3 and SPOT 4, which would continue the program into the late 1990s. The newer satellites will be able to produce color imagery in a fourth spectral band (1.7 microns) with the same resolution as the other bands. SPOT 3 and 4 will also be equipped with a wide-angle, low-resolution imaging camera that will operate in the same spectral bands as the satellites' high-resolution cameras.[80]

When the SAMRO program was cut back in 1982, the proposed satellite was scheduled to use the basic design of SPOT and the U.S. LANDSAT satellite. Major development work had been expected to begin in 1982–83 for the ultimate manufacture of a SAMRO to be launched in 1986–87. After the cutback, however, virtually the only SAMRO contract that was continued was for the camera system.[81]

Plans had called for the retention of the box-shaped main bus of SPOT, with the optical and data transmission systems changed to handle the higher resolution requirements of the military and to provide for secure data transmission. A separate ground receiving and data processing network was to be established to deal with the military information.[82]

In 1984, France and West Germany studied the prospects of jointly developing a military reconnaissance satellite that would be a follow-on to SAMRO. Aerospatiale began ground testing of a high-resolution camera imaging system that was originally developed for SAMRO. German-French negotiations collapsed over the sensors to be carried by the satellite, however, with France favoring an optical system and Germany an imaging radar to allow penetration of the heavy East bloc cloud cover.[83]

Present French plans call for development of a military imaging satellite called HELIOS, able to image objects "smaller than a baseball bat." This program, formally approved in February 1986, calls for the launching of four satellites over ten years, beginning in 1990, to provide a high-resolution capability. The two-ton HELIOS system is being designed to use the platform developed for SPOT and may also employ some common communications links with SPOT.[84]

HELIOS may be developed in conjunction with both Spain and Italy. Italian interest, prompted by the *Achille Lauro* incident, will involve participation in the development of the ground receiving/data processing segment of HELIOS.[85]

In addition to HELIOS, France is considering development of a synthetic aperture radar satellite, as desired by West Germany, that would further increase French reconnaissance capability. The French space agency has awarded a number of initial contracts for this space-cract, designated Radar SAR.[86]

Directorate for Surveillance of the Territory (DST)

The DST, subordinate to the Ministry of the Interior, is estimated to have between two thousand and five thousand full-time employees. The mission of the DST is spelled out by a decree of December 22, 1982. Article 1 of the decree specifies that:

> The Directorate for Surveillance of the Territory is responsible for detecting and preventing, on the territory of the French Republic, the activities inspired, engaged in or sustained by foreign influences of nature that menaces the security of the country and, more generally, and to fight against these activities.[87]

Article 2 specifies that in order to carry out its mission the DST is directed to:

- centralize and exploit all the information reported on the activities mentioned in Article 1 and to transmit it without delay to all services concerned with the security of the country;
- share in the security of sensitive locations and the closed sectors of national activity, so as to protect the secrets of defense; and

- assure the necessary liaison with other services or concerned organizations.[88]

The specific activities that the DST is responsible for countering are espionage and terrorism. In November 1982 the DST was instructed to devote three quarters of its man hours to counterespionage and the majority of the remaining one quarter to antiterrorist work. DST's counterespionage activities involve the surveillance of embassies and their occupants, the protection of classified information, and the monitoring of clandestine radio emissions. One means of monitoring foreign embassies has been the tapping of their phone lines, and DST is believed to tap the phones of both East and West bloc embassies. Apparently, DST wiretaps of the Iranian embassy in Paris proved that an Iranian official, Wahid Gordji, personally issued the orders to the terrorists who planted the bombs during a September 1986 wave of attacks. To monitor clandestine radio emissions, DST maintains intercept stations at Boullay-les-Trois, Marseilles, Toulouse, and Rennes et Lille. In 1984 those stations intercepted 119,824 transmissions.[89]

DST's main counterespionage targets are the intelligence services of Soviet bloc countries. Between 1976 and 1985, twenty-nine court cases involved espionage, twenty-seven of them involving the intelligence services of Warsaw Pact nations and two involving Algeria and the People's Republic of China, as shown in Table 6-2. In February 1986 a former noncommissioned officer in the French Army was

Table 6-2. French Court Cases Involving Espionage, 1976-85.

Nation Involved	Number of Cases	Years
Algeria	1	1978
Bulgaria	2	1978, 1979
Czechoslovakia	1	1985
German Democratic Republic	5	1981, 1982, 1983, 1985
Hungary	3	1978, 1979, 1984
People's Republic of China	1	1985
Poland	4	1976, 1979, 1985
Romania	2	1983, 1985
Soviet Union	10	1978, 1980, 1983, 1984, 1985

Source: Pierre Péan, *Secret d'Etat: La France du Secret, les Secrets de la France* (Paris: Fayard, 1986), pp. 82-83.

charged with handing over information on naval installations to Soviet GRU officers.[90]

A 1984 estimate by the DST broke down the targets of foreign agents in France by percentages:

Military   19%
Scientific and technical   67%
Political   14%

In addition, a 1986 estimate specified the number of intelligence and diplomatic personnel from Soviet bloc (other than the USSR) diplomatic establishments in France, as shown in Table 6-3.[91]

Although normally DST's counterespionage activities are conducted on French territory, in one recent case the organization was involved in running an agent within the KGB. In 1981 a Frenchman delivered to the DST a letter from "a Soviet friend" who offered his services. The friend turned out to be a senior officer of the KGB's Directorate T, which deals with scientific and technical espionage. The KGB officer explained that although he had served in the Soviet embassy in Paris in the 1960s, he would never again be permitted to leave the Soviet Union, because of the senior position he had achieved.[92]

DST accepted the proffered services and code-named the new agent FAREWELL. Beginning in 1981 FAREWELL provided DST

Table 6-3. DST Estimate of Intelligence and Diplomatic Personnel from Non-USSR Soviet Bloc Diplomatic Establishments in France, 1986.

Nation	Diplomats	Intelligence Personnel
Bulgaria	116	26
Cuba	102	12
Czechoslovakia	89	10
German Democratic Republic	110	13
Poland	132	30
Romania	85	12
Total	634	103

Source: Pierre Péan, *Secret d'Etat: La France du Secret, les Secrets de la France* (Paris: Fayard, 1986), pp. 82–83.

with more than four thousand documents on Soviet scientific and technical espionage, including Soviet plans to steal Western technological secrets and Soviet assessments of the value of its covert technology acquisition activities. Specifically, FAREWELL reportedly provided:

- the complete, detailed list of all organizations involved in scientific and technical intelligence;

- the plans, accomplishments and saving effected every year in all branches of the military industry, thanks to the illegal acquisition of foreign techniques;

- the list of all KGB officers in the world, members of "line X," involved in scientific and technological espionage;

- the identity of principal agents recruited by the officers of "line X" in ten western nations, including the United States, West Germany and France.[93]

According to one intelligence official, the operation was "one of the great postwar intelligence coups."[94]

At the July 1981 economic summit in Ottawa, President Mitterrand informed President Reagan about FAREWELL and gave him a sample of intelligence material. Several weeks later, the head of the DST at the time, Marcel Chalet, visited Vice President Bush in Washington to discuss FAREWELL.[95]

FAREWELL ceased providing information at the end of 1982, disappeared without explanation in 1983, and is now believed to be dead. Some French intelligence agents think his disappearance may have been connected with rumors of a vice scandal at the top of the KGB that resulted in the murder of a Soviet police officer.[96]

FAREWELL's information was directly connected with the expulsion of forty-seven Soviet diplomats for espionage activities in April 1983. That such activities have not ceased is indicated by the April 1987 expulsion of three Soviet diplomats for their involvement in an espionage ring at the European Space Agency. Apparently the focus of the ring was on the technology used in some motors for the Ariane space launch vehicle.[97]

DST's antiterrorist function has probably increased in importance since 1982, particularly after a wave of bombings in Paris in September 1986. In the space of ten days, bombs rocked the Gare de Lyon, City Hall, the Cafeteria at la Défense, the Pub Renault, police headquarters, and the Tati store. The goal of the bombers was to obtain the release of Georges Ibrahim Abdallah, leader of the Lebanese Armed Revolutionary Factions (LARF), who was about to be tried for the murders of U.S. and Israeli diplomats. In addition, France's major left-wing terrorist group, Direct Action—responsible for about eighty bombings and shootings in France—killed the head of the state-owned Renault auto company in November.[98]

At the Abdallah trial, DST's judgment and actions were called into question. DST had identified Abdallah as the likely leader of the LARF as early as 1982, when a DST report named him as the probable organizer of the killings of U.S. and Israeli diplomats. DST became aware of Abdallah's presence in France in August/September 1984; in December 1984 he was arrested for possessing false passports, and the gun used in the killings of the diplomats was discovered in his room. DST has been accused of withholding from the police 1982 information about Abdallah's possible role in the killings. The inspector in charge of the investigation said he was "completely in the fog" about the case until 1984, when he was provided with information from DST linking Abdallah to the crimes. It also emerged that the head of the DST had traveled to Syria after the wave of attacks in September 1986 to confer with the chief of Syrian internal security about gaining Syrian help in curbing such bombings.[99]

Other questionable activities of the DST include the bugging, at the urging of its Gaullist superiors, of the satirical weekly *Le Canard Enchaîné*. Although caught in 1973, the DST was not discouraged from continuing such activities. When the magazine moved into new offices in 1980, its staff discovered dozens of microphones, presumably installed by the DST. DST is also alleged to have helped the CIA bug a discussion between Fidel Castro and then President de Gaulle during a Castro visit to France.[100]

General Intelligence Directorate

The General Intelligence Directorate (*Direction de Renseignement Générale*—RG), subordinate to the Ministry of the Interior, serves as an information-gathering service for the government on a wide range of matters. Its official mission was defined in a decree of November 17, 1951: "It acts for the research and centralization of information about the political, social and economic order necessary to inform the government." To carry out its mission, RG maintains a large informer network throughout France, with informers operating in every town and village. As a result, RG is able to keep files on several million noncriminal citizens—journalists, political activists, union militants, and civil servants, including all teachers.[101]

At the headquarters level, RG is divided into four services, or directions: General Information and Foreigners; Political, Social, and Economic Information; Games and Courses; and Administrative Affairs. Locally the organization operates through the police structure and is divided into eight sections and four principal services. These subdivisions focus on all political parties, labor syndicates, economic affairs and finance, the press, terrorism, foreigners, gambling, and the protection of VIPs.[102]

MANAGEMENT STRUCTURE

Several committees are involved in the supervision of the French intelligence community. The GIC (Groupement Interministeriel des Communications), subordinate to the Prime Minister, is the Interministerial Group for Communications, created to supervise the tapping of telephone conversations to and from France. The CIR is the Interministerial Committee on Information (Comité Interministeriel des Renseignement), charged with coordinating the actions of the various information and analysis divisions of the government. The CIR is in turn subordinate to the Superior Committee on Defense under the President of the Republic. Counterintelligence operations are supervised by the Comité Spécial de Contre-espionage (CSC)—special counterintelligence committee.[103]

LIAISON

As with any intelligence organization that seeks to have global reach, the DGSE/SDECE has relied on liaison and joint operations as a means of attaining intelligence and political action objectives. Over the years it has cooperated with the CIA, SIS, Mossad, BND, Portuguese PIDE, and SIFAR and its successors, as well as several other services.

Relations with the BND date back to the late 1940s, when BND's predecessor, the Gehlen Organization, was operating under the control of the CIA. In 1948 agents of the Org were in a position to prove that the Russian, Polish, and Czech secret services were sending agents into the French zone of Germany. Swiss counterespionage authorities offered to arrange a contact between the Gehlen Organization and the SDECE so that they might jointly monitor the espionage lines running between Switzerland and the French zone.[104]

Gehlen was hesitant, believing the SDECE to be still suffering from its penetration by Communists during the resistance. In addition, he regarded the French as amateurs because of their reliance in Berlin on intelligence peddlers who either invented information about the Soviet zone or passed on reports that had been altered by Soviet intelligence. Swiss counterintelligence authorities assured Gehlen that key positions in SDECE were increasingly being staffed by officers who had worked in de Gaulle's counterespionage service during the war; according to the Swiss authorities, the Gaullists within SDECE were waging "savage warfare" against the former members of the Communist resistance. The United States also urged Gehlen to do business with SDECE, partly because of a U.S. desire to gain a view of French policies.[105]

Gehlen relented and a friendly alliance emerged. According to Gehlen, "Long before our transfer to federal control we had entered into informal agreements with out counterparts in France for collaboration in intelligence affairs and the exchange of material. For a long time we supplied the French with our . . . reports in exchange for nothing more than goodwill, to build up West Germany's diplomatic status in French eyes. . . . Relations between the two intelligence services remained constant and cordial." Those relations were formalized by the Franco-German agreement of January 22, 1963.[106]

The SDECE also planned or conducted joint operations with the Portuguese Internal Police for Defense of the State (PIDE). In 1970 they teamed up to plan Operation Mar Verde—a plot to overthrow Sekou Toure in Guinea-Conakry. A second joint project stemmed from the Portuguese interest in maintaining colonial control of Guinea-Bissau, which was in the process of being liberated by the African Party for the Independence of Guinea and the Cape Verde Islands (PAIGC). PAIGC, which had freed almost 75 percent of rural Guinea-Bissau, was being supported by Toure. In the aftermath of the January 20, 1973, assassination of Amilcar Cabral, Secretary General of PAIGC, the head of PIDE African operations decided that it was appropriate to fatally cripple PAIGC.[107]

PIDE and SDECE joined forces, using two provocateurs, code-named PADRE and ANJO, who had penetrated the top ranks of PAIGC. The intention was to stimulate deep divisions within PAIGC, based primarily on supposed differences in ethnicity and ideology between Cape Verdeans and Guineans. It was believed that once a split had developed, Toure would be naturally allied with the leadership of one faction (Cape Verdeans) and the other faction (Guineans) would view him as the enemy and join in ousting him. While the PIDE agents were attempting to destroy PAIGC from within, SDECE was planning the military side of the expected coup d'état. Before the plan could be implemented, however, the Portuguese government was overthrown.[108]

In the 1970s SDECE expanded its contacts with foreign intelligence services in many different directions. It was reported that in 1973–74 a prime objective of the Chinese intelligence community was to attain an exchange of intelligence with France in certain areas of common interest, particularly the Soviet Union. To facilitate the exchange, China passed on to SDECE a large amount of intelligence on Vietnam, as well as a smaller amount of intelligence concerning Soviet moves in the Far East. In 1974 the head of SDECE, Alexandre de Marenches, flew to Peking for talks on arranging a regular system for the exchange of intelligence, with the Soviet Union being the focus.[109]

Marenches also extended liaison arrangements to the Arab world when he joined the Safari Club on September 1, 1976. Marenches signed an agreement with Sheik Kamak Addam of the Saudi External Liaison Bureau, the head of SAVAK (the Iranian National Security and Information Organization), the chief of the Moukhabarat El-Amma of Egypt, and the head of Morrocan secret services. The basic objectives were to prevent the Soviet Union from gaining any political or military foothold in the Middle East and to undertake operations to remove any existing footholds. The SDECE provided logistical support. The Safari Club tried to get Siad Barre of Somalia to expel the Soviets in exchange for weapons, and it organized psychological and guerilla operations against Qadaffi.[110]

Liaison with the United States can be traced to the early 1950s, when Philipe Thiraud de Vosjoli was sent to Washington to organize liaison with the CIA. Coming in the wake of the Philby affair and the consequent damage to U.S.-British intelligence relations, de Vosjoli was assigned a major task: securing for the SDECE the status formerly occupied by the British.[111]

While not being supplied with a great deal of intelligence to negotiate with the United States, de Vosjoli was pressed to request U.S. aid for French operations in Indochina. At the same time, with the Korean War at its height, the United States needed information on the situation in Indochina and on Chinese support of the rebels; thus, de Vosjoli began to negotiate an exchange of intelligence on the Asiatic theater of operations. The intelligence was offered in return for equipment and supplies—an agreement whose final details were worked out with the aid of General Lattre de Tassigny.[112]

Among the information the United States subsequently passed to France and the SDECE was that from 1962 Soviet defector Anatoli Golitsyn, indicating a rather thorough Soviet penetration of the French intelligence apparatus as well as of Charles de Gaulle's cabinet. The first information arrived in a personal letter from President John F. Kennedy to President Charles de Gaulle.[113]

To investigate the charges, the French sent General Jean de Rougement, Director of the Intelligence Division of the National Defense Staff, to Washington. When de Rougement returned to France, he reported that Golitsyn was authentic and that his charges of KGB infiltration required more extensive questioning of Golitsyn by French counterespionage experts. The SDECE and DST assembled their own staffs and interrogation teams.[114]

Golitsyn, assigned the code name MARTEL by the French, was questioned extensively. MARTEL was able to describe in great detail the extensive reorganization undergone by SDECE at the start of 1958. He also knew "how and why specific intelligence functions and objectives had been shifted from one section to another, even the names of certain officers who were running certain intelligence operations—details of a nature that could have come only from a source or sources at or close to the heart of the French intelligence organizations."[115]

In addition, MARTEL asserted the existence in France of a network with the code name SAPPHIRE, consisting of more than a half-dozen French intelligence officers, all of whom had been recruited by the KGB and were operating within SDECE. Further, he informed his French debriefers that a new section would be created (or already had been) within the SDECE for the purpose of obtaining data on U.S. nuclear and other technological advances, the information to be transmitted back to the Soviet Union.[116]

Some recent U.S.-French cooperation has concerned Libya and Chad. The CIA provided information to France to aid it in the previously mentioned attempts to overthrow or assassinate Qaddafi in 1984. Included were satellite photographs and communications intercepts. Both the United States and France provided intelligence to the forces of President Hissen Habre of Chad in his successful battle against Libya in 1987. That information included intelligence based on satellite pictures of the battlefield and intercepted radio messages. At the same time, it was reported that France initially refused to share intelligence obtained from Soviet military equipment abandoned by Libya—equipment that included L-39 ground support jets, MI-24 attack helicopters, two hundred T-55 and T-62 tanks, multiple rocket launchers, entire missile batteries, radar installations, a revolutionary laser guidance system for the SA-6 missile, Russian instruction manuals for the weaponry, and log books of aborted air reconnaissance missions. According to one account, disagreements between French and Chadian officials prevented U.S. acquisition of the MI-24, but the dispute was later resolved to allow for the helicopter's transfer out of the country and for joint U.S.-French analysis.[117]

RAINBOW WARRIOR

At 11:38 P.M. on July 10, 1985, a bomb blew a 3½-by-10-foot hole in the engine room of the *Rainbow Warrior* as it lay docked at New Zealand's Auckland harbor. Shortly thereafter, a second bomb exploded, destroying the ship's propulsion system. It had been intended, by the environmentalist organization Greenpeace, that the *Rainbow Warrior* would lead a group of protest vessels to the vicinity of Moruroa atoll in the South Pacific, where French authorities planned to conduct a round of underground nuclear tests.[118]

The explosions resulted in the disabling and eventual sinking of the *Rainbow Warrior* and the death of Fernando Pereira, a photographer working with Greenpeace who had tried to retrieve his photographic equipment after the initial explosion. The death toll could have been much worse. According to Michael King:

Had the bombs gone off an hour later, when everybody on board had retired for the night, there could have been four deaths from the first explosion, five from the second. Had they detonated an hour earlier, the 14 people at the skipper's meeting would have been trapped in the fish hold. The entire leadership of the Greenpeace Peace Flotilla would have been eliminated.[119]

The *Rainbow Warrior* operation had its genesis in the concern of Admiral Henri Fages, head of the *Centre d'Expérimentations Nucléaires* on Moruroa, over possible Greenpeace attempts to disrupt the French testing program, which was to include testing of both the 60-kiloton warhead for the new Hades tactical missile and the French neutron bomb. The head of the DGSE at the time, Admiral Lacoste, agreed with Admiral Fages that the Greenpeace flotilla should not be allowed to reach Moruroa but believed that the simplest solution was to tow the *Rainbow Warrior* away if it entered French territorial waters. Nevertheless, at a March 4, 1985, lunch Admiral Fages persuaded Defense Minister Charles Hernu that DGSE was not doing enough, and consequently Hernu ordered the secret service, via a memo, to step up its intelligence activities to "forecast and anticipate the actions of Greenpeace." The term *anticipate*, which in French can mean "forestall" or "prevent" was underlined twice. Information leaked to the French press indicated that President Mitterrand's military adviser, General Jean Saulnier, authorized a special budget for the operation.[120]

The *Rainbow Warrior* operation ultimately involved at least nine agents of the DGSE. Christine Cabon, who had previously infiltrated the PLO, was assigned to infiltrate the Greenpeace organization in Auckland. Whereas Greenpeace had announced plans to keep the *Rainbow Warrior* stationed off Moruroa for several weeks, the DGSE wanted to know if that was really likely to happen: Was the ship sufficiently equipped for such a stay? How experienced was the crew? Cabon, who successfully insinuated herself into Greenpeace, was able to report on the organization's activities and to collect maps and information on hotels and car rentals. She was also able to advise on ways of counteracting Greenpeace. Another apparent agent, Francois Verlet, appeared on the ship on the night of the explosion, but his exact mission is not clear.[121]

The actual sabotage mission involved seven to nine agents, including its supervisor, "Jean-Louis Dormand"—Colonel Louis Pierre Dillais, head of the French naval special warfare school—who arrived in New Zealand on June 23. Also involved were the four men who sailed into New Zealand on the yacht *Ouvea*. Roland Verges was an eleven-year veteran of the DGSE-based French Naval Training Center for Combat Frogmen (*Centre d'instruction des Naqueurs de Combat*) at Asperetto in Corsica. Gerald Andries, a six-year DGSE veteran, was similarly based at Asperetto. Jean Michael Barcelo was a four-year DGSE veteran. Less clear-cut was the role of Xavier Christian Maniguet, an expert in diving medicine who previously had worked for Francois Verlet's father; at the very least, Maniguet would seem to have been employed by the DGSE for this mission.[122]

The exact nature of these agents' mission is not clear. The *Ouvea* was certainly employed to bring the equipment required for the bombing into New Zealand, off-loading somewhere on the coast before undergoing customs inspection. Among the equipment were explosives, a Zodiac inflatable raft, and a black Yamaha outboard motor. Some accounts suggest that the equipment was later used by one of the *Ouvea* crew to conduct the sabotage operation. Other accounts suggest that a third team—Alain Tonel and Jacques Camurier, according to Michael King—actually conducted the sabotage operation, with the *Ouvea* being a diversion.[123]

Two other agents unquestionably involved in the operation were Major Alain Marfart and Captain Dominque Prieur, who masqueraded as a married couple. In previous assignments Prieur had infiltrated antinuclear groups in Europe and terrorist movements in Africa. Prieur and Marfat's role was apparently to retrieve the material dropped off by the *Ouvea* before it passed through New Zealand customs and to turn it over to the saboteurs. It was their capture that led to the unraveling of the operation. Subsequently, both were sentenced to ten years in jail, although a $9 million settlement between the French and New Zealand governments involved a provision whereby they would serve three years with their families on the Hao atoll in French Polynesia. The largest circulation paper in New Zealand, the *New Zealand Herald*, responded to the settlement with the statement that "the *Rainbow Warrior* aftermath now stands as a contemptible episode of New Zealand history."[124]

In early December 1987 a new chief of the DGSE was appointed— General François Mermet, head of the South Pacific nuclear test site. Later that month Alain Marfart was evacuated from Hao due to an alleged stomach condition. A Royal New Zealand Air Force plane, which would have carried a doctor to examine Marfart, was denied landing rights at the atoll's French military airport.[125]

NOTES TO CHAPTER 6

1. Henri Navarre, *Service de Reinseignment 1871–1944* (Paris: Edition Plon, 1978), p. 15.
2. Ibid., p. 16.
3. Ibid., p. 18.
4. Christopher M. Andrews, "France and the German Menace," in Ernest R. May, ed., *Knowing One's Enemies: Intelligence Assessment Before Two World Wars* (Princeton, N.J.: Princeton University Press, 1984), pp. 127–49 at p. 129.
5. Ibid., pp. 130–31, 135.
6. Navarre, *Service de Renseignment*, p. 26; Andrews, "France and the German Menace," p. 135.
7. Navarre, *Service de Renseignment*, pp. 39–40.
8. Ibid., pp. 40–41.
9. Navarre, *Service de Renseignment*, pp. 42–44.
10. Ibid., p. 44.
11. Laughlin Campbell, "Genesis of the French Service de Documentation Extérieure et de Contre-Espionage," *Foreign Intelligence Literary Scene* 5, no. 3 (1986): 5, 7–8.
12. Navarre, *Service de Renseignment*, pp. 121–22.
13. Robert J. Young, "French Military Intelligence and Nazi Germany, 1938–1939," in Ernest R. May, ed., *Knowing One's Enemies: Intelligence Assessment Before Two World Wars* (Princeton, N.J.: Princeton University Press, 1984), pp. 271–309 at pp. 278–79.
14. P. L. Thyraud de Vosjoli, *Lamia* (Boston: Little, Brown, 1970), p. 71.
15. Ibid., p. 72; Roger Faligot and Pascal Krop, *La Piscine: Les Services Secrets Français 1944–1984* (Paris: Sevil, 1985), p. 24.
16. de Vosjoli, *Lamia*, pp. 71–72, 74; Faligot and Krop, *La Piscine*, pp. 26–28.
17. de Vosjoli, *Lamia*, p. 77.
18. Ibid.
19. Ibid.
20. Ibid., p. 117; Faligot and Krop, *La Piscine*, p. 31.
21. de Vosjoli, *Lamia*, pp. 133–34; Roger Faligot, "The Plot to Unseat Qaddafi," *The Middle East*, August 1981, pp. 32–36.
22. de Vosjoli, *Lamia*, p. 134.
23. Ibid., p. 135.
24. Ibid., pp. 135–36.
25. Faligot, "The Plot to Unseat Qaddafi"; Faligot and Krop, *La Piscine*, p. 322.
26. "Who's Really Who in Espionage," *Newsweek* (International edition), December 15, 1975, pp. 26–27; Faligot, "The Plot to Unseat Qaddafi."

27. "On His Socialists' Secret Service," *The Economist*, November 27, 1982, pp. 43-44.
28. Ibid., "Goodbye to M," *The Economist*, November 20, 1982, pp. 31-32; Bryan Boswell, "Major Shake-up for French Spy Network," *The Weekend Australian*, November 20-21, 1982, p. 13; Paul Lewis, "Paris Spies: Shady Past of Agency," *New York Times*, September 23, 1985, p. A14.
29. "On His Socialists' Secret Service"; "Goodbye to M"; Boswell, "Major Shake-up for French Spy Network"; Lewis, "Paris Spies."
30. Pierre Péan, *Secret d'Etat: La France du Secret, Les Secrets de la France* (Paris: Fayard, 1986), p. 193.
31. Ibid.
32. Lewis, "Paris Spies"; "On His Socialists' Secret Service."
33. "Le Service de Documentation Extérieure et de Contre-Espionage (SDECE)," *Bulletin d'information sur l'Intervention Clandestine* (July-October 1981): 12-14.
34. Michael Dobbs, "Secret Service Under Fire," *Washington Post*, August 29, 1985, pp. A1, A16.
35. Jean-Marie Pontaut, "Du SDECE à la DGSE: Les Vagues de la Piscine," *L'Express*, August 23, 1985, pp. 25-27; "France's Secret Services," *Foreign Report*, October 10, 1985, pp. 1-3.
36. "Mitterrand Ordering Intelligence Shuffle in Greenpeace Case," *New York Times*, September 20, 1985, pp. A1, A11.
37. "Giscard Ordered U.S. Delegates Bugged, Former Spy Says," *Sydney Morning Herald*, November 26, 1980.
38. Ibid.; Faligot and Krop, *La Piscine*, p. 191.
39. Faligot and Krop, *La Piscine*, p. 193.
40. Ibid., p. 216.
41. de Vosjoli, *Lamia*, p. 286.
42. Ibid.
43. Ibid., p. 296.
44. Steven R. Weisman, "3 Frenchmen Linked to Indian Spy Case," *New York Times*, January 24, 1985, p. A3.
45. Ibid.; Sanjoy Hazarika, "France Recalls Aide in India After Report of Spying Link," *New York Times*, January 21, 1985, p. A9.
46. Péan, *Secret d'Etat*, p. 204.
47. Ibid., p. 207.
48. Faligot and Krop, *La Piscine*, pp. 100-4.
49. Ibid., p. 209.
50. de Vosjoli, *Lamia*, pp. 255-56.
51. Ibid., pp. 256-57.
52. Ibid., p. 261.
53. Lewis, "Paris Spies"; Faligot and Krop, *La Piscine*, pp. 212-13, 219.
54. de Vosjoli, *Lamia*, p. 272.

55. Ibid., pp. 272-73.
56. Ibid., p. 273.
57. Ibid., p. 274.
58. Ibid., pp. 274-77.
59. "New Facts: The Murder of Ben Barka," *Time*, December 29, 1975, pp. 8-11.
60. Ibid.
61. Ibid.
62. Faligot and Krop, *La Piscine*, pp. 150-51.
63. Ibid., p. 245.
64. Ibid., p. 248.
65. Faligot, "The Plot to Unseat Qaddafi."
66. Ibid.
67. Ibid.
68. Ibid.
69. Seymour Hersh, "Target Qaddafi," *New York Times*, February 22, 1987, pp. 16ff.
70. Faligot and Krop, *La Piscine*, pp. 321-22.
71. Ibid., p. 158.
72. Péan, *Secret d'Etat*, pp. 212, 218; Faligot and Krop, *La Piscine*, p. 322.
73. "Schema des Services De Renseignements en France," *Bulletin d'Information sur l'Intervention Clandestine* (July-October 1981): 12.
74. de Vosjoli, *Lamia*, p. 308.
75. Bill Gunston, *An Illustrated Guide to Spy Planes and Electronic Warfare Aircraft* (New York: Arco, 1985), pp. 22-23.
76. Ibid., pp. 18-21.
77. "France Plans Service Start with Elint/ESM C-160 Transalls," *Aviation Week and Space Technology*, August 4, 1986, p. 161; "French Air Force Modified C-160s for ELINT/ESM Mission," *Aviation Week and Space Technology*, February 16, 1987, p. 90.
78. Michèle Chevrel, Michel Courtois, and Gilbert Weill, "The SPOT Satellite Remote Sensing Mission," *Photogrammetric Engineering and Remote Sensing* 47, no. 8 (August 1981): 1163-71.
79. *Satellite-Based Remote Sensing* (Washington, D.C.: SPOT Image, 1985); "France Puts America on the SPOT," *Space World*, June 1984, pp. 27-28.
80. Jeffrey M. Lenorovitz, "France to Fund the Additional SPOT Remote Sensing Satellites," *Aviation Week and Space Technology*, August 5, 1985, pp. 74-75; "Industry Observer," *Aviation Week and Space Technology*, May 26, 1986, p. 13.
81. "French Propose Reduced Defense Spending," *Aviation Week and Space Technology*, September 27, 1982, p. 22; "French to Propose Satellite Imaging System," *Aviation Week and Space Technology*, July 9, 1984, p. 61.

82. "French Proposed Reduced Defense Spending."
83. "French to Propose Satellite Imaging System"; "French Germans Study Recon Satellite Plan," *Aviation Week and Space Technology*, June 4, 1984, p. 23; Sergio Rossi, "Talks Launch French-Italian Cooperation to Build Satellite," *Defense News*, February 7, 1987.
84. Rossi, "Talks Launch French-Italian Cooperation"; Jim Wolf, "French Plan for Joint Satellite Operations," *Jane's Defence Weekly*, October 18, 1986, p. 850.
85. Rossi, "Talks Launch French-Italian Cooperation to Build Satellite"; "Italy to Share in French Satellite System," *Aviation Week and Space Technology*, June 22, 1987, p. 66.
86. "France Studying Synthetic Aperture Radar Satellite," *Aviation Week and Space Technology*, May 11, 1987, p. 34.
87. Péan, *Secret d'Etat*, p. 71.
88. Ibid.
89. Péan, *Secret d'Etat*, p. 214; Daniel Southerland, "Spy Wars: France, the Height of International Intrigue," *Christian Science Monitor*, September 24, 1980, pp. 11ff.; "On His Socialists' Secret Service"; Franco-Iranian Embassy Wars Continue," *Defense Electronics*, October 1987, p. 18.
90. Edward Cody, "Soviet Diplomats Ousted After French Spy Arrests," *Washington Post*, April 3, 1987, pp. A29, A30.
91. Péan, *Secret d'Etat*, pp. 119-21.
92. Paul Lewis, "K.G.B. Figure Called a Spy for France," *New York Times*, January 8, 1986, p. 3.
93. Thierry Wolton, *Le KGB en France* (Paris: Bernard Grasset, 1986), pp. 248-49.
94. Lewis, "K.G.B. Figure Called a Spy for France."
95. Lewis, "K.G.B. Figure Called a Spy for France."
96. Ibid.; Michael Dobbs, "France Expels 4 Soviet Officials for Espionage," *Washington Post*, February 4, 1986, p. A11.
97. "French Seize 6 on Suspicion of Spying on Ariane Rocket," *Washington Times*, March 20, 1987, p. 12B; Richard Bernstein, "France Accuses 6 of Rocket Spying," *New York Times*, March 21, 1987, p. 3; Tom Nuzum, "Spies' Haul at ESA Could Be Extensive," *Washington Times*, March 23, 1987, p. 8B; Paul Lewis, "France Ousts 3 Soviet Diplomats It Calls Spies," *New York Times*, April 3, 1987, p. A7.
98. "The Bombs of September," *Time*, September 29, 1986, pp. 40-42; Edward Cody, "French Arrest Key Terrorists," *Washington Post*, February 23, 1987, pp. A1, A10.
99. Paul Lewis, "French Intelligence Aide Plays Down Terror Role of Suspect," *New York Times*, February 26, 1987, p. A6; Richard Bernstein, "Trial of Suspected Terrorist Leader Opens in Paris Today After 2½ Years," *New York Times*, February 23, 1987; Paul Lewis, "Slain Diplo-

mat's Wife Says French Ignored Leads," *New York Times*, February 25, 1987, p. A9; Richard Bernstein, "Paris Said to Seek Deal with Syrians to Curb Terrorism," *New York Times*, October 30, 1986, pp. A1, A3.

100. "On His Socialists' Secret Service"; Southerland, "Spy Wars"; Faligot and Krop, *La Piscine*, p. 291.

101. "On His Socialists' Secret Service"; André Pacquier, "Les Renseignements Généraux," *Bulletin d'Information sur l'Intervention Clandestine* (July–October 1981): 25–28.

102. Ibid.

103. "La Communauté Francaise du Reinseignement," *Bulletin d'Information Sur l'Intervention Clandestine* (July-October 1981): 11; U.S. Army Intelligence and Threat Analysis Center, *France: A Counterintelligence Assessment* (Washington, D.C.: ITAC, 1984), p. xi.

104. Heinz Höhne and Hermann Zolling, *The General Was a Spy* (New York: Coward, McCann and Geohagen, 1971), p. 187.

105. Ibid.

106. Reinhard Gehlen, *The Service: The Memoirs of General Reinhard Gehlen* (New York: World Publishing, 1972), p. 258).

107. Ken Lawrence, "PIDE and SDECE Plotting in Guinea," in Ellen Ray, William Schaap, Karl van Meter, and Louis Wolf, *Dirty Work 2: The CIA in Africa* (Secaucus, N.J.: Lyle Stuart, 1979), pp. 140–45.

108. Ibid.

109. Richard Deacon, *The Chinese Secret Service* (New York: Ballantine, 1976), p. 418.

110. Faligot and Krop, *La Piscine*, p. 325.

111. de Vosjoli, *Lamia*, p. 216.

112. Ibid.

113. Ibid., pp. 301–2.

114. Ibid., p. 302.

115. Ibid., pp. 304–5.

116. Ibid., p. 307.

117. Hersh, "Target Qaddafi"; Bernard E. Trainor, "France and U.S. Aiding Chadians with Information to Rout Libyans," *New York Times*, April 3, 1987, p. A5; James Dorsey, "U.S. Barred from Chad Intelligence," *Washington Times*, April 28, 1987, p. 10A; "U.S., France Analyze Captured Mi-24," *Aviation Week and Space Technology*, May 18, 1987, p. 19.

118. Sunday Times Insight Team, *Rainbow Warrior* (London: Hutchinson, 1986), p. 20; Michael King, *The Death of the Rainbow Warrior* (London: Penguin, 1986), pp. 11, 48.

119. King, *Death of the Rainbow Warrior*, p. 48.

120. Sunday Times Insight Team, *Rainbow Warrior*, pp. 161–63, 176; John Dyson, *Sink the Rainbow!* (London: Gollancz, 1986), pp. 91, 93; U.S.

Army Intelligence and Threat Analysis Center, *Greenpeace: Repercussions in the French I&SS* (Washington, D.C.: ITAC, 1986), p. 3.

121. King, *Death of the Rainbow Warrior*, pp. 49–50, 64; Sunday Times Insight Team, *Rainbow Warrior*, p. 188.

122. King, *Death of the Rainbow Warrior*, p. 63; Sunday Times Insight Team, *Rainbow Warrior*, p. 207.

123. King, *Death of the Rainbow Warrior*, pp. 75, 108.

124. "Killing of Agents Was Feared, Lange Says," *Los Angeles Times*, July 9, 1986, p. 9.

125. "French Secret Service Gets New Leader," *Washington Times*, December 3, 1987, p. A2; Edward Cody, "New Zealand Angered By Paris," *Washington Post*, December 15, 1987, p. A33.

7 ISRAELI INTELLIGENCE ORGANIZATIONS

ORIGINS

The Israeli intelligence community of today can trace its origins to the underground organizations that existed during the days of the British Mandate in Palestine. The Haganah, the Zionist underground resistance force, maintained the *Sherut Yedioth*, or Information Service, which came to be known as the SHAI. The SHAI had begun to engage in worldwide operations in 1929, with the founding of the Jewish Agency at the Zionist Congress in Zurich.[1]

From 1929 to 1948, the SHAI's objectives were to promote the establishment of an independent state of Israel; to infiltrate British Mandate offices in order to inform the Jewish/Zionist leadership of British attitudes and proposed actions; to collect political intelligence that could be used in Zionist propaganda; to penetrate Arab and anti-Zionist factions in Palestine and surrounding countries; to monitor and control all extremist groups—left and right—among Jewish communities in Palestine and abroad; to provide security for the arms-smuggling and illegal immigration programs of the Haganah; and to collect information on Nazi Germany in order to guarantee the security of Jewish underground and escape channels throughout Europe before, during, and after the Second World War.[2]

The Jewish Division of the SHAI was responsible for surveillance of Jews within Palestine, particularly the rivals of the Haganah.

191

Among the rival organizations subject to SHAI surveillance were the extreme right-wing nationalist group Irgun Zevai Leumi and a breakaway movement from Irgun—the Stern Gang.[3]

Against the British Mandate target, SHAI had considerable success. SHAI agents penetrated customs, police, the postal services, and offices dealing with transport. One consequence was that the Arab guerilla forces had far more of their arms seized than the Haganah did, since SHAI agents were able to provide information of police knowledge of Haganah arms-smuggling activities.[4]

Another institution involved in pre-independence covert operations was the *Mossad le Aliyah Bet*, or Institute of Immigration B. Immigration A was the legal channel for immigration into Palestine as permitted by the British authorities. Because of the small number of immigrants permitted by the British—in 1939 it was announced that seventy-five thousand Jews would be permitted to enter Palestine between 1939 and 1944, and afterward none without Arab consent—the Jewish Agency resorted to Immigration B, illegal immigration. It was the job of the Mossad, operating both in Palestine and abroad, to facilitate this immigration. In Europe the Mossad consisted of exactly ten persons distributed over a half-dozen countries—France, Switzerland, Austria, Romania, Bulgaria, and Turkey. These agents would arrange escape routes, false passports, safe houses, and chartered ships to take the illegal immigrants to Palestine, all without being detected by the British intelligence and security authorities.[5]

Other intelligence, security, and covert operations agencies included Rekhesh, which was responsible for acquiring arms from overseas for the Jewish underground forces. Rekhesh agents set up dummy corporations, assumed false identities, and gained the experience needed to operate as members of a secret intelligence service. The Palmach, an elite full-time military formation, was the strike arm of the Haganah. Its Arab section trained Jewish youths to live and work as Arabs inside the Arab townships. Its maritime branch, Palyam, placed some of its members as mates to the various foreign captains of illegal immigrant ships so as to keep watch on the captains to ensure that no double crosses occurred. Subsequently, Palyam formed the basis of Israel's first naval intelligence service.[6]

On May 14, 1948, Israel became an independent state and on June 30, 1948, began to establish a national intelligence community. The SHAI was disbanded, and the Israeli Defense Forces (IDF) issued an official order creating a military intelligence service as a subdivision of the Operations Branch of the IDF's General Staff. In addition, a classified organization—the Political Department—was organized within the Foreign Ministry and given the mission of collecting intelligence on a worldwide basis. Finally, the *Sherut Bitachon Klali*, or General Security Service, was established to perform internal security functions: counterespionage and countersubversion. The organization is commonly known as SHABAK, a contraction of *Sherut Bitachon Klali*, or Shin Beth, for the first letters of "Security Service" in Hebrew.[7]

The year 1951 saw a major change in the Israeli intelligence structure. Rivals of the Political Department charged that its agents were engaging more in high-living than in intelligence collection. The coordinator of the secret services carried the complaints, which may not have been justified, to the foreign minister, who in turn authorized the coordinator to come up with a solution. The result was dissolution of the Political Department, replacing it with a Research Department charged with researching and studying political questions but stripped of an overseas intelligence network.[8]

The decision of the coordinator, Ruben Shiloach, may not have been based on the validity of the charges against the Political Department. Shiloach had recently been to Washington, where he had been introduced to the workings of the young Central Intelligence Agency. On his return he told Prime Minister David Ben-Gurion that the CIA was breaking new ground in espionage techniques and that Israel needed a similar agency, an independent agency responsible only to the Prime Minister. The Political Department was an impediment to achieving that objective.[9]

Thus, on September 1, 1951, Ben-Gurion issued a directive establishing the *Mossad Letafkidim Meouychadim*—the Central Institute for Intelligence and Special Duties—which has come to be known simply as the Mossad. The Mossad's initial role in special operations was to approve or reject the operations proposed by military intelligence, with military intelligence doing the planning and nominating the targets. In 1953 the status of military intelligence was raised, and it became an independent branch, the *Agaf Modiin* (AMAN), or Intelligence Branch, of the General Staff, with an expanded mission.[10]

Sometime in the mid-1960s another intelligence organization was created to collect scientific and technical intelligence via both open and covert sources. The *Leshkat Kesher Madao* (LEKEM), or Bureau of Scientific Relations, was established by Shimon Peres during his tenure in the Defense Ministry. LEKEM conducted research in science and technology and routinely posted employees to foreign countries to gather data on scientific and technological developments, including those related to weapons systems. LEKEM also nominated the scientific attachés who served in Israeli embassies.[11]

In one instance LEKEM acquired blueprints for essential parts of the Mirage fighter-bomber. As a result of the Six-Day War in June 1967, Israel had lost nineteen planes—10 percent of its Air Force. Israeli defense requirements necessitated that the surviving planes—French Mirage fighter bombers and Mystere fighters—be kept flying until Israel could acquire more or develop its own home-built aircraft. France, however, refused to lift the embargo it had imposed against Israel after the beginning of the war. An attempt to get France to lift the embargo in exchange for information on the performance of the Mirage in the Six-Day War failed. Israel next approached the Swiss government in an attempt to buy spare jet engine parts that could be used in the surviving planes, offering a down payment of 150 million Swiss francs. The Swiss declined because their agreement with the French government prohibited the unauthorized resale of the parts.[12]

LEKEM was able to acquire the blueprints from a Swiss engineer, Alfred Frauenknecht, for $200,000—a fraction of the sum LEKEM would have been willing to pay. Frauenknecht was employed by the Swiss company Sulzer of Winterthor, which had been awarded a contract for building the jet engines to be used in the Mirages being built by the Swiss government under a licensing arrangement with the planes' French manufacturer, Dassault.[13]

Among Frauenknecht's responsibilities was supervision of the incineration of the no-longer-needed blueprints for the Mirage engine machine tools. Every Thursday approximately 110 pounds of the photographed blueprints were packed into cartons and loaded into a Volkswagen van destined for the city incinerator. The van, driven by Frauenknecht's cousin, stopped at a garage located between the Sulzer plant and the incinerator and switched Mirage blueprints for old blueprint patent applications that Frauenknecht had purchased and stored at the garage.[14]

On Saturdays the Mirage plans were loaded into the van and driven in the direction of the Swiss-German border and Kaiseraugst. There the cargo was unloaded in a warehouse belonging to a Swiss transport firm, and an Israeli agent was alerted that the delivery had been made. The agent then transported the documents to West Germany by car, to an airfield in Italy by plane, and to Israel by El-Al. The operation lasted from mid-1968 to Frauenknecht's arrest in September 1969.[15]

As became known in 1985, LEKEM offices had been established at Israeli consulates in New York, Boston, and Los Angeles. Further, LEKEM was running an agent within the U.S. intelligence community—Jonathan J. Pollard, who had served in several naval intelligence units. As a result of the exposure of the Pollard operation, LEKEM was dismantled and its responsibilities probably divided between the Ministry of Science and Technology and the Ministry of Defense.[16]

With the dissolution of LEKEM, the Israeli intelligence community in the late 1980s consists of the same organizations as in the early 1960s: the Mossad, AMAN, Air Force and Navy intelligence units, the Foreign Ministry's Research and Political Planning Center, and Shin Beth.

INTELLIGENCE AND SECURITY ORGANIZATIONS

Central Institute for Intelligence and Special Duties (MOSSAD)

The Mossad is responsible for human intelligence collection, covert action, and counterterrorism. Its principal function is to conduct operations against Arab nations and organizations, their official representatives, and their installations throughout the world but particularly in Western Europe and the United States. The Mossad collects information on Arab military forces—their disposition, morale, armaments, and leadership. It also collects information on the internal politics of and relationships among the principal Arab leaders and on the diplomatic activity of Arab nations. In addition, the Mossad monitors Arab commercial activity, particularly with respect to arms purchases in the West, and attempts to counteract Arab recruitment of military, economic, and political experts. Covert action responsibilities of the Mossad include inciting disturbances calculated to create mutual distrust among Arab states and monitoring and counteracting Arab propaganda.[17]

Other targets of Mossad operations include the Soviet bloc and Western nations as well as activity at the United Nations. In the Soviet Union and Eastern Europe, Mossad intelligence objectives center on determining governmental policy toward Israel, dealing with the problem of Jewish emigration, and recruiting agents in those countries' bureaucracies. In addition, the Mossad seeks to determine the extent and nature of Soviet assistance made available to Arab organizations and nations.[18]

In the Western countries the Mossad collects information about Western, Vatican, and UN policies toward the Near East. It also promotes arms deals for the benefit of the IDF and obtains information for use in silencing groups opposed to Israeli policies in the West. In the United States the Mossad seeks to collect scientific and technical intelligence, gain information about Arab military capabilities, and acquire knowledge of secret U.S. policy decisions concerning the Middle East[19] —such as the Reagan administration's National Security Decision Directives.

As indicated in Figure 7-1, the Mossad, as of 1977, was organized into eight departments: Operational Planning and Coordination; Collection; Political Action and Liaison; Manpower, Finance, Logistics, and Security; Training; Research; Technical Operations; and Technology.[20]

The Operational Planning and Coordination Department is responsible for managing the Mossad's resources, coordinating internal activities and liaison with other elements of the Israeli intelligence community, and handling the requirements and development of overall collection plans. The Collection Department is responsible for overseeing foreign espionage operations and processing the reports obtained; it is the largest unit within the Mossad and has offices abroad under both diplomatic and nonofficial cover. The Political Action and Liaison Department is in charge of political action and relations with friendly foreign intelligence services. It also maintains contact with those nations and political groups with whom Israel does not have normal diplomatic relations, such as Lebanon, Indonesia, and a number of African nations. Apparently subordinate to the department is a Special Operations Division that runs highly sensitive covert action operations against Arab terrorists and former Nazi officials, its operations entailing sabotage, paramilitary, and psychological warfare projects.[21]

Figure 7-1. Organization of the Mossad, 1977.

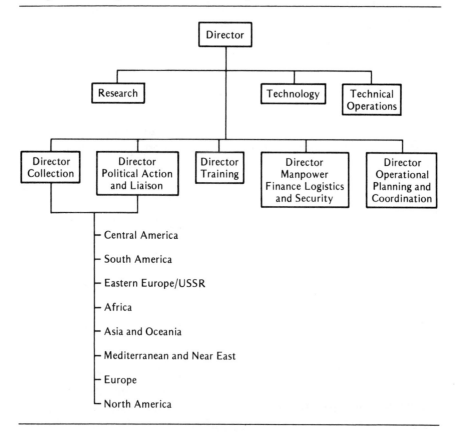

Under the joint control of the Collection Department and the Political Action and Liaison Department are eight regional departments: Central America, South America, Eastern Europe/USSR, Africa, Asia and Oceania, the Mediterranean and Near East, Europe, and North America. Larger stations utilize either two Mossad stations or two compartmentalized components in a single station, one for clandestine collection and one for political action and liaison. In Paris, for example, the Mossad has, under embassy cover, a Collection Department regional controller and a Political Action and Liaison Department regional controller. Mossad stations are located in the United States, in most European capitals, and in the Soviet Union, Turkey, and Iran; strategic centers are located in Africa, the

Far East, and Latin America. The MOSSAD African stations include ones in Khartoum (Sudan) and Abidjan (Ivory Coast), the latter controlling the MOSSAD's West African activities. Stations in Asia include those in Bangkok, Jakarta (operated under commercial cover), and Singapore (the main MOSSAD station in that area). Latin American stations include those in Haiti and Tegucigalpa (Honduras). These stations are generally under diplomatic cover within Israeli consulates and embassies.[22]

As is the case with other countries, Israeli human intelligence operations come to public attention only when an agent is detected. In two cases during the 1960s, detection occurred only after the agent provided the Mossad with significant information.

In 1960 the Mossad recruited Eli Cohen and began to train him for an undercover role in Damascus. Cohen was given a new name—Kamil Amin Taabes—and a new background: He was to be the son of a Syrian who had moved to Lebanon but never renounced his Syrian citizenship. Indeed, the father always urged Taabes to return to his homeland. Instead, Taabes first went to Argentina, joining a brother in the textile business in Buenos Aires. Although the business failed, Taabes proceeded to develop an extremely successful export-import firm in Argentina; still, he desired to return to Syria.[23]

Rather than simply arrive in Damascus with such a story (which a superficial check would show to be a fake), Cohen's first step was to establish himself in Buenos Aires and make contacts within the Syrian community. He did so with astonishing success. Among his many contacts was General Amin el-Hafez, the Syrian military attaché in Argentina and a prominent figure in the rising Ba'ath party. Hafez encouraged Taabes to return to Syria, which he did on January 10, 1962, arriving with letters of introduction from many of his prominent contacts.[24]

Once in Syria, Cohen quickly established himself in the export business and developed a circle of high-level friends. Included were George Seif, head of the radio and press section of the Ministry of Propaganda and Information; Colonel Salim Hatoum; Lieutenant Maazi Zahreddin, nephew of the chief of staff of the Syrian Army; and the returned and soon-to-be-president General Amin el-Hafez.[25]

Through his contacts Cohen was able to accumulate a massive amount of high-level information. In February 1963 Hatoum informed Taabes of an impending coup d'état and in March 1964 showed him a plan of the Israeli Galilee-Negev irrigation system and where Syrian saboteurs were planning to destroy the system. Even more useful were Lieutenant Zahreddin's numerous guided tours of Syria's Golan Heights fortifications; here Taabes was allowed to see areas that an unauthorized person would be shot for entering. Further, because he was accompanied by Zahreddin, commanding officers were willing to show Taabes anything he requested. He was able, on occasion, to extensively tour the deep concrete bunkers built by Syria to house the long-range artillery received from the Soviet Union. On one trip he counted eighty of the latest Soviet 122-millimeter mortars dug in place on the western slope of the Golan Heights. In addition, he was permitted to take photographs looking toward the Jordan Valley, thereby enabling the IDF to determine exactly where the mortars were located and precisely where they were aimed.[26]

In 1964 Cohen sent to the Mossad detailed plans of the entire fortification system defending the key town of Kuneitra. His information included the size, position, and depth of the concrete gun emplacements and the precise siting of the deep trenches in which tanks and other armored vehicles were to be hidden from air attack. Another of his reports concerned the arrival of more than two hundred T-54 tanks, the first such tanks to be sent from the Soviet Union to the Middle East. Subsequently, Cohen provided the Mossad with copies of the entire set of Soviet-devised plans on how Syria would attempt to cut off the northern segment of Israel in the event of a surprise attack. Close-up photographs of the MIG-21 followed.[27]

In January 1965 Cohen was detected by Syrian counterintelligence while in the midst of broadcasting to Tel Aviv. His use of hand Morse radio equipment and extended transmitting time (an hour) apparently contributed to his downfall. Tried and found guilty of espionage, Cohen was publicly hanged in Damascus in May 1965.[28]

Wolfgang Lotz was recruited for a special assignment by the Mossad in 1959. Lotz had emigrated to Palestine with his mother in 1933 and acquired the Hebrew name Zeev Gur Arieh. After being recruited, Lotz received intensive training, including equestrian instruction, in Israel and in early 1960 went to Germany, surfacing as an East German refugee and former African Corps officer. In 1961 he went to Cairo, where he opened a riding academy.[29]

Like Eli Cohen, Lotz was able to establish a circle of high-level friends. Among them were Colonel Abdel Rahman, deputy head of Military Intelligence; Admiral Fawzi Moneim; General Favad Osman, chief of security for Egypt's rocket sites; General Salaam Suleiman; and Youssef Ghorab of the General Police. Other high officials—for example, then General Anwar el-Sadat—although not close friends, attended Lotz's parties.[30]

Lotz's friendship with Osman enabled him to acquire a number of military secrets. In one instance he was able to get an invitation from Osman to tour SAM (surface-to-air missile) rocket bases and see the launching pads in Sinai and on the Negev frontier. Osman was even kind enough to pose in front of one of the new rockets on its launching pad so that Lotz could snap a photograph.[31]

Lotz was also able to obtain a complete list of German scientists living in Cairo, their addresses, the location of their families in Germany and Austria, and their role in the Egyptian rocket and armaments programs. He also provided the Mossad with a microfilm of the blueprints of "project 333" for the design of electronic control systems for Egyptian missiles.[32]

In February 1965 Lotz was arrested. Subsequently, he was tried and imprisoned. In 1968 he was released and returned to Israel in exchange for Egyptian POWs captured in the June 1967 Six-Day War.[33] (The information provided by Eli Cohen played a significant role in Israel's quick victory in 1967.)

It has been reported that information provided by another Mossad agent could have helped Israel avoid the initial setbacks suffered in the 1973 Yom Kippur War. This agent allegedly traveled across Europe and the Middle East under the cover of a professor of languages and arrived on October 4 at Lod airport with a complete set of photostats of the Egyptian-Syrian war plans, as well as the date and time of attack and the code name of the operation, "Badr." Reportedly, the chief of the Mossad believed in the validity of the documents, but Prime Minister Golda Meir and Defense Minister Moshe Dayan considered them disinformation.[34]

In addition to agents such as those described above, the Mossad makes constant efforts to recruit as informants Arabs who are going abroad. Palestinians from the West Bank applying for exit papers to travel and work in Persian Gulf states or other parts of the Arab world may be told by Israeli agents that they must agree to provide information about the country in question in return for their papers. Some are promised money if they cooperate, prison if they do not.[35]

Since the time of Cohen and Lotz, a new aspect of the "Arab target" has appeared in the form of the Palestine Liberation Organization and its offshoots (acknowledged and unacknowledged) as well as OPEC. The PLO is, obviously, a major target, and aspects of its operations that undoubtedly prompt Mossad investigation include internal policy debates and power struggles, relations and aid agreements with foreign governments, and propaganda, training, and planned terrorist activities. Such investigations can be expected to involve Mossad agents in the Soviet bloc, the Middle East, the United States, Western Europe, and elsewhere.

In addition to acquiring intelligence, the Mossad also seeks to acquire military-related equipment, in some cases to allow the analysis of enemy equipment and the design of countermeasures, and in other cases to enhance Israeli capabilities. Among the equipment the Mossad obtained in the 1960s was a MIG-21.

In 1961 the Soviet Union, under conditions of tight security, began introducing the MIG-21 into the Middle East; by early 1963, the plane was in service with the Egyptian, Iraqi, Syrian air forces. Little information about the plane's characteristics or capabilities was available. Israeli intelligence did not know its speed, armaments, performance capabilities, instrumentation, or defensive equipment.[36]

Subsequently, the Mossad was approached by a representative of an Iraqi pilot who offered to fly the plane to Israel for a half-million pounds and a guarantee to bring the pilot's entire family out of Iraq. The Mossad accepted the offer, and on August 15, 1966, the defecting pilot made it over the Turkish border before his escape was detected. After a refueling stop at a secret CIA base in Turkey, the pilot made his way out of Turkey and out over the Mediterranean, where Israeli fighters waited to escort him to Israel.[37]

The Mossad was also employed to circumvent a French embargo. In 1968 at the French port of Cherbourg, eight missile boats were under construction. The builder was Germany and the client was Israel. However, in response to a December 28, 1968, raid by Israeli commandos on Beirut airport and their destruction of thirteen planes—in retaliation for Palestinian attacks on El-Al aircraft—President Charles de Gaulle instructed French customs officials that no French military cargo was to be permitted to leave for Israel. Included were the boats at Cherbourg.[38]

One week later—on January 4, 1969, at 5:00 P.M.—skeleton crews boarded the three missile boats that were almost completed. The Israeli crew members calmly spent three hours of intensive effort to get the boats ready for a sea voyage. When they had completed their preparations and the motors were warmed up, they raised the Israeli flag and sailed off. As a result, the remaining five boats were placed under tight security. Nevertheless, work continued to obtain the boats despite the high level of security as the Mossad initiated Operation Noah's Ark.[39]

The head of the Cherbourg shipyards was informed that Israel no longer desired the boats but wanted them sold off, with Israel reimbursed out of the proceeds of the sale. Shortly afterward, the head of the Cherbourg shipyards was visited by a man who identified himself as Martin Siem, a construction company owner and director of the Norwegian shipping company Starboat and Weill, who claimed to be interested in buying the boats for use in oil exploration. Delivery was requested as soon as possible.[40]

The sale was approved by the Interministerial Committee for the Study of the Export of War Materials. As a result, sailors began arriving at Cherbourg—ostensibly Norwegian and French sailors but in actuality Mossad employees. On Christmas Eve 1969 they sailed the boats out into the English Channel and on to Israel.[41]

Just two days later, the Mossad engineered an even more spectacular acquisition. On December 27, 1969, Israeli commandos landed at the Egyptian naval base at Ras Ghaleb on the Red Sea. After killing the sentries, the commandos disassembled a seven-ton P-12 SPOON REST radar system. This system, which had been installed at Ras Ghaleb to complete Egyptian early warning radar coverage, was capable of detecting an aircraft taking off from an Israeli airbase on the other side of the Suez Canal and tracking it until it was within range of a Fansong SAM-2 radar. The disassembled system was loaded onto helicopters that airlifted the radar and its crew to Israel.[42]

Probably the most important Israeli acquisition was that of nuclear material, apparently acquired in 1965 and 1968. In 1965, the Nuclear Materials and Equipment Corporation, a small nuclear processing plant in Apollo, Pennsylvania, was unable to account for 381.6 pounds of highly enriched uranium, enough to serve as raw material for ten nuclear bombs. Although Zalman A. Shapiro, the founder and first president of the company, repeatedly maintained that the uranium had been lost naturally during processing, the belief of government and private experts is that it may have been transferred to Israel.[43]

In 1968 Israel successfully conducted Operation Plumbat, which had as its objective the acquisition of two hundred tons of uranium oxide from the Société Générale de Belgique, the parent company of Belgonucleaire. Acquisition of the uranium had to be accomplished covertly. Because Israel's Dimona nuclear reactor was not open to international inspection, Euratom, the Common Market nuclear agency, would not have permitted the sale. Hence, Israel had to find a front company to buy the material.[44]

A small West German chemical firm, Asmara Chemie, was induced to serve as the front, telling Euratom that it was about to begin the mass production of petrochemicals and wanted to use the uranium as a chemical catalyst. With the backing of the Société Générale de Belgique, Euratom approved the sale in October 1968. Euratom also agreed that the uranium could undergo special processing and gave permission for Asmara Chemie to send it by ship to Genoa and then on to a paint and chemical company in Milan.[45]

The task of transporting the uranium was assigned to a Turkish-born shipowner who had worked with the Israelis since 1947. The ship he found was the Scheersberg, a ten-year-old, 2,600-ton German-built vessel. In Antwerp the Scheersberg took on 560 specially sealed oil drums marked "Plumbat." Instead of heading for Genoa, however, the Scheersberg headed straight for the eastern Mediterranean between Cyprus and Turkey. According to one account, the ship then transferred the uranium cargo to an Israeli freighter escorted by armed gunboats.[46]

The Mossad also performs a variety of covert action operations, the least violent of which are its political liaison and propaganda activities. The Mossad has often been the vehicle by which Israel maintains contact with governments that do not officially recognize Israel. Since 1967, when the USSR closed its embassy in Tel Aviv, the countries have maintained contact through the Mossad. In spring 1979 the Mossad organized a secret trade mission to China to discuss the interest of the People's Republic of China in acquiring sophisticated technology from Israel. Other nations that Israel maintains contact with via the Mossad reportedly include Ethiopia, Kenya, Zaire, Senegal, Albania, Chile, Argentina, and Turkey.[47]

The Mossad also seeks to plant news stories and analyses that support Israeli foreign and defense policy and discredit and disrupt hostile Arab governments and organizations. One possible example was a report on terrorist activities in Germany, published in the German magazine *Quick* a few weeks after the massacre of Israeli athletes at the 1972 Olympics in Munich. The report revealed new details about the operations of the Fatah and Black September groups; it included a photograph of the man said to be the planner of the massacre and the chief of operations for Black September. Publication of the article, which many German journalists believed was planted by the Mossad, led federal authorities to round up and expel a thousand young Palestinians suspected of having links with terrorist organizations.[48]

A decade earlier the Mossad had been involved in planting stories about Egypt's rocket program. On July 21, 1962, Egypt launched four missiles, developed by German scientists, approximately a year after Israel had tested its first missile. Egyptian President Gamal Abdel Nasser boasted that the missiles had a range of 175 to 350 miles, which would allow them to hit any target "south of Beirut." The Mossad responded by planting numerous stories that the German scientists were producing more than rockets—atom bombs, death rays, chemical warfare microbes, and other exotic weapons that would endanger Israel's survival.[49]

Also among the least violent of Mossad covert action operations is training. The Mossad, along with former British Army commanders, was involved in training Sri Lanka's security forces as part of a 1984 drive by the government to combat the violent Tamil separatist movement in the North. The training programs aimed to overhaul the organization of intelligence gathering, build an effective intelligence-gathering network, and train a paramilitary unit to combat Tamil insurgents. Israel was asked to carry out the training program after the United States, Britain, and West Germany had rejected official requests. About ten Israeli agents trained about one hundred Ceylonese in intelligence tactics in July and August 1984.[50]

The Mossad has supplied arms to various groups and governments. One recipient has been post-Shah Iran, an arrangement the Israelis see as a means of keeping Iraq occupied. Former Carter administration officials have reportedly said that in late 1980 Israel secretly sold to Iran 250 spare tires for American-built F-4 fighter bombers. Between late January 1981 and early 1982, Mossad is reported to have sold between $50 million and $70 million in arms to Iran. In

July 1981 Iran contracted with Israel for the supply, for $27.9 million, of some 360 tons of American-made tank parts and ammunition; they were to be shipped in twelve planeloads, going from Cyprus to Teheran on an Argentine-chartered aircraft. In April 1985 a CIA evaluation stated that Israel was supplying Iran with ammunition for 155-millimeter mortars, spare parts for M60 tanks and tires, and spare parts for Phantom jet fighters.[51] As became known in 1986, Israel served as a go-between in the U.S. attempt to trade arms for hostages with Iran.

At the same time that the Mossad is aiding Iran in its war with Iraq, it may also be aiding Kurdish separatists who wish to break away from Iran. If so, it would not be the first time the Mossad aided Kurdish separatists. Almost as soon as the Hashemite king of Iraq was deposed in a military coup in 1958, the Mossad sent materiel and senior advisers to help the Kurds, some of whom were trained in Israel. Such support apparently continued for a significant period of time with the approval of the Shah of Iran, since Iran was involved in a border dispute with Iraq. The head of the Mossad is said to have entered Iraq secretly and met with Mustafa Barzani, the leader of the rebels. In 1975 the border dispute was settled with the understanding that Iran would stop transshipping Israeli supplies to the Kurds.[52]

Sabotage is apparently also among the covert actions undertaken by the Mossad. In April 1979 a bomb ripped through a warehouse in Seine-sur-Mer, France, where the core structures for the Osirak and Isis nuclear reactors were awaiting shipment to Iraq. Although responsibility for the blast was claimed by the previously unknown "French Ecological Group," French officials speculated that Israeli agents were the actual culprits.[53]

Among the more violent activities engaged in by the Mossad are kidnapping and assassination. One of the most famous Mossad operations was the kidnapping of Nazi war criminal Adolf Eichmann from Argentina in 1960. In 1986 the Mossad ran a sophisticated operation that resulted in the kidnapping of Mordechai Vanunu, a nuclear technician who had been laid off from his job at Israel's Dimona atomic facility in November 1985. Vanunu left Israel for Australia. From there he provided data about Dimona—officially, the Negev Nuclear Research Center—to the *Sunday Times* of London and was subsequently flown to London for further questioning. The story was published on October 5, 1986, occupied almost three full pages, and contained photographs allegedly taken by Vanunu in the control room of the underground bomb factory as well as a detailed cross-section drawing of the entire nuclear complex. According to the article, Israel had a stockpile of at least a hundred nuclear weapons and the capability to build nuclear, atomic, or neutron weapons.[54]

The Mossad, which had advance word of the disclosure, was able to determine Vanunu's location and, according to one account, Vanunu was lured from London by a female Mossad agent calling herself "Cindy." After befriending Vanunu in London she persuaded him, with the promise of sex, to accompany her to Rome. Once there, she took him to an apartment where he was attacked by two men and held down while she injected him with an anaesthetic. He was then chained and smuggled out of Italy in a cargo ship. Vanunu himself claimed, via a message written on his palm and placed against the window of a police van in which he was being transported, that he was kidnapped in Rome on September 30 after arriving there on a British Airlines flight. After first denying any knowledge of the affair, the Israeli government admitted on November 9 that it was holding Vanunu. It offered no explanation of how he was captured but denied his being kidnapped on British soil. Later that month Vanunu was formally charged with treason and aggravated espionage.[55]

The most violent form of covert action is, of course, assassination. Since the 1950s, the Mossad has made occasional use of assassination. The first assassinations were conducted in 1955 in response to Egyptian-directed Fedayeen guerilla raids in which vehicles and buildings were attacked, a Radio Israel transmitter damaged, twenty Israelis wounded, and twenty-two Israelis (five soldiers and seventeen civilians) killed.[56]

As a means of stopping such incidents, it was decided to assassinate Colonel Mustapha Hafez, an Egyptian intelligence officer whom the Israelis considered the true commander and organizer of the Palestinians. The Mossad used a double agent whose allegiance was to Egyptian intelligence to deliver a package to Hafez. The package detonated shortly after being opened, and Hafez died several hours later, after being rushed to the hospital. The second target was Colonel Salah Mustapha, the Egyptian military attaché in Jordan and the person in charge of the Fedayeen in that country. Mustapha received a parcel stamped with the seal of the United Nations headquarters in Jerusalem, where he had numerous friends. The package contained the recently published memoirs of Field Marshall Gerd Von Rondstedt. Concealed within the book was a bomb that blew Mustapha's car in half and killed him.[57]

The next set of assassinations was directed at the German scientists who were involved in the Egyptian rocket program—which, according to some sources, was geared toward giving Egypt the capability of delivering conventional, bacteriological/radiological, and even nuclear warheads onto Israeli territory. In September 1962, after diplomatic attempts to dislodge the German scientists had failed, the head of the Mossad received approval for Operation Damocles.[58]

The first target was Dr. Heinz Krug, the manager of Intra—the main purchasing agency for the rocket program—located at Schillerstrasse in Munich. On September 11, 1962, Krug left his offices with an unknown man. Two days later his car was found, and the police received a telephone call informing them that Krug was dead (his body was never found). On November 27, 1962, a parcel arrived at Factory 333 in Egypt, where the missiles were being constructed. The package was addressed to the factory's director, Dr. Pilz, but opened by his secretary—who was badly injured in the ensuing explosion. The following day another package arrived at the same factory. The explosion that resulted when the parcel was opened killed five people.[59]

On February 23, 1963, an attempt was made to kill Dr. Hans Kleinwatcher, an electronics expert who was working on the crucial guidance system for the missiles. As Kleinwatcher turned into the Lorrach Cul-de-sac, where his house was located, another car suddenly overook Kleinwatcher's and screeched to a halt in front of him, blocking his way. A passenger got out of the car that overtook Kleinwatcher and fired at him through his windshield. Kleinwatcher avoided injury when the bullet was deflected by the windshield and lodged in his scarf.[60]

In 1972 the Mossad again resorted to assassination, this time in response to a massacre at Lod airport in Tel Aviv on May 30, 1972. The massacre, carried out by four members of the Japanese Red Army (JRA) under an agreement with the Popular Front for the Liberation of Palestine (PFLP) and Black September organizations, resulted in twenty-seven deaths. Among the twenty-seven killed by The JRA terrorists were sixteen Roman Catholic pilgrims from Puerto Rico.[61]

The first target of Mossad retaliation was Ghassan Kanafani, a Palestinian poet and novelist residing in Beirut who was also a member of the PFLP's Central Command and helped plan the massacre at Lod. On June 1 Kanafani and his seventeen-year-old niece died when his booby-trapped car blew up. Six weeks later, on July 25, 1972, Bassam Abou Sharif, a member of Kanafani's staff and his likely successor as PFLP information officer, was injured by an exploding package at his home in Beirut. The explosion left Sharif blind in one eye and with damage to the other eye.[62]

The best known and most extensive set of assassinations undertaken by the Mossad was conducted in response to the kidnapping and massacre of ten Israeli athletes at the August 1972 Olympics in Munich. The kidnapping, arranged by the Black September faction of the PLO, was intended to force Israel to exchange two hundred Palestinian prisoners being held in Israel for the athletes who remained alive after the kidnapping (one athlete and one coach were killed in the kidnapping operation). German authorities agreed to the kidnappers' demand that a plane be provided to transport them and their hostages to Cairo, with the intention of having German sharpshooters "take out" the kidnappers at the airport. The kidnappers and hostages were flown to the airport via helicopter. Unfortunately, while some of the Black September terrorists were hit in the initial wave of firings, those who were still holding the hostages at gunpoint in the helicopters immediately killed the athletes.[63]

After the Munich massacre, Black September, led by its operations chief Ali Hassan Salameh, turned its attention to other Israeli-related targets. A letter bomb was sent to the Israeli agricultural attaché at the London embassy, resulting in his death. Similar letter bombs were also sent to Israeli ambassadors, prominent Jews, industrialists and businessmen, heads of Zionist organizations, and the President of the United States. Additionally, Black September operatives assassinated a Mossad officer in Brussels as well as a Mossad informer in Paris. Coming after the events in Munich, these assassinations led to an Israeli government decision to assassinate the leadership of Black September and particularly Ali Hassan Salameh.[64]

The Mossad set up a special unit, known as the Wrath of God, to conduct the operation. Wrath of God consisted of several assassination squads with both primary and support personnel. Its first victim was Wael Abu Zwaiter, the head of the Black September operational base in Rome, who had been involved in the Rome portion of the Lod massacre as well a Black September attempt on El-Al in August 1971. On October 16, 1972, a Mossad operative shot twelve bullets into Zwaiter outside his house after he returned home from an evening with a friend.[65]

In December, Dr. Mahimun Hamchari, the number two Black September official in France, was blown to bits in his Paris apartment by an explosive charge placed in his telephone by Mossad agents while Hamchari was out. The explosives were detonated when Hamchari answered a phone call from a Mossad agent and acknowledged that it was he who was speaking. A few weeks later, Hussein Abdu el Hir, the resident Black September agent in Cyprus, was killed when the explosives placed under his bed by the Mossad were detonated. In April 1973, Dr. Basil al-Kubaisi, an Iraqi professor at the American University in Beirut, was assassinated in Paris. Al-Kubaisi had been responsible, on his European trips, for acting to maintain the proper state of preparedness in Black September's arsenal-arranging for the purchase and delivery of new arms when appropriate.[66]

April 1973 also saw Mossad implementation of Operation Spring of Youth. A Mossad commando squad landed on the beach at Beirut just after midnight on April 9. At 1:30 A.M. on April 10, the commandos broke into an apartment at Rue Verdun and proceeded to kill Muhammad Naggar Abu, the head of Black September; Kamal Nassar, one of the heads of Fatah; and Kemal Adwan, Naggar's deputy.[67]

Next to last on the Mossad list was Mohammad Boudia, the chief of Black September in France. Boudia parked his car in the Latin Quarter, across the street from the apartment of a woman friend he was going to spend the night with. When Boudia returned to the car the next morning, a bomb behind the seat was triggered as he took his place behind the wheel.[68]

Boudia's elimination left the main target, Ali Hassan Salameh. In early 1973 the Mossad obtained information that Salameh would be operating out of a temporary base in Norway, setting up a Black September network that would cover the whole of Scandinavia. The person known to be Salameh's liaison officer was Kemal Benamane. In Lillehammer the Mossad observed Benamane in conference with an Arab waiter who went by the name Ahmed Bouchiki and concluded that Salameh and Bouchiki were one and the same. On his way back to his apartment one evening, Bouchiki was confronted by two members of the Israeli assassination squad, who proceeded to shoot him dead.[69]

Unfortunately for all involved, Bouchiki was truly Bouchiki. Salameh was in Norway but not where the Mossad believed him to be. Although neither of the assassins was apprehended, several members of the support team were, resulting in jail terms for them and extremely embarrassing publicity for Israel.

In early 1979 the Mossad caught up with Salameh in Beirut, where he lived. A Volkswagen packed with explosives was parked on a street by which Salameh was to ride in a Chevolet station wagon. As the Chevrolet passed the Volkswagen, the latter car was detonated by a Mossad agent, killing Salameh, the two bodyguards riding with him, and four persons who were in the vicinity.[70]

It is possible that the October 21, 1986, death of Brigadier Monzer Abu Ghazala, Chief of the PLO's seaborne commando operations against Israel, may have been the responsibility of the Mossad. Ghazala was the victim of a car bombing that sprayed more than 100 ball bearings through the vehicle and set it on fire. Alternatively, Ghazala could have been the victim of inter-Arab rivalry.[71]

Israeli Defense Forces Intelligence Branch (AMAN)

Military intelligence is responsible for the collection, production, and dissemination of military, geographic, and economic intelligence, particularly concerning nations of the Middle East.

As of 1977, AMAN consisted of four departments, as shown in Figure 7-2: Production, Intelligence Corps, Foreign Relations, and Field Security and Military Censorship. The Director of Military Intelligence is also responsible for directing Field Security Units, Territorial Command Combat Intelligence, Air Force Intelligence, and Naval Intelligence.[72]

The Production Department is responsible for preparing national intelligence estimates, versions of which appear as the *Middle East Review* or *Survey* for distribution to friendly liaison services. This department also prepares annual "Risk of War" estimates and produces daily finished intelligence reports, as well as daily bulletins, which contain raw or partially analyzed information. Approximately 2,800 of the 7,000 personnel in AMAN work for the Production Department. Of those 2,800, about 600 (150 of whom are officers and analysts) are involved in production.[73]

Figure 7-2. Organization of AMAN, 1977.

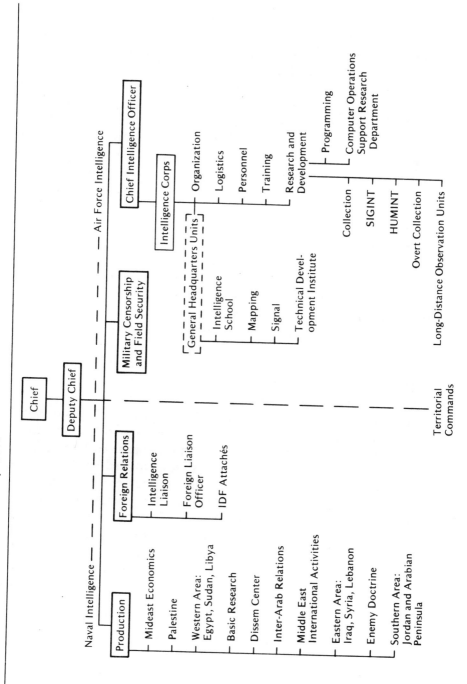

The Production Department is divided into three divisions: Geographical (or Regional), Functional (or Technical), and Documentation (or Registry and Records). The Geographical Division evaluates information and compiles target studies on the Arab countries. It is subdivided into three area desks: Western, responsible for Egypt, Sudan, and Libya; Eastern, responsible for Iraq, Syria, and Lebanon; and Southern, responsible for Jordan and the Arabian Peninsula.[74]

The Functional Division is divided into substantive units that deal with such subjects as Near East Economics, Inter-Arab Relations, Palestinian Affairs, and Near East International Activities. The division produces intelligence on technical and economic matters, including weapons and electronics, and area developments. The Documentation Division employs more than half the personnel in the Production Department. All reports are sent first to the Documentation Division for cataloging and then to the appropriate offices.[75]

Under Meir Amit, Director of AMAN from 1963 to 1968, the Production Department compiled computerized dossiers on every officer in the Egyptian, Jordanian, Saudi, Iraq, and Syrian armies. With information from newspaper stories, military gazettes, informants, and interrogations of prisoners of war, the files are constantly updated. In the event of war, Israeli field commanders can be provided with printouts giving complete profiles of the officers on the opposing side, analyzing their strengths and idiosyncrasies.[76]

The Intelligence Corps is responsible for overt and covert collection operations, including signals intelligence activities for the entire Israeli intelligence community. The corps is organized into divisions for Collection; General Headquarters, responsible for the Military Intelligence School and the Technical Development Institute (communications and cartography); Training; Organization; Logistics; Personnel; and Research and Development.[77]

Responsibility for signals intelligence activities, which include communications intelligence and electronic intelligence gathered via atmospheric and land-line interception, resides with the Collection Division's Signals Branch, with actual operations being performed by the IDF Signal Corps. During the Six-Day War of 1967, the Signal Corps succeeded in intercepting, deciphering, and disseminating a large volume of Arab traffic quickly and accurately. Included was a high-level conversation between Egyptian President Gamal Abdel Nasser and King Hussein of Jordan, who were intercepted talking via radio early in the morning on the second day of the war. The conversation appeared to involve a plan to attribute Israeli success on the battlefield to intervention by the United States and Britain, thus providing an excuse for the Arabs' defeat. Israel released the text of the conversation two days later and gained a diplomatic victory by further alienating Egypt and Jordan from the United States. Over the years the Signal Corps has mounted cross-border operations and tapped Arab land-line communications for extended periods. In addition, the corps on occasion has booby-trapped the land lines.[78]

The Signal Corps operates several ground stations on the Israeli periphery for the interception of communications from the surrounding Arab states. Prior to the 1973 war, one station was located at Umhashida, approximately twenty miles from the Suez Canal. A major station is still in operation at Mount Hermon, forty miles southwest of Damascus; it is equipped with "huge masts, antennas and radar disks."[79]

The Agents Branch of the Collection Division is responsible for all agent operations run by AMAN. Such operations are restricted to those occurring across Israeli borders into neighboring countries. Other subdivisions of the Collection Division are the Open Sources Branch, which collects and collates all material from overt sources, and the Long-Distance Observation Units. The latter units are primarily concerned with visual sightings of Arab activity along the borders and armistice lines. These units also provide support to agent cross-border operations and targeting information to signals intelligence units based on observations of Arab movements across the borders.[80]

The Foreign Relations Department of AMAN is responsible for liaison between the IDF and foreign military organizations and for the activities of IDF attachés. The department is reportedly divided into two components: the Foreign Intelligence Liaison Division and the Attachés Division. The Foreign Intelligence Liaison Division conducts liaison with representatives of those foreign intelligence services which have agreements with AMAN. It is also the official point of contact for all foreign defense attachés in Israel. Within or attached to the Foreign Intelligence Liaison Division is a Secret Liaison Unit that handles all operations outside the larger division's normal charter. The unit may be involved either directly or indirectly in bilateral intelligence operations conducted jointly by AMAN and another nation's intelligence service. Additionally, if the Mossad decides that an Israeli military officer is in the best position to perform a specific foreign operation, it is the Secret Liaison Unit that handles the matter.[81]

The Attachés Division directs the activities of Ministry of Defense missions and attachés. Missions and attachés are located in Washington, New York City, London, Paris, Bonn, Rome, The Hague, Ankara, Bangkok, Buenos Aires, Tokyo, Brasilia, and Caracas. The role of most defense missions and attaché posts is to sell Israeli defense industry products and to purchase defense equipment for the IDF. A few of the posts, such as those in Washington, London, and Paris, are attaché posts in the traditional sense, with information collection being a significant function.[82]

AMAN has been responsible for the two greatest intelligence fiascos in Israel's history—one involving covert action and the other involving intelligence estimation.

The first fiasco occurred in 1954. In 1951 the head of military intelligence, Benjamin Gibli, decided that Israel should create a fifth column inside Egypt to blow up civil and military installations in the event of war. At Gibli's direction, the fifth column was established, headed by an Israeli agent (Avraham Dar) operating under cover as a British businessman ("John Darling"). Subsequently, the Egyptian government of King Farouk was overthrown by Gamal Abdel Nasser, and Nasser's foreign policy—which stressed Arab nationalism and Egyptian control of the Suez Canal, a vital passageway for Israeli commodities—caused consternation within the Israeli government.[83]

Consternation increased in 1954 when it appeared that Britain might be willing to turn over control of the Suez Canal to Nasser. It was under these circumstances that Operation Susanna was conceived, with the goal of damaging Nasser's standing with the United States and Britain and inducing Britain to retain control of the canal. The goal was to be attained by attacking and burning U.S. and British property in Egypt—embassies, information and cultural centers, and commercial buildings. The attacks were to be blamed on Egyptian Communists and the ultra-right-wing Moslem Brotherhood; the operation was to be implemented by the Darling ring in Cairo and Alexandria.[84]

On July 14, 1954, the U.S. Information Service libraries in Alexandria and Cairo were bombed, causing immense damage. A second set of attacks was planned for July 23, although against not U.S. and British but Egyptian targets. Bombs were successfully placed at several locations in Cairo; however, a bomb ignited in the pocket of one of the agents who was to carry out the attacks in Alexandria, and the incident led to the arrest and interrogation of all but one member of the Darling network. The political fallout in Israel resulting from Egypt's exposure of the operation was substantial and long lasting. The Defense Minister, Pinchas Lavon, was forced to resign, as he was believed to be the highest approving authority for the operation. Lavon denied having given his approval, and the issue of his role and that of several other prominent Israeli leaders reemerged on several occasions over the ensuing twenty years.[85]

A more recent disaster was AMAN's failure to provide adequate warning of the Egyptian-Syrian attack on October 6, 1973, that led to the Yom Kippur War and imperiled Israel's existence. AMAN's failure was the result not of inadequate information but of incorrect interpretation of information.

Three weeks before the war began, Israeli intelligence noticed that Syria had begun amassing its forces and was erecting an extremely dense network of anti-aircraft missiles along its border with Israel. Similar reports arrived indicating that Egypt was starting to move units toward the Suez Canal. By the end of September there was clear evidence that SA-6 missiles had been distributed among the armored divisions of the Egyptian Army. There had also been reports of Egypt employing excavations for earth-removing operations along the northern section of the Suez Canal. Additional evidence of an impending attack included the mobilization of Egyptian civil defense, the declaration of blackouts in Egyptian cities, and an appeal for blood donors.[86]

Further indication came when Soviet advisers in Syria made a sudden departure on the night of October 4. In addition, a Mossad agent is reported to have arrived at headquarters on October 4 with detailed information concerning Egyptian-Syrian war plans. It was not until 3:00 A.M. on October 6, however, that the head of AMAN was finally convinced that war was imminent. At that time an agent—an Egyptian Jew in the Canal Zone—radioed to headquarters that Egyptian troops had been ordered to launch an attack at 6:00 that evening. In fact, the attack was launched earlier, at 2:05 P.M.[87]

Responsibility for failing to properly interpret the information acquired by various Israeli intelligence units rested with the Director of AMAN, Eli Zeira. As it had been for many years previously, AMAN was the component of the Israeli intelligence community charged with ultimate responsibility for warning. Zeira, however, had been convinced that no war would occur. He viewed information concerning Egyptian and Syrian military movements through the prism of "the concept," of which he was one of the architects. The concept stated that (1) the Arabs were not ready for an all-out war with Israel, and knew Israel would not fight a limited war, (2) war would be of short duration, and (3) in an all-out war, the Arabs would be quickly defeated—Israel would break through to the other side of the Suez Canal, with options to advance toward Cairo, the Nile Valley, and Upper Egypt; on the Syrian front, Israel would be able to take Damascus if it wished.[88]

Zeira was not alone in his belief in "the concept"; it was a doctrine that most officers inside AMAN believed (although it was not shared by the head of the Mossad or the Chief of Staff). Thus, a report prepared by an intelligence officer attached to the Southern Command and titled *War Preparations of the Egyptian Army?* was suppressed by the officer's superior.[89] On October 4 the director of the Egypt Division of military intelligence concluded:

> Notwithstanding the existence of military strength on the Canal front which appears to be ready for action, to the best of our knowledge there has been no significant change in Egyptian evaluation of their military potential versus [the IDF's]. Therefore the probability of an Egyptian attack is unlikely.[90]

Zeira's view propagated not only downward in AMAN but to higher levels. In May 1973 Moshe Dayan, Israel's Minister of Defense, had issued guidelines to his generals specifying that "a renewal of war in the second half of summer must be taken into account." By summer, however, Dayan predicted no war for ten years. As noted earlier, it was reported that Dayan and Golda Meir dismissed as disinformation the intelligence provided by a Mossad agent indicating an imminent attack. Their views, as well as Zeira's, were certainly reinforced by several previous false alarms in December 1972 and May-June 1973, when Israeli fears of war *apparently* turned out to be unfounded. As was discovered later, President Sadat had intended to launch an attack in May 1973 but held back because of the impending Soviet-American summit and the expectation of additional arms deliveries from the Soviet Union.[91]

Israel's failure to be prepared for the Egyptian-Syrian attack led to significant Arab military gains before the trend could be reversed, to an increase in Arab morale and a decline in Israeli morale, and to the loss of Israeli soldiers. The consequences for AMAN were also notable: Zeira and three of his assistants were cited by the investigating Agranat Commission for their failure to properly interpret the information concerning Egyptian and Syrian mobilization.[92]

In 1983 the Kahan Commission charged the Director of Military Intelligence (DMI) with negligence with regard to the Phalangist massacres in the Sabra and Chatila refugee camps. The DMI was cited for not giving sufficient attention to the potential consequences of sending the Phalangists into the camps and failing to warn, after the murder of President Bashir Gemayel, of the danger that the Phalangists would take revenge against the Palestinian population in West Beirut, and especially in the refugee camps. The commission found implausible the DMI's claim that he was unaware of the role assigned to the Phalangists in connection with the Israeli entry into Beirut until after the massacres.

Air Force Intelligence

The primary functions of Air Force Intelligence are to conduct the intelligence operations necessary to support air activities and to coordinate with the Director of AMAN regarding its collection efforts. Its almost exclusive focus is the order of battle and capabilities of Arab air forces and the compilation of a target base for the Arab nations. The information is largely collected by aerial reconnaissance and signals intelligence.[93]

Planes used in aerial reconnaissance operations are the Grumman Mohawk OV-1D, the McDonnell-Douglas RF-4E Phantom, and the Dassault Mirage III RJ. The Mirage III RJ is a reconnaissance fighter with a speed of Mach 1.8 at 55,775 feet and a radius of 180 miles. The RF-4E is a multisensor reconnaissance plane with a maximum speed of 1,432 mph at 36,000 feet. Six RF-4Es were procured in the initial order of Phantoms placed in 1969, with another six obtained in 1977. The OV-1D is employed for photographic reconnaissance and electronic intelligence. The Israeli Air Force maintains two OV-1Ds. The planes have a maximum speed of 285 mph, a cruising speed of 207 mph, and a service ceiling of 25,000 feet; at a speed of 161 mph, they can operate for almost four and a half hours.[94]

Israel has also made great use of remotely piloted vehicles (RPVs) for reconnaissance. A reconnaissance RPV is essentially a large model aircraft with a variety of electronic equipment that is sent up to observe enemy lines, its movements controlled from the launch site. Israel uses two models—the Scout and the Mastiff.

The Scout, which is launched by catapult from a truck-mounted ramp, has a range of 62 miles and usually operates at 8,000 feet. A Scout mission takes about six hours. On board are two cameras mounted in the belly, one for zoom and one for panorama photography; other payloads such as jamming devices can be inserted if required. The operator controls the vehicle with a joystick. In addition, the controller has an automatic map-plotter, a video and telemetry signals reception capability, minicomputer processing, and a terminal for the display of data received for immediate or later analysis. The Mastiff possesses a package similar to that of the Scout but can carry a heavier load—66 pounds, compared with 48. Its heavier load results in a shorter range, approximately 42 miles. Both vehicles can be recovered and recycled, the Scout by means of a vertically mounted net set up above the ground and the Mastiff by an arresting wire on a road or flat field.[95]

In the Lebanon war, Israel first used RPVs as a substitute for more conventional reconnaissance by ground forces. RPVs were controlled by local battalion commanders, the photographic information obtained being transmitted directly to the commander's field headquarters. The commander was thus able to make immediate decisions on troop deployments without sending out ground reconnaissance units. The RPVs were able to photograph in great detail every enemy position, thereby enabling the Israeli ground forces to outflank their opposition, avoid ambushes, and call up accurate artillery fire. Under present circumstances the Israeli Air Force conducts at least one RPV mission over Lebanon each week.[96]

Naval Intelligence

Naval Intelligence is a small, centralized service—in 1977 it employed some 110 individuals—operating in support of naval units. The service deals largely with naval order of battle, foreign capabilities, and seaborne threats. It operates as a semi-autonomous unit of military intelligence; its personnel are not subordinate to the Director of AMAN except to provide consultative assistance in naval matters.[97]

As indicated in Figure 7-3, subordinate to the Deputy Director of Naval Intelligence are six departments: Organization and Administration, Security, Production, Targeting, Protocol, and Collection.

Figure 7-3. Organization of Naval Intelligence, 1977.

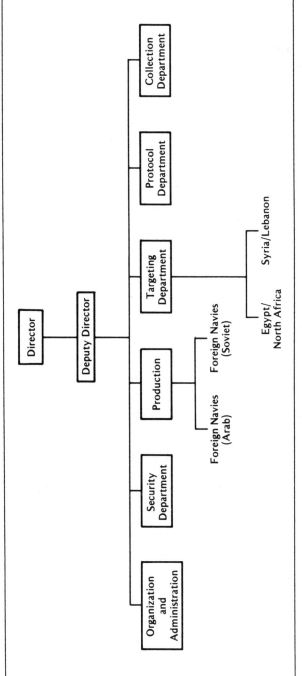

Source: Central Intelligence Agency, *Foreign Intelligence and Security Services: Israel* (Washington, D.C.: CIA, 1977), p. 37.

The Collection Department, with about seventeen employees in 1977 conducts its collection activities via naval attachés, small boat coastal operations, and the merchant marine, as well as in cooperation with Air Force Intelligence. The Targeting Department, with about twenty personnel in 1977, is organized into two divisions: Egypt/North Africa and Syria/Lebanon. These divisions are responsible for preparing coastal studies for naval gunfire missions, beach studies for amphibious assaults, and special target studies to support commando operations as well as maintaining target folders on Lebanese, Syrian, and Egyptian ports.[98]

The Production Department, with a staff of about forty in 1977, is the largest component of Naval Intelligence and consists of two divisions that focus on Arab and Soviet navies. The department is responsible for research, analysis, production, and dissemination of information on all mobile forces associated with the Arab and Soviet navies in the Mediterranean. It is the prime user of the information coming into naval headquarters, particularly SIGINT information. Its finished product is used mainly by naval units operating out of Israel's four naval bases and the commando unit in southern Sinai. Production is generally limited to studies on enemy order of battle and special weapons.[99]

The Security Department, with a staff of about twelve in 1977, performs a limited counterintelligence function within Navy headquarters at all naval bases, while the Organization and Administration Department handles routine administrative duties.[100]

Research and Political Planning Center

The Research and Political Planning Center, formerly the Research Division of the Ministry of Foreign Affairs, prepares for government policymakers analyses based on raw intelligence. The analyses include short papers based on current intelligence and longer analytical memoranda.[101] The center's role is similar to that of the Bureau of Intelligence and Research in the U.S. Department of State.

As of 1977, the center employed fewer than one hundred persons, both analysts and support staff, recruited from the Ministry of Foreign Affairs and from Israeli universities. Its work is divided among six divisions: North Africa, the Fertile Crescent, the Arabian Peninsula, Other Geographic Regions, Economic, and Strategic. Approximately 70 percent of the center's personnel were employed in the three Arab units.[102]

In the aftermath of the Yom Kippur War, the Arganat Commission, citing a lack of diversity in perception as a major problem, recommended that a more pluralistic approach be adopted. Although the responsibility for early warning of impending attack would remain with AMAN, it was intended that political leaders, particularly the Prime Minister, would be provided with information and estimates from the center and the Mossad's Research Department.[103]

Creation of the Research and Political Planning Center led many in the Israeli intelligence community to hope that a new channel had been established to provide Israeli leadership with an overall political perspective of the strategic situation. Yigal Allon, Minister of Foreign Affairs at the time, removed the center from the diplomatic track and replaced those individuals who were not qualified for intelligence work with the best Near Eastern specialists from the ministry and academia.[104]

At present, every Thursday, center researchers prepare summaries of the collection of weekly estimates. On Saturday, one of the heads of the center meet with the Foreign Minister, briefs him, and give him collections to distribute to ministers at the Sunday Cabinet meeting.[105]

Instead of serving the Cabinet, however, the center became a service entity for providing public information to Israeli representatives abroad. The resulting erosion of prestige led to the departure of the best researchers. As was the case with the Research Division, the center's papers ended up in wastebaskets. In the absence of mechanisms for the collection of information, the researchers who remained were unable to base their estimates on independent sources. In 1977 the center played no role in preparing Israeli decision makers for the Egyptian peace initiative. In the Lebanon war of 1982, the Near East specialists of the Lebanese desk provided no information to the Cabinet on the historical and economic background of Lebanon or intergroup relations; instead, they were asked to provide public information material to Israeli representatives abroad on the "just war." The 1983 Kahan Commission, convened to examine Israeli performance in the Lebanese war, reported that the highest officials of the Ministry of Foreign Affairs conceded that the center was not even a marginally pluralist source of analysis.[106]

General Security Service (Shin Beth, or SHABAK)

Shin Beth is the Israeli counterespionage and internal security service. Shin Beth is responsible for collecting information on foreign intelligence organizations, both hostile and friendly, and their activities; ensuring the security of Israeli officials and installations abroad; and investigating all forms of subversion directed by either internal or external foes, including sabotage and terrorism in Israel and abroad. Shin Beth evaluates all information acquired, collates it with openly available information, and submits finished intelligence reports to the appropriate government agencies. The two main targets of Shin Beth activity are the Arab states and the Soviet and Eastern European intelligence and security services.[107]

As shown in Figure 7-4, Shin Beth is organized into eight operational and functional departments: Arab Affairs, Non-Arab Affairs, Protective Security, Operational Support, Technology, Interrogation and Legal Counsel, Coordination and Planning, and Administration.[108] Of special interest are the Arab Affairs, Non-Arab Affairs, Protective Security, Operational Support, and Technology departments.

The Arab Affairs Department is responsible for counterespionage, antiterrorist operations, control of political subversion, research, and maintenance of a counterintelligence index on Arabs. The department operates through field offices controlled by regional officers. Counterintelligence and countersubversion operations involving all other countries are handled by the Non-Arab Affairs Department. Its countersubversion operations are divided between those dealing with Communist subversion and those dealing with non-Communist subversion. The department's counterintelligence activities include the penetration of both hostile and friendly intelligence services and their associated diplomatic installations in Israel. The department is also responsible for foreign liaison and handles all Shin Beth correspondence with other foreign intelligence and security services. Finally, it is responsible for the interrogation of immigrants from the Soviet Union and Eastern Europe.[109]

The Protective Security Department is responsible for the protection of Israeli government buildings and embassies, El-Al and Zim installations and vehicles, defense industries and scientific establishments, and leading personalities. The department is also responsible

Figure 7-4. Organization of the Shin Beth, 1977.

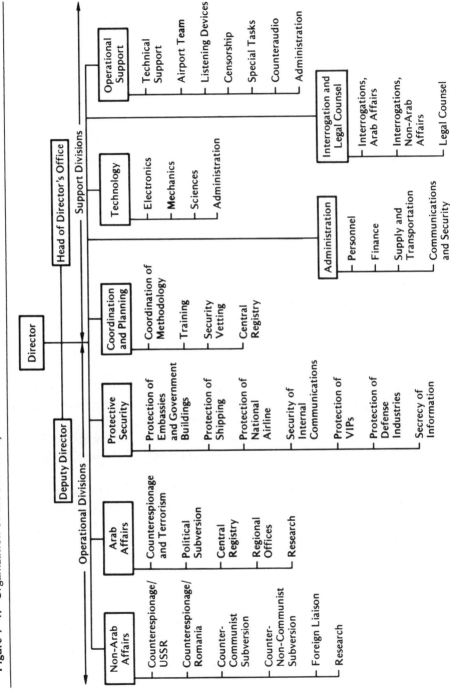

for the security of all important industrial plants and thus attempts to prevent the unauthorized disclosure of industrial secrets such as patents, processes, and statistics.[110]

The Operational Support Department assists the operational departments with surveillance, observation, airport security, censorship, listening devices, special tasks, and counteraudio support. The Technology Department provides support in the areas of audio and visual surveillance, communications, photography, surreptitious entry, telephone tapping, mail censorship, and security devices.[111]

Shin Beth targets within Israel can be organized into four categories: Israelis, Arabs, Communists, and foreigners in general. Aside from the Arab target, Shin Beth is concerned with subversive elements of the left. It has thoroughly penetrated the cells of the Communist MAKI and RAKAH parties, following their activities through informants, surveillance, and technical operations. Shin Beth agents often attend international Communist meetings.[112]

Israelis who are members of extreme right-wing religious groups are targets of Shin Beth surveillance. Such groups have been involved in bombings, such as the one that crippled two West Bank Arab mayors.

All foreigners, regardless of nationality or religion, are viewed as potential threats to Israeli security. Hence, Shin Beth employs a large number of informants among local Israelis who come into contact with foreigners by reason of their employment or activities. Included are bartenders, hotel clerks, telephone operators, secretaries, taxi drivers, caterers, maids, prostitutes, chauffeurs, and waiters; also included are members of trade unions, scientists, and those in the educational field.[113]

Arab informants, too, are recruited for monitoring any organized activity among Arabs with Israel and the West Bank. Arab informers are recruited "by threat and bribe." Arabs also find that their overseas mail arrives appearing to have been opened, read, and resealed. Arab phones are tapped as well.[114]

When an Arab employed by the city of Tel Aviv as a civil engineer assembled some neighbors to promote the preservation of the Arab part of Jaffa, the Shin Beth began repeatedly summoning him for interrogation. The organization's attention to an apparently cultural issue has been attributed to the unwillingness of Israeli authorities to allow a purely Arab organization to operate as a pressure group.[115]

Shin Beth has been involved in a number of espionage cases. One of the first of the East bloc agents to be detected was Professor Kirt Sitte, who held a research post as a nuclear physicist and specialist in cosmic radiation at the Institute of Technology at Haifa. Sitte had been recruited by Czech intelligence prior to joining the Haifa institute in 1954. From 1954 to 1958 he provided Czechoslovakia, and thus the Soviet Union, with intelligence. In 1961 he was sentenced to five years' imprisonment. Another East bloc agent was Aharon Cohen, a Middle East expert of the left-wing Mapam party. In 1962 Cohen was sentenced to five years in prison for his fourteen-month involvement in espionage. In those fourteen months he passed secret information to "a representative of a scientific research mission" whose intelligence role the prosecution claimed Cohen understood.[116]

The most interesting of the spy cases concerned "Israel Beer," who rose to become a principal aide to the Chief of Staff of the Israeli Army in the early days of Israel's existence. Eventually he became deputy chief of AMAN and intelligence liaison officer to the Minister of Defense. In 1962 Beer was arrested and charged with espionage. Beer, who was sentenced to ten years, was apparently a Soviet mole who adopted the identity of the real Beer, who disappeared in 1938.[117]

In 1963 an Egyptian spy, Kaboerak Yaakouvian, was arrested. He had entered Israel in 1960, first joining a kibbutz and subsequently becoming an itinerant photographer around Tel Aviv. Apparently, his cover was blown long before he was arrested, and Shin Beth had been able to feed him false information.[118]

Shortly after Israel occupied the Golan Heights in 1967, a Syrian spy ring began to operate there. The organizer of the ring, Shakib Yousef Abu Jabal, provided Syria with information on troop movements, police and military activity, and even details of the sites of defense posts. The ring was a family affair, involving all of Shakib's family. Ring members were ordered to visit various places in Israel, and they obtained information from places as distant as Eilat and the Sinai Peninsula. The ring was uncovered in 1969 when one of Shakib's sons was arrested in Eilat.[119]

On November 1, 1972, Peter Fulman was convicted by the Haifa District Court of spying for Lebanon and was sentenced to fifteen years' imprisonment. A German electronics engineer, Fulman had immigrated to Israel a year before. Arrested in November were

Ehud Adiv, a former Israeli Army paratrooper, and a friend, Dan Vered. They were charged with spying for Syria. Specifically, Adiv provided information on the deployment of Israeli Army paratroop units and the location of armored units, airfields, anti-aircraft defenses, patrol operations, and radar installations. In addition, he had been given the job of recruiting Jews to be sent abroad for training in sabotage. Vered had been sent to Syria, where he was trained in weapons, explosives, and codes, as was Adiv at a later date. In March 1973, Adiv and Vered were convicted and sentenced to seventeen and ten years, respectively.[120]

By the end of 1972 it appeared to Shin Beth that between 100 and 150 persons—both Jews and Arabs—were involved in the Galilee spy-sabotage ring run by Syrian intelligence. In December, thirty persons, including four Jews, were arrested. On January 24, 1973, in an unrelated case, a British electrical engineer was sentenced to twelve years in jail by a Tel Aviv court for spying for Jordan, the engineer having allegedly passed on information about airfields, security fences, military imports, plans of military bases, and training methods.[121]

A result of its counterterrorist operations the Shin Beth captured a group of Syrian-backed Palestinians in June 1987. The Palestinians were suspected of six attacks in the occupied West Bank, including the assassination of an Israeli-appointed Arab mayor in 1986.[122]

Recently Shin Beth has been involved in two major scandals. On April 12, 1984, four Palestinians who were residents of the occupied Gaza Strip hijacked an Israeli bus near Ashkelon and forced it to travel southward, with all the passengers on board, into the Gaza Strip. The following day Israeli troops stormed the bus. Initial reports stated that one hostage and all four hijackers had been killed in the raid. Among the participants in the raid were several senior Shin Beth officials and security personnel.[123]

Shortly after the event, however, a photograph was published, in defiance of military censorship, showing two of the hijackers being led away. As a result, the Israeli government convened a commission chaired by Meir Zorea to investigate the obvious murders of the two hijackers. The Zorea Commission concluded that although no one had given an order to execute the hijackers, there was enough evidence of wrongdoing in the handling of the terrorists to merit a criminal investigation by the Attorney General.[124]

By 1986 it had become apparent that there was substantial Shin Beth involvement—that the hijackers had been interrogated and then beaten to death by Shin Beth employees. Army men at the scene described how Shin Beth interrogators smashed the head of one of the terrorists against a rock and threw the other terrorist into the air from a stretcher, allowing him to land on the ground. The interrogators claimed they had been acting on orders from the chief of the Shin Beth, Avraham Shalom.[125]

It was further alleged that Shalom tampered with evidence, forging some data and destroying other data, and coordinated all the stories of the Shin Beth witnesses before their appearances at the Zorea and other commissions investigating the incident to make it appear that Shin Beth had no role in the killings. Allegedly involved with Shalom were three of his deputies, including the two top officials in the Shin Beth legal department who were reported to have falsified evidence on Shalom's orders. The falsified evidence apparently shifted the blame for the killings from Shin Beth men to a senior Army officer.[126]

The controversy threatened to go beyond Shin Beth, as Shalom claimed that he had acted with the approval of his political superiors—superiors believed to include then Prime Minister Yitzhak Shamir, who at the time the controversy became public was scheduled to replace Shimon Peres as Prime Minister as part of the arrangement made between the Likud and Labor parties when they agreed to form a unity government in 1984. Further, Peres's role was a subject of concern: While Prime Minister in 1985, he had been approached by Shalom's senior deputy and two other Shin Beth officials, who were concerned over Shalom's actions in the affair. Peres backed Shalom, who forced the resignation of the three men.[127]

In attempting to put the issue to rest, Attorney General Yitzhak Zamir was removed from his post in early June 1986 by the Cabinet after refusing to cede to government pressure to rescind his order for an investigation into the matter. Then, on June 25, Israeli President Chaim Herzog issued blanket pardons to Shalom and the three deputies who had been accused of involvement in the cover-up. In justifying his action Herzog said that he had acted "with the purpose of ending the witch hunt surrounding this affair and to avert additional serious harm to the General Security Service." He further stated that Shin Beth had "uncovered some 320 terrorist groups, which carried out 379 attacks and attempted attacks throughout Israel. . . . The Israeli public has no idea what a debt we owe to all those unknown fighters . . . and how many lives have been saved in Israel thanks to them."[128]

In mid-July the Israeli Cabinet voted on strict party lines, against establishing its own commission of inquiry into the killings. As a result, Zamir's replacement as Attorney General ordered a new police investigation. However, in late August, a few weeks after Israel's High Court of Justice upheld Herzog's pardon of Shalom and the three deputies, Herzog pardoned seven additional Shin Beth employees for their role in the killings. Such a move, it was believed, would eliminate any chances of the Attorney General's probe producing new information or indictments.[129]

The revelations of Shin Beth involvement and the subsequent pardons ignited a huge controversy. Cabinet members such as Trade Minister Ariel Sharon and Labor Minister Moshe Katzav suggested that there was no justification for public concern, with Katzav stating that "Israel is in a state of war against terrorism . . . in a state of war the normal laws don't apply. The Shin Beth, indeed, violates some of the basic laws. This must be recognized and legitimization given to it."[130]

In the wake of Herzog's initial pardons there was a strong reaction from numerous newspapers, with headlines such as "The Plot to Silence" and "Pardon-Conspiracy to Cover Up for Political Echelon." The newspaper Maariv predicted that "the country will not be silent. . . . This guaranteed commotion will be enough to convince the decision makers that the decision is incorrect. . . . The GSS [General Security Service] affair has not ended, it will be with us for a long time yet." And Haaretz wrote that "new norms have been established in Israel. . . . Since yesterday, GSS personnel may murder terrorists. . . . The GSS chief will be allowed to subborn his officials to commit perjury. . . . GSS personnel will also be permitted to give false testimony. . . . These astonishing norms are implicit in the amnesty granted by the President."[131]

In December 1986 Israeli television reported that a Ministry of Justice inquiry found that then Prime Minister Yitzhak Shamir did not order the murders of the two hijackers and was not aware of the cover-up of the killings. The testimony by the former head of Shin Beth was found to be untrustworthy.[132]

In 1987 the Israeli Supreme Court overturned the treason conviction of Izat Nafsu, a former army lieutenant and member of Israel's Circassian Muslim Minority. Nafsu was arrested in 1980, after having served with Israeli forces in southern Lebanon as a liaison officer with the IDF's Lebanese Christian allies. After two weeks of interrogation by the Shin Beth, he apparently confessed to having passed military secrets to Syria—a confession he subsequently withdrew at a secret military trial, claiming that it had been extracted illegally and under duress. The court ruled that the Shin Beth used "unethical interrogation methods" to induce Nafsu's confession and that Shin Beth officers lied before the military tribunal that originally convicted Nafsu in 1981.[133]

MANAGEMENT STRUCTURE

The central body of Israel's intelligence and security community is the Va'adat Rashei Hasherutim—the Committee of the Heads of Services—which has as its primary function the coordination of all intelligence and security activities at home and abroad. The Va'adat consists of the Director of the Mossad (as Chairman), the Director of AMAN, the Director of Shin Beth, the Inspector General of Police, the Director General of the Ministry of Foreign Affairs, the Director of the Research and Political Planning Center of the Ministry of Foreign Affairs, and the political, military, and antiterrorist advisers of the Prime Minister.[134]

Meetings of the Va'adt must be held biweekly but may be held more frequently. At the meetings each director usually provides a briefing on the key activities of his service during the preceding two weeks. The Director of the Mossad chairs Va'adat and in this capacity is directly responsible to the Prime Minister. The members of Va'adat are quasi-equal in status; the term *memune*, used in reference to the Mossad chief, is employed to denote preeminence among equals. According to a CIA study, however, the Director of AMAN overshadows the Director of the Mossad in power and importance.[135]

Figure 7-5 shows the overall structure of the Israeli intelligence community.

Figure 7-5. Structure of the Israeli Intelligence Community.

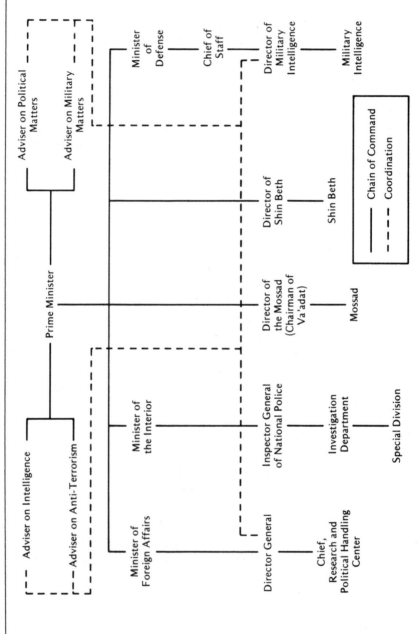

Source: Central Intelligence Agency, *Foreign Intelligence and Security Services: Israel* (Washington, D.C.: CIA, 1977).

LIAISON

The Mossad has liaison relationships with numerous intelligence and security services throughout the world. With a few exceptions, the Mossad's Department of Political Action and Liaison is responsible for relations with foreign organizations. In most instances, the point of contact is in foreign capitals, although some foreign services insist on liaison in Israel.[136]

The Mossad and Shin Beth maintain liaison with some foreign intelligence and security services through membership in the KILOWATT group, whose focus is Arab terrorism. Members of the group include West Germany, Belgium, Italy, the United Kingdom, Luxembourg, the Netherlands, Switzerland, Denmark, France, Canada, Ireland, Sweden, Norway, and Israel. Israel also had, as of 1977, informal connections with other European nations, including Spain, Portugal, and Austria, with respect to terrorism. In October 1986 France and Israel agreed to increase their exchanges of intelligence concerning terrorist activities.[137]

Before the fall of the Shah in 1979, the Mossad was part of a trilateral liaison arrangement called TRIDENT. TRIDENT was established by the Mossad, Turkey's National Security Service (NSS), and the Shah's National Organization for Intelligence and Security (SAVAK) in late 1958. Trident involved intelligence exchanges plus semiannual meetings at the chief of service level.[138]

The terms of the original agreement with the Turkish NSS stated that the Mossad would provide information on the activity of Soviet agents in Turkey and those working against Turkish interests throughout the Middle East. In exchange, the NSS was to provide Israel with information on the Arab nations' political intentions that would affect Israel's security and on the activity and identification of Egyptian agents working against Israel. In addition, the Mossad provided Turkey with counterespionage and technical training.[139]

The primary purpose of Israel's arrangement with Iran was to develop a pro-Israeli and anti-Arab policy on the part of Iranian officials. The Mossad engaged in joint operations with SAVAK beginning in the late 1950s. It aided SAVAK by supporting Kurdish separatists in Iraq, by providing reports on Egyptian activities in Arab countries, and by transmitting to SAVAK reports on trends and developments in Iraq and in Communist countries of concern to Iran.[140]

The Mossad is also reported to have a long relationship with the Moroccan Directorate General for Studies and Documentation (DGED), going back at least to the Ben-Barka affair. Among the areas of cooperation is training, with Israeli experts being involved in training Moroccan intelligence and security units.[141]

Israeli liaison with African intelligence services has varied considerably from country to country. Despite the break in diplomatic relations between Israel and many African countries, the Israelis still maintain good liaison relationships with certain African intelligence services. The Israelis maintain liaison with the Kenyan General Service Unit. In Central Africa they are still active in Zaire, while in West Africa they have trained the Liberian Security Service. They also helped establish the Ghanian Military Intelligence Service. At the same time, the Mossad has had a liaison relationship with South African intelligence services. The South Africa National Intelligence Service, Directorate of Military Intelligence, and Security Police all closely collaborate with their Israeli counterparts in exchanges of information, the transfer of technology from Israel to South Africa, and the training of South Africans by Israelis. Evidence of collaboration concerning intelligence technology surfaced in 1983, when a reconnaissance drone was shot down over Mozambique. The drone, employed by the South African Defense Forces, bore an Israeli Aircraft Industries identification number.[142]

In East Asia the Israelis have provided intelligence training to the Government of the Republic of China and maintain liaison with that nation's intelligence services. In addition, the Mossad may have a liaison arrangement with the People's Republic of China intelligence community. Elsewhere in East Asia, the Mossad maintains liaison with the intelligence services of Japan, Thailand, Indonesia, and South Korea, especially on terrorist matters.[143]

The Mossad has also received information intercepted by an offshoot of Dutch naval intelligence—TICV (*Technische Informatie Centrale Verwerking*—Central Processing of Technical Information)— and passed on by the Dutch IDB (*Inlichtingendienst Buitenland*— Intelligence Services Abroad). IDB has passed on to Israel intercepted messages between Iraq and Italy concerning work at Osirak, the secret plutonium reprocessing laboratory allegedly installed by Italy in an underground facility at the Osirak reactor center. IDB's information is reported to have trigged the timing of the Israeli attack on Osirak on June 7, 1981.[144]

Other nations with which Israel has exchanged intelligence are Egypt, Pakistan, and India. Specifically, the Mossad and the Egyptian General Intelligence Department established liaison subsequent to President Sadat's trip to Jerusalem in 1977; a particular area of exchange concerns anti-Palestinian operations. Israel is reported to have exchanged intelligence with Pakistan by providing Pakistan with information on India that was obtained by Israel's agent within U.S. naval intelligence, Jonathan Jay Pollard. In return, Israel received Pakistani information on Saudi Arabia and the Arab Gulf states. At the same time, Israel has been exchanging information with India concerning Pakistani attempts to develop an atomic bomb.[145]

U.S.-ISRAELI INTELLIGENCE RELATIONS

One of the strongest Western intelligence links is that between the United States and Israel. These arrangements involve the Mossad, AMAN, and a variety of U.S. intelligence agencies—the CIA, FBI, Defense Intelligence Agency, National Security Agency, Foreign Technology Division, and Foreign Science and Technology Center.

The intelligence liaison between the United States and Israel dates back to the early 1960s, when

> the governments of Israel and the United States had agreed to exchange intelligence secrets. . . . Most important of all as far as the Israelis were concerned, the Central Intelligence Agency along with the Federal Bureau of Investigation, had undertaken to supply the Israelis with some top secret equipment, including the most advanced computers for cryptanalysis, as well as to train selected Israeli officers in the use.[146]

The centerpiece of CIA-Mossad cooperation until 1975 was the CIA's Chief of the Counterintelligence Staff, James Jesus Angleton. Angleton had developed extensive contacts with future Israeli intelligence officials during his World War II activities in Europe with the Office of Strategic Services (OSS). In 1957 Angleton set up a liaison unit to deal with the Mossad, and the unit was made responsible for producing Middle East intelligence for both services. In addition, the CIA received intelligence from Mossad networks in the Soviet Union.[147]

After Angleton's dismissal in 1975, the liaison unit was abolished, and the Israeli account was moved to the appropriate Directorate of Operations regional division of the CIA. The CIA also began to operate more independently of the Mossad. In the late 1970s the agency began operating on the West Bank.[148]

Among the present arrangements is Israeli provision of information concerning Soviet weapons systems, particularly those captured in various battles or wars. This exchange has given the United States access to the captured weapons systems themselves, as well as to data concerning their performance.

Such exchanges took place after the 1967 and 1973 Arab-Israeli wars. Israel furnished the United States with captured air-to-ground and ground-to-air missiles and with Soviet antitank weapons. Also furnished were Soviet 122 and 130-millimeter artillery pieces, along with ammunition for evaluation and testing. After the 1973 war, the furnished material included a Soviet T-72 tank. Upon examination, it was discovered that the T-72 was equipped with a special type of air filter to defend against germ warfare. Additionally, extensive joint analyses were done after the 1973 war: Eight volumes of between two hundred and three hundred pages apiece were produced. These analyses influenced subsequent developments in U.S. weapons tactics and military budgets.[149]

In early 1983 the Israeli government offered to share military intelligence gained during the war in Lebanon. The offer included details of an "Israeli invention" that was alleged by Prime Minister Menachem Begin to be the key to Israel's ability to destroy Syria's Soviet-made surface-to-air missiles during the war. However, Secretary of Defense Caspar Weinberger rejected a proposed agreement for sharing that information because he felt it would have trapped the United States into long-range commitments to Israel that he wanted to avoid. Administration officials argued that the information had already been learned through normal military contacts.[150]

As a condition for sharing the information, Israel insisted on sending Israeli experts to the United States with captured weapons and receiving whatever analysis came from U.S. research. Israel also insisted on the right to veto the transfer of information and analysis to third-party countries, including members of NATO, and on measures to ensure that sensitive data remained secret. According to diplomats, the Israelis expressed fears that Soviet intelligence agents who had penetrated Western European governments would find out what Israel had learned and would then pass that information along to Arab allies of the Soviet Union. Subsequently, an agreement was reached that continued the flow of information.[151]

A late 1983 reassessment of U.S. policy in the Middle East, following the deteriorating situation in Lebanon and continued Syrian intransigence, resulted in National Security Decision Directive 111, which specified a "tilt" toward Israel and expanded U.S.-Israeli strategic cooperation.[152]

The expanded cooperation reportedly involved a higher degree of sharing of reconnaissance satellite data, including such data on Saudi Arabia and Jordan. William J. Casey, in his first three years as CIA Director (1981–84), provided Israeli intelligence with access to sensitive photographs and other reconnaissance information that the Israelis had been denied under the Carter administration. The head of AMAN from 1979 to 1983, Major General Yehoshua Saguy, said in early 1984 that the CIA was providing Israel with access to data from reconnaissance satellites, and "not only the information but the photos themselves." Under the Carter administration, Director of Central Intelligence (DCI) Stansfield Turner refused to provide the satellite imagery that had been furnished when George Bush was DCI in 1976 and 1977.[153]

Upon becoming DCI in 1981, William Casey decided to resume supplying Israel with actual photographs. Inside the Israeli intelligence community, the satellite photos were often referred to as "Casey's gift" and were considered invaluable. After Israel used some of those photos to aid in targeting the Osirak reactor, however, Casey restricted Israeli access to only those photographs which could be used for "defensive" purposes relating to Arab states directly on or near the Israeli border.[154]

Another aspect of the expanded cooperation was reported to be greater Israeli access to the "take" of Cyprus-based SR-71 flights. The United States had been sharing such data with Israel, Egypt, and Syria on a "highly selective basis" as a result of an agreement signed in 1974 after the October War of 1973. The information previously transmitted to Israel primarily concerned Egyptian or Syrian military developments but was now to be expanded to cover a "broader range."[155]

Israel did not, however, receive everything it wanted. Among the items it did not receive were a dedicated satellite and a system of ground stations that would "directly access" the KH-11 as it passed over the Middle East.[156]

Another area of expanded U.S.-Israeli cooperation involves the large number of émigrés who arrive in Israel from the Soviet Union each year. Information obtained by interviews conducted by the Mossad is now reportedly passed on to the CIA.[157] Although it is unlikely that any startling revelations are produced, the collective data can be quite valuable.

Most recently, Israel has been involved in supporting U.S. covert action in Central America. At the request of the United States, Israel has supplied to Honduras weapons captured from the PLO and slated for eventual use by the contras. The arms shipments include artillery pieces, mortar rounds, mines, hand grenades, and ammunition. The deliveries to the contras were reportedly part of a joint U.S.-Israeli project involving the covert deliveries of captured Soviet arms to anti-communist insurgent groups. In addition to the contras, groups receiving the arms are reported to include the Mujahedeen in Afghanistan, UNITA in Angola, and the MNR forces in Mozambique. Israel has also consulted with Central American governments about intelligence operations.[158]

In addition, Israel has supplied the United States with intelligence on the Middle East—both reports from agents and finished intelligence analyses. Some U.S. officials have not been impressed by the political intelligence, however. One CIA official said that he was "appalled at the lack of quality of the political intelligence on the Arab world. . . . Their tactical military intelligence was first rate. But they didn't know their enemy. I saw this political intelligence and it was lousy, laughably bad. . . . It was gossip stuff mostly."[159]

Both the United States and Israel have received intelligence aid from the other during crises situations. During the 1973 war Israel received data obtained by the U.S. signals intelligence satellite known as RHYOLITE. In 1976 the United States supplied Israel with both aerial and satellite reconnaissance photographs of Entebbe airport to supplement the information obtained by Israeli agents in preparation for the Israeli hostage rescue mission. During the 1985 hijacking of the *Achille Lauro*, Israel provided the United States with the location of the ship on several occasions, the location of the ships hijackers when they were in Israel, and the identification number and calls signs of the plane carrying the hijackers seconds after it took off from Egypt.[160]

Despite the high level of cooperation between the U.S. and Israeli intelligence communities, each has treated the other as a target for penetration. In the early 1950s the CIA attempted to use American Jews to collect intelligence on Israel as well as conducting electronic eavesdropping operations within Israel and against Israeli institutions abroad, some of which were detected by Israel. In addition, there were some unsuccessful efforts to recruit Israeli Army officers sent to the United States for advanced military training and other studies. Early in the 1950s the United States also tried to penetrate the Mossad operation in Vienna.[161]

At the same time, U.S. institutions within Israel have been the target of Israeli penetration attempts. In one instance, Shin Beth tried to recruit an employee of the U.S. Consulate General in Jerusalem who was having an affair with an Israeli girl. Shin Beth rigged a fake abortion case against the employee in an unsuccessful attempt to recruit him. Before this attempt at blackmail, Shin Beth had tried to get the girl to elicit information from her boyfriend. In addition, there were two or three attempts to recruit Marine Guards for monetary reward. In 1954 a hidden microphone planted by the Israelis was discovered in the office of the U.S. ambassador in Tel Aviv. In 1956 telephone taps were found connected to two telephones in the residence of the U.S. military attaché.[162]

In 1979 the Mossad acted abroad in a combination of intelligence collection and covert political action, according to one account. During that year, U.N. Ambassador to the United States Andrew Young indicated to a PLO representative that he wished to talk informally. The account states that the telephones of both the PLO representative and Young were tapped by the Mossad, and the story was "leaked" to *Newsweek*. Young lost his job and the dialogue with the PLO was dropped.[163]

The most recent known case of Israeli operations against the "American target" became public in 1985, when Jonathan Jay Pollard, an employee of the Naval Investigative Service's Anti-Terrorist Alert Center (ATAC), made a mad but unsuccessful dash for asylum in the Israeli embassy. Pollard, who had been under FBI surveillance after being reported to superiors by colleagues who considered some of his activities suspicious, was arrested and charged with espionage. Subsequently, Pollard pleaded guilty.[164]

Pollard was first hired by the Navy in September 1979 to be an analyst for the Navy's Fleet Operational Intelligence Office (now the

Navy Operational Intelligence Center). In June 1984 he was assigned as a watch officer for ATAC, with a focus on potential terrorist threats in the United States and the Caribbean; he received high-level clearances, giving him access to intelligence produced by photographic and signals intelligence systems. Shortly afterward Pollard requested that an associate put him in touch with Aviem Sella, a high-level Israeli Air Force officer attending graduate school at New York University, whom Pollard's associate had recently met. Pollard and Sella then met in Washington, D.C., in early summer 1984. There Pollard informed Sella that he wanted to provide Israel with classified documents and information, and proceeded to describe the data he could furnish, including signals intelligence and technical information that he said could be used by Israel to strengthen its defensive capabilities.[165]

Shortly thereafter, Pollard and Sella again met in Washington, and Pollard delivered the classified documents. Sella informed him that he could arrange for Pollard to be paid for providing additional classified information. Pollard was ultimately promised more than $300,000 for delivering suitcases full of classified information; he was to receive $30,000 a year for ten years in addition to monthly cash payments. The monthly payments started out at $1,500 and were later increased to $2,500 a month. Before being arrested, Pollard had received more than $45,000, according to prosecutors.[166]

The information Pollard provided included not only naval intelligence data but information produced by the Defense Intelligence Agency and other U.S. government agencies. His courier card allowed him to walk out of his Navy office complex with documents he was not authorized to have. According to a U.S. Justice Department memo:

> During the approximately 18 months that [Pollard] was selling U.S. secrets to Israel, more than a thousand classified documents were compromised, the majority of which were detailed analytical studies containing technical calculations, graphs and satellite photographs. . . .
> A substantial number of these documents were hundreds of pages in length. More than 800 of these documents were classified top secret.[167]

According to one account, those documents provided information on:

- PLO headquarters in Tunisia (including a description of all the buildings);
- the specific capabilities of the Libyan air defense system;

- Iraqi and Syrian chemical warfare production capabilities (included were detailed satellite pictures and maps showing the location of factories and storage facilities);

- Soviet arms shipments to Syria and other Arab states, including specifics on the SS-21 ground-to-ground and SA-5 anti-aircraft missiles;

- Pakistan's program to build an atomic bomb (including satellite photographs of its nuclear facility outside Islamabad).

The information on the PLO headquarters in Tunisia and the Libyan air defense system, along with Pollard-provided information, helped the Israeli Air Force evade detection in its bombing attack on PLO headquarters on October 1, 1985.[168]

Pollard delivered his weekly take of classified documents to the apartment of Irit Erb, the secretary to the science attaché in the Israeli embassy in Washington; the material was then photocopied in another apartment in the building. Also involved was Joseph Yossi Yagur, the science consul at Israel's New York City consulate and Sella's successor as Pollard's contact. Both Erb and Yagur were employees of LEKEM. Along with Sella and Rafael Eitan, the head of LEKEM, they were named as unindicted coconspirators in the indictment of Pollard.[169]

The Israeli government denied that the espionage operation had been approved by the highest authorities, dismissed Eitan from his positions as head of LEKEM and special adviser on terrorism to the Prime Minister, and disbanded LEKEM. An Israeli embassy spokesman stated:

> The Pollard affair was an unauthorized deviation from the clear-cut Israeli policy of not conducting any espionage whatsoever in the United States or activities against the interests of the United States, given that the United States is a true friend of Israel.
> The unit, which was involved . . . has been disbanded and the head of the unit has been relieved of his duties.[170]

The credibility of the Israeli government's denial was questioned—in part, because of Eitan's subsequent appointment as the head of Israeli Chemicals, a large, government-owned corporation, and because of Sella's position as a brigadier general and commander of Rimon Air Force Base (one of Israel's largest) in the Negev. In the midst of the controversy, Sella was promoted to commander of Israel's second largest air base, Tel Nof.

Statements by several participants in the case and by U.S. intelligence officials cast doubt on the Israeli assertion of "unauthorized deviation." Rafael Eitan claimed that the operation was approved by higher levels in the government, while Pollard stated that "the type of collection guidance I received suggested a highly coordinated effort between the naval, army and air force's intelligence services."[171]

As a result of the controversy that continued even after Pollard was sentenced to life imprisonment, the Israeli government set up a two-member commission to investigate the case, and Colonel Sella resigned from the Air Force. John Davitt, head of the Justice Department's internal security section until his retirement in 1980, said that the Israeli intelligence services were "more active than anyone but the KGB. . . . They were targeted on the United States about half the time and on Arab countries about half the time." Other U.S. intelligence officials said that they were aware of a number of cases of Israeli intelligence operations in the United States, some of which involved leaks of classified information to Israeli agents by Americans who were pro-Israel but not paid agents.[172]

NOTES TO CHAPTER 7

1. Central Intelligence Agency (CIA), *Foreign Intelligence and Security Services: Israel* (Washington, D.C.: CIA, 1977), p. 7.
2. Ibid., p. 7.
3. Stewart Steven, *The Spymasters of Israel* (New York: MacMillan, 1980), pp. 42–43.
4. Richard Deacon, *The Israeli Secret Service* (New York: Taplinger, 1977), p. 39.
5. Steven, *The Spymasters of Israel*, p. 4; Stanley A. Blumberg and Gwinn Owens, *The Survival Factor: Israeli Intelligence from World War I to the Present* (New York: G. P. Putnam, 1981), pp. 69–70.
6. Deacon, *The Israeli Secret Service*, pp. 38, 40.
7. Steven, *The Spymasters of Israel*, pp. 16–17; Ze'ev Schiff, *A History of the Israeli Army: 1874 to the Present* (New York: MacMillan, 1985), pp. 192–93.
8. Blumberg and Owens, *The Survival Factor*, pp. 154–55.
9. Steven, *The Spymasters of Israel*, p. 31.
10. Ibid., pp. 32–33; Central Intelligence Agency, *Foreign Intelligence and Security Services: Israel*, p. 8; Schiff, *A History of the Israeli Army*, p. 194.

11. Dan Fisher and Ronald J. Ostrow, "Little-Known Israeli Unit Linked to Pollard Spy Case," *Los Angeles Times*, November 29, 1985, pp. 1, 2; Ze'ev Schiff, "Israel Breaks the Rules," *Washington Post*, December 8, 1985, pp. B1, B2; William Claiborne, "Israel to Allow Questioning by the U.S.," *Washington Post*, December 3, 1985, pp. A1, A2; William Claiborne, "Israel Offers to Return Documents," *Washington Post*, November 30, 1985, p. A23; Thomas L. Friedman, "Israeli Antiterror Aide Reportedly Had Two Jobs," *New York Times*, November 30, 1985, p. 9.

12. Blumberg and Owens, *The Survival Factor*, p. 256.

13. Ibid., p. 262.

14. Ibid., pp. 260–65.

15. Ibid., pp. 264–65.

16. Fisher and Ostrow, "Little-Known Israeli Unit Linked to Pollard Spy Case"; Schiff, "Israel Breaks the Rules"; Claiborne, "Israel to Allow Questioning by the U.S."; Claiborne, "Israel Offers to Return Documents"; Friedman, "Israeli Antiwar Aide Reportedly Had Two Jobs."

17. Central Intelligence Agency, *Foreign Intelligence and Security Services: Israel*, pp. 15–16.

18. Ibid., p. 16.

19. Ibid., pp. 9, 16.

20. Ibid., p. 17.

21. Ibid., p. 16.

22. Ibid., pp. 16-19, 24-25; Benjamin Beit-Hallahami, *The Israeli Connection: Who Israel Arms and Why* (New York: Pantheon, 1987), pp. 26, 32, 33, 48, 69, 76-77, 98.

23. Blumberg and Owens, *The Survival Factor*, pp. 211-12.

24. Ibid., pp. 213, 215.

25. Ibid., pp. 218-19, 221.

26. Dennis Eisenberg, Uri Dan, and Eli Landau, *The Mossad: Israel's Secret Intelligence Service* (New York: Signet, 1978), pp. 111-12.

27. Ibid., p. 116.

28. Central Intelligence Agency, *Foreign Intelligence and Security Services: Israel*, p. 18.

29. Ibid.

30. Deacon, *The Israeli Secret Service*, pp. 143-44.

31. Ibid., p. 144.

32. Eisenberg, Dan, and Landau, *The Mossad*, p. 143.

33. Central Intelligence Agency, *Foreign Intelligence and Security Services: Israel*, p. 18.

34. Deacon, *The Israeli Secret Service*, p. 263.

35. David Shipler, *Arab and Jew: Wounded Spirits in a Promised Land* (New York: Times Books, 1986), pp. 407-8.

36. Steven, *The Spymasters of Israel*, pp. 172–73.
37. Ibid., p. 183.
38. Eisenberg, Dan, and Landau, *The Mossad*, p. 182.
39. Ibid., p. 183.
40. Ibid., pp. 185–86.
41. Ibid., pp. 186–87.
42. Craig S. Karpel, "Tales of the Mossad, Part Three," *Penthouse*, May 1980, pp. 129 ff.; Mario de Arcangelis, *Electronic Warfare* (London: Blanford, 1985), pp. 182–83.
43. David K. Shipler, "Close U.S.-Israel Relationship Makes Keeping Secrets Hard," *New York Times*, December 22, 1985, pp. 1, 12.
44. Steven Weismman and Herbert Krosney, *The Islamic Bomb: The Nuclear Threat to Israel and the Middle East* (New York: New York Times Books, 1981), p. 125.
45. Ibid.
46. Ibid., p. 126.
47. Andrew Weir and Jonathan Bloch, "Mossad's Secret Rivals," *The Middle East*, December 1981, pp. 24–26.
48. Michael Bar-Zohar and Eitan Haber, *The Quest for the Red Prince* (New York: Morrow, 1983), p. 159.
49. Donald Neff, *Warriors for Jerusalem* (New York: Linden/Simon & Schuster, 1984), p. 101.
50. Sanjoy Hazarika, "Israel and Britain Said to Aid Sri Lanka Force," *New York Times*, August 26, 1984, p. 8.
51. Leslie H. Gelb, "Iran Said to Get Large-Scale Aid from Israel, Soviet and Europeans," *New York Times*, March 8, 1982, pp. A1, A10; Glenn Frankel, "Israeli Report Links Peres Aide to Contra Support," *Washington Post*, January 11, 1987, p. A21.
52. Weir and Bloch, "Mossad's Secret Rivals."
53. Leonard Spector, *Nuclear Proliferation Today* (Cambridge, Mass.: Ballinger, 1984), p. 176.
54. "A Mossad Caper," *Newsweek*, October 27, 1986, p. 5; Thomas L. Friedman, "Israel Said to Abduct Seller of A-Bomb Secrets," *New York Times*, October 27, 1986, p. A6; "Revealed: The Secrets of Israel's Nuclear Arsenal," *Sunday Times*, October 5, 1986, pp. 1 ff.
55. "How Israeli Agents Snatched Vanunu," *The Sunday Times*, August 9, 1987, pp. 1, 3; Glenn Frankel, "Treason Suspect in Israel Flashes Message on Kidnapping," *Washington Post*, December 23, 1986, pp. A1, A14; for other accounts see "The Long Arm of the Mossad," *Newsweek*, November 10, 1986, p. 39; Glenn Frankel, "Israel Says It Holds Technician," *Washington Post*, November 10, 1986, pp. A1, A26; "Mossad Agent Tied to Fugitive's Arrest," *Los Angeles Times*, November 17, 1986, p. 6; Dan

Fisher, "Israeli Charged with Treason in A-Plant Case," *Los Angeles Times*, November 29, 1986, pp. 1, 15.
56. Steven, *The Spymasters of Israel*, pp. 87–88.
57. Ibid., pp. 90–92.
58. Ibid., p. 145.
59. Ibid.
60. Ibid., p. 146.
61. Ibid., p. 265; Bar-Zohar and Haber, *The Quest for the Red Prince*, pp. 116–17.
62. Steven, *The Spymasters of Israel*, p. 265.
63. Blumberg and Owens, *The Survival Factor*, p. 249; Bar-Zohar and Haber, *The Quest for the Red Prince*, pp. 129–30.
64. Bar-Zohar and Haber, *The Quest for the Red Prince*, pp. 132–35.
65. Ibid., pp. 146–49; Blumberg and Owens, *The Survival Factor*, pp. 249–50.
66. Steven, *The Spymasters of Israel*, pp. 270–71; Bar-Zohar and Haber, *The Quest for the Red Prince*, pp. 153–54; Blumberg and Owens, *The Survival Factor*, p. 250.
67. Bar-Zohar and Haber, *The Quest for the Red Prince*, pp. 167–77.
68. Ibid., pp. 187, 189; Blumberg and Owens, *The Survival Factor*, pp. 250–51.
69. Steven, *The Spymasters of Israel*, p. 286.
70. Ibid., p. 292; Bar-Zohar and Haber, *The Quest for the Red Prince*, pp. 218–19.
71. "Cutting Arafat's Sea Link," *Newsweek*, December 1, 1986, p. 46.
72. Central Intelligence Agency, *Foreign Intelligence and Security Services: Israel*, p. 30.
73. Ibid., p. 30; *Jane's Defence Weekly*, January 11, 1986, p. 4.
74. Central Intelligence Agency, *Foreign Intelligence and Security Services: Israel*, p. 31.
75. Ibid., p. 32.
76. Weir and Bloch, "Mossad's Secret Rivals."
77. Central Intelligence Agency, *Foreign Intelligence and Security Services: Israel*, p. 32.
78. Ibid., p. 32; Neff, *Warriors for Jerusalem*, p. 218.
79. John Kifner, "Matching Israel: Syrian Goal Seen as Unlikely," *New York Times*, December 14, 1986, p. 25.
80. Central Intelligence Agency, *Foreign Intelligence and Security Services: Israel*, pp. 32–33.
81. Ibid., pp. 33–34.
82. Ibid., p. 34.
83. Steven, *The Spymasters of Israel*, pp. 64–67.
84. Ibid., p. 69.

85. Ibid., pp. 75-77.
86. Schiff, *A History of the Israeli Army*, p. 212; Deacon, *The Israeli Secret Service*, pp. 262, 264; Steven, *The Spymasters of Israel*, p. 298.
87. Jacques Derogy and Henri Carmel, *The Untold Story of Israel* (New York: Grove Press, 1979), p. 281; Steven, *The Spymasters of Israel*, pp. 303-4.
88. Steven, *The Spymasters of Israel*, p. 297.
89. Derogy and Carmel, *The Untold History of Israel*, pp. 280-81.
90. Ibid., p. 281.
91. Steven, *The Spymasters of Israel*, p. 298; Schiff, *A History of the Israeli Army*, pp. 209-10; Janice Gross Stein, "The 1973 Intelligence Failure: A Reconsideration," *The Jerusalem Quarterly* 24 (Summer 1982): 41-54.
92. Steven, *The Spymasters of Israel*, p. 305.
93. Central Intelligence Agency, *Foreign Intelligence and Security Services: Israel*, p. 36.
94. Bill Gunston, *Spy Planes and Electronic Warfare Aircraft* (New York: Arco, 1983), pp. 86, 109, 138.
95. James Adams, *The Unnatural Alliance* (New York: Quartet, 1984), p. 113; Geoffrey Manners. "Israel's Intelligence Units," *Jane's Defence Weekly*, June 20, 1987, pp. 1318-19.
96. Adams, *The Unnatural Alliance*, p. 113.
97. Central Intelligence Agency, *Foreign Intelligence and Security Services: Israel*, p. 36.
98. Ibid., pp. 37-38.
99. Ibid., p. 38.
100. Ibid., p. 38.
101. Ibid., p. 42.
102. Ibid.
103. "Development, Role, Conception of Intelligence Agencies Viewed," *Joint Publications Research Service*-NEA-84-102, July 2, 1984.
104. Ibid.
105. Ibid.
106. Ibid.
107. Central Intelligence Agency, *Foriegn Intelligence and Security Services: Israel*, p. 25.
108. Ibid., pp. 25-26.
109. Ibid., p. 25.
110. Ibid., p. 27.
111. Ibid.
112. Ibid., p. 29.
113. Ibid.
114. David K. Shipler, *Arab and Jew*, pp. 130, 431-32.
115. Ibid., p. 432.

116. Deacon, *The Israeli Secret Service*, p. 161.
117. Ibid., pp. 162–63.
118. Ibid., p. 189.
119. Ibid., p. 190.
120. Ibid., pp. 192, 193–94.
121. Ibid., pp. 195–96.
122. "Israel Captures West Bank Ring," *New York Times*, June 20, 1987, p. 28.
123. Thomas L. Friedman, "Security Official Focus of Debate in Israeli Furor," *New York Times*, May 27, 1986, pp. A1, A7; Thomas L. Friedman, "Dispute over Shamir Role in '84 Case," *New York Times*, May 30, 1986, p. A4.
124. Friedman, "Dispute over Shamir Role in '84 Case."
125. Dan Fisher, "Israeli Security Chief Resigns Amid Scandal," *Los Angeles Times*, June 26, 1986, pp. 1, 18; Moshe Brilliant, "New Reports on Scandal Rock Israel," *New York Times*, June 18, 1986, p. A3.
126. Friedman, "Dispute over Shamir Role in '84 Case"; Thomas L. Friedman, "Israeli Lawyers in a Dispute: Ministry vs. Security Agency," *New York Times*, September 30, 1986, p. A14.
127. Friedman, "Dispute over Shamir Role in '84 Case"; Glenn Frankel, "Israelis Pardon 7 in Slaying," *Washington Post*, August 25, 1986, pp. A1, A23.
128. Dan Fisher, "Shin Bet Affair Revives Israeli Dispute of Security Needs versus the Law," *Los Angeles Times*, June 27, 1986, pt. 1, p. 8.
129. Thomas L. Friedman, "Inquiry Ordered in Israeli Scandal," *New York Times*, July 15, 1986, p. A10; Glenn Frankel, "Pardon of 4 Upheld in Israeli Bus Deaths," *Washington Post*, August 7, 1986, pp. A25, A27; Glenn Frankel, "Israelis Pardon 7 in Slaying."
130. William Clairborne, "Israeli Debate Focuses on Security vs. Law," *Washington Post*, May 31, 1986, p. A16.
131. Fisher, "Shin Bet Affair Revives Israeli Dispute," p. 8.
132. "Israeli Investigation Clears Shamir in Killing of 2 Arabs or Cover-Up," *New York Times*, December 29, 1986, pp. A1, A6.
133. Dan Fisher, "Treason Case Stirs Furor in Israeli Legal Circles," *Los Angeles Times*, May 18, 1987, pt. 1, p. 5; Michael Ross, "Israeli Court Deals Blow to Security Agency," *Los Angeles Times*, May 25, 1987, pp. 1, 13.
134. Central Intelligence Agency, *Foreign Intelligence and Security Services: Israel*, p. 10.
135. Ibid.
136. Ibid., p. 24.
137. Ibid.
138. Ibid.
139. Ibid.
140. Ibid.

141. "Mossad and the DGED," *Defense and Foreign Affairs Weekly*, August 4–10, 1986, p. 1.
142. Central Intelligence Agency, *Foreign Intelligence and Security Services: Israel*, p. 24; Beit-Hallahmi, *The Israeli Connection*, pp. 118, 126.
143. Central Intelligence Agency, *Foreign Intelligence and Security Services: Israel*, p. 24; Beit-Hallahmi, *The Israeli Connection*, pp. 118, 126; Deacon, *The Israeli Secret Service*, pp. 198–200.
144. Robert Schouten, *Haagsche Courant*, March 30, 1985 (summary of article provided by Paul Rusman).
145. Private information.
146. Steven, *The Spymasters of Israel*, p. 27.
147. Judith Perera, "Cracks in the Special Relationship," *The Middle East*, March 1983, pp. 12–18.
148. Ibid.
149. Blumberg and Owens, *The Survival Factor*, p. 272; Richard Halloran, "U.S. Offers Israel Plan on War Data," *New York Times*, March 13, 1983, pp. 1, 13.
150. Edmund Walsh, "Begin Offers to Give War Intelligence to U.S.," *Washington Post*, October 15, 1982, p. A18; Richard Halloran, "U.S. Said to Bar Deal with Israel," *New York Times*, February 10, 1983, pp. A1, A7.
151. Halloran, "U.S. Said to Bar Deal with Israel"; Bernard Gwertzman, "Israelis to Share Lessons of War with Pentagon," *New York Times*, May 22, 1983, pp. 1, 11.
152. Bernard Gwertzman, "Reagan Turns to Israel," *New York Times Magazine*, November 27, 1983, pp. 62ff.
153. Bob Woodward, "CIA Sought 3rd Country Contra Aid," *Washington Post*, May 19, 1984, pp. A1, A13.
154. Bob Woodward, "Probes of Iran Deals Extend to Roles of CIA, Director," *Washington Post*, November 28, 1986, pp. A1, A33.
155. "U.S. to Share More Recon Data, Tightens Air Links with Israel," *Aerospace Daily*, December 8, 1983, pp. 193–94.
156. Ibid.
157. "Is the CIA Hobbled?" *Newsweek*, March 5, 1979, pp. 18–20.
158. Philip Taubman, "Israel Said to Aid Latin Arms Race to U.S.," *New York Times*, July 21, 1983, pp. A1, A4; Beit-Hallahami, *The Israeli Connection*, p. 204.
159. Charles Babcock, "Israel Uses Special Relationship to Get Secrets," *Washington Post*, June 15, 1986, p. A1.
160. Desmond Ball and Jeffrey Richelson, *The Ties that Bind: Intelligence Cooperation Between the UKUSA Countries* (London: Allen & Unwin, 1985), p. 304; "How the Israelis Pulled It Off," *Newsweek*, July 19, 1976, pp. 42–47; David Halevy and Neil C. Livingstone, "The Ollie We Knew," *The Washingtonian*, July 1987, pp. 77ff.

161. Wolf Blitzer, *Between Washington and Jerusalem: A Reporter's Notebook* (New York: Oxford, 1985), p. 96.
162. Central Intelligence Agency, *Foreign Intelligence and Security Services: Israel*, pp. 29-30.
163. Weir and Bloch, "Mossad's Secret Rivals."
164. "Jay Pollard's Peculiar Tale," *U.S. News and World Report*, June 1, 1987, pp. 23-25.
165. "Test of Federal Government Summary of Espionage Case Against Pollard," *New York Times*, June 5, 1986, p. B11.
166. Ibid.; Joe Picharello, "Ex-Analyst Pollard Pleads Guilty to Spying for Israel," *Washington Post*, June 5, 1986, pp. A1, A37.
167. Philip Shenon, "U.S. Describes Data that Spy Provided Israel," *New York Times*, January 7, 1987, p. A14.
168. Wolf Blitzer, "Pollard: Not a Bumbler, but Israel's Master Spy," *Washington Post*, February 15, 1987, pp. C1, C2.
169. Ibid., Philip Shenon, "Spy Telling of Israeli Operations; Pelton Convicted of Selling Secrets," *New York Times*, June 6, 1986, pp. A1, B5.
170. Philip Shenon, "Israel Denies Running a Widespread Espionage Operation in U.S.," *New York Times*, June 2, 1986, p. A12.
171. Wolf Blitzer, "Pollard Says Top Israeli Officials Authorized His Spying," *Jerusalem Post International Edition*, March 7, 1987, pp. 1-2.
172. Charles R. Babcock, "U.S. an Intelligence Target of the Israelis, Officials Say," *Washington Post*, June 5, 1986, pp. A1, A38; Shenon, "Spy Telling of Israeli Operations"; William Claiborne, "Israelis Criticize Spy Case Leaks by U.S. Officials," *Washington Post*, June 7, 1986, pp. A1, A11.

8 JAPANESE INTELLIGENCE ORGANIZATIONS

ORIGINS

The origins of the present-day Japanese intelligence community are difficult to trace. Japan's defeat in World War II and its demilitarization by the Allies left it without any surviving military or intelligence establishment. And for Japan there was no Reinhard Gehlen to parlay his World War II intelligence file on the Soviet Union into a postwar arrangement. Nevertheless, it is clear from an examination of the Japanese intelligence establishment in World War II that it was a worthy predecessor for a modern-day intelligence community. According to a U.S. study:

> Prior to the Pearl Harbor attack the Japanese Government had developed a vast organization throughout the world for the collection of intelligence, using diplomatic, commercial, and military representatives together with literally thousands of enthusiastic amateur spies. Their efforts were by no means confined to the uncovering of military secrets. Every activity—commercial, social and cultural—merited investigation and reporting, the natural effect of the characteristic Japanese thirst for knowledge, and his fear that his nation might not keep pace with technological developments of the western world.[1]

Japan maintained a variety of military and civilian agencies that engaged in numerous types of intelligence collection, analysis, and covert action operations. Organizations that housed intelligence units were the Army General Staff, the Navy General Staff, the Air Force, the Foreign Office, and the Greater East Asia Ministry.

The Second Division of the Army General Staff was responsible for intelligence, and it received intelligence reports from units in the field as well as from military attachés stationed in neutral and Japanese-controlled countries. These attachés accounted for a large portion of the information collected by Japanese intelligence, particularly in Europe. Originally formed in 1878 and designated the *Kanseikyoku*, the organization became the Second Division in 1896. In 1908 a Western Section and a China Section were established. In 1936 the Russian group of the Western Section was transformed into a Russia Section. In that same year an Espionage Section was also established.[2]

The various sections of the Second Division produced reports on: (1) enemy strength and dispositions; (2) enemy capabilities and intentions; (3) the general situation in enemy countries, including production, morale, and the ability to wage war; (4) the performance and characteristics of enemy equipment; and (5) aircraft and ship recognition material. The reports were based on information derived from a variety of sources: attachés, COMINT, technical research studies, reports from area armies and air general headquarters, civilian agencies such as the Foreign Ministry, and accounts of Allied ship, plane, and submarine movements.[3]

The evaluations of the different sections of the Second Division varied in quality. The China Section consistently provided poor evaluations of China's capabilities. The Russian Section did much better, at least during the summer of 1937, when the section closely followed Stalin's purge of the Red Army. Its tracking of Soviet military movements was aided by reports from outposts along the Manchurian border that used high-powered telescopes, by additional information on train schedules, and by some aerial reconnaissance.[4]

Besides its intelligence collection network, the Army maintained special service organizations at the theater level. These organizations were variously referred to as the Special Service Agency (*Tokumu Kikan*), the Liaison Department (*Renraku Bu*), and the Army Department (*Rikugun Bu*), and their intelligence functions included conducting covert action operations and working with puppet governments and local leaders in occupied areas.[5]

Army signals intelligence activities were the responsibility of the Central Special Intelligence Department (*Chūō Tokushu Jōhō-Bu*), or CSID, which may have been subordinate to the Second Division. The CSID supervised all the Special Intelligence sections assigned to area armies and air armies. Apparently subordinate to the CSID was the Central Signal Examination Department, which conducted technical analyses of Allied signals. Among its products were summaries of the characteristics of B-29 traffic, issued to the Special Intelligence sections of field commands.[6]

In addition to military signals, the CSID was heavily involved in the cryptanalysis of diplomatic messages. Thus, the 23rd Area Army at Canton, China, monitored diplomatic traffic and transmitted the intercepted messages to the CSID in Tokyo. It is likely that the CSID decoded whatever traffic it could and then passed the results on to the Foreign Office.[7]

General naval intelligence responsibilities were lodged in the Third Department of the Naval General Staff. An Intelligence Section (*Chōhō-ka*) had been established in the Naval General Staff in 1896, shortly after the Sino-Japanese War, to compile reports of foreign fleet dispositions. By 1915 the section had become the Third (Intelligence) Group and acquired a section to organize reports on the U.S. Navy, including information from the Imperial Navy's attaché in Washington. In 1932 the Third Group became the Third (Intelligence) Department and acquired a section to compile data on the British Navy.[8]

The main function of the Third Department was the analysis of data. To carry out this function, the department was organized into four analytical sections: the Fifth Section for North and South America and U.S. Territories; the Sixth Section for China and Manchuria; the Seventh Section for Russia, Germany, and Europe; and the Eighth Section for Britain, Indochina, Australia, and the East Indies.[9]

Naval intelligence collection using human sources and sabotage operations were assigned to organizations variously known as the Special Service Department (*Tokumu Bu*) and the Office of the Resident Officer (*Zaijin Bukan Fu*). These organizations were responsible to the Naval General Staff and the appropriate geographical sections of the Intelligence Division. Naval signals intelligence collection was directed by the Special Service Section of the Naval General

Staff and carried out by the Fourth (Communications) Department of the Naval General Staff. The headquarters organization was divided into three sections (General Affairs, Communications Security, and Code-breaking Research), while interception activities were conducted by a number of communications units stationed at various Japanese bases, including those at Truk, Saipan, Wake, Rabual, Shimushiro, Yokosuka, and Owada.[10]

The full set of sources employed by the Third Department was diverse. Communications intelligence, captured documents (which proved to be the most accurate source of information), and prisoner of war information were just three of those sources. In addition, the department received technical intelligence developed by the Naval Air Technical Arsenal; reports from monitoring U.S. and foreign news broadcasts, which provided a great deal of information on production, strength, and losses; and newspapers and magazines, which were useful in developing long-term estimates of U.S. strength. Prior to the war, naval attachés were a valuable source of information, but the flow dried up almost completely once diplomatic relations were severed. Finally, combat information from the fleet also contributed to the department's store of knowledge.[11]

The success of the Japanese code-breakers varied from target country to target country. They evidently had little success with high-grade American or British codes. Japanese success in reading American codes was apparently confined almost entirely to codes used by the Air Force. Special intelligence personnel were able to derive important information on aircraft movements and unit dispositions. In the southwest Pacific area, Japanese Navy signal units in China were for several months able to determine the probability of B-29 attacks by reading messages giving instructions to turn on homing beacons. Against Soviet systems the Japanese did not have great success. A signal intercept station in the northern part of the Japanese half of Sakhalin sent out periodic messages based on the reading of Soviet messages, principally traffic between Petropavlovsk and Vladivostok. Much greater success was obtained against the cipher systems employed by the Chinese Nationalist government and Chinese Communist forces. Chinese tactical traffic, military attaché traffic, and diplomatic traffic were all read by Japanese cryptanalysts.[12]

Aerial reconnaissance was a primary source of intelligence for the Japanese with respect to Allied naval movements and air force deployments. Only one unit existed exclusively for the performance of aerial reconnaissance missions, the 1st Air Photographic Unit. The principal emphasis was on the surveillance of ships and harbors. Nearly half the aerial reconnaissance reports intercepted and read by Allied cryptanalysts fell into that category. The remainder of the decrypted reports described the location of Allied airfields and the number of planes located at airfields. Little attention was paid to the use of aerial reconnaissance to determine the location of ground troops or the location and size of Allied reserve units and supply stocks.[13]

The intelligence responsibilities of the Foreign Office were housed in the Investigation Bureau (*Chōsa Kyoku*), which was divided into three sections. Section I was responsible for the study of diplomatic history, the collection and organization of data, and the evaluation of areas outside Russia and West Asia; Section II was responsible for the Soviet Union and West Asia; and Section III was responsible for collection. Section III operated through embassies, legations, and consulates. Among the establishments used for espionage purposes was the consulate in Hawaii. When President Roosevelt based the American fleet in Hawaian waters in May 1940, the Japanese Foreign Ministry, at the urging of the Naval General Staff, asked consul General Kiichi Gunji to send regular reports on the fleet's size, disposition, and activities. To accomplish this mission, Gunji relied heavily on a far-from-secret source: the Honolulu newspapers, which reported on the size, numbers, and movements of warships.[14]

The Investigation Bureau's collection operations were located not only in Asia but also in Europe. Intelligence gathered in Spain concerned the United States and England; Portugal, Sweden, and Switzerland were other countries where the Foreign Office was engaged in active collection operations. Japanese collection activities concerning the United States focused on U.S. military and diplomatic activities in the Far East—U.S. strategy in the war in the Far East, the locations and conditions of airfields, and U.S. relations with the Chinese government.[15]

Communications intelligence work in the Foreign Ministry was the responsibility of the Cable Section (*Denshin-ka*). The section's Code Research Group (*Ango Kenkyu-han*) housed the cryptologists who broke various U.S. and British cipher systems.[16]

In 1942 the Greater East Asia Ministry was founded to handle all business, other than "purely diplomatic" business, relating to political, economic, and cultural affairs in Greater East Asia. The ministry was also given primary responsibility for intelligence collection concerning countries in the Far East, excluding Asiatic Russia. The Ministry's General Affairs Bureau, and within it, the General Affairs Section, was the unit most concerned with intelligence and its collection. The principal areas of operation were Siberia, Manchukuo, China, French Indochina, and Thailand, with the greatest amount of activity taking place in China.[17]

Following the war, as Japan resumed its place as a sovereign nation it began to establish a variety of intelligence and security units. The organizations that were established included one directly responsible to the Cabinet, several within the armed forces, and additional units in three civilian ministries.

INTELLIGENCE AND SECURITY ORGANIZATIONS

Cabinet Research Office (Naichō)

The Cabinet Research Office, known as Naichō, is Japan's premier intelligence organization, in that it is under the direct control of the Prime Minister and provides him with studies and analyses to aid in making foreign and defense policy decisions.[18]

Naichō is an extremely small organization to be the premier intelligence unit of a nation like Japan. In 1982 it was estimated that as of 1978 Naichō had only 84 regular employees, with an additional 70 being seconded from other ministries; its budget was estimated at $6 million. A 1986 estimate gave figures of 122 employees and a budget of $25 million. The Director of Naichō, Morimasa Taniguchi, proposed that the practice of seconding bureaucrats to the organization should be ended and intelligence analysts should be employed on a full-time basis.[19]

Naichō depends for information on private news and business organizations as well as the intelligence collected by the military. Among those organizations, as of 1975, were the World-Politico Economic Research Council, the Kyodo News Service, the Radio Press, and the Jiji Press. Such groups gather and collate information from domestic newspapers and magazines; they also collect foreign publications and monitor foreign television and radio broadcasts.[20]

Information may also come from attachés, business people, or scholars traveling to a location of interest. On occassion the Soviet

Union has alleged that some information on the USSR is obtained by Japanese travelers or diplomats. In 1967 Masatomi Uchikawa, an employee of the World Politico-Economic Research Council, was arrested on a trip through the Soviet Union for having taken photographs of a military installation. In 1986 a Japanese-owned railway container filled with electronic surveillance equipment was discovered on the Trans-Siberian railroad. In 1987 the Soviet Union expelled two Japanese—a naval attaché and a businessman—accusing the attaché of conducting "intelligence activity" during a July 1987 visit to the Black Sea port of Odessa. Earlier in the year four Soviet officials were expelled from Japan.[21]

The data gathered are analyzed by Naichō, the resultant products then distributed to the appropriate officials. Each week Naichō issues a classified report, *Military Information Data*. It also publishes reports on specific topics. Past papers have included *Organizations and Individuals in the People's Republic of China*, *Registry of Soviet Leaders*, *Examination of the Chinese Communist Party's Cultural Revolution*, and *The Economic Effects of the Vietnam War*.[22]

The great majority of Naichō reports deal with the Soviet Union and other Communist countries. It is rumored that in order to facilitate the preparation of such reports, research fees are given to scholars before they leave for trips to Communist nations, or high prices are paid for papers written after they return to Japan.[23]

Second Section, Investigation Division, Ground Self-Defense Forces

The Second Section, or *Nibetsu*, is responsible for the collection and analysis of pure military intelligence. Accordingly, the section collates material from the thirty Japanese military attachés stationed at overseas embassies as well as from the representatives of friendly governments who serve as liaison at their Tokyo embassies.[24]

Another source of information for Japanese military intelligence has been that obtained by analyzing photography produced by the civilian LANDSAT earth resources satellite. Beginning in March 1985, the Japanese government began buying LANDSAT photographs and passing them on to the 101st Survey Battalion in Tokyo that analyzes it. The battalion's analysts have been able to glean information of value from the photos. Satellite photos indicated that improvements were being made to the Soviet air base in a Siberian coastal area. Photos also indicated that the Zavitinsk base west of Khabarovsk had been extended and that work was continuing on support facilities. These changes meant that bases were being constructed for the operation of larger aircraft, such as the TU-22M Backfire.[25]

Annex Chamber, Second Section, Investigation Division, Ground Self-Defense Forces (Chobetsu)

The role of signals intelligence in Japanese defense activities is acknowledged in the 1986 *Defense of Japan* white paper: "the SDF [Self-Defense Forces] is endeavoring to gather and analyze military communications radio waves from abroad and those emitted from electronic weapons, thus obtaining information and preparing data necessary for Japan's defense."[26]

Established in 1958, the *Chosa Besshitsu*, or Chobetsu, is Japan's signals intelligence agency. The Chobetsu is located at Ichigaya Camp in Tokyo and draws its director from the National Police Agency. Because of the importance of the intelligence it collects, the Chobetsu is directly responsible to the Cabinet Research Office.[27]

The Chobetsu dwarfs Naichō in size, with approximately 1,000 employees drawn from all three branches of the Japanese armed forces as well as a modest number of civilians. A 1982 estimate suggested that there were 950 Chobetsu personnel: 480 from the Ground Self-Defense Forces, 190 from the Maritime Self-Defense Forces, 230 from the Air Self-Defense Forces, and 50 civilians. Among these employees are specialists in interception, cryptanalysis, and foreign languages. The major targets of the Chobetsu's interception operation are the communications of China, North Korea, and the Soviet Union. To conduct this activity the Chobetsu operates ten ground stations in Japan.[28]

Among the stations is one at Shiraho on Ishigaki, one of the southernmost islands of the Ryuku archipelago near Taiwan. An unmanned, circularly disposed antenna array (CDAA) only a few years old, the facility may be operated by the Japanese Post Office for the military. On Miho Peninsula is a Wullenweber-type CDAA, with typical reflector screen and sheathed monopoles; in addition, the Miho Peninsula site contains some highly directional rhombic antennas. The Miho and Shiraho antennas are employed to help monitor the patrol zone over which Japanese forces are supposed to be guarding the sea lines of communication between Japan and Guam. The antennas at Miho and Shiraho are located at apexes of the triangular patrol zone, providing ideal lines of intersection for triangulating onto radio emissions from the patrol zone. The Shiraho antennas would also provide ideal lines of intersection for emitters from the People's Republic of China, as well as for intercepting signals from Taiwan.[29]

At Higashi Chitose, on Hokkaido, is a CDAA identical to the one at Miho, as well as a couple of radomes that cover satellite antennas. The radomes help reduce radio interference and thus enhance satellite reception. The antennas may be employed to intercept signals from the Soviet Union's elliptically orbiting Molniya military communications satellites.[30]

Another station is located on the northern tip of Hokkaido, at Wakkanai. This station was heavily involved in the monitoring of Soviet Air Force activities during the September 1983 shooting down of a Korean Air Lines passenger jet. During its normal activities, the Wakkanai facility is targeted on Soviet Air Force activities, including the conversations between pilots and ground control.[31]

Altogether, the stations include five in the north (on Rebunto Island, at Higashi Chitose, at Nemuro at Higashi Nemuro, and at Nemuro Shibetsu), two in the middle of Japan (at Ohi and Kofunato), two in the south (Miho and Tachiarai), and one in the Ryukus (at Kikaijima Island).[32]

Yet another signals intelligence facility is to be built on Hokkaido. This station will be established on the west coast of the island to monitor Soviet communications in Siberia, four hundred miles east of Vladivostok. It is expected to be completed in 1989.[33]

Japan also employs aircraft to conduct signals intelligence operations. The Maritime Self-Defense Forces 81st Squadron at Iwakuni Air Base operates two EP-2J signals intelligence aircraft, which deploy to Machinoc Air Base near Misawa for electronic intelligence missions versus Sakhalin. In 1986 remodeled U.S. C-130 Hercules aircraft with electronic intelligence-gathering equipment and given the designation YS-11, began operations. The plane had undergone testing since 1982, and new planes will be deployed through a five-year period ending in 1990. Most likely the planes will be deployed on Hokkaido and fly over the Sea of Japan and the northwestern Pacific, intercepting signals emitted from Soviet land bases, airfields, and operational aircraft and warships in the soviet Far East. The planes will be particularly valuable in monitoring Soviet radars, which cannot be easily monitored by Chobetsu's ground stations.[34]

Several of Chobetsu's accomplishments have been noted in press accounts. When China began to assemble two hundred of its six hundred fishing boats near the disputed Senkaku Islands, Chobetsu monitored the exchange of radio signals between the Chinese fishing base and its ships. Chobetsu also monitored Soviet landing operation maneuvers on the northern territories islands from the inception of the operation, having picked up an unusually large volume of military communications from Etorofu Island.[35]

In September 1971 Chobetsu intercepted Chinese military communications canceling the leave for key Army units and grounding Air Force flights. Those communications turned out to be signs of the immediate aftermath of Lin Piao's alleged coup attempt against Mao Tse-tung. In January and February 1979, Chobetsu detected that call signs from Chinese Air Force squadrons normally stationed near the Soviet border were emanating from the far south of China. This was an indication that Deng Xiaoping was going to attempt to carry out his promise to punish Vietnam for its invasion of Cambodia.[36]

More recently, in 1984 Chobetsu apparently monitored an unauthorized coded signal of the Soviet Far East Army stating that the United States and the Soviet Union were going to war. The signal, which was sent from the Soviet part of Vladivostok to a nearby troop unit and intercepted in Tokyo, was issued two days after Ronald Reagan joked that he had ordered the bombing of the Soviet Union. Also monitored by Chobetsu were North Korean communications during the December 1986 reports of Kim-Il Sung's death, with Chobetsu's stations not picking up any unusual radio communications or troop movements.[37]

Intelligence Division, Air Self-Defense Forces

The Intelligence Division, Air Self-Defense Forces, is responsible for producing intelligence on the air forces of regional powers—their aircraft, deployments, and tactics.

The unit probably also supervises the airborne imaging program for the Japanese military. Airborne operations are carried out by the 501st Flight Squadron, located at Hyakuri air base. The squadron flies RF-4E Phantoms, which replaced the RF-86F. The RF-4E is equipped with side-looking radar, an infrared imaging system, and an optical camera—in contrast to the RF-86F, which possessed only an optical camera. Thus, the replacement of the RF-86F with the RF-4E greatly expanded the conditions under which Japanese forces could conduct aerial reconnaissance.[38]

The RF-4E carries a crew of two and has a maximum speed of at least Mach 2. With its 63-foot wingspan, height of 16 feet 5 inches, and weight of 30,400 pounds, the RF-4E can fly at maximum speeds of 910 mph at sea level (Mach 1.19) and 1432 mph at high altitude (Mach 2.17).[39]

Intelligence Division, Maritime Staff Office, Maritime Self-Defense Forces

The Intelligence Division, Maritime Staff Office, Maritime Self-Defense Forces, is responsible for producing basic naval intelligence on the navies of the Soviet Union, China, and other countries of regional interest. The division is probably also responsible for supervising the monitoring of naval movements in the vicinity of Japan. The importance of such monitoring, in the view of the Japanese Defense Agency, is stressed in the agency's 1986 report:

> It is extremely important for Japan, which takes an exclusively defensive posture, to maintain constant surveillance over its territory and waters and airspace surrounding Japan and to collect and process information necessary for defense, both in peacetime and emergencies. . . .
>
> Vessels passing through main straits are under vigilance and surveillance from land. Moreover, as a measure to make up for constraints stemming from weather conditions and other factors, vessels are constantly deployed in the Straits of Tsugaru, Tsushima and Soya.[40]

One major target of Japanese monitoring are Soviet submarines. Japan operates several airborne antisubmarine warfare aircraft—for example, the Shin Meiwa PS-1, a flying boat with a crew of nine. Production of the PS-1 followed from a decision by the Self-Defense Force in 1966 that a flying boat was a nearly ideal antisubmarine warfare (ASW) platform because it could sit on the water to conduct sonar searches, resulting in a more effective sonar capability and saving on the cost of sonobuoys. The first of two PS-1 prototypes flew on October 5, 1967. Because of increasing costs, only twenty-three were built, nineteen of which remained in operation in 1984. Since land-based ASW aircraft have proved more effective, it is not expected that there will be a follow-on plane.[41]

The PS-1 has four turboprop engines, a fuselage length of 109.9 feet, a wingspan of 108.7 feet, a height of 31.9 feet, a weight of 58,000 pounds when empty, and a maximum weight of 94,800 pounds. It can operate up to 29,500 feet and has a maximum speed of 295 knots. Its range when loaded is 1170 nautical miles (nm). It can operate in wave heights up to 14 feet, allowing operations in the Pacific for 80 percent of the time.[42]

The payload of the PS-1 includes four depth bombs, four MK 44/46 homing torpedoes, and wingtip launchers for triple groups of 5-inch rockets. The plane is also equipped with sonobuoys and magnetic anomaly detection equipment for detection and tracking purposes. The crew consists of two pilots, a navigator, a radio operator, a Magnetic Anomaly Detector (MAD) operator, two sonar operators, and a tactical coordinator.[43]

Also soon to be replaced is the Kawasaki P-2J, a land-based aircraft. This plane was a follow-on to the P-2H, in itself an adaptation of the Lockheed P-2. The P-2H entered the design phase in 1961. Between 1969 and 1979, eighty-nine P-2Hs were delivered. Driven by two turboprop and two turbojet engines, the P-2J has a maximum speed of 350 knots and a range of 2,400 nm. Its service ceiling is 30,000 feet, while its typical cruising speed is 217 knots. The plane has a length of 95.9 feet, a wing span of 101.3 feet, and a height of 29.3 feet. It weighs 42,000 pounds empty and 75,000 pounds full.[44]

The P-2J's weapons systems include MK 44/46 homing torpedoes, depth bombs, and rockets. Its sensors include the Julie/Jezebel acoustic system, the ARR-52A(V) sonobuoy receiver, and the HSQ-101 MAD installation. Originally the planes were equipped with APS-80J search radar, but this was subsequently replaced by the APS-80(N) in later aircraft.[45]

The most important Japanese ocean surveillance aircraft is the P-3C Orion. The Maritime Self-Defense Forces (MASDF) had sixty-nine planes in service as of August 1987. In early 1987 Japan announced its intention to buy nine more, and an additional thirty will be purchased between 1988 and 1991. The version flown by the MASDF is the Update II, which can carry up to eighty-four sonobuoys, sixteen of which can be monitored at a time. Additionally, the P-3C is equipped with a MAD and infrared detection system. P-3Cs purchased in 1988 and after will be the Update III version.[46]

One ASW aircraft flies over the Sea of Japan daily and over waters around the East China Sea and Hokkaido every two days. This surveillance is supplemented by vessels and other aircraft when considered necessary.[47]

Japan will also augment its ocean surveillance capability by the purchase of nine EP-3C electronic intelligence planes beginning in 1988. The nine planes will fly from Iwakuni air base, near Hiroshima, before the mid-1990s.[48]

In addition to its airborne submarine detection and tracking systems, Japan also operates underseas listening devices similar to those which make up the U.S. SOSUS system. In 1971 the Japanese Defense Agency announced that it was going to establish submarine detection devices on the sea bottom at the entrance to the Soya, Tsugaru, and Tsushima straits. In addition to a single array at Soya, arrays were established at Tsushima North and Tsushima South. Arrays at Matsumne, Tappi Point, and Hachinobe cover the Tsugaru Straights. Furthermore, the Ocean Environmental Observation Facility has been established at White Beach, Okinawa. And under the Maritime Self-Defense Force's Oceanographic Command in Yokosuka, Kanagawa Prefecture, are ten buildings and a staff of about a hundred engaged in submarine detection operations.[49]

A probable source of surface ocean surveillance information is the Marine Observation Satellite (MOS-1), launched on February 18, 1987, into a 564-mile sun-synchronous orbit. The MOS carries microwave, multispectral, thermal infrared, and visible radiometers, including charged-coupled detectors comparable to those on the SPOT satellite. An MOS-1 image of Kyushu Island shows runways and taxiways at Nagasaki airport. Resolution is 165 feet but may be better for many details.[50]

Figure 8–1 shows the location of Japanese ocean surveillance and SIGINT sites.

Information Analysis, Research and Planning Bureau, Ministry of Foreign Affairs

The Information Analysis, Research and Planning Bureau is responsible for the collection, distribution, and analysis of information on international affairs, research, and surveys on foreign countries, and

Figure 8-1. Japanese Ocean Surveillance and SIGINT Sites.

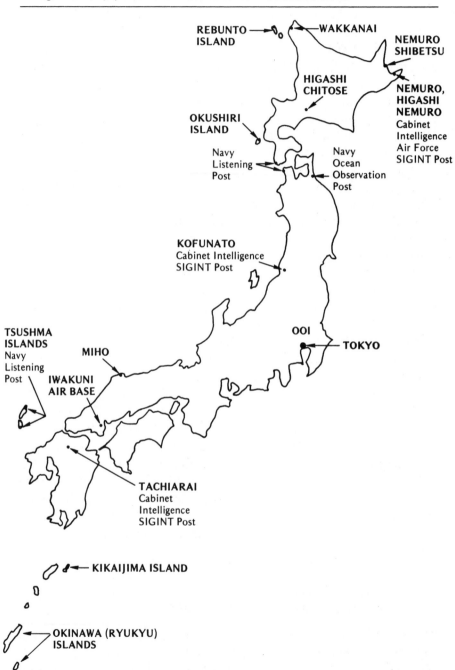

planning work connected with the formulation of general diplomatic policies. It is divided into the Overseas Information Division, the Policy Planning Division, and the Analysis Division.[51]

Ministry of International Trade and Industry

Within several of the bureaus of the Ministry of International Trade and Industry (MITI) are units that perform research and analysis of issues pertaining to international trade. Included are the General Affairs sections of the Secretariat, the International Trade Policy Bureau, and the Machinery and Information Industries Bureau. Additionally, the Research and Statistics Department of the Secretariat, the Trade Research Section and International Economic Affairs Department of the International Trade Policy Bureau, and the Research Section of the Industrial Policy Bureau may have intelligence analysis functions. According to one account, a Special Survey Group of the Information Room of the MITI Bureau of Heavy Industries (since merged with another bureau) was at one point set up to report on the U.S. computer industry.[52]

Another organization with commercial intelligence functions is MITI's Japanese External Trade Organization (JETRO). JETRO has an information-gathering network of 270 employees distributed through 81 cities in 59 countries. The information is then subject to analysis by 1,200 analysts. Altogether, JETRO has a budget of $130 million a year.[53]

Public Security Investigation Agency

With 2,000 employees, the Public Security Investigation Agency (PSIA) is the successor to the Special Investigation Bureau of the Ministry of Justice. Its functions include both counterespionage and countersubversion. In pursuit of the latter function, the PSIA places a number of groups under surveillance, among them the Japanese Communist Party, a variety of leftist social and labor organizations, radical new left organizations and factions, the North Korean-oriented Chosen Soren (the General Federation of Korean Residents in Japan), and rightist activist groups.[54] Undoubtedly the Japanese Red Army is among the groups under surveillance.

Because the agency does not have the power to compel cooperation, it tries to attain cooperation via economic incentives. On one occasion, in an attempt to detail the movements of a leader of the Communist party, the PSIA tried to gain the cooperation of the leader's wife. A PSIA official offered the wife, who was a struggling insurance agent, a deal: he would purchase a life insurance policy on his brother in exchange for information on the activities of her husband. Other reports claim that the agency has attempted to recruit informants by offering them women or, in the case of a student activist who was close to a target of investigation, by indicating that he could pass the teacher's employment exam if he provided information.[55]

The PSIA is also active in counterespionage operations. As might be expected, the primary nations involved in espionage operations in Japan are North Korea, the Soviet Union, and China. North Korea and the Soviet Union are interested in U.S. defense capabilities in the area, Japanese policy, and advanced technology. The Chinese areas of interest include Japanese policy toward the Soviet Union as well as high technology.

In June 1983 Soviet First Secretary Arkhadii A. Vinogradov was strongly requested to leave Japan for activities "incompatible with his status as a diplomat." According to Japanese authorities, he had tried to steal computer secrets from Hitachi. According to the police, who had been investigating Vinogradov as a suspected KGB officer since 1978, Vinogradov, together with B. N. Kakorin, an engineer with a private trading firm, had approached an unidentified computer company executive with a scheme to gain confidential high-technology information. The KGB officers asked him to establish a special company, financed by Moscow, to tap Japanese industrial secrets. Unknown to the KGB officers, their meetings were filmed.[56]

In April 1987 two Polish researchers at the Technical University of Szczecin who had entered Japan in October 1986 on tourist visas were expelled. They had been staying on the premises of K.K. Integra, a Tokyo computer-related company that a Pole naturalized in Japan had set up the same month the researchers arrived. The two researchers were accused of using the company as a base for espionage operations. The technology they obtained related mostly to computer graphics and high-speed tracing.[57]

In June 1987 four Japanese—an adviser to the privately run China Technical Center in Tokyo, an employee of the technical library of the U.S. Yokota Air Base, a military affairs expert, and an executive of a Japanese trading firm conducting business with China—were arrested and charged with selling U.S. military documents to Soviet diplomats and Chinese buyers over several years. One of the four was arrested after passing documents to an official of the Soviet trade mission. According to Japanese police officials, the papers and equipment confiscated at the homes of the four included technical manuals for the U.S. F-16 Falcon jet fighter, radio receivers, maps, and recordings of Morse Code signals.[58]

The most devastating allegations concerning Soviet bloc espionage and covert activities in Japan came from Major Stanislav Levechenko, who alleged that twenty-six Japanese were conducting activities—both influence and intelligence collection activities—for the KGB. Included in the twenty-six named were several members of the Japanese Diet, businesspeople, journalists, and a Foreign Ministry code clerk "who photographed or photocopied hundreds of messages from Japanese embassies around the world for the KGB."[59]

In addition to its domestic role, the PSIA prepares reports on Communist nations. Among its reports have been *The Recent International Federation of Communism* and *A Study of the Czechoslovakian Incident.*[60]

National Police Agency

The Foreign Affairs Section of the National Police Agency is concerned with operations carried out by China, North Korea, the Soviet Union, and other nations from the East bloc. The Agency's Security Section monitors the movements of political activists and extremists, such as members of the Japanese Red Army, who are based overseas.[61]

LIAISON

Among the countries of Asia with which Japan has intelligence relations is Australia. In May 1976 the Australian Secret Intelligence Service (ASIS) sought approval from the Australian Foreign Minister to establish a liaison relationship with Japan's Cabinet Research Office. Approval was given, and formal contact was established in August 1976. Between 1971 and 1975 the possibility of a liaison relationship between ASIS and the Cabinet Research Office had been raised but was rejected for a variety of reasons.[62]

As would be expected, the country with which Japan has the most extensive intelligence exchange relationship is the United States. One aspect of that relationship is the sharing of signals intelligence, as indicated by the Japanese sharing of Soviet communications intercepted on the night the Soviets shot down Korean Air Lines flight 007. Signals intelligence sharing is based on mutual interests and as partial payment by the United States to Japan for the SIGINT facilities the U.S. maintains on Japanese territory.

Japan has also received satellite photographs from U.S. authorities. In 1982 Secretary of Defense Caspar Weinberger presented the chief of the Japanese Defense Agency with satellite photographs "showing a Japanese-made floating dock being used in the repair of the Soviet aircraft carrier *Minsk*."[63] The purpose of that revelation was to convince the Japanese that technology made available to the Soviets for nonmilitary purposes was being misused.

In addition, it is likely that the Japanese Defense Agency is the recipient of satellite photographs or at least satellite photograph-derived information on a regular basis. Such information would concern Soviet naval capabilities and movements in the vicinity of Japan, Soviet air activity in Siberia, and the deployment of Soviet troops and weapons systems (particularly the SS-20) in the vicinity of Japan.

But the most extensive exchange undoubtedly occurs with respect to ocean surveillance information, particularly regarding Soviet naval movements. One aspect of such cooperation is the CINCPACFLT [U.S. Commander-in-Chief Pacific Fleet]-JMSDF [Japanese Maritime Self-Defense Forces] Intelligence Exchange Conference. Likewise, a responsibility of the Intelligence Liaison and Production Section of the Intelligence Division, U.S. Naval Forces Japan is to "coordinate Commander in Chief, U.S. Pacific Fleet and Commander U.S. Naval Forces, Japan intelligence exchange with the Chief of the Intelligence Division, Maritime Staff Office and the Intelligence Officer, CINCSDFLT [Commander-in-Chief Self-Defense Fleet]."[64]

Information derived from U.S. worldwide ocean surveillance assets—especially from White Cloud satellites and the SOSUS network—can substantially increase the effectiveness of Japan's surface ship and submarine detection efforts. Among the information likely to be passed on to Japan is much of that coming into the Fleet Ocean Surveillance Information Center at Kamiseya, Japan. At the same time, the Japanese share information obtained by their sonar arrays and P-3Cs. According to the staff manual for U.S. Naval Forces Japan, the Operations Special Projects officer of the Operations Division, U.S. Naval Forces Japan, conducts liaison with cognizant Japanese officials with respect to Operations Special Projects 6100, 6200, and 6300 Oceanographic Station Detachments.[65]

JAPANESE INTELLIGENCE AND FLIGHT 007

Japanese intelligence, particularly Chobetsu, was heavily involved in monitoring the communications of Soviet fighter pilots on the night that Korean Air Lines flight 007 was shot down.

On September 1, 1983, at 3:38 A.M. the Japanese radar station at Wakkanai, which had been tracking an unidentified aircraft's progress through the Soviet Union, saw the blip disappear from the screen when the plane was less than fifty miles away from the station. The trackers thought it was possibly a Soviet plane that had gone down. At 7:30 A.M. the Korean government asked Japan to find out, through its Moscow embassy, whether the Soviets had forced the missing plane down over Sakhalin.[66]

Japanese intelligence was not of immediate help in producing information on the incident, despite the presence of Chobetsu's Wakkanai intercept facility twenty-seven miles across the La Perouse Strait from Sakhalin. Wakkanai was a manned intercept facility only in the daytime, with its recording systems being voice-activated at all other times. Only a skeleton crew operated at night. No one in that crew listened to what was being recorded, and therefore no one triggered the high-speed secure communications link between Wakkanai and the U.S. signals intelligence facility at Misawa. Yet even if someone had listened to the tape, in crisis situations the Japanese pass intelligence through their own chain of command before forwarding it to Misawa.[67]

The Japanese station at Wakkanai also recorded radar tracks showing the sudden disappearance, at 3:29 A.M., of the flight path of an unidentified aircraft over Sakhalin Island. It was several hours after the airliner was declared missing at 5:30 A.M., however, that the station surveyed its recorded intelligence and discovered that the Soviet Union had scrambled interceptors to chase an intruder near

Sakhalin. Thus, the United States relied initially on the intercepts obtained by a small and highly secret U.S. unit at Wakkanai, Project CLEF.[68]

Ultimately, the Japanese tapes, which were of better quality than those of Project CLEF, were translated. At about 7:30 the Wakkanai listening post began an arduous search of the tapes of Soviet radio transmissions for the crucial time period. Hours later, the tape and radar chronologies were matched up. Japan had monitored not only what the pilots said but also the hard-to-obtain ground commands to the pilots—revealed because of slips of the tongue by U.S. and Japanese officials. The contents of the tape in which the Soviet pilots discussed in detail the "target" and its destruction were withheld from Prime Minister Nakasone for an hour by Chief Cabinet Secretary Masharu Gatudo. The Prime Minister ordered that they be made available to the United States.[69]

The tapes were later played at the UN to bolster the U.S. indictment of the Soviet Union. In a letter to Prime Minister Nakasone, President Reagan stated that the tapes made for an effective presentation. Some Japanese staff officers are reported to have opposed disclosure, fearing that it would harm Japan's ability to monitor Soviet military communications in the future. And according to one Japanese official, the Soviet Union promptly changed the codes and radio frequencies used by its aircraft in the Far East. One report indicated that the Chobetsu could monitor and understand only 60 percent of what it could before the disclosures.[70]

NOTES TO CHAPTER 8

1. The United States Strategic Bombing Survey (Pacific), *Japanese Military and Naval Intelligence* (Washington, D.C.: U.S. Government Printing Office, 1946), p. 1.

2. J. W. Bennett, W. A. Hobart, and J. B. Spitzer, *Intelligence and Cryptanalytic Activities of the Japanese During World War II* (Laguna Hills, Calif.: Aegean Park Press, 1986), p. 2; Michael A. Barnhart, "Japanese Intelligence Before the Second World War: 'Best Case' Analysis," in Ernest R. May, *Knowing One's Enemies: Intelligence Assessment Before the Two World Wars* (Princeton, N.J.: Princeton University Press, 1984), pp. 424–55 at 428.

3. United States Strategic Bombing Survey (Pacific), *Japanese Military and Naval Intelligence*, pp. 9–16.

4.   Barnhart, "Japanese Intelligence Before the Second World War," p. 435.
5.   Bennett et al., *Intelligence and Cryptanalytic Activities of the Japanese*, p. 3.
6.   Ibid., p. 7.
7.   Ibid., p. 10.
8.   Barnhart, "Japanese Intelligence Before the Second World War," pp. 427–28.
9.   Ibid., p. 427.
10. Bennett et al., *Intelligence and Cryptanalytic Activities of the Japanese*, pp. 3, 11; Barnhart, "Japanese Intelligence Before the Second World War," p. 427.
11. United States Strategic Bombing Survey (Pacific), *Japanese Military and Naval Intelligence*, pp. 21–22.
12. Bennett et al., *Intelligence and Cryptanalytic Activities of the Japanese*, pp. 12–15.
13. Ibid., pp. 44–45.
14. Ibid., p. 4; Gordon W. Prange, *At Dawn We Slept: The Untold Story of Pearl Harbor* (New York: McGraw-Hill, 1981), p. 70.
15. Bennett et al., *Intelligence and Cryptanalytic Activities of the Japanese*, pp. 63–64, 121–27.
16. Barnhart, "Japanese Intelligence Before the Second World War," p. 426.
17. Bennett et al., *Intelligence and Cryptanalytic Activities of the Japanese*, pp. 4, 92–113.
18. Hamish McDonald, "Japan to Lift Spying Effort After Being Caught Short," *Sydney Morning Herald*, October 27, 1982.
19. Ibid., Murray Sayle, "The 122 Japanese Spooks: Must They Be Multiplied?" *The Sampson Letter*, January 21, 1986; "On the Way to Securing a World Position?: Japan's Intelligence Agencies and Their Activities," *Japan Quarterly*, June 1982, pp. 159–62.
20. "On the Way to Securing a World Position?"
21. Ibid.; Bill Keller, "Soviet Expels 2 Japanese as Spies: Tokyo Reacts by Ousting Russian," *New York Times*, August 21, 1987, pp. A1, A7; "Japan's Naval Attaché Expelled for Spying," *Jane's Defence Weekly*, September 5, 1987, p. 446.
22. "On the Way to Securing a World Position?"
23. Ibid.
24. McDonald, "Japan to Lift Spying Effort"; Japanese Defense Agency, *Defense of Japan 1986* (Tokyo: JDA, 1986), p. 122; Sam Jameson, "747 Disclosure Costly to Japan's Security Effort," *Los Angeles Times*, September 19, 1983, pt. 1, pp. 1, 15.
25. "Japan Maintains Military Intelligence via Landsat Satellite," *Defense Electronics*, January 1986, p. 18.
26. Japanese Defense Agency, *Defense of Japan 1986*, p. 122.
27. Jameson, "747 Disclosure Costly to Japan's Security Effort."

28. "On the Way to Securing a World Position?"
29. Jameson, "747 Disclosure Costly to Japan's Security Effort"; personal communication from Owen Wilkes.
30. Personal communication from Owen Wilkes.
31. Jameson, "747 Disclosure Costly to Japan's Security Efforts."
32. Asahi Newspaper Co., *Neo Information War* (Tokyo: Asahi, 1978).
33. "Filter Center," *Aviation Week and Space Technology*, December 19, 1983, p. 73.
34. "ASDF Plane to Gather Data on Soviets: Sources," *Japan Times*, April 26, 1985; "Japan ELINT Aircraft to Be Deployed," *Defense and Foreign Affairs Daily*, May 3, 1985, p. 2.
35. "On the Way to Securing a World Position?"
36. Ibid.; McDonald, "Japan to Lift Spying Effort."
37. Howard Kurtz, "Reagan Joke Said to Cause Soviet Alert," *Washington Post*, October 12, 1984, p. A10; "Kim II-Sung's Death: Greatly Exaggerated," *Newsweek*, December 1, 1986, p. 43.
38. Bill Gunston, *An Illustrated Guide to Spy Planes and Electronic Warfare Aircraft* (New York: Arco, 1983), pp. 44–45.
39. Ibid., p. 44.
40. Japanese Defense Agency, *Defense of Japan*, p. 121.
41. David Miller, *An Illustrated Guide to Modern Sub Hunters* (New York: Arco, 1984), p. 110.
42. Ibid.
43. Ibid.
44. Ibid., p. 112.
45. Ibid.
46. "Industry Observer," *Aviation Week and Space Technology*, November 25, 1985, p. 11; "Japan to Strengthen Air and Sea Defenses," *Defense Electronics*, March 1987, p. 16; "Japan's Navy Weighs E-3, Additional E-2Cs for AEW Mission," *Aviation Week and Space Technology*, May 11, 1987, p. 59; Miller, *An Illustrated Guide to Modern Sub Hunters*, p. 125; "Industry Observer," *Aviation Week and Space Technology*, August 24, 1987, p. 13.
47. Japanese Defense Agency, *Defense of Japan 1986*, p. 121.
48. "Japan's Navy Weighs E-3, Additional E-2Cs for AEW Mission."
49. Richard Deacon, *Kempei Tai: The Japanese Secret Service* (New York: Berkeley, 1983), p. 242.
50. "Japanese MOS-1 Satellite Images Kyushu Island," *Aviation Week and Space Technology*, March 23, 1987, pp. 62–63; "Commerce Urged to Divert Weather Satellite Funding to Save Landsat," *Aviation Week and Space Technology*, March 23, 1987, pp. 61–63.
51. *Organization of the Government of Japan, 1984* (Tokyo: Institute of Administrative Management, 1984), p. 55.

52. Chalmers Johnson, *MITI and the Japanese Miracle: The Growth of Industrial Policy, 1925–1975* (Stanford, Calif.: Stanford University Press, 1982), pp. 336–38; Deacon, *Kempei Tai*, p. 259.
53. "On the Way to Securing a World Position?"; McDonald, "Japan to Lift Spying Effort"; Sayle, "The 122 Japanese Spooks."
54. "On the Way to Securing a World Position?"
55. Ibid.
56. "Japan Fingers a Soviet Spy," *Asia Week*, July 1, 1983, p. 14.
57. "Computer Spies" (Intelligence Report), *Washington Times*, April 6, 1987, p. 3A.
58. "Passage," *Asia Week*, June 7, 1987, p. 36.
59. "The Levchenko List," *Asia Week*, April 22, 1983, pp. 28–38.
60. "On the Way to Securing a World Position?"
61. Ibid.
62. Australian Royal Commission on Intelligence and Security, *Fifth Report* (Canberra: Australian Government Printer, 1977), pp. 5-E, para. 46.
63. "U.S. Warns Japan Not to Increase Soviet Military Power," March 30, 1982, Xinhau General Overseas News Service.
64. U.S. Naval Forces Japan, COMNAVFORJAPAN STAFF INST. 5450.1G, Subj: Staff Organization Manual, May 13, 1983, p. V-5.
65. Ibid., p. VI-8.
66. Jack Anderson, "Japan Discloses Dialogue on Downed Jet," *Washington Post*, April 3, 1984, p. C13.
67. Seymour Hersh, *"The Target Is Destroyed": What Really Happened to Flight 007 and What America Knew About It* (New York: Random House, 1986), pp. 57, 60.
68. Ibid., pp. 57–58, 64.
69. Ibid., pp. 63–72; Anderson, "Japan Discloses Dialogue on Downed Jet"; Jameson, "747 Disclosure Costly to Japan's Security Effort."
70. Jameson, "747 Disclosure Costly to Japan's Security Effort."

9 CHINESE INTELLIGENCE ORGANIZATIONS

ORIGINS

The intelligence and security apparatus of the People's Republic of China (PRC) can trace its origins to the Communist party's days as an underground movement. From the late 1920s until at least 1930, Chinese Communist Party (CCP) intelligence was directed by Chou En-lai. By the early 1930s, two security/intelligence organs existed. One, located in Shanghai, was formally affiliated with the CCP apparatus and associated with the "returned student group." The other, the Political Security Bureau, was officially a government office, although in reality it represented Mao Tse-tung's power base in Kiangsi. Eventually the Shanghai organization declined in importance, possibly becoming subordinate to the Political Security Bureau.[1]

In 1937, K'ang Sheng, a follower of Mao's who had been undergoing training overseas, returned to China and the new Communist capital of Yenan in North Shensi. Upon his return he apparently resumed work in the intelligence field, in which he had been active prior to his sojourn overseas. He was reportedly attached to the CCP's Organization Department and subsequently replaced the director of the Political Security Bureau.[2]

In November 1938, after the Sixth Central Committee Plenum, the CCP's central units were reorganized. The Political Security Bureau was abolished, and intelligence and security functions were consolidated within the newly formed Social Affairs Department (SAD). SAD operated under the direction and jurisdiction of the Politburo, with K'ang Sheng as its director, and was assigned both internal and external functions: to conduct espionage operations and to conduct surveillance over all Communist party, government, and military organizations.[3]

SAD's internal and external responsibilities meant that it was charged with formulating the CCP's security policies and plans, supervising their execution, providing centralized leadership to subordinate units, directing security control and purges within the CCP, furnishing guidance and supervision through the CCP mechanism to government and military organs with regard to public safety, assigning secret service cadres for covert action and espionage activities outside the CCP, training secret cadres, and devising secret codes.[4]

At the headquarters level, SAD was commanded by a Director, a Deputy Director, and a Secretary General and was organized into four sections. The First Section was responsible for organization, the Second Section for intelligence collection, and the Third Section for examination and trial. The Fourth Section was the General Service Section. In addition there was a Cadre Training Corps.[5]

SAD's power increased in 1941 with the beginning of an all-out intelligence campaign directed against the Japanese while maintaining the previous high level of operations directed against Chiang Kai-shek's Koumintang (KMT). An August 1, 1941, Central Committee "Decision on Investigation and Research" called for a movement away from overreliance on the subjective evaluation of enemy intentions and toward greater emphasis on objective investigation. The decision called for the stepping up of investigation and research into the history, environment, and events within and outside the country; it mandated that the Central Committee set up a research organization to gather and study information about the international and domestic political, economic, and cultural situation and social relations. Included were open sources of information—the decision specified that any information found in newspapers, magazines, and books concerning the political, economic, and cultural situation and social relations in "enemy, friendly and our own territories" should be excerpted and compiled for study. This led to an expansion of SAD's analysis and research offices, establishment of a new Fourth Section for analytical study, and enlargement of the intelligence section.[6] Figure 9-1 shows SAD's structure after the reorganization.

Figure 9-1. Organization of the Social Affairs Department, 1942.

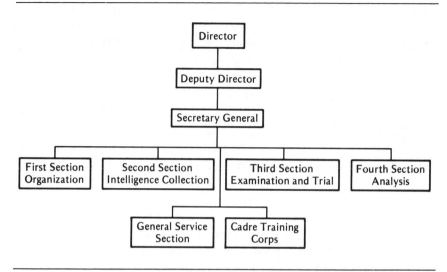

Although SAD was the central intelligence unit, a variety of other party and military units were engaged in intelligence and security activities. An intelligence service was attached to the Chief of Staff's office, while a "Meteorological Bureau" performed communications intercept operations. And the CCP Political Department had two divisions: the Anti-Subversion Division, responsible for eliminating enemy agents, traitors, and undercover elements, and the Division for Work on Enemy and Puppet Armed Forces, which handled prisoners of war and ran agitation-propaganda and sabotage operations within the enemy's military.[7]

The Sixth Central Committee Plenum also resulted in the creation of United Front Work departments within party organizations at all levels. These departments were responsible for penetrating the KMT and the Japanese in order to conduct espionage and subversive operations. Similarly, a Liaison Bureau was established. Although the bureau was ostensibly charged with liaison with the KMT in their "common" war against Japan, it also provided cover for CCP intelligence gathering directed at the KMT.[8]

In August 1940 the CCP's Secretariat issued a "Directive on United Front Operations" calling for a friendship drive to win over at least two million troops to agitate for the defection of Nationalist

(KMT) armed forces. In September 1940 a Committee for Work Behind Enemy Lines was founded, with Chou En-lai as its chairman and K'ang as his deputy. This committee conducted intelligence and subversive operations behind Japanese lines; in 1945 its emphasis was redirected toward subversive operations against the KMT.[9]

With the fall of Chiang Kai-shek in 1949 and the attainment of power over the entire mainland, the CCP had to create a full-fledged governmental structure, including intelligence units. By October 1949 an Intelligence Administration had been established under the Government Affairs Council; among its components was the External Affairs Investigation and Research Bureau. Although officially the Intelligence Administration was abolished in 1952, in fact it became a covert organization until its disbandment several years later.[10]

In October 1949 the Ministry of Public Security (MPS) was created. The MPS was assigned responsibility for countersubversion, counterintelligence, surveillance of Chinese returned from overseas and of the politically suspect, monitoring of internal travel, protection of economic and military installations, border patrol, management of "labor reform" camps, census registration, and routine police administration and investigation of criminal cases. The MPS was also responsible for conducting intelligence operations within Macao, Hong Kong, and Taiwan.[11]

The first Central Committee meeting to study the intelligence and security system took place in May 1951, on the eve of the Third National Public Security Conference. Among the results was the continuation of SAD as the nation's premier foreign and domestic intelligence service. In addition, two new organizations were established. First was a new United Front Work Department, charged with maintaining links with Chinese citizens overseas and using them, when desirable, for covert operations. The department was probably also involved in inducing prominent exiles to return to the mainland, e.g., General Li Tsong-jen, former Nationalist Vice President. (In the area of nuclear weapons and space programs, K'ang Sheng, the head of SAD, was given the responsibility of bringing back Chinese living outside of China who were working in the relevant technologies. An early recruit was Chien Wei-Chung, who later became deputy head of the Chinese rocket program.)[12]

Second was an International Liaison Department, created to maintain relations with out-of-power Communist and revolutionary groups. This department performed covert operations by funding, training, and supplying arms to some of those groups.

Other agencies that may have been involved one way or another with intelligence work were the Liaison Department of the People's Revolutionary Military Council (abolished in 1954), the Foreign Ministry's Commission for Cultural Relations with Foreign Countries (created in 1958), and the Department of Information within the Foreign Affairs Ministry.[13]

Further changes evolved over the following years. As noted, the Intelligence Administration was abolished in the 1950s. The General Staff Department of the People's Liberation Army (PLA) formed two intelligence units, the Military Intelligence Department and the Technical Department, with the latter responsible for collecting signals intelligence. In 1962 SAD was apparently divided into two units—the (Central) Investigation Department and the Administrative and Legal Work Department—with the former responsible for intelligence and security work.[14] In addition, the MPS assumed a significant worldwide intelligence function.

In 1983 the Ministry of State Security was created (for reasons discussed later in this chapter) to take over the counterespionage and political police functions of the MPS, which was left with common police functions. It has been suggested that the Ministry of State Security absorbed not only the MPS's foreign intelligence functions but also the Investigation Department in an attempt to centralize and improve the PRC's foreign intelligence operations. In a 1986 espionage case in France, a member of the French counterespionage service testified that an espionage operation had been conducted by a CCP intelligence unit that no longer exists.[15] It therefore appears that the major units of the present Chinese intelligence community are as follows:

International Liaison Department, CCP Secretariat
United Front Work Department, CCP Secretariat

Ministry of State Security, State Council

Military Intelligence Department, PLA General Staff Department
Technical Department, PLA General Staff Department

In addition, several other organizations, including the New China News Agency and a number of research institutes, either have or may have intelligence functions.

INTELLIGENCE AND SECURITY
ORGANIZATIONS

International Liaison Department

The International Liaison Department (ILD) is a tool of Chinese foreign policy that has both overt and covert functions. In the past it was responsible for maintaining contacts with other Communist parties and revolutionary groups, including those which were out of power, and its covert action activities involved funds, training, and support for such groups. The ILD was not, however, indiscriminate; it generally supported only those groups it believed could substantially influence events and refused to support groups simply for diversionary or terroristic purposes.

In recent years the ILD has been given a broader mandate with respect to its overt operations. In addition to developing relationships with Communist and revolutionary groups, it also develops contacts with socialist, social democratic, and labor parties as well as with varied political parties in Third World nations. Moreover, the ILD provides support to Chinese mass organizations that develop relationships with foreign labor, women's, youth, and student groups.[16]

As indicated, in the past the covert action activities carried out by the ILD largely involved support to revolutionary groups seeking to overthrow some government by insurrection or coup d'état. In 1961 the ILD targeted, in Africa, Guinea, Mali, Ghana, Cameroon, Congo, and Guinea-Bissau. In 1965 China gave either explicit or implicit endorsement to twenty-five revolutionary armed struggles, including those in Portuguese Africa, the Congo, Malayasia, Thailand, and South Vietnam. Camps established to provide guerilla training for revolutionaries were reported to be located in several countries, particularly in the Congo (Brazzaville) and Tanzania, which both border the Congo (Kinshasa), "site of the continent's most active antigovernment struggle in early 1965." It was also reported that investigations in Ghana, undertaken after the fall of Kwame Nkrumah in February 1966, revealed Chinese-staffed guerilla training facilities in Ghana that had allegedly been established in connection with a continent-wide underground network for the training of exiles from both independent and colonial African nations.[17]

Other covert actions attributed to the PRC in this time period include support for Watusi refugees in Kenya and Uganda who had been dispossessed from their native Rwanda in central Africa and financial support for dissident Malawian government officials in an effort to overthrow the government there. Chinese agents were also alleged to be responsible for the assassination of the Premier of Burundi in 1964 because he represented an obstacle in using the country as an arms pipeline to Congolese rebels.[18]

In the years since, Chinese revolutionary zeal has diminished and the nature of Chinese covert action operations have shifted accordingly, with the main objective being the advancement of China's "national interest." These operations include black propaganda and arms sales.

Among more recent covert actions conducted by China are those directed against Singapore and Malaysia. On November 15, 1969—six months after race riots in Kuala Lumpur—a Chinese-run clandestine radio station, Voice of the Malayan Revolution (VMR), began operating. VMR was apparently closed down on June 30, 1981, in response to a promise made to Prime Minister Lee Kuan Yew of Singapore when he visited Peking in 1980. On July 1, however, VMR was replaced by the Voice of Malayan Democracy (VMD), whose broadcasts, unlike those of VMR, were made not from China but from near Bammar Sata in the Thai province of Yala. The speed with which the switch was made and VMR's carefully worded announcement in which it handed over operations to VMD indicate coordination between the CCP and the Communist Party of Malaysia (CPM).[19]

Observers saw the thrust of the propaganda effort as an attempt to enhance the CPM's position. More effective joint operations by Malaysian and Thai forces had resulted in a series of reverses for the CPM, and the VMD campaign was designed to propagandize against the joint operations and to persuade Muslim separatists to cooperate with the CPM.[20]

A 1976 campaign had had an effect. About ten thousand of Betong's mostly Sino-Thai residents demonstrated in the name of a "sovereignty protection group," demanding that the Malaysian Police Force stationed in that border area be withdrawn. In Bangkok simultaneous demonstrations protested the presence of American troops in Thailand. Semi Pramoj, then Premier of Thailand, gave Kuala Lampur four days to withdraw its police from the salient.[21]

One reflection of China's changed position in the world is that the country no longer trains or supports the Maoist *Shining Path* guerillas of Peru, as it did in the early part of the 1970s, but does support at least four guerilla groups that are fighting Communist or Socialist regimes. According to contra leader Adolfo Calero, the contras have purchased weapons, including the SAM-7 Strella, from China to aid them in their attempt to unseat the Sandinistas. And Cambodian guerillas fighting the North Vietnamese occupation forces have been offered new weapons by China to supplement past aid, training, and weapons. Norodom Sihanouk, the Cambodian resistance leader, stated in September 1986 that China had promised unspecified amounts of weapons, ammunition, and other military supplies to his guerrilla coalition.[22]

China has also supported guerrilla groups fighting in the Soviet- and Cuban-supported MPLA (Popular Movement for the Liberation of Angola) in Angola. In 1975 those forces were engaged in a civil war to determine which of three groups would take over from the Portuguese; today, they are the government. China has provided assistance to the two groups that have opposed the Soviet-backed forces: the FNLA (Front for the National Liberation of Angola) and UNITA (National Union for the Total Independence of Angola). In 1973 and 1974 the FNLA received large arms deliveries and advisers from China, while UNITA received arms. In May 1974, 112 Chinese advisers joined the FNLA in Zaire, and China shipped 450 tons of arms to the FNLA.[23] In the aftermath of the MPLA victory, China continued to support UNITA.

China's largest covert operation at present is support of the Afghan rebels who are battling the Soviet troops trying to "pacify" that country. Chinese involvement apparently began in early 1979 when the rebels were battling the Soviet-style government that had come to power but before the Soviets actually invaded the country. Officials of the U.S. Drug Enforcement Agency (DEA) came upon a group of suspicious-looking Chinese in Pakistan. Fearing that the Chinese were Hong Kong heroin dealers in Pakistan to buy up the Afghan-Pakistan opium crop, the DEA officials requested that the Pakistani government take action. The Pakistani officials explained, off the record, that the Chinese were there to train Afghan insurgents on Pakistani soil. In addition, Afghan insurgents are being trained in Xinjiang province to use rockets and anti-aircraft missiles.[24]

Since then, Chinese support has continued, involving both training and the supply of weapons. In May 1980 Chinese Defense Minister Geng Biao visited Washington and, along with U.S. Secretary of Defense Harold Brown, urged both nations to formulate a common strategic response to the Soviet invasion.[25]

United Front Work Department

Like the ILD, the United Front Work Department (UFWD) is a covert action agency with no intelligence collection functions. The UFWD is responsible only for covert action with respect to overseas Chinese, who in many countries can represent a powerful lobby. Not only do they frequently represent a significant portion of the population, but they often control an even greater portion of the wealth.

In establishing the UFWD, the Chinese leadership made a conscious decision to separate covert action activities employing overseas Chinese from the normal course of covert action, such as the support of coups and insurrections. The leadership feared that using overseas Chinese in such operations would result in the neutralization of overseas Chinese communities as elements of influence and the perception of the communities as Chinese "fifth columns."

Ministry of State Security

The Ministry of State Security (MSS) was established in June 1983. A "Report on Government Work," delivered to the First Session of the Sixth National People's Congress on June 6, stated that "to protect the security of the state and strengthen China's counterespionage work . . . the State Council is submitting to the present congress for approval a proposal to establish a Ministry of State Security which will provide effective leadership over such work."[26]

In an interview with the New China News Agency, the new Minister of State Security stated that:

> the struggle between espionage and counterespionage is very acute in the world today. . . . Since China adopted the policy of opening to the outside world, intelligence agencies or secret services of some foreign countries have stepped up their activities to obtain China's state secrets and sent special agents into China for subversive and destructive purposes.[27]

The new ministry took over the counterespionage and security functions of the Ministry of Public Security. The MSS was apparently created because of the annoyance and concern of high Chinese officials in regard to espionage and leaks to the foreign press from within the Chinese government.

One reason for widespread "leaks" in China is the enormous amount of information that is considered classified. The "Provisional Regulation on the Protection of State Secrets," enacted in 1951, lists seventeen categories of classified information, including that pertaining to defense matters; foreign affairs; economic data ranging from the country's development program to the budgets of planned construction projects; scientific discoveries of all sorts; education, culture, and public health programs; and legislative and judicial proceedings. In addition, the regulation specifies that "all state affairs that have not yet been decided upon," or that have been decided upon but not announced, and "all other state affairs that should be kept secret" are state secrets, with disclosure punishable by imprisonment.[28]

During the five years preceding the establishment of MSS, Chinese leaders were increasingly alarmed about the unauthorized and widespread disclosure of Communist party debates as well as the steady flow of confidential and sometimes embarrassing reports on economic, social, and cultural affairs. Attempts to stop the leaks proved frustrating and unsuccessful. At one meeting of senior officials in 1981, Hu Yao-bang, the party's Secretary General, complained that "everything we say in here we can read in the Japanese press two days later. Is nothing confidential, nothing secret?" Certainly not Hu's remarks, which were reported within a week by a Japanese newspaper, citing "well-informed Chinese sources."[29]

Plans for the new ministry were reported to include a nationwide network of security agents to halt the widespread information leaks. A professor at China's People's University feared that "every major office, factory, laboratory, school and library will probably have a security officer on its staff now to make sure no secrets leak out and nobody learns what he is not supposed to know. We will have thousands upon thousands [of] more policemen spying on us."[30]

Other concerns for the new ministry include dissidents, journalists, and spies. In December 1985 Chinese students marched from Tienanmen Square to Zhongnanhai compound, where Chinese leaders have their homes and offices. Two hundred to three hundred students protested atomic weapons tests by the PRC government. Students from the Xinjiang Uigur Autonomous Region, where the Lop Nor test facility was located, presented a list of demands that included a call to halt atmospheric testing of nuclear weapons.[31]

December 1986 witnessed a number of student demonstrations in Peking and Shanghai. On December 13 students at Peking University put up posters on campus calling for greater democracy and said they wanted to stir up a national movement to pressure the CCP into implementing democratic reforms. The posters called for freedom of the press and democratic elections in the countryside, to be followed by similar elections in the cities. The posters at Peking University followed demonstrations earlier in the week in the provincial capitals of Wuhan and Hefei, where thousands of students took to the streets to demand greater freedom and democracy.[32]

During a three-day period on December 19–21, 1986, a series of student protests took place in Shanghai. On December 20 some twenty thousand students marched to municipal government offices to demand more extensive and rapid democratic reforms than those under consideration by the CCP. Students from at least six Shanghai universities participated in the December 20 march, increasing by almost sevenfold the approximately three thousand protesters who demonstrated on December 19.[33]

On December 21, fifty thousand students and workers demonstrated in Shanghai's People's Square, unveiling white banners demanding "Law, Not Authoritarianism" and "Long Live Democracy." The demonstrations subsequently expanded in size and scope. On December 23, Peking University students joined in the protests, with more than a thousand students from Qinghua University (the equivalent of MIT in China) taking part in a demonstration that ran more than four hours. More than two thousand students marched in northwest Peking on December 29, while January 1 saw a demonstration in Peking's Tian An Men Square that was described as "the largest public protest since the end of the Cultural Revolution in 1976."[34]

Chinese dissidents living overseas—particularly students—are likely to be one of the targets of MSS's foreign operations. In 1978 and 1979 the Peking Spring movement produced widespread criticism, within China, of the CCP. In 1983 a China Spring movement was created by Chinese students studying in North America. The movement publishes a monthly journal, *China Spring*, which first appeared in New York in December 1982. According to one student involved in the movement, China Spring forms the platform of a movement dedicated "to change the system in China completely and give our people [including those in Taiwan and Hong Kong] a real opportunity to choose what they want in terms of government and political beliefs. We want democracy, rule of law, liberty and human rights."[35]

In response to the demonstrations in China in late 1986, nearly seventeen hundred Chinese nationals studying at more than a hundred U.S. universities signed open letters criticizing the government's response to the demonstrations, which included the removal of Hu Yao-bang as the Communist party leader and the disciplining of Chinese intellectuals.[36]

Like the Soviet KGB, the Chinese MSS is also concerned about the activities of foreign diplomats, tourists, and reporters, particularly those reporters who attempt to make contact with Chinese citizens and visit off-limits areas. The ministry is reportedly populated with conservative, xenophobic, and authoritarian officials who are loyal to the legacy of Mao and oppose Western influences and the domestic reforms of Deng Xiao Ping. Western diplomats believe that one of the first priorities of the ministry was to pin espionage charges on Western journalists and other foreigners to justify its bureaucratic existence and demonstrate the dangers of an open door policy. Journalists are an attractive target because they do not have diplomatic immunity. Thus, American reporters have received mysterious telephone calls from Chinese requesting a meeting, and at face-to-face meetings Chinese have offered to deliver classified documents. One Westerner with ties to the CCP was asked to inform on foreign correspondents in Peking.[37]

In 1984 Tiziano Terzani, the Peking correspondent of *Der Spiegel*, was expelled from China. Terzani was stripped of his press credentials for allegedly smuggling antiques and defacing a portrait of Mao. Western diplomats believed that the charges were simply a pretext for expelling Terzani after the ministry failed to uncover any evidence of espionage, despite nineteen hours of hostile interrogation, the search of Terzani's apartment and office, and threats of jail.[38]

In July 1986 John F. Burns, the Peking bureau chief for the *New York Times*, was taken into custody by MSS officials in connection with a trip he had recently made through the Chinese countryside. PRC officials informed the U.S. embassy that Burns was being investigated on suspicion of "entering an area forbidden to foreigners, gathering intelligence information and espionage." Burns and three companions were first detained on the Sichuan border for two days by local officials who informed them they had not been authorized to travel freely by road.* Burns was subsequently held and questioned for fifteen hours in a room at the Peking airport. He was later taken, along with his wife, to his apartment in Peking, where ten security men with videotape cameras conducted a systematic search.[39]

Burns admitted that he had not made arrangements or received permits to enter an area closed to foreigners. Within a week of his first arrest, he was expelled from China while Chinese officials informed the executive editor of the *New York Times* that they considered Burns guilty of an "act of spying and intelligence gathering which will not be tolerated by any sovereign state." In addition to expelling Burns, Chinese authorities confiscated the film he had taken of the trip.[40]

On January 30, 1987, Lawrence MacDonald, a reporter for the AFP (French Press Agency) news service, was also expelled. In September, MacDonald had reported on the defection to the United States of the chief of the MSS's Foreign Affairs Bureau, which apparently caused considerable embarrassment to officials of the ministry. On January 26 Chinese officials asked the AFP to transfer MacDonald, maintaining that "MacDonald's recent activities did not accord with his status as a journalist and were harmful to friendship between the Chinese and French people." Specifically, MacDonald was alleged to have obtained secret intelligence information from a Chinese student in the city of Tianjin.[41]

MacDonald's departure was apparently hurried at the insistence of the MSS. Although the Ministry of Foreign Affairs had been willing to allow MacDonald several days, the MSS, in a show of strength, was able to force him out with only his passport. In addition, the MSS arrested Lin Jie, a student at Tianjin University, for his "secret collusion with and providing intelligence to Lawrence MacDonald." MacDonald interpreted the events as "part of an effort to intimidate foreign journalists and the Chinese citizens with whom they come in contact."[42]

Burns, Terzani, and MacDonald were not the only journalists to feel the attention of the MSS. In May 1987 a Japanese reporter,

---

*There are 244 cities, towns, and tourist areas that foreigners can visit without permission. But because of the presence of military units or an embarrassing level of poverty, many areas between the cities are off limits unless foreigners travel straight through via railway or receive permission to drive through.

Shuitsu Henmi, was expelled for having obtained "intelligence" data. Henmi had reported a few months earlier on confidential documents issued by the CCP Central Committee. Another journalist left China in 1986 in despair at the monitoring of her activities. Other journalists working in Peking reported that they and their Chinese friends had been followed by plainclothes officers (assumed to be with the MSS). On one occasion an American journalist was bicycling to visit a Chinese friend when a Chinese man on a bicycle began to follow him. The journalist tried to lose the man by darting down a side street but failed to do so. Finally, the Chinese bicyclist gave up the chase, but then the journalist noticed that he was being watched by two other men in a battered Citroen. He decided to forego visiting his Chinese friend.[43]

MSS surveillance of foreigners also involves monitoring embassy personnel. Foreign embassies (and firms) cannot hire Chinese employees of their own choosing but must have individuals allotted to them by state agencies. Diplomats assume that the first loyalty of their Chinese employees is to the Chinese government and that Chinese employees are involved in mail openings and phone tappings. One Asian diplomat reported that listening devices had been found in a wall of his embassy many years ago.[44]

In one case in Shanghai in 1986, MSS officers held overnight and interrogated a Chinese woman for having accompanied an American male on a walk from and back to a hotel. The woman did not enter the man's room but was simply a hotel employee trying to help him find a restaurant.[45]

Espionage has also been a concern. In July 1983 it was reported that an alleged Soviet spy had been arrested in the Northeast and that a Hong Kong newspaper editor had been convicted of passing secrets to the United States. In May 1983 CCP Secretary General Hu Yao-bang said that about two hundred Chinese accused of spying for the Soviet Union had been arrested during the previous year.[46]

In 1985 it became apparent that the United States had a source with significant access to information concerning Chinese nuclear activities, including information about Chinese help given to Pakistan in the building of an atomic device. The source apparently reported that Chinese technicians had been helping at a suspected Pakistani bomb development site, such help including commenting on bomb designs. The source had also provided information about Chinese nuclear dealings with Iran, Argentina, and South Africa.[47]

In 1986 a case of Taiwanese espionage came to light with the conviction of Roland Shensu Loo and three associates. Loo, who immigrated to the United States in 1980, was apparently recruited by an agent of the Taiwanese Military Intelligence Bureau to be part of an intelligence net based in the United States. According to the MSS, Loo came to China in 1984 and 1985, collecting information from an engineer at the Peking Construction Engineering Institute and from her husband, a director of the Peking Science and Education Film Studio. In 1985 Loo allegedly recruited Zhu Junyi, a resident of Hangzhou, Zhejiang Province.[48]

Particularly embarrassing for an agency set up to stem leaks and combat foreign espionage is to suffer the defection of a major official within the first years of its existence—which is exactly what happened to the MSS in 1986. Yu Zhensan, the former head of MSS's Foreign Affairs Bureau, defected and was debriefed by U.S. intelligence and given a new identity. Zhensan, the son of two prominent Chinese revolutionaries, was reported to be in his late thirties and able to provide the United States with extensive information about Chinese intelligence operations abroad, including the names of Chinese agents and suspected agents from other nations working in China. Before defecting, he apparently provided the United States with information leading to the arrest of Larry Wu-Tai Chin, an employee of the CIA's Foreign Broadcast Information Service, as a long-term Chinese mole.[49]

Military Intelligence Department

The Military Intelligence Department (MID) is responsible for basic order-of-battle intelligence, studies of foreign weapons systems, and analyses of the capabilities of foreign armies. One account suggests that most of the department's work is in these areas rather than broad political-military or military-strategic questions.[50]

The MID would also be the logical department to manage China's photographic reconnaissance program. China has been conducting photographic reconnaissance operations since April 24, 1970, when China 1, a satellite weighing only 354 pounds, was placed into orbit. China 2, placed into orbit a year later, weighed 484 pounds. China 4 and 5 were far heavier spacecraft: China 4's estimated weight was 5,940 pounds, while China 5's was 9,900 pounds. China 4 ejected a capsule, presumably containing film. China 5's orbital parameters included a 68-degree inclination, a perigee of 114 miles, and an apogee of 237 miles.[51]

Between 1970 and September 7 1987, ten of the twenty-one Chinese space launches were associated with military photographic reconnaissance. (See Table 9–1) Chinese officials have acknowledged that on six of the flights, capsules were recovered at the conclusion of the mission. Recovery takes place in southwestern China, on a southbound pass, within approximately five days of a launch. The satellites do not maneuver once they have obtained orbit. The 10-foot tall nose-cone shaped spacecraft is divided in two sections. The lower section, which is the widest, holds the reconnaissance camera, altitude control gas, and a solid propellant rocket for reentry braking. The opening for the reconnaissance camera is about 20 inches wide, with the film being automatically routed from the camera into the forward rounded nose cone for return to earth. Return of the film takes place when the 5-by-6-foot capsule is ejected, leaving behind a large bus. The satellites are launched no more than once a year, in late summer or early winter. In the period 1981–84, the satellites were launched no earlier than August 19 and no later than September 19. For example, on September 12, 1984, China 16 was launched from Shuang Cheng Tzu into a 107-by-248-mile orbit with a 67.94-degree inclination. The capsule was recovered on September 17.[52]

With an inclination exceeding 60 degrees, the Chinese photographic reconnaissance satellites are able to cover all of the world, except for the most northerly parts of the Soviet Union, Canada, and Scandinavia. Figure 9–2 shows the ground tracks of the photographic reconnaissance satellite launched on October 21, 1985.

In addition to the film-return satellites, one or more of China's previous low-altitude satellites has used a different imaging system, transmitting pictures to earth by radio signals; a 10-foot-diameter tracking dish for receiving such imagery was observed at the Xian Institute of Radio Technology. A more advanced system is under development for a planned launch in the period 1988–90. The new spacecraft will apparently be similar to the French SPOT satellite and will use charged-coupled device technology being developed at the Xian Institute.[53] Presumably, a high priority of such a satellite, once in operation, would be the monitoring of the Sino-Soviet border and areas in Southeast Asia where China might find itself directly or indirectly involved in a military confrontation, for example, in Vietnam or Cambodia.

Table 9-1. Basic Data on Chinese Photographic Reconnaissance Satellites.

Designation	Date of Launch Lifetime	Inclination	Perigee (MI)	Apogee (MI)
China 1 1970-34A	April 24, 1970 100 years	68.44	273	1,479
China 2 1971-18A	March 3, 1971 3,028 days	69.90	166	1,135
China 4 1975-111A	November 26, 1985 33 days Capsule recovered December 2	62.95	110	289
China 5 1975-119A	December 16, 1975 42 days	69.00	115	240
China 7 1976-117A	December 7, 1976 26 days Capsule recovered December 9, 10	59.45	107	297
China 8 1978-11A	January 26, 1978 12 days Capsule recovered January 30	57.02	99	291
China 13 1983-86A	August 19, 1983 15 days Capsule recovered August 24	63.31	107	237
China 16 1984-98A	September 12, 1984 17 days Capsule recovered September 17	67.94	109	247
China 17 1985-96A	October 21, 1985 17 days Capsule recovered November 7, 1985	62.98	106	239
China 21 1987-75A	September 9, 1987	63.00	127	193

Sources: Royal Aircraft Establishment (RAE), *RAE Table of Earth Satellites 1957-1980* (New York: Facts on File 1981); RAE, *The RAE Table of Earth Satellites 1981-1982* (Farnsborough, England: RAE 1983); RAE, *The RAE Table of Earth Satellites 1983-1986* (Farnsborough, England: RAE 1987).

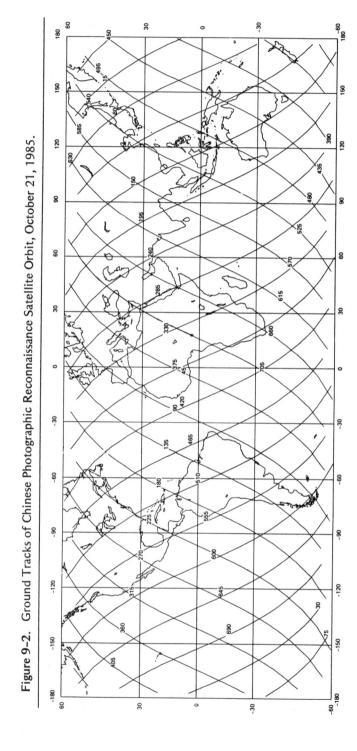

Figure 9-2. Ground Tracks of Chinese Photographic Reconnaissance Satellite Orbit, October 21, 1985.

China relies on aerial reconnaissance, as well as space reconnaissance, to provide military intelligence. In early 1987 China purchased five Gates Learjets from the United States to be fitted with KS-157 Long-Range Oblique Photography (LOROP) cameras for long-range high-altitude reconnaissance. The LOROP cameras are able to photograph other countries from 25,000 to 30,000 feet at a distance of more than forty miles. India and the Soviet Union are likely targets.[54]

Technical Department

The Technical Department is the Chinese signals intelligence agency, responsible for managing China's signals intelligence network.

The estimated location of four Chinese SIGINT stations are shown in Figure 9-3. As indicated, one is located in the very Northeast, across from the Sino-Soviet border, while another is just off the Sino-Mongolian border.

The two stations in western China, located at Qitai and Korla in the Xinjiang Uighur Autonomous Region, are the result of U.S.-Chinese intelligence cooperation. The United States initially suggested setting up such posts in 1978, prior to the establishment of diplomatic relations. At first the Chinese, apparently concerned about cooperating too closely with the United States, were reluctant to agree. The issue was raised again after the overthrow of the Shah in January 1979. In an April 1979 meeting with a visiting U.S. Senate delegation, PRC Vice Premier Deng Xiaoping indicated that China was willing to use U.S. equipment "to monitor Soviet compliance with a proposed new arms limitation treaty." Deng also indicated that the monitoring stations would have to be run by the Chinese and that the data would have to be shared with the PRC.[55]

The United States and the PRC reached a basic agreement in January 1980. According to a TASS report, the selection of Qitai and Korla resulted from an exercise called Karakoram-80. Actual operations began in the fall of 1980. The stations were constructed by the CIA's Office of SIGINT Operations (part of the agency's Directorate of Science and Technology), whose personnel trained the Chinese technicians and now periodically visit the stations to advise them and to service the equipment as required.[56] The initial set of equipment allowed for the interception of telemetry from Soviet missile test and space shots conducted from two major Soviet launch sites—at Tyuratam near the Aral Sea and at Sary Shagan near Lake Balkash. While

Figure 9-3. Location of Chinese SIGINT Sites.

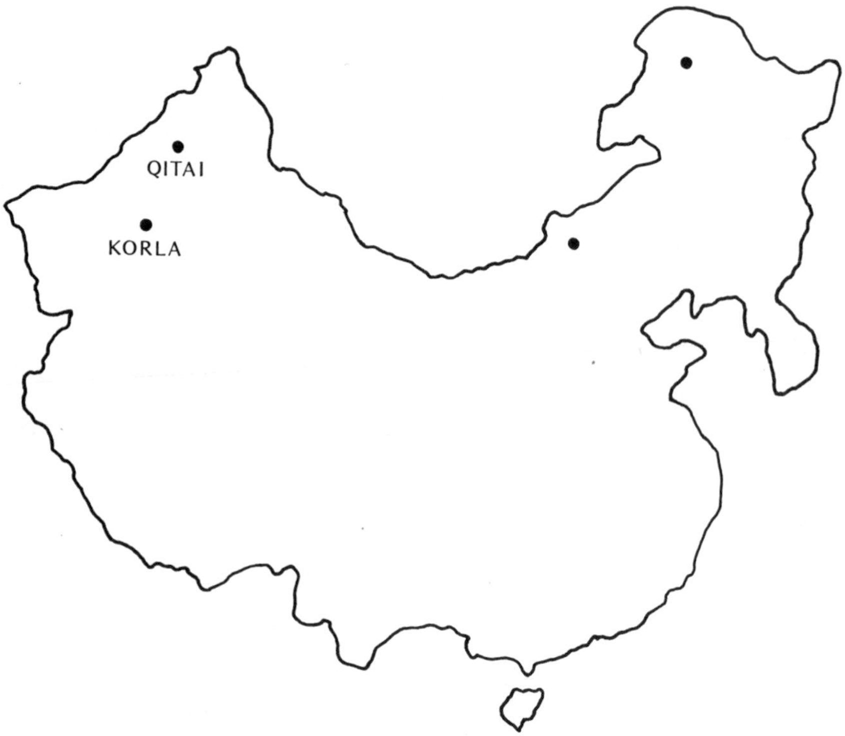

Sources: Jim Bussert, "China's C³I Efforts Show Progress," C³I Handbook, Vol. 1 1986, p. 173; Mario de Arcangelis, Electronic Warfare: From the Battle of Tsushima to the Falklands and Lebanon Conflicts (Dorset, England: Blanford, 1985), p. 289.

somewhat farther from Tyuratam than the Iranian sites, the Chinese sites are closer to the Sary Shagan ABM test site.

The Technical Department, along with the Navy, is probably also responsible for signals intelligence activities conducted from PRC surface ships and submarines. Among the ships that may be employed for such activities are frigates and some of the Xiangyang Hong class of research ships; the Xiangyang Hong 10, for example, is equipped with several log-periodic antennae that could be used for COMINT purposes. In addition, the Yuan Wang 1 and 2 spaceships may be employed not only to support Chinese space activities but also to monitor Soviet space and missile activities.[57]

New China News Agency

Another organization with an intelligence role is the New China News Agency (NCNA), whose origins date to 1931, when a "Red China News Agency" was founded in Ruijin (Jianjxi Province). The agency adopted its present name in 1937 and became a state organization in 1949. Since then, it has been the primary PRC vehicle for the collection and dissemination of news at home and abroad.[58]

The NCNA, in 1972, had a staff of five thousand at home and abroad; its ninety-plus foreign bureaus employed three hundred workers. One component of the NCNA's main headquarters operation is responsible for monitoring foreign news, particularly about the West, and has access to all the major wire services. A 1957 report stated that the NCNA "takes down the broadcasts of more than 40 stations of 30 foreign news agencies, totalling about 300,000 words (English) and 281 hours per day in radio-teletype, Hellschreiber and Morse code." When necessary, NCNA can focus its monitoring of news on specific events or regions.[59]

Of the total flow of foreign news into the main office of NCNA, only a bare minimum goes out to the public media for mass dissemination after it has been edited and the original source identification eliminated. The bulk of monitored foreign news is published in two news circulars, the top-secret *Reference Materials (Canka Ziliao)* and the *Reference News (Tsan-kao Hsia-hsi)*. *Reference Materials* is a classified daily complilation of news and articles from foreign newspapers and journals, is quite comprehensive, and includes a wide range of articles, some critical of China and Chinese policies. Two issues of *Reference Materials* appear daily, in print form, and each averages between forty and fifty pages, although an issue may run to eighty or even a hundred pages. In addition, a daily four-page digest of major world developments accompanies *Reference Materials*. The second circular, *Reference News*, is smaller and less restricted than *Reference Materials*, having become an open publication in 1985.[60]

The NCNA is also used, on occasion, as a cover for outright espionage. In 1957 the DST claimed that NCNA correspondent Yang Xiaonong was a top agent of Chinese intelligence. In 1964 the Brazilian security service charged that several NCNA employees were, in fact, intelligence agents involved in both collecting information and financing local communist groups. The deputy head of the NCNA office in Hong Kong has traditionally been an intelligence officer.[61]

Research Institutes

Like the Soviet Union, China supplements its intelligence analysis activities with a variety of research institutes. While not formally members of the intelligence community, such institutes perform certain intelligence functions.

Under the CCP Secretariat is the *Party Research Office*, and within it, a group that deals with foreign affairs. Some observers believe that this group has a close relationship, and possibly a personnel overlap, with the research staff of the Secretariat's Foreign Affairs Small Group.[62]

Within the Foreign Ministry are two organizations. The *Foreign Policy Research Office* has ten to twenty staff members who address international issues that transcend bilateral relationships or regional boundaries. The *Institute of International Studies*, although officially independent, is closely affiliated with the ministry and largely staffed with former diplomats and past employees of the ministry. It produces policy-related reports that in the United States would be done by in-house research units.[63]

The institute's staff of 250 members, more than two-thirds of whom are researchers, are organized into both geographic and functional divisions: the Americas, the Soviet Union and Eastern Europe, Western Europe, East Asia and the Pacific, Africa and the Middle East, International Economic Issues, and Comprehensive Research (which deals with broad international issues, including security matters).[64]

The consumers of the institute's products are not limited to Foreign Ministry personnel; rather, the studies and reports circulate throughout the entire official foreign affairs establishment and the national leadership. Some of the institute's reports are prepared at its own initiative, while others are commissioned by leaders of other institutions.[65]

The *College of International Politics*, established in Peking in 1978, currently has about six hundred students. Originally under the control of the Ministry of Public Security, the college was probably taken over by the Ministry of State Security when that organization was formed.[66]

The *Beijing Institute for International Strategic Studies* was created by the Ministry of National Defense in 1979 with a mandate to conduct research concerning strategic questions and national security issues. This institute is fairly small and has a limited research output. The institute's constitution describes it as "an academic body for research on international strategic problems" established "to study strategic questions in relation to national security and world peace and to develop academic exchange with strategic research establishments, organizations and academics abroad." Several of the institute's top officials have a background in intelligence. The institute's director, Wu Xiquan, formerly headed the ILD, while his senior deputy was previously a deputy chief of staff at ILD. Other members of the institute's staff divide their time between the institute and the Military Intelligence Department.[67]

In 1985 the institute was reportedly beginning to develop five projects, related to (a) the strategic and security situation in Southeast Asia, (b) Soviet military aims and activities in the Asian Pacific region, (c) trends and conflicts in the Middle East, (d) U.S.-Soviet strategic relations (including arms control), and (e) relations between the Soviet Union and Western Europe.[68]

Finally, the *Institute of Contemporary International Relations*, established in 1979, is the largest international affairs research institute in China, having a staff of three hundred. The origins of the institute can be traced to the 1940s, although it has undergone several reorganizations and name changes since then. Currently it is directly affiliated with the State Council and responsible to the council's Center of International Studies. It also has ties to the Ministry of State Security and performs classified research for China's premier and other officials.

The institute has eight divisions: Comprehensive Research, North America, Latin America, the Soviet Union and Eastern Europe, Western Europe, East Asia, South and Southeast Asia and West Asia and Africa. Each division has a staff of about thirty.[69]

MANAGEMENT STRUCTURE

The closest thing to a management organization for the Chinese intelligence community is the General Office of the CCP Central Committee. In 1966 the office's functions were defined as being to "protect Chairman Mao and the Party Centre, and safeguard the inner secrets of the Party." All foreign intelligence reports sent from government, PLA, and CCP organs pass through the General Office.[70]

LIAISON

Chinese liaison and exchange relationships include those with France, the United Kingdom, Israel, and the United States. According to one report, during the early 1970s China passed a great deal of information about Vietnam to the French SDECE; it also provided the French with information on Soviet activities in the Far East. As a result, the chief of SDECE, Alexander de Marenches, flew to Peking in the early 1970s for talks with Chinese intelligence officials in order to arrange a regular exchange of information focusing on the Soviet Union. He also set up an SDECE liaison unit at the French Embassy in Peking.[71]

In the same time period, Chinese intelligence was involved in a liaison relationship with the British SIS, at least in part through the SIS station chief in Hong Kong. SIS-Chinese cooperation led to the dismantling of a large KGB operation in Hong Kong. At the same time, the Australian-British listening post in Hong Kong, targeted on the PRC, was a target of Chinese intelligence operations, Chinese intelligence having successfully penetrated the operation in the early 1960s.[72]

The Chinese and Israeli intelligence communities may have been involved in a liaison relationship since the early 1970s. In particular, Khartoum and areas of West Africa appear to be locations where Chinese and Israeli agents make contact. During that time period the Mossad, SDECE and Chinese intelligence operated in the Sudan with the common objective of eliminating Soviet influence.[73]

China's intelligence relationship with the United States began with the visit of Morton Abramowitz, Deputy Assistant Secretary of Defense for International Affairs, to China. In a meeting with a senior Chinese defense official, Abramowitz gave him a highly classified briefing on the deployment of Soviet forces along the Chinese border as well as providing information about Soviet strategic weapons. Abramowitz provided more than information, pulling out of his briefcase satellite photographs of Soviet military installations and armor facing China. China has apparently continued to receive such photography. According to one U.S. official, the Chinese reconnaissance satellite's "footprint is very small, and they want mapping support, especially of the Soviet Union" in addition to photographs of Soviet forces deployed along their border.[74]

Another aspect of U.S.-Chinese intelligence cooperation involves a joint project to set up nine monitoring stations in China, primarily for studying and predicting earthquakes. These U.S. seismic devices will also allow monitoring of Soviet nuclear tests. One device is located in Urumqi in Xinjiang province and is approximately 600 miles from the Soviet nuclear test site at Semipalatinsk in Central Asia. A second device, in Manchuria, will help U.S. analysts learn more about the geology of the Soviet Union, which in turn will increase the accuracy of intelligence estimates of Soviet test explosions.[75]

A third aspect of cooperation lies in the covert action area. The International Liaison Department and CIA have both been active in conducting coordinated operations against Soviet-backed forces in Angola, Cambodia, and Afghanistan. Some camps in Pakistan for training at Mujahdeen guerrillas operate under the joint direction of the CIA and ILD.[76]

CHINESE HUMAN INTELLIGENCE AND COUNTERINTELLIGENCE OPERATIONS AGAINST THE UNITED STATES

Although Chinese intelligence services concentrate their human intelligence efforts on Far East neighbors such as Vietnam, Taiwan, and the Soviet Union, they are also active in the United States. In 1983 it was reported that the counterintelligence division of the FBI was troubled by the growing number of Chinese diplomats and trade officials—a number, 866, that represented a 24 percent increase from 1981.[77]

Since then, the number has increased by 65 percent, amounting to some fifteen hundred diplomatic and commercial representatives located at some seventy PRC offices in the United States. In addition, those representatives have some degree of access to the approximately fifteen thousand Chinese students (some of whom are "45-year-old physicists," according to former FBI Director William Webster) and ten thousand other individuals arriving in twenty-seven hundred delegations each year. The ethnic Chinese community in the United States is also a target of PRC intelligence activities. Recruited students can significantly aid the official diplomats, who are free to travel in only twenty-nine cities. Said an FBI official: "If each of these students is given a small task, it's much easier, less obtrusive for them to gather what they want." The information sought by such students would include both open source and classified information.[78]

According to a study by the Senate Select Committee on Intelligence, the primary target of Chinese HUMINT collection in the United States is advanced technology not approved for release that would further PRC military and economic modernization in the 1990s and beyond. Concern over such activity resulted in a protracted battle when China wanted to open a consulate in Los Angeles. It took twenty-one months before the United States approved the request, in early 1987—in large part because U.S. counterintelligence agencies were concerned about the potential for Chinese spying in an area of heavy defense contracting.[79]

In 1985 Assistant Secretary of Defense Richard Perle suggested that some Chinese technology acquisition operations might be unnecessary. Perle stated that "it is entirely possible of the Chinese intelligence operations of not being informed that we have so liberalized our trade policy with China that they probably could have obtained what they wanted through a formal, legal transaction."[80]

The Chinese have also sought to penetrate the United States intelligence community—and in one case had spectacular success. Larry Wu-Tai Chin began his employment with the U.S. government in 1943 with the U.S. Army Liaison Mission in China. In 1948 he worked as an interpreter in the American consulate in Shanghai and two years later took a job as a secretary-interpreter at the American embassy in Hong Kong. During the Korean War, Chin interviewed Chinese prisoners captured by U.S. and Korean troops.[81]

In 1952 Chin began his employment with the CIA in Okinawa, monitoring Chinese radio broadcasts for the agency's Foreign Broadcast Information Service (FBIS). He remained in that position until 1961, and then moved to Santa Rosa, California, where he continued to work for the FBIS. From 1970 until his retirement in 1981, Chin worked as an analyst in the FBIS office in northern Virginia and also served as the FBIS document control officer. From 1981 to 1985, he worked with the U.S. Joint Publications Research Service, a division of the CIA that does translation work for FBIS.[82]

Chin's career as a spy may have begun in the early 1940s, when he allegedly received espionage training while still a student in college.

In 1952 Chin was paid two thousand dollars by Chinese intelligence agents for having located Chinese POWs in Korea. Moreover, he provided Chinese agents with information on the intelligence being sought from Chinese prisoners by U.S. and Korean intelligence officers. In 1967 he is alleged to have begun regular meetings with PRC controllers in Hong Kong. Between 1976 and 1982, Chin met four times with a courier for Chinese intelligence, "Mr. Lee," at a shopping mall near Toronto International Airport. Speaking in Cantonese, Chin handed over undeveloped film of classified documents from the FBIS.[83]

In addition to his Toronto meetings, Chin also held clandestine meetings with Chinese agents in Macao, Hong Kong, and Peking. In 1981 he met with the Vice Minister of China's Ministry of Public Security in Hong Kong and Macao. In February 1982 Chin went to Peking, where high government officials honored him at a banquet, promoted him to Deputy Bureau Chief in the MPS, and awarded him fifty thousand dollars. As late as February 1985 he met Chinese intelligence officials in Hong Kong.[84]

The information Chin provided led the PRC to pay him several hundred thousand dollars over his thirty-year career. Although the FBIS is best known for its translations of the public broadcasts of foreign nations (and less known for its translations of the broadcasts of clandestine and black radios), the service's analysts also used classified intelligence reports to help assess the importance of foreign broadcasts. Further, Chin's skill as an interpreter and his long tenure gave him access to a great deal of highly classified data. Thus, Chin "was more than a guy . . . listening to People's Republic of China broadcasts and translating the People's Daily." According to testimony given at his indictment, Chin "reviewed, translated and analyzed classified documents from covert and overt human and technical collection sources which went into the West's assessment of Chinese strategic, military, economic, scientific and technical capabilities and intentions," and in 1979 passed on that assessment to "Mr. Lee." In helping to produce such as assessment, Chin would have had access to documents provided by Chinese sources (which could help identify them) as well as intercepts of Chinese communications obtained by satellites, aircraft, and ground stations.[85]

FBI testimony at a hearing for Chin stated that Chin's deliveries to Chinese intelligence were so voluminous that it took two translators two months to translate each shipment.[86] Chin was eventually arrested, possibly as a result of information provided by Yu Zhensan, and convicted of espionage. Shortly after his conviction he committed suicide in his jail cell.

NOTES TO CHAPTER 9

1. David Anthony Reynolds, "A Comparative Analysis of the Respective Roles and Power of the KGB and Chinese Intelligence/Security Apparatus in Domestic Politics" (M.A. thesis, Brown University, February 1984), pp. 61–62.
2. Ibid., p. 62.
3. Ibid., pp. 62–64; Warren Kuo, "CCP Wartime Secret Service and Underground Struggle, Part 1," *Issues and Studies*, August 1970, pp. 57–75.
4. Reynolds, *A Comparative Analysis*, pp. 62–64; Kuo, "CCP Wartime Secret Service and Underground Struggle, Part 1."
5. Reynolds, *A Comparative Analysis*, p. 63.
6. Reynolds, *A Comparative Analysis*, p. 65; Kuo, "CCP Wartime Secret Service and Underground Struggle, Part 1."
7. Kuo, "CCP Wartime Secret Service and Underground Struggle, Part 1."
8. Ibid.; Reynolds, *A Comparative Analysis*, p. 64.
9. Kuo, "CCP Wartime Secret Service and Underground Struggle, Part 1"; Reynolds, *A Comparative Analysis*, p. 64.
10. Reynolds, *A Comparative Analysis*, p. 81.
11. Ibid., p. 72.
12. Ibid., pp. 78–79; P. S. Clark, "The Chinese Space Programme," *Journal of the British Interplanetary Society* 37 (1984): 195–206.
13. Reynolds, *A Comparative Analysis*, pp. 79–81.
14. Ibid., p. 80.
15. Richard Bernstein, "France Jails 2 in Odd Case of Espionage," *New York Times*, May 11, 1986, p. 7. The case in question was the Boursicot case. Testimony at the trial of Bernard Boursicot, a former French diplomat, established that he had spied for the Investigation Department at various intervals since 1969. The foundation for his espionage activities occurred in 1964, while he was stationed in Peking. Boursicot fell in love with a male opera singer who played female roles. The singer, Shi Peipu, began an affair with Boursicot—who not only continued to believe that Shi was a woman but that he fathered a son by "her." His confusion, he explained in 1986, stemmed from the fact that his meetings with Shi were hasty affairs that always occurred in the dark.
    His espionage activities began in 1969, when he returned to China after being away for three years. The cultural revolution was at its height in that year, making it virtually impossible for a foreigner to have a personal rela-

tionship with a Chinese citizen. It was under these circumstances that Bouriscot was approached by a member of Chinese intelligence (presumably from the Investigation Department) and informed that the price for being allowed to continue his relationship with Shi would be securing intelligence information from the French embassy. From 1977 to 1979 Boursicot was assigned to the French embassy in Ulan Bator, Mongolia, from which he made weekly trips to Peking with the diplomatic pouch. Before reaching Peking he photocopied the documents contained in the pouch and turned them over to Shi. Boursicot apparently gave some 150 documents to Shi, who in turn passed them on to the Chinese agent who approached Boursicot. At his trial Boursicot claimed that the documents were, in general, not very sensitive and publicly available.

16. A Doak Barnett, *The Making of Foreign Policy in China: Structure and Process* (Boulder, Colo.: Westview Press, 1985), p. 47; Roger Faligot and Remi Kauffer, *Kang Sheng et les Services Secrets Chinois, 1927-1987* (Paris: Robert Laffont, 1987), p. 351.

17. Peter Van Ness, *Revolution and Chinese Foreign Policy: Peking's Support for Wars of National Liberation* (Berkeley, Calif.: University of California Press, 1970), pp. 90, 114.

18. Ibid., p. 114; Sterling Seagrave and Robert A. Jones, "From China, with Love," *Esquire*, January 1966, pp. 42ff.

19. K. Das, "New Faces, Old Hearts," *Far Eastern Economic Review* (August 14, 1981): 24-25.

20. Ibid.

21. Ibid.

22. Faligot and Kauffer, *Kang Sheng et les Services Secrets Chinois*, p. 378; Jack Anderson and Dale Van Atta, "Red China Sells Arms to Contras," *Washington Post*, May 5, 1986, p. C8; Daniel Southerland, "China Said to Increase Guerrilla Aid," *Washington Post*, September 12, 1986, p. A31.

23. John Stockwell, *In Search of Enemies: A CIA Story* (New York: Norton, 1978), pp. 67-68.

24. Jay Peterzell, *Reagan's Secret Wars* (Washington, D.C.: Center for National Security Studies, 1984), p. 14; Faligot and Kauffer, *Kang Sheng et les Services Secrets Chinois*, p. 505.

25. Peterzell, *Reagan's Secret Wars*, p. 10.

26. "'Ministry of State Security' Set Up on Mainland China," *Issues and Studies*, July 1983, pp. 5-8.

27. Ibid.

28. Michael Parks, "China Setting Up Security Unit to Curb Leaks, Spying," *Los Angeles Times*, June 19, 1983, pp. 1, 22-24; "Spy Fever: A Security Crackdown," *Asia Week*, July 22, 1983, p. 10.

29. Parks, "China Setting Up Security Unit."

30. Ibid.

31. John F. Burns, "Students in Peking Protest Atom Arms Tests," *New York Times*, December 24, 1985, pp. A1, A7.

32. "Peking Students Call for Democracy," *Washington Post*, December 14, 1986, p. A44.

33. Daniel Southerland, "20,000 Students Protest in Shanghai," *Washington Post*, December 21, 1986, pp. A1, A39.

34. Edward A. Gargan, "China Denounces Student Protests as 'Illegal Acts,'" *New York Times*, December 22, 1986, pp. A1, A14; Edward A. Gargan, "Students in Beijing, Defying Police Warnings, Stage a Mass Protest," *New York Times*, January 2, 1987, p. A8; Daniel Southerland, "Students in Peking Join Protest for Democracy," *Washington Post*, December 24, 1986, pp. A1, A12; Daniel Southerland, "Peking Students Defy Ban; Government Threatens Arrests," *Washington Post*, December 30, 1986, p. A15.

35. Mary Lee, "The Mouse that Roared," *Far Eastern Economic Review* (March 10, 1983): 28–29.

36. Lena H. Sun, "Chinese Students, Academics in U.S. Protest Beijing Move Against Three," *Washington Post*, February 25, 1987, p. A31; Douglas Martin, "1,000 Chinese in U.S. Endorse a Protest," *New York Times*, January 20, 1987, p. A3.

37. Michael Weisskopf, "Expulsion of Journalist Raises Fear of New Campaign by Chinese Police," *Washington Post*, March 18, 1984, p. A14.

38. Ibid.

39. "Times Reporter Held in Peking," *New York Times*, July 18, 1986, p. A3.

40. "Times Reporter Is Expelled from China," *New York Times*, July 24, 1986, p. A3; Margaret Scott, "Ousted Times Reporter Counters Spy Charge," *Washington Post*, July 24, 1986, p. A30.

41. "Beijing Expels American Reporter for French News Agency," *New York Times*, January 27, 1987, p. A10; Daniel Southerland, "Reporter's Ouster Said to Show Strength of Chinese Security Office," *Washington Post*, January 31, 1987, p. A10.

42. Southerland, "Reporter's Ouster Said to Show Strength"; Daniel Southerland, "Chinese Accuse U.S. Reporter," *Washington Post*, January 26, 1985, p. A15.

43. Daniel Southerland, "How China Watches China Watchers," *Washington Post*, September 7, 1986, p. C2; "Westerners Get Rare Glimpse at China's Secret Services," *New York City Tribune*, September 15, 1987, p. 2; Lawrence MacDonald, "My Expulsion from China," *Washington Post*, February 8, 1987, p. C3; Jim Mann, "China Tells Japan Reporter to Leave as Tension Mounts," *Los Angeles Times*, May 9, 1987, p. 12; Daniel Southerland, "Expulsion Baffles Japanese Diplomats," *Washington Post*, May 10, 1987, p. A21; Daniel Southerland, "China Expels Japanese Reporter," *Washington Post*, May 9, 1987, p. A15; Daniel Southerland, "Chinese

Police Surveillance of Foreigners Said to Increase Sharply," *Washington Post*, April 8, 1987, p. A16.

44. Southerland, "How China Watches China Watchers"; "Westerners Get Rare Glimpse at China's Secret Services."

45. Southerland, "How China Watches China Watchers."

46. Michael Weisskopf, "Peking Goes on Spy Alert," *Washington Post*, July 7, 1983, p. A21.

47. Jack Anderson and Dale Van Atta, "Nuclear Exports to China?" *Washington Post*, November 3, 1985, p. 7; Patrick E. Tyler and Joanne Omang, "China-Iran Nuclear Link Is Reported," *Washington Post*, October 23, 1985, pp. A1, A19; Joanne Omang, "Nuclear Pact with China Wins Senate Approval," *Washington Post*, November 22, 1985, p. A3; Patrick Tyler, "A Few Spoken Words Sealed China Atom Pact," *Washington Post*, January 12, 1986, pp. A1, A20–21.

48. "China Convicts American, 67, as Taiwan Spy," *New York Times*, August 24, 1986, pp. 1, 11; David Holley, "Father Held by Chinese Admits Spy Role to Son," *Los Angeles Times*, September 23, 1986, pp. CC1–CC2.

49. "Chinese Official Said Exposer of CIA Turncoat," *Washington Post*, September 5, 1986, p. A18; Michael Wines, "Spy Reportedly Unmasked by China Defector," *Los Angeles Times*, September 5, 1986, pp. 1, 12; Daniel Southerland, "China Silent on Reported Defection of Intelligence Official," *Washington Post*, September 4, 1986, p. A30.

50. Barnett, *The Making of Foreign Policy in China*, p. 100.

51. Russell Spurr, "Enter the Spooks," *Far Eastern Economic Review* (February 25, 1977); "News Digest," *Aviation Week and Space Technology*, December 22, 1975, p. 38.

52. Nicholas Johnson, *The Soviet Year in Space 1984* (Colorado Springs: Teledyne Brown Engineering, 1985), p. 84; P. S. Clark, "The Chinese Space Year of 1984," *Journal of the British Interplanetary Society* 39 (1986): 29–34; "China to Launch Satellite with Wooden Heat Shield," *Aviation Week and Space Technology*, July 27, 1987, pp. 52–53.

53. Craig Covault, "Austere Chinese Space Program Keyed Toward Future Buildup," *Aviation Week and Space Technology*, July 8, 1985, pp. 16–21.

54. "PRC Looks Deep," *Defense and Foreign Affairs Weekly*, February 9–15, 1987, p. 1.

55. Philip Taubman, "U.S. and Peking Jointly Monitor Russian Missiles," *New York Times*, June 18, 1981, pp. 1, 14; Murrey Marder, "Monitoring Not So-Secret-Secret," *Washington Post*, June 19, 1981, p. 10.

56. Robert Toth, "U.S., China Jointly Track Fixings of Soviet Missiles," *Los Angeles Times*, June 18, 1981, pp. 1, 9; David Bonovia, "Radar Post Leak May Be Warning to Soviet Union," *London Times*, June 19, 1981, p. 5; Taubman, "U.S. and Peking Jointly Monitor Russian Missiles."

57. Stephen Ladd, "The Chinese Naval Sigint Threat," *Naval Intelligence Quarterly* 7, no. 4 (1986): 30–34; *Jane's Fighting Ships, 1984–1985* (London: Jane's Publishing Co., 1984), pp. 105–6.

58. Barnett, *The Making of Foreign Policy in China*, p. 112.

59. Alan P. Liu, "Ideology and Information: Correspondents of the New China News Agency and Chinese Foreign Policy Making," *Journal of International Affairs* 2 (1972): 131–41.

60. Ibid.; Barnett, *The Making of Foreign Policy in China*, pp. 83, 115.

61. Faligot and Kauffer, *Kang Sheng et les Services Secrets Chinois*, pp. 372, 412, 419.

62. Barnett, *The Making of Foreign Policy in China*, p. 37.

63. Ibid., pp. 78, 84–85.

64. Ibid., p. 121.

65. Ibid., pp. 84–85.

66. Ibid., p. 91.

67. Ibid., pp. 101, 124–25.

68. Ibid.

69. Ibid., p. 123.

70. Reynolds, *A Comparative Analysis*, p. 102.

71. Richard Deacon, *The Chinese Secret Service* (New York: Ballantine, 1974), p. 418; Faligot and Kauffer, *Kang Sheng et les Services Secrets Chinois*, p. 463.

72. Faligot and Kauffer, *Kang Sheng et les Services Secrets Chinois*, pp. 398, 464.

73. Ibid., p. 463.

74. "Washington Round-Up," *Aviation Week and Space Technology*, March 19, 1984, p. 15; Daniel Southerland, "U.S. Navy Call at Chinese Port Symbolizes Growing Military Relationship," *Washington Post*, November 5, 1986, pp. A23, A29; Nayan Chandra, *Brother Enemy: The War After the War* (New York: Harcourt, Brace and Jovanovich, 1983), p. 280.

75. Michael R. Gordon, "U.S. Uses Seismic Devices in China to Estimate Size of Soviet A-Tests," *New York Times*, April 4, 1987, pp. 1, 4.

76. Faligot and Kauffer, *Kang Sheng et les Services Secret Chinois*, p. 505.

77. George Stuckenbroker, "Chinese Spies Lurk Outside Spotlight of Publicity," *Hampton Roads Daily Press*, October 28, 1985, pp. A1, A3; "The FBI's China Syndrome," *Newsweek*, September 5, 1983, p. 13.

78. Stuckenbroker, "Chinese Spies Lurk Outside Spotlight of Publicity"; Ruth Marcus, "Experts Begin Task of Assessing Damage," *Washington Post*, December 8, 1985, pp. A1, A24–25; Senate Committee on Governmental Affairs, *Foreign Missions Act and Espionage Activities in the United States* (Washington, D.C.: U.S. Government Printing Office, 1986), p. 57.

79. Senate Select Committee on Intelligence, *Meeting the Espionage Challenge* (Washington, D.C.: U.S. Government Printing Office, 1986), p. 27; Don

Oberdorfer, "Carlucci Reviewing Secret Operations," *Washington Post*, February 26, 1987, p. A23.

80. Senate Committee on Governmental Affairs, *Foreign Missions Act and Espionage Activities*, p. 89.

81. Ruth Marcus and Joe Pichirallo, "Chin Believed Planted in U.S. as Spy," *Washington Post*, December 6, 1985, pp. A1, A22; Philip Shenon, "Former C.I.A. Analyst Is Arrested and Accused of Spying for China," *New York Times*, November 24, 1985, pp. 1, 31; Joe Pichirallo, "Ex-CIA Analyst Gave Secrets to China for 30 Years, FBI Says," *Washington Post*, November 24, 1985, pp. A1, A24.

82. Pichirallo, "Ex-CIA Analyst Gave Secrets to China"; Stephen Engelberg, "30 Years of Spying for China is Charged," *New York Times*, November 27, 1985, p. B8.

83. Pichirallo, "Ex-CIA Analyst Gave Secrets to China"; "A Chinese Agent in the CIA?" *Newsweek*, December 2, 1985, p. 49.

84. Joe Pichirallo, "Retiree Kept Close CIA Ties," *Washington Post*, November 27, 1985, pp. A1, A10; Robin Toner, "Bail Denied Ex-CIA Worker in China Spy Case," *New York Times*, November 28, 1985, p. B8; Pichirallo, "Ex-CIA Analyst Gave Secrets to China."

85. Marcus and Pichirallo, "Chin Believed Planted in U.S. as Spy"; Philip Shenon, "U.S. Says Spy Suspect Had Access to Highly Classified Data," *New York Times*, January 3, 1986, p. A12; Michael Wines, "Bigger Role Laid to Suspected Spy," *Los Angeles Times*, November 28, 1985, pp. 1, 10; *United States of America v. Larry Wu-Tai Chin aka Chin Wu-Tai* in the United States District Court for the Eastern District of Virginia, Alexandria Division, Criminal No. 85–00263–A, January 2, 1986, pp. 2–3, 14.

86. Marcus and Pichirallo, "Chin Believed Planted in U.S. as Spy."

10 CONCLUSION

The intelligence and security activities of the nations examined in this book are the products of many factors—national interests, international obligations (such as participation in the UKUSA Agreement or NATO), the technology available for intelligence collection, and the resources a particular nation can afford to devote to intelligence and security activities. National interests and international obligations determine the desired targets and priorities for intelligence and security activities. The nature of the targets (for example, a terrorist group versus a missile system), together with the available resources, determines the means by which collection is undertaken.

One hundred years ago intelligence and security activity consisted of the lone agent seeking to purloin military plans or infiltrate a "subversive" domestic or exile group, or of the codebreaker laboriously attempting to decipher, by hand, the communications of a foreign government. Today, the human agent can still play a significant role—whether as a spy infiltrated into a terrorist group, a mole such as Larry Wu-Tai Chin, or a defector-in-place such as FAREWELL or Oleg Gordievsky. However, with the development and increasing use of technology for intelligence activities, the lone agent is now generally overshadowed by the land-based antenna farm, the airborne signals or photographic intelligence collector, and, for some nations, either now or in the future, the reconnaissance satellite.

The intelligence activities of the middle-ranking powers often have international ramifications. Information that one country collects on terrorist groups can help prevent attack within other nations as well. A FAREWELL or Oleg Gordievsky provides information that is useful not only to France or Britain but is also quite valuable to the United States.

The increased technical collection capabilities—and particularly satellite capabilities—of the middle-ranking powers may well contribute to a more stable world by diminishing the possibility of surprise attack. In 1968 the Soviet forces headed toward Czechoslovakia were temporarily "lost" by U.S. intelligence. A U.S. reconnaissance force augmented by a French-Italian-Spanish Helios satellite and other West European collection systems (such as a German radar satellite), however, will reduce the likelihood of a similar event.

Crises—such as those that periodically occur in the Middle East, between India and China, or between Turkey and Greece—would be subject to closer monitoring. A cease-fire agreement, whether between Iran and Iraq, Israel and Syria, or Libya and Chad, could be monitored with greater frequency and the results more widely distributed than they are at present. Just as countries today contribute to peacekeeping operations by sending troops, they could in the future contribute their intelligence capabilities to the same cause.

The monitoring of arms levels, particularly of mobile arms, would be facilitated and the ability to verify compliance with arms limitation treaties adequately would also improve. In the Far East, for example, a Japan that possessed its own reconnaissance satellite would certainly find it in its own interest to supplement U.S. coverage of Soviet compliance with any limits on SS-20s.

At the very least, enhanced technical collection capabilities will allow national leaders to make more informed and independent judgments. It may spare them embarrassment such as that suffered by French President Mitterrand when he insisted, based on the assurances of the SDECE, that Libya was complying with her promise to withdraw her troops from Chad—only to be presented with U.S. satellite photos indicating quite the opposite.

The internal operations of intelligence and security organizations can also contribute to stability, both domestically and internationally. The proclivity of various expatriate groups, such as the Sikhs, to resort to violence in their native and adopted lands presents a very real threat to citizens of those nations. Likewise, terrorism, conducted by independent groups or by the secret service of a foreign nation such as Iran or Syria, is a significant threat to many nations. The 1986 wave of bombings in Paris, during which ten attacks in only nine months killed 10 people and wounded 25 more, clearly demonstrates the value of a security service that could prevent such events.

While it is important to recognize the contribution that intelligence and security activities can make to eliminating international and domestic conflicts, it is also important to acknowledge the dark side often associated with these activities.

In terms of internal repression, none of the democratic nations considered here can match China. However, several have less than commendable records when it comes to using their secret and security services for repressive purposes. As noted in Chapter 4, Italy's intelligence services have been involved in a variety of neo-Fascist plots and terrorist incidents—actions that hardly contribute to the preservation of a free and democratic Italy. Israel's General Security Service has recently been exposed as having been involved in the murder of two terrorist prisoners and the framing of an Israeli military officer for espionage. In the later case, the GSS used a variety of illegal interrogation techniques, including cold showers, sleep deprivation and blackmail threats, to extract a false confession. The security service then lied about its actions in court.[1]

Even the United Kingdom and Canada, with their reputed heritage of tolerance, have seen their security services target individuals and groups on extraordinarily flimsy grounds. The British Security Service has conducted surveillance of both unionists and antinuclear campaigners. The RCMP Security Service was revealed in 1981 to have conducted surveillance of groups such as the Canadian Association of University Teachers and the National Farmer's Union; the infiltration of agent provocateurs into black and Indian groups; and break-ins at the office of the Parti Québecois, the Free Press Agency of Quebec, and the Movement for the Defense of Political Prisoners of Quebec.[2] Further, the Canadian government's Security Intelligence Review Committee has indicates that the CSIS is still having problems differentiating dissent from subversion. Thus, the SIRC noted that one CSIS report spoke of a certain organization's "attack on the anti-communist, pro-U.S. government of El Salvador . . . in direct support of . . . policy objectives . . . to blunt American foreign policy initiatives." The SIRC commented that "we cannot agree that a non-violent attack on U.S. foreign policy is necessarily a threat to the security of Canada." In contrast, the committee noted that "there seems to have been minimal CSIS interest in fund raising inside Canada for the Contra rebels in Nicaragua—although this seems to meet section 2's criterion of "activities within or relating to Canada directed toward or in support of the threat or use of acts of serious violence against persons or property for the purpose of achieving a political objective within Canada or a foreign state.'"[3]

Externally, various intelligence services have conducted missions that have put innocent individuals at risk. The Israeli Wrath of God operation may have been motivated by more than a desire for revenge—specifically, by the desire to eliminate the PLO leaders who stood in the way of an accommodation between Israel and at least parts of the Arab world. Irrespective of the motive, the operation resulted in the deaths of one target's niece and of several bystanders unfortunate enough to be in the vicinity when Ali Hassan Salameh drove past the car rigged by the Mossad with explosives. The French *Rainbow Warrior* operation caused one death, and could have caused another ten.

The intelligence services involved in those activities are not solely responsible for their outcome. A significant share of the blame—indeed, the primary blame—falls on the shoulders of national leaders who condone or order such activities. It was the French Minister of Defense, if not President Mitterrand himself, who approved the *Rainbow Warrior* operation. The Israeli government's failure to pursue criminal cases against those in the General Security Service involved in the murder of the captured terrorists, and the pardons awarded by President Chaim Herzog, certainly send a message to the GSS that such activities are condoned by the highest authorities.

Also responsible is the attitude, whether held by government officials or citizens, that the activities of the intelligence and security services must not fall under public scrutiny. Of course, certain aspects of national security activities require secrecy. Delicate negotiations to establish relations with a foreign country, the methods by which a stealth capability is obtained, and the identities of agents in a foreign government are all good examples. There is no reason, however, why citizens cannot be informed of the missions and structures of their intelligence and security services, as well as some details on intelligence targets and methods of collection. The West German BfV prepares an annual report, for instance, as does the Canadian

Security Intelligence Review Committee. Other intelligence and security agencies should be encouraged to prepare similar reports.

The current practice of shielding intelligence and security services from legislative and public oversight can engender a dangerous arrogance, the belief that those possessing secret knowledge should also have secret power. Such a belief can lead to security service involvement in the obstruction of justice, surveillance of individuals who are simply exercising their democratic rights, coups, and outright murder. It also allows public officials to conduct two policies—one for public consumption, another in the shadows. The necessity for some form of oversight has been recognized in Canada and Italy, and recent scandals involving the intelligence and security services in the United Kingdom and Israel may result in increased oversight in those countries.

Whether subject to increased oversight or not, it is certain that the intelligence and security services will continue to perform a variety of tasks, both in response to national authorities and international obligations, and that the consequences of their activities will be felt— for good or for ill—within and outside of their national boundaries.

NOTES TO CHAPTER 10

1. Glenn Frankel, "Israel's Security Service Has Found New Enemy: Itself," *Washington Post*, July 2, 1987, pp. A1, A32–33.
2. Jeffrey Richelson and Desmond Ball, *The Ties that Bind: Intelligence Cooperation Between the UKUSA Countries* (London: Allen & Unwin, 1985), pp. 283–300.
3. Security Intelligence Review Committee, *Annual Report 1986–87* (Ottawa: Minister of Supply and Services, 1987), p. 37.

INDEX

Guillaume, Gunter, 145
Guinea, 167, 178, 278
Gunji, General Kiichi, 253

Habre, Hissen, 181
Hafez, Colonel Mustapha, 206
Haganah, 191
Hamchari, Dr. Mahimun, 209
Handawi, Nezar, 33
Hassan, King, 166-167, 169
Heinz, Colonel Friedrich Wilhelm, 143
HELIOS satellites, 114, 172, 308
Hernu, Charles, 159, 182
Herzog, Chaim, 227-228, 310
High-Frequency Direction-Finding
    (HF-DF) equipment, 18, 19, 80,
    142
Hinsley, F. H., 70
Hitler, Adolf, 106, 129
Hoke, Margarete, 145
Holland, 153
Hong Kong, 20, 22, 276, 280, 284,
    286, 296, 298
Hooper, Sir Leonard, 36
Houghton, Harry, 32
Human intelligence (HUMINT)
    Chinese intelligence and, 297-300
    Israeli intelligence and, 195, 198
    West German intelligence and, 139,
    143
Hungary, 33, 42, 139, 152
Hunt, P. R., 79
Hussein, King, 212

Imbot, General Rene, 158
India, 231, 306
    Canadian intelligence and, 3, 75, 76,
    92
    French intelligence and, 162
Indochina, 157, 180
Indonesia, 33, 196, 232
Industrial Intelligence Centre (IIC)
    (U.K.), 12-13
Information Analysis, Research and
    Planning Bureau (Japan), 261-263
Information Service (SHAI) (Israel),
    191-192
Information Service (SR) (France),
    151, 152, 153, 154, 155
Information Service for Operations
    and Situations (SIOS) (Italy), 107,
    116

Informers, see Agents
Intelligence, use of term, 10-11
Intelligence Advisory Committee
    (IAC) (Canada), 86, 87
Intelligence collection, 1
    Canadian intelligence and, 74
    French intelligence and, 156-157,
    159, 160, 162, 176-177
    Israeli intelligence and, 193, 195,
    196, 220
    Italian intelligence and, 103,
    107-108, 109, 114
    Japanese intelligence and, 250-252,
    253-254
    United Kingdom intelligence and,
    10, 13-14
    West German intelligence and, 138,
    144, 146
Intelligence Department (U.K.), 11
Intelligence organizations, see Canadian
    intelligence organizations; Chinese
    intelligence organizations; French
    intelligence organizations; Israeli
    intelligence organizations; Italian
    intelligence organizations;
    Japanese intelligence organizations;
    United Kingdom intelligence
    organizations; West German
    intelligence
Intelligence Policy committee (IPC)
    (Canada), 85, 86
INTELSAT communications, 18
Interdepartmental Committee on
    Security and Intelligence (Canada),
    86, 87
International Committee of the
    Central Committee (Soviet Union),
    87
International Liaison Department
    (ILD) (CXX), 278-281, 295
Inter-Services Intelligence Committee
    (ISIC) (U.K.), 13
Iran, 5, 20, 26, 173, 308, 309
    French intelligence and, 79, 173
    Israeli intelligence and, 204-205,
    231
Iraq, 20, 26, 201, 205, 212, 239, 308
Ireland, 19, 26-27, 33, 35, 231
Irgun Zevai Leumi, 192
Irish Republican Army, 2
Irish Special Branch (U.K.), 11, 35
Israel, 20, 75, 118, 139, 158, 296, 308

Rezun, Vladimir, 28
Richter, Ursula, 147
Robertson, Norman, 70, 85
Room 40 (U.K.), 12
Roosevelt, Franklin D., 107, 130, 155, 253
Royal Air Force (RAF) (U.K.), 14, 18, 21, 27, 29, 47
Royal Canadian Mounted Police (RCMP), 70, 71, 72, 74, 76–78, 83–84, 85, 309
Royal Canadian Signal Corps, 68, 69
Royal Flying Corps (U.K.), 11–12, 14
Rumania, 114, 139, 163, 192
Russia, *see* Soviet Union

Sabotage
  French intelligence and, 182–183
  Israeli intelligence and, 205
Sadat, Anwar, 216
Saeed, Lieutenant Colonel Haithem, 146
Safari Club, 179
SA-5 Gammon missiles, 147–148
Saguy, Major General Yehoshua, 235
Salameh, Ali Hassan, 209, 210–211, 310
SAMRO satellite system, 170, 171
Satellite communications
  Canadian intelligence and, 79, 94
  Chinese intelligence and, 287–291
  French intelligence and, 170–172
  Israeli intelligence and, 236
  Italian intelligence and, 114
  Japanese intelligence and, 255, 261, 266
  United Kingdom intelligence and, 18, 19, 21–22, 25, 27–28, 56
Saudi Arabia, 20, 235
SAVAK (Iran), 179, 231
Schellenberg, Walter, 131
Scientific information exchange, 44
Schiller, Warner, 140
Schlieffen Plan, 152
Scotland Yard, Special Branch, 35
Scout aircraft, 218
Second Section (Nibetsu) (Japan), 255–256
Secret Information Service (SIS) (Italy), 104, 105–106

Secret Intelligence Service (SIS) (U.K.), 2, 37, 42, 52, 168, 171, 296
  organization of, 22–28
  origins of, 11, 13, 14
Secret Intelligence Service, Australia (ASIS), 42–43, 265
Secret Service (Italy), 101
Security Advisory Committee (SAC) (Canada), 86–87
Security clearances, Canadian, 78
Security Intelligence Review Commission (SIRC) (Canada), 30, 76, 309
Security Panel (Canada), 85–86
Security Planning and Research Group (SPARG) (Canada), 83
Security Service (Canada), 71–72, 74, 76–78
Security Service (U.K.), 2, 11, 13, 14, 30–34, 35
Sella, Aviem, 238, 239
Senegal, 165, 167, 203
Service de Documentation Extérieure et de Contre-Espionage (SDECE) (France), 156–157, 159–160, 163, 165, 167, 168, 177, 178, 179, 180, 296, 308
Service de Renseignement (SR) (XFF), 151, 152, 153, 154, 155
Service for External Documentation and Counterespionage (SDECE) (France), 156–157, 159–160, 163, 165, 167, 168, 177, 178, 179, 180, 296, 308
Service for Information and Democratic Security (SISDE) (Italy), 110, 111–113, 116, 118, 119, 122
Service for Information and Military Security (SISMI) (Italy), 110, 113–115, 118–122
Service of Information Security (SIS) (Italy), 110
Servizio Informazioni Aeronautiche (SIA) (Italy), 104
Servizio Informazioni Difesa (SID) (Italy), 108–110
Servizio Informazioni e Sicurezza (SIS) (italy), 110
Servizio Informazioni Forze Armate (SIFAR) (Italy), 107–108, 118, 177

Underwater surveillance, 93
Union of Soviet Socialist Republics
(U.S.S.R.) *see* Soviet Union
UNITA, 236, 280
United Front Work Department
(UFWD) (CXX), 281
United Kingdom
Canadian intelligence and, 67, 68
Chinese intelligence and, 296
French intelligence and, 152, 161,
179-180
Israeli intelligence and, 191, 192,
214, 231
Italian intelligence and, 105, 106
West German intelligence and, 130,
131, 132, 133, 140, 141
United Kingdom intelligence organi-
zations, 2-3, 9-58, 309, 311
counterintelligence in, 27-28
Falklands War and, 45-58
French intelligence and, 179-180
liaison and, 39-45
management structure of, 35-39
origins of, 9-15
Soviet Union and, 21-22, 25,
27-28, 32
specific intelligence and security
organizations in, 15-35
West German intelligence and, 140,
141
World War II and, 13-14, 19, 26
United Nations, 28
Falklands War and, 47, 48, 51, 52,
58
Israeli intelligence and, 196, 206
United States, 7, 308
agents of, 237-239, 240, 264,
298-300
Canadian intelligence and, 69-70,
80, 81, 87, 90-91
Chinese intelligence and, 6,
280-281, 291, 296-297, 298-300
Cuban missile crisis and, 161-162
drugs and terrorism and, 118
Falklands War and, 50, 56-57
French intelligence and, 154, 155,
160, 161-162, 168, 169, 170-171,
179-181
Israeli intelligence and, 196, 213,
214, 233-240
Italian intelligence and, 105, 107,
111, 113, 114, 118

Japanese intelligence and, 251, 252,
253, 261, 264-265, 266-267
Korean Air Lines flight 007 and,
266, 267-268
radio and television broadcast monitoring and, 41-42
satellite systems of, 170-171
United Kingdom intelligence and,
19, 20, 24, 25, 26, 29, 33, 39,
40-41, 41-42, 45
West German intelligence and, 129,
130, 133-135, 141-142
U.S. Information Service, 214
U.S.S.R., *see* Soviet Union

Va'adat Rashel Hasherutim (Israel),
229
Vanunu, Mordechai, 205-206
Vassall, John, 32
Vered, Dan, 226
Versailles treaty, 128, 129
Vichy government, France, 68, 69-70,
154
Vinogradov, Arkhadii A., 264
Vulcan bombers, 29

Wallesch, Captain Durt Heinz, 138
Walsingham, Sir Francis, 9-10
War Office (U.K.), 10-11, 14, 30
Warsaw Pact nations, 4
Canadian intelligence and, 91
French intelligence and, 169, 173
Italian intelligence and, 113, 119
United Kingdom intelligence and,
19, 21
West German intelligence and, 141,
142, 147
Washington Naval Conference (1921-
22), 12
Webster, William, 297
Weinberger, Caspar, 234
Welles, Sumner, 107
Wessel, General Gerhard, 136
West German intelligence organiza-
tions, 3-4, 127-148
monitoring of Baltic by, 147-148
origins of, 127-136
specific intelligence and security
organizations in, 136-147
World War I and, 127-128
World War II and, 130-133

ABOUT THE AUTHOR

Jeffrey T. Richelson is an author and consultant. He received his M.A. and Ph.D. in political science from the University of Rochester in 1974 and 1975, respectively. He has taught at the University of Texas, Austin and The American University. He was also a senior fellow at the Center for International and Strategic Affairs, UCLA.

Richelson's publications are in the areas of intelligence, defense, policy, and social choice theory. He is author of *The U.S. Intelligence Community* (Ballinger, 1985), *Sword and Shield: The Soviet Intelligence and Security Apparatus* (Ballinger, 1985), *The Ties that Bind: Intelligence Cooperation Between the UKUSA Countries* (with Desmond Ball), *American Espionage and the Cold War: The Soviet Target*. His articles have appeared in the *Review of Economic Studies, Journal of Economic Theory, Political Science Quarterly, Journal of Strategic Studies*, and *Journal of Conflict Resolution*.